THE God OF Jesus

THE
God
OF
Jesus

The Historical Jesus and the Search for Meaning

Stephen J. Patterson

TRINITY PRESS INTERNATIONAL
Harrisburg, Pennsylvania

Trinity Press International, P.O. Box 1321, Harrisburg, PA 17105
Trinity Press International is part of the Morehouse Group

Cover: Henry Ossawa Tanner, *The Savior*, ca. 1900–1905,
National Museum of American Art, Washington, D.C. / Art Resource, New York

Library of Congress Cataloging-in-Publication Data
Patterson, Stephen J., 1957–
    The God of Jesus : the historical Jesus and the search for meaning /
Stephen J. Patterson.
        p. cm.
    Includes bibliographical references and index.
    ISBN 1-56338-228-8
    1. Jesus Christ – Historicity. 2. Jesus Christ – Biography – History
and criticism. 3. Desire for God. I. Title.
BT303.2.P38   1998
232.9′08–dc21   97-45196
                                                                  CIP

Printed in the United States of America

98   99   00   01   02   10   9   8   7   6   5   4   3   2   1

In Gratitude

To the Jesus Seminar,
who drew me in.

To Christ in the City,
who opened my eyes.

To Deborah,
who made it all real.

Contents

Preface

There are two experiences from my time as a graduate student at Claremont in the 1980s that even today stand out so clearly for me that they never quite leave my consciousness whenever I am working on an ancient text. The first is a conversation with James M. Robinson about how Rudolf Bultmann used to conduct his graduate seminars in exegesis. Whether the text in view was from the New Testament, or a Greek philosopher, or a Jewish hymn, or an ancient amulet, he always came around finally to a single question: what is the understanding of human existence that comes to expression in this text? For those familiar with Bultmann's theology, this question will immediately be recognizable as a question ultimately about God. Bultmann was always interested ultimately in the *meaning* of a text. The second experience is a seminar with Burton Mack, in which we undertook to study the early Christian traditions surrounding the Lord's Supper. In due course we came to the phrase "This is my body, broken for you." Mack put the question in a most disarming and challenging way: what could it possibly mean for someone to look at a piece of bread and say, "This is my body, broken for you"? Collectively we searched high and low for anything in the ancient world that might help us to understand this peculiar statement, but to no avail. In the end, we had simply to struggle with the *meaning* of this text at some basic human level.

Why another book on Jesus? Somewhere in the myriad of books and articles that have appeared even in the past few years one would think that just about everything that could have been said about Jesus has been said, and perhaps more than once. Can one more droplet make a difference in an atmosphere already saturated with proposals? This book is not another new proposal for reconstructing the life and teaching of the historical Jesus. It contains a few new proposals, but for the most part one will recognize my presentation of the historical Jesus as a summary of scholarship ground out over several years by others, whose work I have come to regard as eminently reliable. In fact, one of the aims of this book was to present common biblical scholarship in a way that would be accessible to persons not conversant with its fine points and jargon. More than this, however, in presenting this work I

wanted to pose an additional question that scholars are less and less willing
to pose of their work today: what does it *mean?* To decide on the authenticity of the first beatitude is one thing. But beyond that, what did it mean
for Jesus to pronounce a blessing on the poorest of the poor? What vision of
reality is presented in the parable of the Prodigal? Why did Jesus cavort with
prostitutes or lepers? What did Jesus' death mean to his followers? And why
did they say, "God raised Jesus from the dead"? These questions of meaning
are for me inescapable, for they come with the texts and traditions of early
Christianity, inextricably tied to them. To ignore them is to ignore the very
raison d'être for these artifacts of the past, and for our interest in them. They
exist today because they meant something to someone, and might still mean
something today.

New Testament scholarship in North America is currently involved in
a great struggle and a fundamental realignment. This struggle, which has
been developing behind the scenes and in polite conversation, has now been
forced out into the open, as groups like the Jesus Seminar and individuals
like Mack have produced materials for public consumption, exposing a wide
audience to some of the most challenging critical work being done in New
Testament scholarship today. To this has come an equally public and strident
response from persons such as Luke Johnson and Ben Witherington, who,
more than challenging the work of Mack or the Jesus Seminar, really have
expressed basic misgivings about the value and validity of critical scholarship
as it has emerged in the late twentieth century. This is where we are today.
Critical scholarship — not only *historical* critical scholarship, but also newer
approaches to the Bible using critical theory — has pressed our understanding
of the texts and traditions of ancient Christianity to the point where organized Christianity, if it were to be guided by such work, would have to begin
to rethink some of its basic theological commitments. However, most scholars pressing the critical edge have not been willing to address the question
of what this work might really mean for Christian self-understanding. At the
same time, conservatives like Johnson are beginning to insist that this critical work has gone too far, and that biblical interpretation ought to draw
back and be guided more by church tradition than critical scholarship. And
so the gulf widens. Critical scholarship eschews any interest in the church,
and conservatives tell the church that it ought to have no interest in critical
scholarship.

This is intolerable. Biblical scholarship that ignores the church risks losing
the one genuine constituency that could take what it has to say to heart.
Apart from the church, does anyone really care about the Bible or biblical
scholars and their work? And a church that adores the Bible but ignores

biblical scholarship is a house built on sand, and its foundations are already beginning to fall away. The church must take seriously what scholars today are saying about the Jesus tradition. But for this to happen, scholars must also be willing to say what they think their work means.

This is what I have attempted to do in this book. Its purpose is to show how scholars have come to the conclusions they have reached over many years, and what these conclusions might mean for someone — or a church — who wants to take seriously their implications for the big questions that make life worth while: Who am I? What is life for? What is real? Who is God? Whether one agrees with what I say the Jesus tradition means is not as important to me as the act of raising these questions themselves. It is the questions that matter. Scholars should not shrink from asking them. The church should not fear their answers.

Many persons have helped me understand the Jesus tradition and how it might address these questions, and to them I owe a debt of gratitude: to the Jesus Seminar, and especially to Robert W. Funk, who encouraged my participation in the Seminar; to those outside the Seminar who tried to keep me honest, especially James M. Robinson, Helmut Koester, and Charles Bobertz; to those who encouraged this work in church settings, especially Jon Daniels, Valerie Russell, Peg Jacobs, Jim Smucker, William Hulteen, and Bob Mesle; and to my colleagues in St. Louis, especially Deborah Krause, John Riggs, Richard Valantasis, and Philip Devenish. Thanks go also to Peg Doherty, who helped in proofreading the final manuscript. And finally, thanks to the Monday night cabal, who made sure the book had a decent title. For that, they are responsible. For any other lapses in judgment, *mea maxima culpa.*

STEPHEN J. PATTERSON
November 29, 1997

Who Needs the Historical Jesus?

*The critical study of the life of Jesus
has been for theology a school of honesty.*

— ALBERT SCHWEITZER,
The Quest for the Historical Jesus (1906)

The Historical Jesus

"The historical Jesus." It is a peculiar expression. It seems overwrought. To speak of any person is to speak of a *historical* person. This is true of Jesus as well. Like every person who ever walked the earth, Jesus was historical. And yet through the course of Western history he has become so much more than a figure of history. He has become the object of faith. Millions worship him as God. The literature of Christian faith presumes his divinity and assumes it is speaking to an audience that will agree fully with this presumption. The four gospels of the New Testament present his story as that of a divine human being, whose destiny begins and ends in another world that is not our own. Here is a life that is not merely a life; a person who is not merely a person; a history that has become so much more than his/story.

For ancients, such paradoxes would not have posed the sort of difficulty they do today. That a person might be at the same time both human and divine was quite conceivable. The world, as ancients conceived it, was an open universe, with gods coming and going and interfering regularly in the lives and histories of human beings. To think of Jesus as such a figure was no great leap. But moderns no longer think of the world in this way. We live in a closed universe. It behaves in consistent ways that we know to be immutable, at least for all practical purposes. Newton's apple, once dropped, always falls. God does not sometimes step in to catch it. Only insurance companies still factor "acts of God" into their day-to-day conduct of business. When we speak of history today, we are speaking of unfolding events that proceed through processes of cause and effect, however chaotic and complex the routes may be. We do not assume that history is filled with combatants from Mt. Olympus, unseen forces that secretly determine the fate of the world, as well as our own personal destinies.

But the gospels come from the ancient world, where gods do come and go, a world in which God does sometimes catch the apple, a world in which humans and gods converse in normal tones, sometimes contend, wrestle, and even engage in sexual intercourse. The gospels are at home in that world, not our own. They are foreign territory to us. The questions we bring to these texts, questions like "What was Jesus like, historically speaking?" or "How did this or that really happen?" are questions that would not have arisen in that world. These are our questions, and they reflect distinctly modern interests.

Since the nineteenth century, when it really began to sink in with scholars of the New Testament that the gospels do not share our view of the world, theologians have commonly drawn a distinction between the "historical Jesus" and the "Christ of faith." That is, it is commonly assumed that the portrayal of Jesus we have in the gospels is not an accurate depiction of what one would have experienced in meeting him on the street. The gospels we have are not historical in any modern sense. Rather, they intend to speak of Jesus in all his significance to believing Christians. They are documents that were written "out of faith for faith," to borrow a phrase from another biblical author, the apostle Paul. Jesus' significance for the earliest Christians was not primarily historical, comparable, say, to the significance of Thomas Jefferson in shaping the Constitution of the United States. It was more than that. Much more. It was that in Jesus they had come to know who God is. The gospels reflect this point of view, this conviction, this faith, entirely. And so, they do not depict Jesus as a normal human being, someone we might encounter buying vegetables in the marketplace. The Jesus we meet in the gospels is nothing less than a god descended to earth, wielding the divine thunderbolt even as he mixes in with the market crowds.

Now, initially, this realization that the gospels are not plain and simple history produced a crisis. For, while our ancient saints do not seem to be so interested in history, many moderns, even modern Christians, most definitely are. We have come to associate, even equate, history with truth, often at the expense of older ways of expressing religious truth, such as through poetry or hymnody. For good or for ill, modern sensibilities are attuned to history. This was true especially in the eighteenth and nineteenth centuries, when the shine had not yet worn off the new methods of doing history along rational, objective lines. In view of these new emerging standards of truth, theologians began to ask the obvious questions, "In what, then, are we interested, the Jesus of history, or the Christ of early Christian confession? Are we interested in what Jesus taught, or what the early church taught about Jesus?"

The First Quest

In the eighteenth and nineteenth centuries many scholars chose to focus their interest on the Jesus of history. But knowing what we do about the gospels, it became clear that to speak of the historical Jesus would involve not just a simple reading of the gospels — *that* would yield the Christ of faith — but a critical analysis of the gospels using modern historical methods. This period produced literally hundreds of books and articles on the historical Jesus, which sought to explain as much of the gospels' story of Jesus as possible in rational, reasonable terms. But the focus of most of this work was not to explain away the New Testament. Rather, it sought to uncover the original teaching of Jesus and to construct a Christian ethic and social program that would faithfully continue that teaching. Some of the results of that research, known today as "liberal theology," sound remarkably contemporary. For example, Albrecht Ritschl, one of the leading lights of this early liberal theology in Germany, could write as a summary of his views in 1883 that the Kingdom of God consisted in

> those who believe in Christ, inasmuch as they treat one another with love without regard to differences of sex, rank or race, thereby bringing about a fellowship of moral attitude and moral properties extending through the whole range of human life in every possible variation.[1]

No one could fault such sentiments. But they could doubt whether this vision might ever become reality. By the turn of the century, as Europe slid inevitably closer to the conflict that would eventually engulf the whole planet in the first of two world conflagrations, almost everyone began to doubt it. As human communities collapsed into violent self-destruction, many theologians became convinced that what we needed was not a teacher, but a savior. The Jesus unearthed by the historically oriented theologians of the nineteenth century could not step up to this role. And so the first quest for the historical Jesus came to disappointing end, as theology turned away from history and back to the texts of the New Testament, and the Christ of faith, in search of a divine savior who could somehow rescue us from ourselves.

Theology without the Historical Jesus

This legacy from almost one hundred years ago survives to this day. For most of this century, theologians have not been very interested in the historical Jesus, but rather in the Christ of faith. In other words, it is not what Jesus taught that is of significance, but what the church taught about Jesus. This

---

1. *The Christian Doctrine of Justification and Reconciliation*; trans. H. R. Mackintosh and A. B. Macauley (Edinburgh: T. & T. Clark, 1902; German original published in 1883), 285.

has been true of liberals and conservatives alike. This was the position of both Karl Barth, the patron saint of conservative theologians today, as well as Rudolf Bultmann, his counterpart among liberals. Both began not with Jesus' teaching, but with the early Christian preaching about Jesus, especially its emphasis on the saving act of God effected in the cross and resurrection. It was the Christ of faith that really mattered, not the Jesus of history. This meant that the gospels could be read without ever asking the troubling historical question: Did this or that really happen? With the exception of a brief interlude in the 1950s and '60s, twentieth-century theology has managed to function without the historical Jesus by focusing on the preaching and confessions of the early church. And what is wrong with this? After all, as many have observed, if the gospels are not history, then we really do not have a historical Jesus. He is lost to the ravages of time. What we do have are the gospels, a clear record of the preaching and confessions of the early church. Here, at least, is a stable starting point, a fixed text, much more secure than the shifting sands of historical research. For this reason, *biblical* theology, not "Jesus theology," has been the staple of twentieth-century Christian thought.

This comfortable situation might have gone on forever, had it not been for the activities of a group known as the "Jesus Seminar." I joined in the work of the Jesus Seminar in 1988 because I had become troubled about this theological situation. The church has always rejected theologies that do not take seriously the incarnation — the idea that Jesus really was a human being. Could we really forget about the historical Jesus, forget about what he said and did as a real person without risking this age-old heresy? Could we really embrace the idea that the foundation of Christianity is to be found in the gospel *texts*, in narratives, as though Christian faith were a literary phenomenon, a matter of consulting the right authors and their stories? I became involved in the Jesus Seminar because I feared that twentieth-century Christianity was veering dangerously close to docetism, the idea that Jesus' historicity is not really important. In my view, it is important, very important. The idea that we have discovered who God is in a real person, in a human life and destiny, is what connects Christian faith so closely to human life and experience. To sacrifice the historical Jesus is to put at risk the relevancy of Christian faith for human existence. As I began my career as a theologian, the church of which I was a part was risking irrelevancy — or so the rapid decline in participation and membership in mainline Protestant churches would suggest. Some have said that this was because these churches had ceased to believe anything. I think that it was because these churches had ceased to believe anything important. Believing in the authority of the biblical texts was simply not enough. Expounding their stories was not enough. Something important was missing: the very real, historical person by whom the earliest Christians had initially been moved to faith, Jesus of Nazareth, the historical Jesus.

By now, most readers of this book will be familiar with the Jesus Seminar, a group of New Testament scholars who have gathered twice a year over the past ten years to study the words and deeds ascribed to Jesus in early Christian literature and to ask which, if any, of them, were actually said or done by Jesus, and which were attributed to him by early Christians.[2] In principle, the work of the Jesus Seminar was not new or revolutionary. The quest for the historical Jesus has been going on among New Testament scholars for more than two centuries. And some of the broad conclusions reached by the Jesus Seminar are also not new — for example, that only a small percentage of the things one reads about Jesus in the gospels are actually historical. This is the view that most New Testament scholars have held for many generations. But, while these things are not new, they did turn out to be *news*. That is because the Jesus Seminar did do one thing new in this project: it invited others to listen in on this work: lay people, pastors, the news media. Scholars seldom do this. They prefer the library or the classroom to *public* debate. This has meant that over many years the only public voice speaking out on matters of religious faith in our culture has been a very conservative voice and, for the most part, one ignorant of biblical scholarship or opposed to it on ideological grounds. The result has been that disciplined, thoughtful biblical and theological discourse has seldom been brought into the public discussion of religion in our culture. We live in a peculiar situation of cultural ignorance,

---

2. For those who are not familiar with the Jesus Seminar and its work, an introduction may be found in the initial report of the Seminar edited by Robert W. Funk and Roy Hoover, called *The Five Gospels* (New York: Macmillan, 1993). This report focused on the words of Jesus. Soon the Seminar will publish a second report on the work done on the things Jesus is thought to have done, the "deeds" of Jesus. There has also been much discussion of the Jesus Seminar, both critical and laudatory, both in popular literature and on the Internet. For a rancorous critique of the Seminar, see Luke Timothy Johnson's *The Real Jesus: The Misguided Quest for the Historical Jesus and the Truth of the Traditional Gospels* (San Francisco: HarperSanFrancisco, 1996). For a response to Johnson see John Dominic Crossan, "Why Christians Must Search for the Historical Jesus," *Bible Review* 12, no. 2 (April 1996): 34–38, 42–45. *Bible Review* published another lively exchange on the Seminar between Robert J. Miller ("Battling over the Jesus Seminar: Why the Ugly Attacks?") and Ben Witherington III ("Buyer Beware!") in *Bible Review*/ 13, no. 2 (April 1997): 18–26. Meanwhile, the founder of the Jesus Seminar, Robert W. Funk, published his defense of the Seminar and offered his own understanding of Jesus and his contemporary significance in *Honest to Jesus: Jesus for a New Millennium* (San Francisco: HarperSanFrancisco, 1996). A compelling account of the whole contemporary debate is to be found in Russell Shorto's *Gospel Truth: The New Image of Jesus Emerging from Science and History, and Why It Matters* (New York: Riverhead Books, 1997).

in which overwhelming numbers of people will agree to the simple proposition that "the Bible is the Word of God," but very few can even name the four gospels found in the New Testament.

The brunt of this situation of scholarly timidity and cultural ignorance has been borne by pastors and priests educated in reputable divinity schools, schools of theology, and seminaries, where the Bible is never taught as though it were simple history. Having received the finest education in biblical studies, they leave the ivy-covered walls of the academy to encounter a church in which almost no one has any idea what they are talking about. Most people in our culture know more about nuclear physics than they do about the Bible. Biblical scholars' failure to take seriously their responsibility to participate in public discourse and to contribute to the common understanding of our sacred religious texts has created a situation in which the basic foundation of most mainline Christian theology must lurk in the background, locked in dusty volumes shelved in the pastor's study. Biblical scholarship has become a secret body of knowledge, a kind of *gnosis*, access to which cannot be risked on common lay folk. This situation has come about not as the result of some elaborate conspiracy, but from a simple failure of nerve. Pastors have been left to go it alone, while scholars stayed in the back room, protected from controversy and criticism. One of the main goals of the Jesus Seminar was to force biblical scholars out of the back room and into the fray. It worked. Suddenly critical biblical scholarship was in the news. *Time, Newsweek,* and *U.S. News and World Report* were raising questions that had heretofore been safely guarded in the cloistered classrooms of the academy. Countless pastors and teachers found themselves having to answer difficult questions about history and the Bible, about miracles, about Jesus' birth and death, and even the resurrection. Those of us in the Jesus Seminar wanted a public discussion, and we got it. But it has not always been pleasant. Was it worth it?

Why the Historical Jesus?

Since its origins in the eighteenth century, the discussion of the historical Jesus has always led to controversy and turmoil. Anyone wishing to take up the subject again had better know the consequences ahead of time and have a very good reason for rudely awakening sleeping dragons. So before we begin, I want to be clear about my own reasons for taking part in such a potentially troubling discussion.

First, it is important for theologians, especially interpreters of scripture, to be absolutely clear with lay people that the narratives we find in scripture are, for the most part, not historical. This conclusion rests on many generations of biblical scholarship, most of it carried on under church sponsorship. Most mainline clergy simply assume this today; the theology they espouse presupposes it. Yet, of the hundreds of lay people I speak with every year, very few have ever heard a theologian say this. In other words, we as theologians have not been honest with the church. We have allowed a generally conservative spirit within American religion to frighten us into a fundamental breach of trust with our lay constituents. If we cannot be honest with the church and the public, if we have to fudge on even our most basic presuppositions, then there can be no integrity in our work as theologians.

Second, the fact that the biblical narratives are not historical is itself *theologically* significant. It reminds us that faith is not grounded in the certitude that this or that story narrated in scripture is historically accurate. Faith is grounded, rather, in the experience of the living spirit of God working in and through communities of faith. Faith that requires historical verification for its claims is not faith at all. Faith is always a risk to trust in a transcendent reality. This is the reason why theologians must reiterate again and again that the Bible is not history. If this embarrasses or troubles us, it is because we have become confused about this aspect of faith and need to rediscover the risk involved in authentic faith.

Third, most gospels scholarship today presumes that even though the gospels are not historical, they do indeed contain historical elements. This mixture of history and confession in the gospels is also *theologically* important. That which is historical gives us a glimpse of what the earliest Christians experienced in the presence of Jesus that so transformed their lives. The non-historical elements — the confessional elements — proclaim that what they experienced was not just the effective ministry of a fine teacher, but the very love and acceptance of God. This confessional material is just as important as the historical. In it, the "what" of history is transformed into a confession of who God is. However, so often Christians have focused on the confessional elements of the gospels, such as the virgin birth or the resurrection, but ignored that which is being confessed. The earliest Christians did not simply proclaim that *someone* was raised from the dead, but that God had raised *Jesus* from the dead — Jesus, who pronounced blessings on beggars, who ate with prostitutes and sinners, who parabled his listeners into a new way of thinking. These things are not incidental. They are among the fundamentals of Christian faith, for they define for us who God is.

The search for the historical Jesus should not be about replacing the biblical stories with history, throwing out the "confessionally biased gospels" in favor of the "indisputable facts of history." If this were the case, the quest would be a false one, a futile search for certainty in the realm of faith, a realm that does not allow the comfort of certainty. Rather, the search for historical materials embedded in the gospels can be helpful, even crucial for the understanding of Christian faith, when in the end we can see the interplay between history and its interpretation in scripture. History and interpretation — they work together in these sacred texts, the gospels. The interpretive element tells us that the gospel writers saw in the events surrounding Jesus' life a significance deep enough to be called "Immanuel...God with us." The historical element tells us what it was about Jesus that moved them so deeply that they could only name it as "God with us."

This interplay between history and interpretation, events and their meaning, is crucial to what follows in this book. Our own reaction to a recent event might help to illustrate this interplay between events and their interpretation. Not long ago in our own history, someone drove a truck full of explosives up to a federal office building in Oklahoma City and blew it up, killing 168 workers and children inside. What did this mean, this event? I recall those first zealous news reporters fast on the scene asking staggering victims and passersby for their "thoughts on what has just happened." No one could answer. No one knew what had just happened. There was only the shock of an event, the raw feelings, the fear, the excitement. What did this event mean? The answer to this question would emerge only after months of contemplation, and it would not be the same for everyone. It would mean different things for different people, depending on their own histories and their own involvement with the event itself. Ultimately, the meaning of this event will depend on how people experienced it. In the months and years to come, as people begin to comment on what this event might mean, it will always be important to ask about the event itself and how people experienced it. This is the task of history. It is an imprecise task. There will be many things that no one will ever know about this event. So it is with almost every truly significant event. Nonetheless, in order to fully understand what people say it meant to them, one will always have to ask as best one can about the event itself and how people experienced it.

Jesus was just such an "event" for many people. They experienced him as meaningful for their lives. In this book I want to ask what we can know about the historical Jesus, what he did and said, the stories he told, the people he gathered around him, that really meant something to people. It is my attempt to work out what the earliest Christians meant when they said that in this person they had come to know who God is. Who was Jesus? Who is God? For the earliest Christians, these questions became the same question. They were linked, not through abstract speculation about Jesus' inner nature or because of prodigious displays of the miraculous. They were linked simply in the experiences people had of Jesus that moved them to a clearer idea of who God is — so clear that they could give themselves over to this theological vision and allow it to determine who they would become if they chose to live faithfully to it. In this book I do not wish to replace early Christian claims with new claims of history. I wish, rather, to clarify why it was that early Christians made their claims about Jesus in the first place.

The Search for God

As I worked on this book I found voices from two worlds constantly playing in my head. On one side were the voices of people I have known in the Jesus Seminar and other professional colleagues engaged in New Testament scholarship. On the other side were the voices of people I have known through my involvement in the church, theologians and leaders in the United Church of Christ, Eden Seminary, where I teach, and my students past and present, most of whom are or intend to become pastors in local churches. Both of these worlds have made legitimate demands on how I should direct my attention in the writing of this book. Both sets of voices raised interesting and important questions as I worked through its various chapters. On the one hand, Jesus and the impression he made on people is a historical question of purely scholarly interest to me. On the other hand, I am also part of a church which still claims to have come to know who God is in this person's life and words. So I am not interested just in the impression Jesus made on people as a historical question. I am also interested in why some people who heard and experienced him claimed to have experienced him as God. What sort of experience was this? What was its character? How did it feel to people? What sort of God would one believe in if this God were to be seen in Jesus' words and deeds? These questions are not purely historical. They come from my own search for meaning in the Christian tradition.

In the following chapters I will be carrying on a conversation with both of these voices at once. I will be working through the traditions designated red and pink in the work of the Jesus Seminar to construct as much of a cogent historical impression of Jesus as these materials will allow. Occasionally I will include materials that were designated gray or black by the Jesus Seminar, indicating my own divergent assessment of these materials. When I disagree in this way with the consensus of my colleagues, I will note that fact and try to explain why I was led to a different conclusion.[3] As I work toward a reconstruction of the historical impression left by Jesus on his followers, I will be asking another sort of question as well. I will also be asking what it was about this person, Jesus, and their experience of him, that so moved his followers to have faith in him and to say that in him they had come to know God in a deeper and more authentic way. What did Jesus mean to people? This question is not an idle one. I ask it because I am a Christian and I, too, think that Jesus means something. For me, the quest for the historical Jesus is also about my own search for God. And so it is that history and theology become perilously intertwined, perhaps to the detriment of both. But as perilous as this path might be, it is the only one I can take with any honesty and integrity. I cannot step out of my own skin to assume the role of a disinterested, objective researcher. I can only strive to be fair to history itself and to allow it to address me without prejudice. As I have done this over the past several years in the context of the Jesus Seminar, however, I still find that I am moved and inspired by this material, and cannot help, from time to time, pleading its case. But I believe that a historian ought to be moved, one way or the other, by the past. A theologian ought to be moved, one way or the other, by religious tradition. Being moved, one way or the other, is a necessary consequence of engaging and being engaged by the Jesus tradition. For the claims it makes are on the human sphere of meaning. When one hears them, one cannot remain neutral — that is, *I* could not.

Fortunately, I am not alone in this search for meaning in the life and words of Jesus of Nazareth. The quest for the historical Jesus has been pursued for more than two centuries. And that quest for the historical Jesus has always also been about the search for God. There is much to be learned from these years of effort. That is where I shall begin: the historical Jesus and the search for God.

---

3. For those unfamiliar with the system of the Jesus Seminar, it works like this: The Fellows of the Seminar voted to designate each saying or "deed" with one of four colors:

> red: Jesus said/did something like this.
> pink: Jesus probably said/did something like this.
> gray: Jesus probably did not say/do something like this.
> black: Jesus did not say/do something like this.

The votes were tabulated on a system of weighted averages and each item assigned a color accordingly.

Usually I will not offer much comment on those sayings or "deeds" on which I was in agreement with the voting of the Jesus Seminar, but simply state how the Seminar voted and note my agreement. For more information regarding the voting on particular traditions the reader may consult *The Five Gospels* (see previous note), the report of the Jesus Seminar. Where I disagree with the Seminar I will note the fact, and briefly state the basis of my position. In this way I hope to avoid repeating extensive argumentation for each piece of information I wish to incorporate, and yet still give the reader some sense of what I think is historical and what is not, and why.

Chapter 1

The Historical Jesus and the Search for God

On the Quest for the Historical Jesus

Anyone who has followed the debate about the historical Jesus during the last decade must have been astonished or even horrified to observe how, as in a volcanic area, the earth was suddenly everywhere spewing forth fire, smoke, and differently-sized masses of lava, where, for a generation past, pleasant gardens had been planted on the slopes of ancient craters. Exegetes and systematic theologians, Protestants and Catholics, one's own school and its opponents (not least what was once the New World), our students and even the so-called lay people have been drawn into the uproar and have made strenuous efforts to extend the fireworks display.

— Ernst Käsemann,
New Testament Questions of Today (1965)

The Problem of the Historical Jesus

Who was Jesus, historically speaking? Every generation or so scholars of the Bible find themselves returning again to this very old, yet very important question. For Christians — and to a lesser extent, anyone involved in the course and flow of Western history — it is a question about origins, about roots, about beginnings. It is an orienting question that takes us back to basics. How did Christianity begin? Who was this person in whom genera-tion upon generation of Christians have claimed to see God, in whose name Christians have risen to the heights of what it means to be human in acts of care and compassion, and sunk to the very depths of demonic possession in acts of brutal oppression and violence? These questions draw us back time and again because they are foundational to our understanding of who we are as a culture, and what we would like to be. The quest for the historical Jesus involves more than mere historical inquiry into the life of a famous and influential person. It is a loaded question. It has become a question about ourselves and our search for God.

With stakes so high, one would think that the question of the historical Jesus would have been answered long ago. But it has not been — at least not to everyone's satisfaction. We are once again in the midst of a renaissance of interest in the historical Jesus.[1] New proposals are being offered from every quarter, with counterproposals and impassioned backlash demonstrating that this is indeed a question that still has the power to strike at the very heart of Christian self-understanding. But even while it is an enormously important question, it is also one of the most difficult historical questions to answer. We simply do not have very much historical information about Jesus. The ancient historians leave us helpless; the Christian texts at our disposal leave

---

Parts of this chapter were presented as a paper to the Spring '96 meeting of the Jesus Seminar in Santa Rosa, California, on February 28, 1996.

1. The resurgence of interest in the historical Jesus is well documented by Marcus Borg, *Jesus in Contemporary Scholarship* (Valley Forge, Pa.: Trinity Press International, 1994), 3–43.

14

us confused. To ask about the historical Jesus is to begin with a problem. Let us begin with the historians.

The Historians

Jesus came of age and spent his brief career under the reign of Tiberius Caesar, who succeeded Augustus in the year 14 C.E., and ruled until 37 C.E., well after Jesus' execution. Burton Mack deftly called attention to this problem using the words of Tacitus, one of our most thorough Roman historians, who summarizes the significance of this period with but three words: "Sub Tiberio quies" ("Under Tiberius, nothing happened," *History* 5.9).[2] This illustrates the problem: Jesus was an obscure figure in a remote part of the world. For centuries he would go unnoticed and unknown. Outside of Christian circles, virtually no one took note of his life or death — virtually, that is, for we do have a few brief notices. For example, in speaking of Christians Tacitus does write in his *Annals* (15.44):

> The founder of this sect, Christus, was given the death penalty in the reign of Tiberius by the procurator, Pontius Pilate; suppressed for the moment, the detestable superstition broke out again, not only in Judea where the evil originated, but also in [Rome], where everything horrible and shameful flows and grows.

As one can see, Jesus did not make much of an impression on the Roman cultural elite. In such circles he was remembered, if at all, as a criminal. Nor did those who claimed allegiance to him make a good impression. They were, after all, foolish enough to claim to see God in the career of a criminal. These impressions, of course, were not cast in a neutral field. Tacitus was Roman. Jesus was Jewish, a peasant from among a folk known for its rebellious resistance to outside efforts to subdue and exploit it. Among the provincial holdings of imperial Rome, Palestine required more than its fair share of subduing.

We might expect fairer and more extensive treatment from a Jewish historian. There is one, Flavius Josephus, and he is more complimentary about his cultural cousin than is Tacitus. However, he is not so complimentary as the Christian monastics (who preserved the manuscripts of Josephus) would have us believe. When reading Josephus one must always be wary of the presence

---

2. Burton L. Mack, *A Myth of Innocence* (Philadelphia: Fortress Press, 1988), 25.

of interpolations added by Christian scribes to bring this important voice to bear witness to the Christian gospel. In the following quotation from Josephus's *Antiquities of the Jews* I have indicated (in brackets) those places where scholars agree that a Christian hand has intruded:

> About this time there lived Jesus, a wise man [if indeed one ought to call him a man]. For he was one who wrought surprising feats and was a teacher of such people as accept the truth gladly. He won over many Jews and many of the Greeks. [He was the messiah.] When Pilate, upon hearing him accused by men of the highest standing among us, had condemned him to be crucified, those who had in the first place come to love him did not give up their affection for him. [On the third day he appeared to them restored to life, for the prophets of God had prophesied these and countless other marvelous things about him.] And the tribe of Christians, so called after him, has still to this day not disappeared. (*Ant.* xviii.63)

Josephus tells us more than Tacitus, but not much more. Jesus was a Jewish religious figure (the reference to his wisdom and "surprising feats" indicate the category), who was arrested and crucified under Pontius Pilate. That is all we know from Josephus. The handful of other Jewish references to Jesus scattered through the later rabbinic literature do not add much. Among the most important of these references, this one comes from the Babylonian Talmud:

> On the eve of Passover they hanged Yeshu [of Nazareth] and the herald went before him forty days saying, "[Yeshu of Nazareth] is going forth to be stoned, since he practiced sorcery and cheated and led his people astray. Let everyone knowing anything in his defense come and plead for him." But they found nothing in his defense and hanged him on the eve of Passover. (b. Sanhedrin 43a)

Then, a little later the same text continues:

> Jesus had five disciples: Mattai, Maqai, Metser, Buni, and Todah. (b. Sanhedrin 43a)

Not the traditional twelve, but interesting nonetheless.

Still, all of these sources tell us precious little.[3] All we learn from them is that Jesus was a Jewish teacher of wisdom with a reputation for sorcery, who

---

3. There is little else in the non-Christian record. Contrary to recent tantalizing theories, there are no obvious references to Jesus or Christians in the Dead Sea Scrolls from Qumran.

had a few disciples, and perhaps a somewhat larger following, which, after his execution at the hands of Roman authorities, did not entirely give up on him. For some, that much is enough. For those who want more, we must turn to the documents produced by those unflappable hangers-on — in the words of Josephus, that "tribe of Christians."

Paul the Apostle

Of that tribe, the first person to have left behind anything in writing was Paul of Tarsus. But in all his letters Paul never speaks of Jesus' life and seldom even refers to something Jesus might have said during his lifetime.[4] This is understandable, for Paul never knew Jesus personally. Paul became part of the following of Jesus only after Jesus had been crucified. His direct experience of Jesus was limited to spiritual experiences, which he understood to be "revelation" from Jesus Christ, whom he believed God had raised from the dead (Gal 1:11–17). Therefore, any help Paul may offer the historian interested in the historical Jesus will be only indirect help. As the earliest Christian voice we hear in the New Testament, Paul provides a perspective on things that can sometimes help us to piece together otherwise disparate information gathered from other sources. Paul came into the Jesus movement, after all, just a few years after the death of Jesus, when the memory of him would have still been relatively fresh. Paul knew things about Jesus we would very much like to know today, even if he is not so considerate as to share them with us. So it is important to keep an eye on Paul as one works through the Jesus tradition; occasionally it pays off.

In any event Paul will not be a primary source of information about the historical Jesus. His interests simply lie elsewhere most of the time. Like it or not, to hear anything of Jesus' life, we must wait several years for the writing of the first gospels.

---

4. On just three occasions does Paul actually quote a saying of Jesus known from the gospels: 1 Cor 7:10–11 (cf. Mark 10:11–12||Matt 5:32; 19:9||Luke 16:18); 1 Cor 9:14 (cf. Mark 6:8–9||Matt 10:10||Luke 9:3; 10:7); 1 Cor 11:23–26 (cf. Mark 14:22–25||Matt 26:26–29||Luke 22:14–20). He seems to allude to familiar sayings of Jesus in a handful of other passages: Rom 12:14 (cf. Matt 5:44); Rom 12:17 (cf. Matt 5:39); Rom 13:7 (cf. Matt 22:15–22); Rom 14:13 (cf. Matt 18:7||Mark 9:42||Luke 17:1–2); Rom 14:14 (cf. Matt 15:11||Mark 7:15); 1 Thess 5:2 (cf. Matt 24:43||Luke 12:39); 1 Thess 5:13 (cf. Mark 9:50); 1 Thess 5:15 (cf. Matt 5:38–48). For a discussion of the relationship between Paul's version of Christianity and the earlier followers of Jesus see Stephen J. Patterson, "Paul and the Jesus Tradition: It is Time for Another Look," *Harvard Theological Review* 84 (1991): 23–41.

The Synoptic Gospels and Q

There are four gospels in the New Testament: Matthew, Mark, Luke, and John. The last of these, John, is probably of little value to the historian. Its view of Jesus is quite different from the others, both in terms of the events it describes and the message its Jesus preaches. Since the nineteenth century scholars have regarded John as more of a spiritual reflection on Jesus, with only loose connections to the historical person.[5] Today, many regard it as a quasi-Gnostic interpretation of Jesus. In any event, it seldom comes into the current discussion.

The other three, Matthew, Mark, and Luke are closely related. Since the eighteenth century, scholars have noticed that they share a common view of Jesus' ministry. This is why they are called the *synoptic* gospels, from the Greek word meaning "seeing together."[6] In 1776 Johann-Jakob Griesbach noticed that with respect to the biographical outline of Jesus' life, Matthew and Luke agree only when they also agree with Mark. Griesbach explained this by suggesting that Matthew wrote his gospel first. Then Luke wrote, making use of Matthew loosely. Finally, Mark wrote his gospel, combining Matthew and Luke, but using only those things which they share in common (Fig. 1).[7]

For fifty years this hypothesis held sway — and in a few circles it is still preferred today.[8] But a majority of scholars began to feel dissatisfied with it.

---

5. Earlier work on the historical Jesus tended to favor John as the most comprehensive of all the gospels, rather than bracket it out. Friedrich Schleiermacher, for example, relied heavily on John in his lectures on the historical Jesus given in Berlin in 1832 (published posthumously in 1864 by his student K. A. Rütenik as *Das Leben Jesu* [Berlin: Georg Reimer, 1864]). The earlier, historically positive view of John was dislodged by the great Tübingen scholar F. C. Baur in his 1847 book, *Kritische Untersuchungen über die kanonischen Evangelien* (Tübingen: Osiander, 1847). Thereafter, the synoptic gospels gained the center stage in historical work.

6. These relationships may be seen in any number of synopses of the gospels, reference tools in which the parallel texts of the gospels are placed in adjacent columns. A convenient English-language synopsis is that of Burton H. Throckmorton, *Gospel Parallels* (Nashville: Nelson, 1979). A new kind of synopsis, distinctive for its inclusion of all early Christian gospels, not just the canonical four, was created by Robert W. Funk, *New Gospel Parallels*, 2 vols. (Philadelphia: Fortress Press, 1985).

7. Griesbach introduced his theory in one of the earliest gospel synopses, which he published in Latin: *Synopsis evangeliorum Matthaei, Marci, et Lucae* (Halle, 1776). He later published his conclusions in a book entitled *Commentatio qua Marci evangelium totum e Matthaei et Lucae commentariis decerptum esse monstratur* (Demonstration in which the entire Gospel of Mark is shown to be excerpted from the memoirs of Matthew and Luke; Jena, 1789–90). This work has recently been translated into English in B. B. Orchard and Thomas Longstaff, eds., *J. J. Griesbach: Synoptic and Critical Studies 1776–1976* (London: Cambridge University Press, 1979), 74–135.

8. In recent years this hypothesis has been revived by William Farmer and a number of his students. For a critical appraisal see C. M. Tuckett, *The Revival of the Griesbach Hypothesis* (Cambridge: Cambridge University Press, 1983).

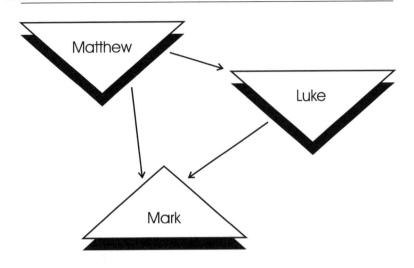

Fig. 1. The Griesbach Hypothesis

It could simply not account for the evidence, even on its own terms. For example, both Matthew and Luke begin with accounts of Jesus' birth and end with his resurrection, hardly inconsequential matters. But Mark includes neither of these. Perhaps more astonishingly, however, both agree in opening Jesus' ministry with the Sermon on the Mount (the Sermon on the Plain in Luke). Mark says nothing of it. Scholars also began to notice that Mark's Greek was much less polished than that of Matthew, and especially of Luke. Could one imagine Mark ruining the perfectly good prose of his predecessors?

To account for these and a myriad of similar, though less obvious problems, C. H. Weisse, H. J. Holtzmann, J. Weiss, and other scholars of the nineteenth century proposed another hypothesis.[9] Rather than Matthew, *Mark* wrote first. Then, Matthew and Luke wrote independently of one another, each making use of Mark as a source. That would explain why Matthew and Luke agree in terms of their general outline only when they also agree with Mark: they both used Mark as a source. This is called the hypothesis of Markan priority (Fig. 2). It is the basis for most synoptic gospels scholarship today.

9. C. H. Weisse, *Die evangelische Geschichte kritisch und philosophisch bearbeitet*, 2 vols. (Leipzig: Breitkopf und Hartel, 1838); H. J. Holtzmann, *Die synoptischen Evangelien* (Leipzig: Wilhelm Engelmann, 1863); J. Weiss, *Jesus' Proclamation of the Kingdom of God* (Philadelphia: Fortress Press, 1971 [German original published in 1892]).

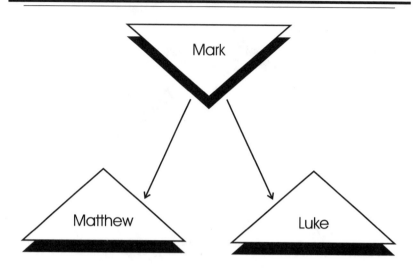

Fig. 2. The Hypothesis of Markan Priority

But there were still problems. The most pressing was a large amount of material shared by Matthew and Luke, but not found in Mark. This material was most intriguing. In it there is a relatively high degree of verbal agreement between Matthew and Luke. Each also uses it in more or less the same order. However, they almost always insert it differently into Mark's outline. It is as though they shared a list of sayings, parables, and the like, but no blueprint for where these things should go in the life of Jesus.[10] Based on these observations, Weisse, Holtzmann, Weiss, and others proposed a second hypothesis: that in addition to Mark, which provided the basic outline for a life of Jesus, Matthew and Luke also had a second source, consisting primarily of sayings and parables. Since this source did not survive the ancient period, Weisse simply called it the "Source," in German "Quelle." Later this was shortened to the simple siglum "Q."[11] Thus was born the two-source hypothesis (Fig. 3),

---

10. Attention was called to the common relative order of these texts originally by Vincent Taylor in two essays: "The Order of Q," *Journal of Theological Studies*, n.s. 4 (1953): 27–31, and "The Original Order of Q," pp. 246–69 in A. J. B. Higgins, ed., *New Testament Essays: Studies in Honor of T. W. Manson* (Manchester: Manchester University Press, 1959). Both essays are reprinted in Taylor's *New Testament Essays* (Grand Rapids: Eerdmans, 1972), 90–94 and 95–118, respectively.

11. For an introductory discussion of Q, see John S. Kloppenborg, Marvin W. Meyer, Stephen J. Patterson, and Michael G. Steinhauser, *A Q–Thomas Reader* (Sonoma, Calif.: Polebridge, 1990), 3–27. Also helpful is Helmut Koester's discussion in *Ancient Christian Gospels:*

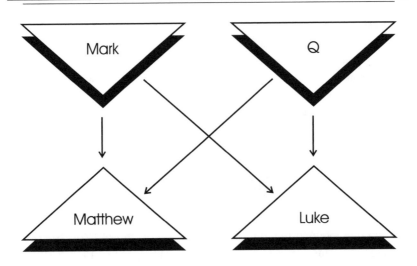

Fig. 3. The Two-Source Hypothesis

namely, that Matthew and Luke had two sources: Mark and a second source, now lost, which we call Q. Since it did not survive, this second source, Q, must be reconstructed rather imperfectly by extracting it from Matthew and Luke.[12]

These four sources were all written in the last half of the first century. The earliest was probably Q, around 50–60 C.E. Mark was written a short time later, near the end of the Jewish War for independence from Rome, in about 70 C.E. References in Mark 13 to the events surrounding the war, especially the destruction of the Jewish Temple in Jerusalem, are the clearest indication for dating any of these gospels. Matthew and Luke were written a generation or so later, or at least long enough for Mark to have circulated and

---

Their History and Development (Philadelphia: Trinity Press International; London: SCM, 1990), 49–171.

12. In recent years the reconstruction of Q has reached a new state of the art. Since the mid-1980s a team of scholars has been working under the direction of James M. Robinson, John Kloppenborg, and Paul Hoffmann to survey scholarship on this technical art and to produce a new critically reconstructed Q for scholarly use today. The results of their team, The International Q Project, have been published in the *Journal of Biblical Literature* in installments beginning in 1990: JBL 109 (1990): 499–501; JBL 110 (1991): 494–98; JBL 111 (1992): 500–508; JBL 112 (1993): 500–506; JBL 113 (1994): 495–99; JBL 114 (1995): 475–485; and JBL 116 (1997): 521–25. The complete work of the Seminar is being published in the series *Documenta Q: Reconstructions of Q through Two Centuries of Gospel Research, Excerpted, Sorted, and Evaluated* (Leuven, Peeters Press).

gained some currency. Matthew seems to be in dialogue with Jews involved in the reorganization of Judaism that was taking place in the 80s C.E. The year 85 C.E. is a date commonly assigned to it. Luke is harder to date since it lacks even weak gestures to contemporary events. Luke's generally positive attitude toward Roman officials may be an indication that it was written after the reign of the Roman emperor Domitian (81–96 C.E.), under whom Christians suffered persecution. This would suggest a date in the last few years of the first century, or even a bit later.

The Gospel of Thomas

In addition to these sources, there is yet another source to which scholars are turning more and more in the quest for the historical Jesus, the Gospel of Thomas.[13] This noncanonical gospel was widely known in antiquity, but due largely to its content (considered heretical by many ancient church authorities) it fell into disuse and gradually dropped from sight in the early Middle Ages. It reappeared as part of a spectacular discovery of ancient manuscripts in 1945 — not the Dead Sea Scrolls, but a lesser-known discovery of even greater significance for the study of Christian origins than the scrolls themselves: the Nag Hammadi Library.[14] This small library of thirteen leather-bound codices was discovered by villagers in Upper Egypt near the town of Nag Hammadi, which now lends the collection its name. Among the more than fifty tractates which fill these ancient books there is a complete text of the Gospel of Thomas.

The Gospel of Thomas is an early Christian gospel, written at about the same time that Mark, Matthew, and Luke were being written. But unlike these gospels, Thomas contains no real narrative. It consists of sayings — 114 in all — attributed to Jesus. These sayings are for the most part simply listed,

---

13. For a general introduction to the Gospel of Thomas see Kloppenborg et al., *Q–Thomas Reader*, 77–123. For the current state of research on the Gospel of Thomas see F. T. Fallon and R. Cameron, "The Gospel of Thomas: A Forschungsbericht and Analysis," *Aufstieg und Niedergang der Römischen Welt* 2/25.6; W. Haase and H. Temporini, eds. (Berlin/New York: de Gruyter, 1988), 4195–4251, and G. J. Riley, "The Gospel of Thomas in Recent Scholarship," *Currents in Research: Biblical Studies* 2 (1994): 227–52. For a thoughtful consideration of future prospects for research, see Philip Sellew, "The Gospel of Thomas; Prospects for Future Research," in John D. Turner and Anne McGuire, eds., *The Nag Hammadi Library after Fifty Years: Proceedings of the 1995 Society of Biblical Literature Commemoration*, Nag Hammadi and Manichean Studies 44 (Leiden: Brill, 1997), 327–46.

14. For an English translation of these texts and an account of their discovery see James M. Robinson, general editor, *The Nag Hammadi Library in English*, 3d rev. ed. (San Francisco: HarperSanFrancisco, 1988).

each introduced briefly by the words "Jesus said." Occasionally two or more sayings will be clumped to form a brief dialogue. Once in a while a saying will be introduced with a very brief narrative setting. Generally speaking, however, Thomas is a sayings gospel. It is in this respect closer to the earliest synoptic source, Q, than to the gospels now found in the New Testament.

Thomas has become more and more important since its discovery in 1945 owing to its remarkable content. Of its 114 sayings, roughly half have parallels in the synoptic gospels. For this reason it has sometimes been called the "fourth synoptic gospel." It is not really very synoptic-like, however, for its lack of narrative and its peculiarly esoteric outlook — the prologue to Thomas declares: "These are the secret words of the living Jesus" — make it really quite different in both form and content. But the fact that in spite of these differences, Thomas still has many, many parallels to the synoptic tradition makes this gospel as important as the synoptic tradition for this work. One factor that makes Thomas so interesting to the historian is its apparent lack of dependence on the synoptic gospels or their sources. This means that Thomas is more or less an independent witness to the sayings of Jesus found in Q, Mark, Matthew, and Luke, as well as some of the tradition thought at one time to have been unique to Matthew or Luke. Sometimes Thomas even presents us with a saying known already from the synoptics, but in a more original form.[15]

All of these sources can be of use in the discussion of the historical Jesus, but only with the help of critical scholarship. For as will soon become clear, though they all share our interest in Jesus, none of them shares our interest in history. For the historian, this can pose difficulties.

The Making of Mark

The problem of finding history in these sources will perhaps best be illumined if we focus attention for the moment on Mark. Of the three gospels that seem to present us with a narrative account of Jesus' life, it is the earliest. It is also the source upon which Matthew and Luke drew in constructing their

---

15. So I have argued in *The Gospel of Thomas and Jesus* (Sonoma, Calif.: Polebridge, 1993), 9–110. This view of Thomas is followed by most North American scholars. European scholarship tends not to regard Thomas as an independent tradition. For a review of the extensive discussion of the relationship between Thomas and the synoptic gospels, see Stephen J. Patterson, "The Gospel of Thomas and the Synoptic Tradition: A Forschungsberichte and Critique," *Forum* 8, nos. 1–2 (1992): 45–97.

narratives of Jesus' life. Therefore, what we find out about Mark's narrative
will be of relevance for them as well.

To assess Mark as a source for historical research we must first ask what
sort of document it is. We call it a "gospel," an Old English word traditionally used to render the Greek *euangelion*, which means literally "good news."
But this tells us little. On the one hand, so many different things are called
"gospel" in ancient Christianity it is well nigh impossible to define just what is
meant by the term.[16] On the other hand, Mark, or any of the books we now
call "gospels," were not originally referred to by this term. Originally they bore
only an ascription (*Kata Markon*: "According to Mark"; *Kata Lukan*: "According to Luke"; etc.). Marcion, an unorthodox Christian teacher active in the
second century, was probably the first to have used this term with reference
to one these texts. He applied it to Luke — specifically to Luke, but not to
the others. In Marcion's view only Luke got the "good news" of Jesus right,
along with Paul. He rejected the Hebrew scriptures and most early Christian
writings as being "too Jewish." Luke alone was "good news." Eventually most
Christians rejected Marcion's views, asserting that Matthew, Mark, and John
were also good news, and so they also came to be called "gospels." But none
of this tells us what these books were originally — how and why they were
written, and what ancient Christians thought of them.

We are fortunate to have at least one ancient account of the making of
a gospel, and it happens to be Mark. It comes to us rather indirectly from a
certain elder who is claimed to have known Mark. His remarks are preserved
in the work of Eusebius, the fourth-century church historian, who got them
from Papias, a church elder who lived around the turn of the first century,
who in turn got them from that elder who knew Mark. Now, historians are
not usually inclined to trust third-hand accounts. Nonetheless, this little fragment is worth our attention, for it illustrates how ancient Christians thought
about these texts and challenges the assumptions moderns often bring to
them. Papias's brief account reads as follows:

> And the presbyter would say this: Mark became Peter's interpreter and
> wrote accurately whatever he remembered, not, however, in the order
> in which things were said and done by the Lord. For he had not heard
> the Lord, nor had he followed him. Rather, as I said, later on he fol-
> lowed Peter. And he used to give instruction as the need arose, but did
> not make something like an arrangement of the Lord's sayings. So Mark
> did nothing wrong in writing down single points as he remembered

---

16. For a discussion of the term "gospel" and its varied use in earliest Christianity, see Koester,
Ancient Christian Gospels, 1–48.

them. For to one thing he gave attention, to leave out nothing of what he had heard and to falsify nothing in them. (Eusebius, *Ecclesiastical History* 3.39.15)

From the modern point of view, the intriguing thing about this account is that, on the one hand, it plainly says that Mark did not write things down in the right order — that is, he did not write a historically accurate life of Jesus. He simply did not have the necessary information to do so: "For he had not heard the Lord, nor had he followed him." But on the other hand, he seems to insist that Mark wrote things down accurately and did not falsify anything. When many people read this passage they typically hear the last part — about Mark being accurate. They like that; it gives them a sense of security that, in our culture, only historical accuracy can bring. But when their attention is directed to the first part — about Mark not writing things down in the right order — now it gets interesting! For when a modern person reads Mark, it reads for all the world like a short biography. How could Mark write a biography in which none of the events or sayings were in the right order and still be regarded as having written "accurately"? The explanation is not difficult, but for the historian it spells trouble.

First of all, one must realize that there is nothing in antiquity that roughly approximates our own concept of historical biography. Such classics as Plutarch's *Lives* are not easily transported into our world. These are not biographies, but aretalogies, that is, works whose purpose is to recount the wondrous deeds of great persons. Their purpose is not to report history, but to glorify the figures who appear in them as great heroes. That is true of Mark as well. It cannot be considered historical biography in any meaningful modern sense. But if the Gospel of Mark is not a historical document, then how can Papias claim that it is nonetheless accurate? Or perhaps we might better put the question this way: What could "accurately" mean to Papias? To answer this question we must turn our attention briefly to the phenomenon of oral tradition in ancient Christianity.

The Oral Tradition

Accuracy is not an absolute concept, but a relative one. One's accuracy in achieving a goal depends on the goal one is seeking to achieve. We tend to associate accuracy in a literary milieu with verbatim, objective accuracy. We can expect that kind of accuracy today because it is achievable — with writing, recording devices, computers, and the like. But this was not the case in antiquity. In Mark's cultural milieu only about 10 percent of the people could read or write. People operated orally. No thought was given to writing things down. This was simply an expensive, technological luxury too costly to be part of most people's reality. Ninety percent of the people in first-century Roman society never wrote or read anything.[17] In such a milieu "accuracy" comes to mean something quite different. In a culture that is for the most part oral, verbatim accuracy is not achievable for most people. Thus, most people in antiquity would never have tried for verbatim accuracy — it barely exists as a concept in antiquity. The famous studies of Albert Lord on oral cultures in rural Yugoslavia showed that oral tradition is never repeated with verbatim accuracy, even though the bards charged with preserving these traditions claim vociferously that they are indeed rendered accurately.[18] Without texts around to define what "accurate" means, it can and does mean something else altogether. For Lord's poets it meant rendering their traditional songs and poems differently in various times and places in such a way that the original intent of the tradition was preserved. They understood that nothing distorts a tradition more than simple wooden repetition under new and quite different circumstances. Mark and the other early Christians who passed along the Jesus tradition understood this as well.

The predominantly oral culture in which our gospels were written is one of the major barriers to working with them as though they were historically accurate accounts. Because so few people had access to the basic tools of literacy, most of what we read in the gospels was passed along by word of mouth for generations before it was ever written down. And once gospels like Mark or Q were written, the oral tradition did not cease to be the source of most people's information about Jesus. Even in the second century, when the written gospels were gaining in popularity and authority, Papias still preferred the oral tradition to these early written documents. The study of how traditional stories about Jesus were passed along orally is called form criticism. Form criticism attempts to take seriously the realities of an oral culture. For example, in the absence of widespread literacy, most of what is not useful on an ongoing basis in an oral culture is simply forgotten. Whatever is not repeated is lost. This means that the things that were remembered about Jesus were remembered because they were useful in the ongoing life of early Chris-

---

17. William V. Harris, *Ancient Literacy* (Cambridge: Harvard University Press, 1989), 1–24, esp. 22. Harris has reversed the long-held assumption that ancient Greece and Rome were highly literate cultures. For a fascinating discussion of the difference between cultures that operate orally and cultures like our own, in which the availability of texts is assumed, see Walter Ong, *Orality and Literacy: The Technologizing of the Word* (New York: Methuen, 1982).

18. Albert Lord, *The Singer of Tales* (Cambridge: Harvard University Press, 1960).

tian communities. Moreover, the use to which some tradition about Jesus was put often determined the form in which the tradition was preserved. For example, the fact that early Christians worshiped together means that some early traditions about Jesus are preserved in the form of hymns, confessional statements, or prayers (the Lord's Prayer is a good example of this). The instruction of persons new to the Christian movement necessitated the collection of materials into didactic forms (such as Luke's Sermon on the Plain).[19]

But there was one overriding concern that pervades all of Christian tradition; indeed, it is the concern that makes it "Christian" in the first place. That is the conviction that Jesus was significant, ultimately so. The early Christian tradition is dominated by the concern to show — in many and various ways — that in Jesus we have come to know who God is. This means that virtually nothing preserved in the years of oral traditioning that preceded and continued on past the writing of gospels could be described as "just the plain facts." Like the gospels themselves, the oral tradition upon which they were based was shaped and transformed by the overriding Christian concern to proclaim to themselves and to others what they believed was the real significance of Jesus.

All of this is good news to the theologian. The early Christian tradition, as well as the gospels themselves, holds great stores of early Christian theology and preaching. But for the person interested in history, these findings are ominous. They indicate that there can be no easy access to the historical Jesus, if one may have access to him at all.

The Quest for the Historical Jesus and the Search for God

For these reasons the question of the historical Jesus has become in our time less a question and more of a quest. But the quest did not first arise in our time. Problems with the historicity of the gospel texts have plagued scholars since the eighteenth century, when the full force of the Enlightenment began to make itself felt, especially in areas of religious faith. The origins of the problem are not mysterious. The idea that everything we read in scripture is literally, historically true simply could not be maintained in the face of new information about the way the world works that was turned up by the new

---

19. The classic study of early Christian oral forms and their corresponding settings in the life of the early church is still that of Rudolf Bultmann, *The History of the Synoptic Tradition*, trans. John Marsh (New York: Harper & Row, 1963; German original published in 1921).

disciplines of history, geography, and science. The question of the historical Jesus arose when scholars first began to notice that the gospel texts come with an entire worldview, an ancient worldview that grants the plausibility of things a modern worldview simply will not.[20] For example, for ancients, who thought about heaven as a vaulted space above the sky, it made sense to speak of Jesus' final "ascent" into heaven. For modern persons, whose worldview includes space and planets, atmosphere and ozone, this no longer makes sense. But if this part of scripture cannot be literally true, then what is true? And in what way can something be considered true? And how shall that be determined, and by whom? The intellectual challenge of the Enlightenment was really about the ability and authority to name what is true and what is not. Insofar as the Bible is finally about ultimate reality, that is, ultimate truth, the question of the historicity of the Bible, and with it the question of the historical Jesus, has always been bound up closely with the search for Truth. The quest for the historical Jesus has, from its very beginning, also been about the search for God.

The Enlightenment and Religious Faith

To many people today the Enlightenment, with its emphasis on reason and natural law as the basis for understanding all that there is to know about the world, now seems like a vain attempt to subjugate everything to human control and validation, to impose arbitrary structure on what is ultimately chaos. However, whatever its shortcomings and moments of hubris might have been, one should not forget what the Age of Reason meant as an advance over what had preceded it, especially in the realm of religious faith. The Enlightenment was about the democratization of authority to name what is true and what is not. Prior to the Enlightenment, the power to say what is true lay with vested authority. In the church it lay with priests and bishops, and ultimately the Pope. The Protestant reformers had begun to challenge this authority already in the Reformation age using the tools of reasonable argument and criticism. In his dispute with Cajetan, for example, Martin Luther

---

20. A masterful description of this basic cultural difference and the problems it poses for the modern interpreter of scripture is to be found in Rudolf Bultmann's classic essay "New Testament and Mythology." Published originally in German in 1941, this essay has been translated and reprinted in a number of different forms. An excellent translation is to be found in Rudolf Bultmann, *New Testament and Mythology and Other Basic Writings*, selected, edited, and translated by Schubert M. Ogden (Philadelphia: Fortress Press, 1984), 1–44.

could argue that "any one of the faithful" has authority above that of the Pope "if armed with a better authority and reason."[21]

In the Enlightenment this principle reigned. The power to name what is true fell to anyone who could make a reasoned defense of an idea. This was true, of course, especially in the study of the natural world, which was discovered more and more to behave according to consistent "laws of nature." But science in the seventeenth and eighteenth centuries was not a discipline altogether separate from religion. Renaissance heroes like Galileo and Spinoza were not only scientists; they were philosophers and theologians as well. After all, the Bible had its own theories about how the universe was created and sustained. When new scientific ideas grounded in reason and criticism came into conflict with the Bible, scientists found themselves standing before the Inquisition defending the theological implications of their views. Galileo paid for the advances we all owe to him with the final years of his life, spent under house arrest and in forced seclusion in Florence. Spinoza was excommunicated from the synagogue, and for a century after his death was *persona non grata* in the cultured circles of Europe.

By the eighteenth century the Enlightenment was in full swing. Challenge to ecclesiastical authority was no longer a life-threatening adventure, but it could still land one in plenty of hot water. The battle and the booty were still the same: who has the authority to name what is true? The church claimed this authority for itself. Scientists, philosophers, and breakaway theologians claimed it for anyone with a reasonable argument. Their attitude toward the church was frequently hostile and distrustful. They saw its defense of supernaturalism and the literal truth of the scriptures as an attempt to shore up its authority in the face of spreading populism and *egalité*.

Reimarus and the Beginning of the Quest

In this atmosphere the forebear of modern critical scholarship on the gospels labored in secret. Hermann Samuel Reimarus was a German Deist, theologically trained, but posted in the philosophical faculty at Wittenberg and later as a professor of oriental languages in Hamburg. His was not a stellar academic career. In fact, no one would have known of this obscure figure had his private notes on Jesus and Christian origins not been published posthumously

---

21. As quoted from Luther's correspondence with Cajetan by Roland Bainton in *Here I Stand: A Life of Martin Luther* (Nashville: Abingdon, 1950), 96. Luther and Calvin were not hostile to scientific advancement and the use of reason in the service of Christian faith. See B. A. Gerrish, *The Old Protestantism and the New* (Chicago: University of Chicago Press, 1982), 163–78.

and anonymously by G. E. Lessing in installments between the years 1774 and 1778. But in the fragmentary notes of this unknown professor, there lurked a revolution. The crucial final installment, entitled "On the Intentions of Jesus and His Disciples," provoked the duke of Brunswick to demand that Lessing immediately turn over his mysterious manuscript and cease all further publication.[22]

Reimarus assessed the Enlightenment struggle between reason and church authority and read it into the problem of gospel origins. Reading the gospels with enlightened eyes, he saw in them the simple story of a martyred teacher that had been augmented and aggrandized by adding tales of the miraculous, supernatural intervention, and, in the end, a resurrection. He attributed these accretions to the apostles, who, according to Reimarus, created such legends around Jesus in order to transform Jesus' simple moral teaching into a supernatural religion. Turning the idea of apostolic succession on its head, he saw the apostles as the first bishops, establishing and defending their position of authority by asserting divine sanction for their views. In short, he argued that the church was, from the very beginning, a fraud. Small wonder that even after his death, Reimarus's family was reluctant to allow the publication of his notes, for fear that the reputation of his entire family would be ruined.

In retrospect one can see that Reimarus's theory of gospel origins was grounded in his own struggle with the church. The story of gospel origins is in fact much more complicated than Reimarus imagined it. But his work did make a lasting impact. His relentless application of the standards of consistency and reasonableness left little in the gospels that could stand up as evidence in a court of law. No one could read Reimarus and come away unshaken in the notion that the gospels could somehow be construed as modern, reasonably constructed history. To anyone interested in the historical Jesus, it had become abundantly clear that the gospels posed a serious problem.

The Quest for the Historical Jesus

Many who followed Reimarus held out the hope, however, that somehow buried in these incredible stories of miraculous feedings, walks on the sea, and corpses rising from the grave one could find a historical kernel beneath

---

22. Reimarus's fragment "On the Intentions of Jesus and His Disciples" is available in an English translation by Ralph S. Fraser, edited by Charles H. Talbert, *Reimarus: Fragments* (Philadelphia: Fortress Press, 1970). Talbert's excellent introduction is the source of most of the information about Reimarus presented here.

the embellished husk. The quest for the historical Jesus was on. The late eighteenth and early nineteenth centuries saw the publication of hundreds of books and articles on the historical Jesus. But unlike Reimarus, many of these studies were done not in critical opposition to the church, but as a way of revitalizing the church by uncovering the pure moral religion of Jesus, freed from its ancient supernatural encasement. Like Reimarus, however, they were all doggedly rationalistic in their approach. Among them one finds some of the most creative and fanciful explanations for Jesus' best-known miracles. For example, it was once proposed that the Feeding of the Five Thousand was accomplished with the help of a secret band of co-conspirators, who planted themselves with a large quantity of bread in a cave that day on the hillside, which they passed out to Jesus as was needed. Or there is the theory that Jesus walked on water with the help of an extremely long raft extending out into the Sea of Galilee.[23] This is also the origin of any number of theories explaining Jesus' resurrection (coma, physical shock, drug-induced stupor — the list is as endless as the imagination) many of which are themselves periodically resurrected and repackaged as astonishingly new and bold ideas. They are not.

This was the first quest for the historical Jesus. The assumption of most of the early questers was that the gospels were at least intended to be read as historical reports. The only problem was that their authors were ancients, with naive and primitive assumptions about the world, unenlightened about the laws of nature and unfamiliar with rational thought. They were trying to write history, but were simply ill-equipped for the task. If one could only see through their naive and primitive assumptions, one could find a historical core nestled beneath the layers of ancient naiveté. All of this work was chronicled by Albert Schweitzer at the end of the nineteenth century in his classic study, *The Quest of the Historical Jesus*.[24] It is often thought that Schweitzer brought the first quest to an end in this famous book, through his devastating review and dismantling of virtually every critical proposal from Reimarus to William Wrede. But this is not true. It is true that Schweitzer was devastatingly critical of his predecessors, but he did not fundamentally challenge their approach. He, too, thought that the gospels could be read critically to glean from them a historical kernel. He simply disagreed with the results of those

23. These creative ideas come from the work of Karl Friedrich Bahrdt, who wrote a weekly newsletter on the Bible in the 1780s and '90s. His views are reported by Albert Schweitzer in his classic treatment of the first quest for the historical Jesus, *The Quest of the Historical Jesus* (London: Adam and Charles Black, 1948), published in German originally in 1906 with the title *Von Reimarus zu Wrede*. Schweitzer's masterful treatment of the quest during this period is widely regarded as the standard. For Bahrdt's views on miracles see p. 41.

24. See previous note.

whose work preceded his. For his part, Schweitzer offered his own historical reconstruction of Jesus' life and ministry. We shall return to Schweitzer
presently.

Strauss's Attack on History

The end of the first quest for the historical Jesus came only when scholars began to realize that the gospels are not really historical sources at all.
While the first questers were busy constructing reasonable lives of Jesus, the
source of their undoing was already at work. He was David Friedrich Strauss.
Strauss was not a product of the Enlightenment, but of its successor, Roman-
ticism. The romantics did not repudiate the worldview of the Enlightenment
so much as they sought to supplement pure reason with a more humanistic approach to human culture and existence: human beings also "feel"
things (Kant); they have a certain "sensibility" (Rousseau); they have "ideas"
(Hegel). Strauss was impressed with the notion that truth might be borne in
"ideas" and that ideas might find their representation in mythic stories and
themes. In reading the gospels, Strauss became convinced that at base their
story is not a history, but the mythic expression of an idea: that God is incarnate in humanity. The problem is that the gospels had become historicized
in our thinking, so that the universal truth of God's incarnation in all of
humanity had come to be seen as a unique event associated only with Jesus.

Strauss set out to prove his case through a thoroughgoing critical assessment of the gospels themselves in a massive, two-volume manuscript, first
published in 1835 and 1836 when he was just twenty-seven years old.[25]
His plan, though thorough, was quite simple. First, he joined the rationalist
questers in dismantling the traditional supernaturalist position by discounting
the historicity of anything in the gospels that involved supernatural powers,
direct intervention by God, or miraculous feats by Jesus. But then he turned
around and attacked with equal vigor the rationalist position, by showing that
once those transcendent elements of the story are eliminated, there is virtually nothing left. There is nothing in our gospels upon which to construct a
reasonable, historical life of Jesus. If the gospels are not history, then what are

---

25. The original two-volume work was called *Das Leben Jesu, kritisch bearbeitet* (Tübingen:
Osiander, 1835–36). The book appeared in three subsequent editions. In the third edition
(1838–39), Strauss softened his position, moving closer to the great spokesperson for liberal
Christianity, Friedrich Schleiermacher. But in 1840, a new edition appeared, in which these
changes were withdrawn. An English translation by George Eliot first appeared in 1846. This
was recently reprinted, with an introduction and notes by Peter C. Hodgson, as *The Life of Jesus
Critically Examined* (Philadelphia: Fortress Press, 1972).

they? Strauss argued that they are myth — myth, not in the sense of "fairy tale" or "falsehood," but in the religious sense, as described by Hegel. Hegel spoke of myths as narratives that bear in themselves the content of eternal, universal "ideas." In Strauss's view, the gospels are mythic narratives that bear in themselves the universal idea of God's incarnation in humanity. To historicize them is to miss their point. The early church created them not to recount a history, but to give expression to what it had learned about God in Christ.

Strauss's position that the gospels are myth, not history, did not meet with warm regard. In attacking the supernaturalist position, he incurred the wrath of a still conservative state church. In attacking the rationalists, he alienated anyone who might have lent support to his position from a more liberal point of view. Though his book turned out to be very popular — owing to its controversial nature — its popularity could not save him. He lost his teaching position at Tübingen almost immediately and found himself blacklisted when others tried to find a position for him elsewhere. His own teacher denounced him as the "Judas Iscariot of our time."[26] He spent much of his life bitter and depressed, and eventually withdrew from a career in theology out of sheer frustration.

But Strauss had planted the seed of an idea: that perhaps the gospels had not been written with the intention of recounting a history at all. It was this basic idea that turned out to be the undoing of the first quest, as well as the traditional orthodox view that the gospels are literally, historically true. At the end of the nineteenth century this idea would be taken up again, but made more palatable by another German theologian, Martin Kähler, who was not a radical, but a conservative. What had been anathema to the church in the first half of the nineteenth century would at its end become the basis for a new orthodoxy.

The Quest Falters

Throughout the nineteenth century, in spite of Strauss's insights, the quest for a rational, reasonable life of Jesus continued. But its results became increasingly meager, and the figure that emerged seemed less and less compelling as a complacent nineteenth-century church struggled to find a Jesus with whom it could be comfortable. In 1892 the quest for a Jesus who was

---

26. As noted by Leander Keck in the introduction to his translation of Strauss's *The Christ of Faith and the Jesus of History: A Critique of Schleiermacher's "Life of Jesus"* (Philadelphia: Fortress Press, 1977), xvii. Keck notes that the epithet so effectively took that it apparently generated a legend that Strauss was red-haired, as was Judas in traditional portrayals of the time.

both historically plausible and theologically relevant was dealt a critical blow. This was the year Johannes Weiss published his study of the preaching of Jesus, in which he argued that Jesus was a preacher of apocalyptic doom, a prophet of the end time, who believed that the end of history was coming to pass in his own lifetime.[27] This hypothesis, made more popular by Albert Schweitzer after the turn of the century,[28] has persisted unchallenged until our own day.[29] But its impact on the quest for the historical Jesus was devastating. It meant that when all was said and done, the quest had yielded a Jesus whose preaching, to the extent that it can be known at all, was motivated by notions about the end of the world to which we can no longer subscribe. As Schweitzer so deftly put it at the end of his masterpiece of deconstruction, this Jesus

> will not be a Jesus to whom the religion of the present can ascribe, according to its long-cherished custom, its own thoughts and ideas, as it did with the Jesus of its own making. Nor will He be a figure which can be made by popular historical treatment so sympathetic and universally intelligible to the multitude. The historical Jesus will be to our time a stranger and an enigma.[30]

To its credit, the first quest for the historical Jesus had sought to make Jesus relevant to a culture vastly different from the world of Jesus. But in Schweitzer's view, in their search for relevance, the questers had been forced to overlook something so crucial to the preaching of Jesus that without it, it would collapse into an unrecognizable heap: apocalypticism. Could a Jesus who saw himself as standing on the edge of apocalypse, turning the wheel of history forward to its final hour with the force of his own shoulder, could such a Jesus still mean something to our world?

Schweitzer himself was not troubled by this. He wrote, "Jesus means something to our world because a mighty spiritual force streams forth from him and flows through our time also."[31] That spiritual force is to be found in the radically world-negating sayings, the so-called "hard" sayings of Jesus, which are quite in tune with apocalyptic's hostile stance over against the world.

---

27. Johannes Weiss, *Jesus' Proclamation of the Kingdom of God* (Philadelphia: Fortress Press, 1971; German original published in 1892).

28. Schweitzer, *The Quest of the Historical Jesus*, (see p. 31, n. 23 above.

29. The question of Jesus' commitment to apocalypticism has reemerged as a question in the most current phase of the discussion. The field, once united around the Weiss/Schweitzer hypothesis, is now divided. For the current state of the question and how some have begun to turn away from the apocalyptic hypothesis, see chapter 5 below.

30. Schweitzer, *The Quest of the Historical Jesus*, 396–97.

31. Ibid., 397.

The problem with the nineteenth-century lives of Jesus was that they offered a Jesus

> who was too small, because we had forced Him into conformity with our human standards and human psychology. To see that, one need only read the Lives of Jesus written since the [eighteen] sixties, and notice what they have made of the great imperious sayings of the Lord, how they have weakened down His imperative world-contemning demands upon individuals, that he might not come into conflict with our ethical ideals, and might tune His denial of the world to our acceptance of it. Many of the greatest sayings are found lying in a corner like explosive shells from which the charges have been removed. No small amount of elemental religious power needed to be drawn off from His sayings to prevent them from conflicting with our system of religious world-acceptance.[32]

For his part, Schweitzer accepted his own challenge and allowed the radical sayings of Jesus to explode his own world. He gave up his academic post and found the reign of God in deepest Africa, where he lived a life of radical world-negation. His convictions were legendary.

But what of those left behind amid the exploding shells, who could find comfort neither in the all too human and now apparently failed attempt to secure faith through historical research, nor in the "mighty spiritual force" streaming forth from Schweitzer's Jesus? Had the search for God come to a dead end in the quest for the historical Jesus?

The End of the Quest

In the midst of this despairing scene, Martin Kähler's little book *The So-Called Historical Jesus and the Historic, Biblical Christ*,[33] written ten years earlier, now appeared like a knight in shining armor. Kähler was well-versed in the advances that had been made in the critical study of the Bible and had accepted these largely negative results. But he also grasped the problem that modern critical scholarship posed for Christian theology, which had always sought its authoritative grounding in scripture (for Kähler, a German Protestant, this was especially true). In his small but enormously influential

---

32. Ibid., 398.

33. Martin Kähler, *The So-Called Historical Jesus and the Historic, Biblical Christ*, trans. and ed., with an introduction by Carl E. Braaten (Philadelphia: Fortress Press, 1964; German original published in 1896).

book, he posed the question in a way that is still relevant for many Christians today. As Carl Braaten phrased it in his introduction to the modern edition of Kähler:

> How can the Bible be a trustworthy and normative document of rev-
> elation when historical criticism has shattered our confidence in its
> historical reliability? And how can Jesus Christ be the authentic basis
> and content of Christian faith when historical science can never attain
> to indisputably certain knowledge of the historical Jesus?[34]

These were everyone's questions, not just Kähler's. But Kähler was not satisfied with the way in which they had been answered in his generation. In spite of warnings to the contrary, liberal theologians were still attempt-ing to address them by treating the gospels as sources for a life of Jesus, using critical analysis to reconstruct a reasonable account of Jesus' life and career. Orthodox theologians were still attempting to address them by assert-ing ecclesiastical authority, insisting that the Bible is historical because the church says that it is. Faith in the Bible, in the form of biblical inerrancy, became a necessary prerequisite to faith in Jesus Christ. Both positions, how-ever different, nonetheless shared a set of basic assumptions, and it was these assumptions that Kähler questioned: (1) that the gospels were intended to be read as history in the first place, and (2) that Christian faith should even be interested in a historical Jesus as its ground and starting point.

Kähler did not accept either of these propositions. The results of histori-cal criticism for Kähler indicated that the gospels were never intended to be read as history in the first place — certainly not history in the way we have come to understand the concept since the Enlightenment. But never mind, said Kähler. The church is not really interested in the historical Jesus. It is not interested ultimately in where he went, what he did, or what he said. These things, while interesting, simply do not have any bearing on Jesus as he is seen to be significant to the church. The church is interested in that which makes Jesus significant for our lives. Its interest is not in the *historical* Jesus, what he really did and said, but in the *historic* Jesus. What makes Jesus significant to the church, to humanity? For Kähler it was his *death and res-urrection*. This is the content of the gospel, for Kähler; it is also the content of the gospels. They are not histories intending to convey a teaching or an ethic, but "passion narratives with extended introductions."[35]

So it matters not that the gospels are not historical. To insist that they are is to press upon them a requirement that they cannot, and need not, fulfill.

---

34. In his introduction to Kähler, *The So-Called Historical Jesus*, 10.
35. Kähler, *The So-Called Historical Jesus*, 80, n. 11.

But Kähler went further still. To insist, with orthodoxy, on the historicity of the gospels is to insist that their claims be judged by a criterion established arbitrarily by our own particular human culture. History is our criterion, not the Bible's. He leveled the same criticism at the liberal quest for the historical Jesus. To search for a historical element within the text that could serve as the objective foundation for faith would be to put in danger the very nature of faith itself. Faith is always a risk to believe, to venture a life lived out of a transcendent reality. Kähler saw the quest for the historical Jesus as an attempt to minimize the riskiness of faith, to establish a kind of historical proof for one's claims. That would not be faith, but a flight from faith. The authority of the gospels, said Kähler, lay not in their historical accuracy, but in their ability to call forth faith in Jesus through generation after generation of Christians.

Kähler's approach to the problem proved compelling and persuasive for many generations of Christian theologians. In retrospect we can now see that it was really his work that brought to an end the first quest for the historical Jesus. As the search for God continued, it did so completely under his influence. The next generation of theologians would be dominated by persons profoundly influenced by him, most notably Karl Barth and Rudolf Bultmann. These two giants of early twentieth-century theology, often seen as opposite poles in the theological field of that time, were actually much more deeply connected than they were separated — and the connection lies in Kähler. Both Barth and Bultmann assumed that the starting point for Christian faith is not the historical Jesus, but the saving action of his death and resurrection. This, for them, was the heart of Christian faith and preaching — it was the *kerygma*. Each worked out the implications of this early Christian kerygma in very different ways, Barth using the categories of traditional orthodoxy, Bultmann using existentialist philosophy. However, these two camps within kerygmatic theology shared one thing: the historical Jesus was not a necessary part of the equation. For the time being, the quest was off.[36]

---

36. In view of this it may seem somewhat incongruous that Bultmann in fact wrote a very well-known book on Jesus, *Jesus and the Word* (New York: Charles Scribner's Son's, 1934; German original published in 1926). This is especially so since it will be recalled that Bultmann first published his *History of the Synoptic Tradition* in 1921, a book that is frequently credited with creating a new standard of skepticism about the historicity of the gospel tradition. But in fact it is not so incongruous. In *The History of the Synoptic Tradition* Bultmann is far more positive about the historicity of the tradition than is frequently realized, especially when it comes to discrete sayings assigned to Jesus. It is such sayings that are the focus of his attention in *Jesus and the Word*. The justification for this focus on Jesus' words, which would come to characterize the work of Bultmann's students in the later new quest (see below), can be found already in Kähler, who generally despaired of historical work, but allowed that the words of Jesus provide a

The New Quest

The quest has remained off for most European and American theologians for most of this century. European and American scholarship still stands under the influence of Barth and Bultmann, as the two schools of thought spawned by these compelling thinkers have branched into multiple forms and found a home in other lands. One might easily say that the success of these theological paradigms and their ability to unfold ever new aspects of Christian faith and its significance for modern people has proven that Christian theology does not really need the historical Jesus. That is where the matter stands for many theologians today. Christian theology begins with scripture, not history.

But a trip to the local bookstore will tell even the most casual observer of this drama that the problem of the historical Jesus has not really gone away. We are in the midst of a great resurgence of interest in the historical Jesus; seldom has scholarship so potentially arcane attracted such a broad popular audience. Where has this new interest come from?

It began more than forty years ago when a former student of Rudolf Bultmann raised the question: Can Christian theology really manage without the historical Jesus? The student's name was Ernst Käsemann, and he raised his question at a meeting of Bultmann's former students known as the "Old Marburgers," in 1953.[37] Käsemann answered his own question with a resounding "no." The sources themselves, argued Käsemann, will not allow us to renounce all interest in the historical Jesus. To be sure, the gospels as we have them are filled with Christian theology; they are not history. But they all cast that theology, give it expression, in terms of a life of Jesus. In other words, they all locate what they had come to see as decisive for our understanding of God within the very real life of a real person, Jesus. It matters not that their confessional way of recounting that life has all but obliterated any actual facts about Jesus. The one fact, that they cast their insights in the form of a life, says that the historical reality of this person is indispensable to the Christian understanding of who God is and how God works.

For Käsemann, the historical Jesus is theologically indispensable. In his historicity lies the particularity with which God encounters humanity. It is not in the abstract that one knows God, or through general principle, but in history, with all the particularity and challenge to decision that is found

---

kind of historical reference point to check our fantasies about the kind of person Jesus was (*The So-Called Historical Jesus*, 82).

37. Käsemann published the essay in German in 1954; it appeared in English as "The Problem of the Historical Jesus," pp. 15–47 in Ernst Käsemann, *Essays on New Testament Themes*, Studies in Biblical Theology, trans. W. J. Montague (Naperville, Ill.: Allenson; London: SCM, 1964).

only in a human life. The gospels declare that in this life, the life of Jesus, we have come to know God in a new way. The early Christian preaching about Jesus does not replace that life and render it superfluous; it confirms it and makes it decisive. It presents Jesus' life as *kairos*, a moment in history that demands a decision.

Käsemann also argued that historicity itself is important. It represents the claim that God chooses to reveal Godself in history, in the corporeality of human existence. In Jesus, God is near, not far. Käsemann thus called for a renewed effort to learn what we can about the historical Jesus, even though he knew that the methodological difficulties in evaluating the sources would be considerable.

Käsemann's call led to a new phase in historical Jesus research, known as the new quest. This term was coined by James M. Robinson, who also served as its chronicler and principal architect.[38] The New Questers did not simply take up where the first quest had left off. They did not return to a pre-Kähler understanding of the texts, treating them as naive history, whose facts need simply to be straightened out. They understood the theological nature of the texts. At the same time, however, they brought to their project a new understanding of history, which itself is not interested simply in the *bruta facta*. Drawing on the insights of R. G. Collingwood and Wilhelm Dilthey, they argued that a genuine interest in the past is motivated not by simple curiosity about what happened when, but by the desire to explore events in their significance for human beings, then and now. This new philosophy of history directed attention not to the *bruta facta* of history, but to the significance of the past for the present. But this is exactly the interest one finds expressed in the gospels. They, too, are not interested simply in preserving the facts about Jesus' life, but in presenting Jesus' life in all its significance for all who claim the name "Christian." So when the gospel writers selected materials and presented them in a way that emphasized the significance of Jesus, they did not thereby block all possibility for the modern historian to do his or her work. In a sense, their interest and that of the historian coincide: both are interested in that which makes Jesus significant for human existence.[39]

One might rightly sense in this program quite a different attitude toward the early church than that which characterized the first quest. The first quest, it will be recalled, was interested in Jesus before the church transformed him into an object of veneration, the Christ of faith. In the historical Jesus, they

---

38. James M. Robinson, *A New Quest of the Historical Jesus*, Studies in Biblical Theology (Naperville, Ill.: Allenson; London: SCM, 1959).

39. Ibid., 66–72.

believed, one could find that originally pure moral religion that should claim our only true loyalty as Christians. The New Questers saw things differently. In their view, the early Christian proclamation did not replace Jesus' own preaching, but confirmed and continued it in a new form. The New Questers asked whether and to what extent the preaching of the early church was anticipated already in the preaching of Jesus himself. Käsemann, for example, believed that Jesus did not think himself to be the Messiah. Nonetheless, the first, second, and fourth antitheses of the Sermon on the Mount (Matt 5:26–30, 33–37), which Käsemann takes to be authentic words of Jesus, indicate that in his teaching Jesus elevated himself above the authority even of Moses. He thus concludes, "The only category which does justice to his claim (quite independently of whether he used it himself and required it of others) is that in which his disciples themselves placed him — namely, that of Messiah."[40] In this way the New Questers could stress the continuity between the preaching of Jesus and the preaching of the early church, even while making historical judgments about what could rightly be ascribed to each.

To make such distinctions the New Questers began what has become a long tradition of rigorous historical methodology to be applied to the gospel texts. First, they assumed what biblical scholarship had shown over the previous hundred years, that the texts were not primarily intended to be read as history. They were interested, rather, in interpreting the significance of Jesus for their own communities in their own time and place some thirty-five to sixty-five years after the death of Jesus. If this is the case, they argued, then anyone wishing to use the gospels for historical purposes would have to face a stiff burden of proof. They would have to show that in spite of a gospel writer's lack of historical focus, he had nonetheless included this or that piece of historical information in the narrative. This the New Questers did in a variety of ways, developing certain criteria for identifying historical remnants in the texts. For example, they argued that something that could not be traced readily to the interests of the gospel writers themselves or their communities, but is nonetheless present in the text might reasonably be ascribed to Jesus.[41] They also looked for multiple attestation of material in two or more independent gospels texts, so that one could readily see that a single gospel

40. Käsemann, "The Problem of the Historical Jesus," 38.

41. This criterion, commonly referred to as "dissimilarity," naturally posed problems for the New Questers in exploring the lines of continuity between the preaching of Jesus and that of the early church. For example, the continuity Käsemann saw between Jesus' preaching in the antitheses of the Sermon on the Mount and the early church's claim that Jesus was the Messiah rests on the assumption that the antitheses of the Sermon on the Mount do in fact go back to Jesus. But given Matthew's general interest in presenting Jesus as an interpreter of the law, it is quite plausible to suppose that these antitheses do not go back to Jesus, but come from Matthew

writer was not responsible for creating this or that particular saying, parable, or story. Multiple attestation indicates that material is at least older than the gospels themselves, thus placing it one step closer to the historical Jesus. The New Questers also became wary of material with close parallels in the popular culture of antiquity, on the assumption that as Jesus became ever more significant to Christians, they would have ascribed various popular sayings and authoritative words to him, even if he had not himself uttered them. The Golden Rule is a good example of this. Many people advised treating others as one would like to be treated, some long before Jesus arrived on the scene. But Jesus became for Christians *the* source of all wisdom; thus, they gradually attributed all sorts of common wisdom to him. These commonplace sayings tended to be overlooked in favor of the more unusual, odd, clever, or difficult sayings in the tradition, for which there are no parallels in popular lore, but which could still fit plausibly into the first-century Galilean world of Jesus.

When conscientiously and rigorously pursued, such a methodology will of necessity be more complicated than can be dealt with here. The general picture of the procedure started by the New Questers, and in large measure continued today, is enough.[42] Above all, one can see that any attempt to find in the gospels anything like a complete portrait of Jesus will be something of a disappointment. The portrait will not be a portrait at all, but a fragmentary picture — like a jigsaw puzzle with most of the pieces missing. Neither will this fragmentary picture be an "objective" view of Jesus, any more than any historical procedure can claim objectivity. As participants in the human drama, all of us are much too involved in the human subject matter of history to claim objectivity. We can and must try to be fair, unprejudiced, and self-critical in viewing the past, but pure objectivity lies beyond our grasp. This is the problem historical criticism has left us with. We cannot undo it, try as we might, even with new discoveries like the Dead Sea Scrolls or the

---

himself. In this case, Käsemann overlooks his own criterion on the way to achieving the desired result.

42. Scholars do not always spell out clearly the criteria they actually use in determining what is historical and what is not. One recent attempt at clarity is Robert Funk's listing of all the "Rules of Evidence" used at one time or another by the Jesus Seminar in its deliberations (Robert W. Funk and Roy Hoover, eds., *The Five Gospels* [New York: Macmillan, 1993], 16–34). This part of the Jesus Seminar's work has been criticized because it seems to preprogram the results. In fact, however, this was not so. Funk's Rules of Evidence were compiled deductively, by looking back over the work of the Seminar and identifying the trends that developed over the course of several years. Another approach is offered by John Dominic Crossan in *The Historical Jesus: The Life of a Mediterranean Jewish Peasant* (San Francisco: HarperCollins, 1991). Rather than using strict criteria, Crossan uses a combination of historical and cross-cultural anthropological information to complement a critical reading of the pregospel tradition. My own criteria and method are spelled out in Appendix 1B of this volume.

Nag Hammadi Library. Of the historical Jesus we have only pieces, and for the most part, pieces of our own choosing. If we want to work theologically with the Jesus of history, this will have to do.

For many theologians, this would not do. For this reason, the new quest lasted about ten years, but then faded and passed from the scene. Its practitioners were interested in theology, but they could not ultimately sustain the project with such a fragmentary base of operations. New Testament theology went back to the texts of the New Testament and began exploring the theology of the evangelists, Matthew, Mark, Luke, and John, quite apart from the preaching of Jesus himself. Form criticism gave way to redaction criticism — the study of how the gospels are put together — and eventually to full-fledged literary criticism, leaving the problem of the origins of the gospel tradition behind. Historical theology gave way to narrative theology, in which authoritative texts could provide a solid normative foundation for a linguistically based theology of story. As for Käsemann, who issued the call for a new quest in the first place, he steered his career toward Paul, where extant letters give us access to the voice of the apostle himself. The quest for fragments of Jesus' life and preaching was too difficult and yielded results that were too meager and unsatisfying.

The Renewed Quest

The end of the new quest created a problem. Professional theologians had a bit of knowledge they did not know what to do with. They knew that the gospels are not history, and to recover history from them would be a task too complex and difficult to be useful for churches. And yet, just to explain this problem to a lay audience would itself be difficult, and troubling. Theologians, and the pastors they trained, shuddered to think of how one might effectively break the news to an ordinary congregation that the gospel stories they had come to treasure were not history, but fiction. And facing this question in the 1960s and '70s posed its own risks and difficulties. This was a period in which the historic Protestant denominations began losing members in droves. The cultural turmoil of that time had called into question modern institutional life in general, and the church, as an institution, suffered through a crisis of confidence along with other stalwarts of public life. Within the church, a new conservatism began to assert its grip on those who were left, hoping to stem the tide with a brave show of confidence in the past. This was not the time for theologians to come clean about the nature of the biblical texts. Fortunately, there was a way out. Narrative theology provided an easily misunderstood professional discourse, in which one could speak of the biblical narratives with the tacit understanding that they were stories, not history, but without ever explicitly addressing the troubling question of historicity. It became fashionable to dismiss the historical question as unimportant or beside the point.[43] The result was an ever widening gap between lay Christians and professional theologians. Most lay people continued to assume that the church still considered the gospels to be historical, a comfort to conservative Christians, but a scandal to more progressive, critically minded persons, who either left the church in dismay or simply held their peace in discomfort with one more institution that could not deal honestly with difficult questions.

This was the situation within which Robert W. Funk declared the quest on again with the founding of the Jesus Seminar in 1985. Funk had come to the end of a long and productive professional life in a variety of institutions — colleges, seminaries, universities — educating people into the ways of critical biblical scholarship, only to realize that his and the collective efforts of an army of biblical scholars working with the same critical presuppositions were not making any difference at all. The only public voice addressing the issue of the Bible, or of religious faith in general, was the conservative voice of the Christian right wing, represented by popular preachers and television evangelists. Mainline denominational leaders knew they could not agree with these new evangelicals but were not sure enough of their own position to really make any clear response to the growing wave of conservatism. Scholars had abandoned the field altogether, preferring the classroom and the library to public debate.

Funk stepped into the breach by assembling a group of about one hundred biblical scholars interested in pursuing the question of the historical Jesus. They came from a variety of backgrounds, both Catholic and Protestant, from various denominations, and from teaching posts in seminaries, colleges, and universities, both private and public. Funk's idea was to take on a central question, like the historical Jesus, in a self-consciously open forum in order to educate the broader public into the ways of biblical scholarship. He invited the press. He created a process — the much ballyhooed voting on sayings of Jesus using different colored beads — that was easy to understand and

---

43. Much of this school of thought grew up around a cluster of theologians at the Yale Divinity School, including George Lindbeck (see his *The Nature of Doctrine* [Philadelphia: Westminster, 1984]), Brevard Childs (see esp. his *Introduction to the Old Testament as Scripture* [Philadelphia: Fortress Press, 1979]), and Hans Frei (see his *The Eclipse of Biblical Narrative* [New Haven: Yale University Press, 1974]). All are heavily indebted to Karl Barth's view of scripture, as interpreted by Frei.

easily published.[44] It worked. Soon the subject of the historical Jesus was once again on everyone's agenda. Those who did not have anything to say about Jesus himself had plenty to say about keeping Jesus and the Jesus Seminar off the agenda and out of the news. Churches were caught off guard, wary of airing the critical basis of most mainline theology in public, and yet unable to repudiate what was being taught as a matter of course in most seminaries. Theologians committed to putting history aside in favor of a more narrative approach dismissed the new discussion and its promoters as unimportant and insignificant. But with Jesus once again on the cover of *Time* magazine, the protest rang hollow. The historical Jesus was turning out to be important after all.

The Jesus Seminar was not the only new scholarly effort to address the question of the historical Jesus. For example, in the same year that the Jesus Seminar began its deliberations, E. P. Sanders published his study *Jesus and Judaism* to critical acclaim.[45] But like the Jesus Seminar, Sanders and others consciously avoided any attempt to make their work relevant for theology. The quest for Jesus was on, but not the search for God. In the case of the Jesus Seminar, the participants were simply too diverse in their religious backgrounds and commitments to be able to offer anything like a coherent theological interpretation of their work. Others working within the con-fines of professional biblical scholarship had long since learned that revealing any theological agenda in connection with their historical work would only compromise their credibility within the academy. As the quest for Jesus con-tinued, it appeared as though it would go on without the theological interest that had always characterized it.

But the theological stakes associated with the figure of Jesus in Western culture do not go away just because historically oriented scholars choose not to address them. Whenever Jesus is the subject, someone in the discussion is thinking also about God. Culture has made Jesus more than simply an interesting historical figure; he is at the same time a religious symbol. As the discussion of the renewed quest broadened, its theological aspects began to emerge. Church groups began to study the results of the Jesus Seminar.

---

44. The Jesus Seminar published its results in a popularly accessible form in *The Five Gospels* (see p. 6, n. 2 above). In addition it published a small volume on parables (R. W. Funk, Bernard Brandon Scott, and James R. Butts, eds., *The Parables of Jesus: Red Letter Edition* [Sonoma, Calif.: Polebridge, 1988]), and the Gospel of Mark (R. W. Funk and Mahlon Smith, eds., *The Gospel of Mark: Red Letter Edition* [Sonoma, Calif.: Polebridge, 1991]). Volumes on Matthew, Luke, and Thomas are also planned. In addition, a second popularly accessible volume on the deeds of Jesus is planned for 1997.

45. E. P. Sanders, *Jesus and Judaism* (Philadelphia: Fortress Press, 1985).

The Five Gospels[46] became the centerpiece of seminars on spirituality. Marcus Borg's autobiographical pilgrimage, *Meeting Jesus Again for the First Time,*[47] became a religious best-seller. A colloquium was convened to discuss the theological implications of John Dominic Crossan's work.[48] And a vociferous backlash began among conservatives, which by its very force demonstrated that Jesus was by no means a matter of simple historical interest. Even the a-theological Jesus Seminar itself has now decided to broach the question of what the quest for Jesus might mean. Theology is once again on the table. The question is, how can we carry on a theological discussion about Jesus that is historically responsible, that makes sense in a pluralistic world, and yet still has the character of a *theological* discussion?

A Jesus Theology?

Throughout its history the problem of the historical Jesus has been received as a question of choices: *either* the historical Jesus *or* the church's Christ of faith. The initial discovery that these might not be the same thing, that the church's portrait of Jesus the Christ might not be a historical portrait of Jesus of Nazareth, produced among Christians a kind of disappointment and a resulting suspicion that has never really gone away. In the nineteenth century, this attitude of suspicion led to a fascination with the historical Jesus at the expense of the Christ of Christian faith. Back to Jesus! Forget Paul and the rest of the church's theologians who have obscured, then forgotten, the clear voice of Jesus and his remarkable vision. This was the clarion call of nineteenth-century liberal theology. One still hears this today as a kind of first response to the work of the Jesus Seminar and others who are reintroducing the problem of the historical Jesus to a broad public audience.

But the new world of liberal theology never came. In fact, as Christendom entered a new century its vision seemed more distant than ever. A new voice, advocating a different choice, was soon to be heard in the new advocates of orthodoxy. These neo-Orthodox theologians, such as Karl Barth, argued that what the world needed was not a teacher, but a savior with the power to lift

---

46. See n. 39 above.

47. Marcus Borg, *Meeting Jesus Again for the First Time* (San Francisco: HarperCollins, 1994). Borg, perhaps more than any other person involved in the current discussion, has been concerned to relate Jesus to contemporary religious faith. See, for example, his essays, "The Jesus Seminar and the Church," and "Does the Historical Jesus Matter?" 160–81 and 182–200, respectively, in his collected essays, *Jesus in Contemporary Scholarship.*

48. Jeffrey Carlson and Robert Ludwig, eds., *Jesus and Faith: A Conversation on the work of John Dominic Crossan* (Maryknoll, N.Y.: Orbis, 1994).

humanity from out of its utter sinfulness. A new call went out: forget Jesus, fast forward to Paul, the first person really to see the significance of Jesus, the Christ, our savior. One still hears this view expressed today among the critics of the renewed quest. The Jesus who emerges from this newest phase in the quest for the historical Jesus, they argue, is little more than ordinary, a mere human being incapable of inspiring the faith we know to have been the result of his life, death, and resurrection.

But to pose the problem of the historical Jesus as a choice is, in my view, a mistake. After all, the earliest Christians did not see the necessity of making a choice between the historical Jesus and the Christ of faith. The historical Jesus *was* their Christ of faith. As the new quest advocates of the 1950s and '60s rightly pointed out, the earliest Christian preaching about Jesus did not *replace* him with something new and different. The new things they said about Jesus, they still said *about Jesus*.[49] Nonetheless, the earliest Christians did say things about Jesus that Jesus himself did not say. Christian preaching was indeed something different, not a repetition of what Jesus said. So how are we to understand the relationship between the preaching of Jesus and the preaching of the earliest Christians? What is the structure of the earliest Christian faith and what are the real choices it offers us?

The Structure of the Earliest Christian Faith

Solving this problem takes some imagination — not much, but some. Let us imagine an encounter with the historical Jesus. Like most itinerant preachers/ teachers Jesus would have been found on occasion in the marketplace of an ancient town. Let us imagine such a situation. As he begins to teach, a small crowd gathers. Willi Marxsen liked to remind us that among those first hearers of Jesus there would have been various reactions.[50] We cannot imagine that everyone who heard Jesus was so taken with his words that immediately they fell down and worshiped him. His fate just does not bear this out. He was, after all, tried in a court of law, convicted, and sentenced to death, and all this, presumably, for something he said or did. Nor can we imagine that at the end of every speech Jesus performed some miraculous deed to prove the

---

49. See, for example, Käsemann, "The Problem of the Historical Jesus," 30–34; also Robinson, *A New Quest*, 78–79.

50. See especially Marxsen's essay "Jesus Has Many Names," pp. 1–15 in his collected essays, *Jesus and the Church: The Beginnings of Christianity*, selected, translated, and introduced by Philip E. Devenish (Philadelphia: Trinity Press International, 1992; German original published in 1968). The following approach is owed entirely to Marxsen and to Schubert Ogden, *The Point of Christology* (San Francisco: Harper & Row, 1982), 20–40.

veracity of what he had just said. Again, remember his fate. As Crossan has more recently remarked, any plausible historical reconstruction of Jesus must take into consideration that when people heard him and saw what he was doing, some said "Let's execute him," while others said "Let's worship him."[51] And there were other responses, from offense, to excitement, to indifference. But whatever the response was, it was always a *response to Jesus*. This is true of both the negative and the positive responses, the "Let's execute him" and the "Let's worship him," and even the "Who cares?"

This is the structure of the earliest Christian faith. The confessions of faith uttered by Jesus' followers did not replace what Jesus had said and done with new claims that were unconnected to their experience of him. Their confessions of faith in Jesus were a response to what he had said and done. Unlike those who were moved to anger by Jesus, or those for whom his words and deeds were a matter of complete indifference, those earliest Christians claimed that in his words and deeds they had come to know who God really is, what God is really like. Why? Simply because they had experienced Jesus that way. They heard Jesus' words and risked calling them the Word of God because they chose to believe in the kind of God they saw in him. Their responses of faith did not replace what Jesus had said and done with something new. Rather, they elevated what they had experienced in Jesus to a new kind of status: a claim about who God is, a *theological* claim.

If this is true, then one can see that the difference between the historical Jesus and the Christ of faith does not force us into a choice between the two. Rather, in order to have Christian faith one needs both. On the one hand, the historical Jesus by himself does not necessarily yield Christian faith. He is only a teacher, to whom many different responses were/are possible. A teaching, a life, is not yet a religion. It must move us, utterly so, beyond mere interest or fascination, to the point of risking the claim that in this person we have seen God.

On the other hand, early Christian declarations of faith in Christ are, by themselves, also inadequate. To say "Jesus is the Son of God" means nothing, unless, of course, one knows something about this Jesus. The point, after all, is not simply to assert that there is a Son of God. Ancient people would have taken this for granted. The notion of divine offspring walking among us on the face of the earth belonged to the common religious mentality of the ancient world. Asclepius, Heracles, Augustus Caesar — they were all sons of a god. So why would one say that *Jesus* was a son of a god, or even *the* Son

---

51. John Dominic Crossan, *Jesus: A Revolutionary Biography* (San Francisco: HarperSan-Francisco, 1994), 199–200.

of God? It could only be because one had chosen not to believe in a God of perfect health (Asclepius), of infinite strength (Heracles), or of wealth and brutal power (Augustus). One had chosen to believe in a God whose character is seen in Jesus. But who is that God? What is the substance of the theological claim being made in such a confession of faith? This can only be supplied by Jesus himself, what he said and what he did that so moved people to make the claim that in him they had come to know who God is. As Crossan has so succinctly put it: "Christian belief is always (1) an act of faith (2) in the historical Jesus (3) as the manifestation of God."[52]

What's in a Title?

We can illustrate this point by looking at the titles early Christians commonly ascribed to Jesus, titles such as "Christ," "Lord," or "Savior." These titles have become familiar to us as Christian titles. But they did not start out that way. Non-Christians used them long before they were applied to Jesus. So what makes Christianity any different from other forms of Judaism that proclaimed the arrival of the Messiah, or from the imperial cult of the caesars, which hailed Augustus as its lord and savior? The distinctiveness of Christianity lay not in these titles, but in the fact that early Christians applied them to Jesus, who said and did certain things. To get at the substance of the claims Christians were making when they applied these titles to Jesus, one must first take seriously what Jesus said and did that made this seem like the appropriate response to Jesus.[53] For example, Jesus once said that the Empire of God is like this:

> A person once gave a great banquet, and invited many guests. And when it came time for the banquet, he sent his servant around to the invited guests to say, "Come, for everything is now ready." But they all, one after another, began to make excuses. The first guest said to him, "I've bought a field and must go out to look it over. Please pass along my regrets." And another said, "I've bought five yoke of oxen and must go examine them. Please pass along my regrets." And another said, "I

---

52. Ibid., 200.

53. As Marxsen says so clearly, "We need to pay attention precisely to the direction in which the statement 'Jesus is the Messiah' came into being. It was not a matter of transferring all current messianic conceptions to Jesus, but rather of rediscovering (in the Messiah-concept) experiences one had had with Jesus. The name that Jesus receives has to be filled with content from the experiences one had had with Jesus — not from current messianic conceptions" ("Jesus Has Many Names," 7).

have just gotten married and so cannot come." So the servant went and reported this to his master. Then the householder got angry and said to his servant, "Go out right away into the streets and alleys of the city and bring in the poor, the blind and the lame." And the servant said, "What you have commanded has been done, but there is still more room." So the master said to the servant, "Go out to the highways and hedges and compel people to come in, so that my house might be filled. For I tell you, none of those who were invited shall ever taste my banquet."[54]

Now we have something to work with. Let's go back to those titles: what did early Christians mean by calling Jesus names like "Christ," "Lord," and "Savior"?

The first of these, "Christ," is just the Greek word for "Messiah." Both mean "the anointed one." In Jewish culture, anointing was part of the ceremony for installing the king. The anointed one is the king. So Messiah or Christ is a common title having nothing to do originally with Christianity. In Jesus' time the hope for a new Messiah was bound up with the hope for a new kingdom in which Israel might be freed from Roman rule and turn once again to live in faithfulness to God. So what does it mean to call Jesus "Christ" or "Messiah"? It is to proclaim that with Jesus the reign of God was here, that it was and is just as he described it. But can we believe that this is true? Can we believe that the reign of God is like a banquet in which the blind, the poor, and the lame find a place? Can we believe that God will welcome into it anyone who dares to come in? That is what it means to call Jesus the Christ. It is to accept his vision of the banquet and the God who comes with it.

The title "Lord" is also common and early in Christianity. What does it mean to say "Jesus is Lord"? Is this a different order of claim? A lord — in Greek *kurios* — is one who has servants at his disposal. Like Messiah or Christ, Lord is a common title not having to do originally with Christianity. In fact, it is not always a religious term at all. To say, "so and so is my lord," is to place oneself at the disposal of someone, to do that person's work, to respond to that person's commands. So to confess Jesus as one's Lord is simply to ask, "What am I to do in the service of Jesus?" What does Jesus command one to do? "Go out into the streets, and gather in the poor, the blind, and the lame." "Bring in anyone you find. . . . Fill up the banquet hall!" Is it possible to

---

54. This is Luke's version of the parable of the Great Feast (Luke 14:16b–24), versions of which are also found in Matthew (Matt 22:2–13) and the Gospel of Thomas (Thom 64). Luke's version, which the Jesus Seminar designated "pink" (="Jesus probably said something like this"), is close enough to an original parable of Jesus for our purposes here.

do this? Is it possible to open up the table so that all may come? Is it possible to enact the vision of the reign of God Jesus offers? This is what it would mean to claim Jesus as one's Lord.

And what about "Savior"? What does it mean to say "Jesus is my Savior"? The ancient world was full of saviors: Isis, Atargatis, Sarapis, Asclepius, Zeus, Augustus Caesar. Saviors were so plentiful in antiquity because antiquity was so rough. Ancient life was "nasty, brutish, and short," to appropriate the aphorism of Hobbes. Many people asked, "Is there anyone who cares about me? Is life more than random violence with brief interludes of tolerable peace? Is there a God who cares what happens to me personally, who loves *me?*" These are the questions behind the quest for a savior. A savior is one who cares about me, who loves me, who will protect me. Where is that care to be found? Where can one find that kind of love and security? In the military power of the emperor? In the healing touch of Asclepius? In the mysterious inner sanctum of the Isis temple? When early Christians claimed Jesus as their Savior, they were claiming that the love of God was to be found around the open tables of the Jesus movement. It was there that they experienced care. It was there that they experienced love. It was there that they experienced the safety and security that comes only from knowing experientially that there is a God who cares about me personally. Jesus created an experience of the unmitigated love of God for those in his world who had experienced it least: the poor, the blind, the lame, the homeless. They in turn confessed him as "Savior."

So the historical Jesus is important. And so are the confessions of the early church. That Jesus' reign is the reign *of God,* that he makes demands on my life, that in him I find refuge — these are the things that come from the confessional language of the early church. But what is that reign *like?* *What* does Jesus demand of me? What does it *feel like* to be embraced by God? These questions can be answered only if we pay close attention to the person whom early Christians confessed as Christ, Lord, and Savior: Jesus of Nazareth, the historical Jesus.

A Resurrection or the Resurrection?

This point may be further illustrated by exploring one of the most important and basic Christian confessional claims about Jesus: that God raised him from the dead. Many Christians assume that "the resurrection" is that one, great miraculous event that gave Christian faith a jump-start and proves once and for all that Christians have a unique claim on the truth about God. But to someone living in the ancient world, such an attitude would not have made much sense. The problem is this: when one speaks today of "the resurrection," no one ever asks what he or she is talking about. We all know *whose* resurrection *the* resurrection is. Since the resurrection of famous people is no longer part of our worldview (excepting, perhaps, the worldview of the tabloids), we have reserved a special and unique place for Jesus' resurrection. It appears to us like an utterly unique event, the likes of which even Elvis cannot hope seriously to attain. By itself it appears quite adequate to inspire faith in Jesus as the Son of God, regardless of what he said or did.

But to ancient ears, the resurrection of Jesus would not have sounded quite the same. You could never say "the resurrection" and expect that everyone would know what you were referring to. The first question an ancient would want to ask is: Whose resurrection? That there *was* a resurrection would not have been the question. Everyone knew about famous resurrections. Resurrection was a confessional element of most ancient religions. So to say that God raised someone from the dead . . . well, by itself, it really does not say much. It depends on who: Who was raised from the dead? What did he say? What did she do? What did he stand for that God would raise him from the dead?

Most people in Jesus' day believed that the emperor Augustus had been raised from the dead. Now, there was a religion. All over the Mediterranean world one can find its legacy still today in grand temples and arches, dedicated to the gods "Roma and Augustus." Rome was very clear about what it believed in. It believed in power. No one embodied that more than Augustus. He conquered lands far and wide, from which great treasures were extracted. He subjugated cultures, gave them a new language and new institutions. He quashed rebellions. His life was one great manifestation of power. The imperial cult was about power. And the great thing about a religion of power is that it provides its own authentication: victory reveals the favor of the gods. Resurrection became the ultimate symbol of that religion: the final victory. The ultimate bestowal of power was to rise beyond the limits of this world to join the great pantheon of the gods in heaven.

Now, if one looked just at the resurrection in Christianity, one might get the impression that Christian faith was about this too, about power. And many have made the mistaken assumption that the resurrection shows that the Christian god is the most powerful god, and that this power is to be used to subjugate inferior, less powerful cultures. If one looks critically and honestly at the history of bringing Christian faith to Africa, Asia, the Americas, or Hawaii, one has to admit that Christians have indeed been confused about this at certain times in our history. Let's be honest about modern American faith claims. The doctrine of manifest destiny is a statement of faith. The *Wealth of Nations* is a religious tractate.

But the earliest Christians did not just proclaim *a* resurrection, as though the power of such a demonstration was the point. No, this confessional statement was attached to a history, the history of a person, Jesus of Nazareth. He was not powerful, but the victim of power. He did not believe in the Empire, but proclaimed another Empire, the Empire of God. He said things like:

> Blessed are you beggars, for the Empire of God belongs to you;
> Blessed are you hungry, for you will be satisfied;
> Blessed are you who cry and are depressed, for you will laugh;
> Blessed are you when people despise you, and exclude you, make fun of
>   you, and curse you, for prophets have always been treated like this.[55]

He said to religious leaders: "Prostitutes and sinners go into the Empire of God before you."[56]

God raised . . . him? He said what? Who is this God, whose empire belongs to beggars? What kind of religion focuses on these marginal, pathetic creatures? These are the questions posed by the claim that God raised *Jesus* from the dead.

An Existential Christology

So, if one proclaims that God raised *Jesus* from the dead, that *Jesus* is the Son of God, then it makes a difference what he said and did, what people experienced of him that moved them to say such things. Jesus' words and deeds in this way give definition and character to Christian theology — they make it *Christian!* And for this same reason, for the Christian, the quest for the historical Jesus will also always be about the search for God. However, this way of coming to see God in Jesus will involve coming to see Jesus and his significance for Christians in a way that is profoundly different from what many have assumed to be normative, orthodox thinking. Let me explain.

---

55. These are the beatitudes more or less as they appear in Luke's Sermon on the Plain (Luke 6:20b–23). They are also found in Matthew's Sermon on the Mount (Matt 5:3–4, 6, 10–12) and the Gospel of Thomas (Thom 54, 69:2, 68:1). The Jesus Seminar designated the first three beatitudes in their Lukan form "red." The fourth I have modified to remove the early Christian apologetical motifs that caused the Jesus Seminar to designate it "gray." In this form I would designate it "pink."

56. Matt 21:31b. A small majority of the Fellows in the Jesus Seminar designated this saying "red" or "pink," but the stronger feeling of the minority against attributing it to Jesus led ultimately to a weighted average in the "gray" designation. I would assign it a "pink" designation.

When most people today say something like "Jesus is God's Son," they mean to say that there was something about Jesus that was essentially different from all other human beings. It is not just that he behaved in an unusual way. He was different in his essence, in his being. This idea may be seen in the words of a placard hoisted aloft several years ago by a protester outside an Atlanta theater during the showing of the controversial Scorsese film *The Last Temptation of Christ*. It read, "My Savior is not human!" These are the words of a zealot, but they express with a clarity afforded only in hyperbole what many Christians think about Jesus. They think that in his essence Jesus was not really human after all. He was divine. The problem with this essentialist approach to Christology, an approach encouraged throughout the last generation of positivist theologians, such as Karl Barth, is that for many modern folk it has become incredible in a way that was not so for the ancient folk who created the texts of the New Testament. For ancients, the idea that a human being might essentially be divine made sense. In a worldview in which Gods sometimes mated with human beings, the offspring of such a conjugation, a divine human being, was a distinct possibility. Today, of course, no one believes this. But many still believe that Jesus was essentially divine, accepting this as an article of faith, even though the mythic framework within which such belief might have made sense has long passed from our cultural consciousness. It remains as the text of a placard, a rallying cry. But it is a claim without much meaningful content in the modern world. It is perhaps the centerpiece of a modern Christianity that has been drained of most of its content and meaning.

What I have been describing in the final pages of this chapter is an alternative to this essentialist approach to Christology. I will call this approach an "existential Christology." It is based on the idea that the early followers of Jesus did not make claims about him because they had somehow sensed in him a different essence, a palpable divinity. When they said of him, "Behold, the Son of God," it was not because they had seen a halo circling his head. It was because they had heard him say and seen him do certain things. They experienced him acting in their lives. And what they experienced in the company of this person, Jesus, moved them deeply. They heard in his words profound truth about the world, about human nature, and about God. They experienced in his actions what authentic human being can and should be. In his life they experienced a depth of meaning that tapped into what they knew to be true, ultimately true. Such truth is called, in normal religious parlance, God. God is that ultimate reality running through and beyond all things, in which all things have their grounding, in which life, if it is to have any meaning at all, must also be grounded. In their experience of Jesus, the followers of Jesus had experienced God. In his followership they had found the true meaning of their lives. And so they said of him, "Behold, the Son of God."

An existential approach to Christology takes this basic experience as the foundation of Christian faith. Christian faith began with a decision to see in Jesus' words and deeds the deepest of all truths, the truth that is God. This is what Christian faith was, and must become if it is ever again to have any meaning in the modern world. In the coming chapters I wish to present the words and deeds of Jesus, to the extent that responsible historical scholarship makes this possible, in such a way that reveals what they meant to those who decided that in Jesus they had come to know who God is. What did he do? What did he say? And why did these things matter to people? Can they matter again in our own time? The quest for the historical Jesus is part of my own search for meaning . . . for truth . . . for God.

Chapter 2

Jesus and the Empire of God

On Dirt, Shame, and Sin
in the Expendable Company of Jesus

The Jesus who was preached to us was barely human. He seemed to float above history, above all human problems and conflicts. He was pictured as a high and mighty king or emperor who ruled over us, even during his earthly life, from the heights of his majestic throne. His approach to the poor was therefore thought of as condescending. He condescended to make the poor the objects of his mercy and compassion without sharing their oppression and their struggles. His death had nothing to do with historical conflicts, but was a human sacrifice to placate an angry God. What was preached to us was a completely other-worldly Jesus who had no relevance to this life.

— The Kairos Document (1989)

The Gospel of Jesus

What did the followers of Jesus experience in his company that moved them to claim that in his words and deeds they had come to know who God is? What was the goodness they saw in his deeds? What was the good news — the "gospel" — they heard in his words? And how did some people find such ultimate goodness in Jesus, while others experienced him quite differently? Indeed, not everyone experienced Jesus as *good* at all. For some, Jesus was an enigma, an oddball; what he said and did was to them meaningless nonsense. And among those who did understand him, the meaning of what he said and did was not all the same. For some he was interesting, perhaps even amusing in his novelty. For others, Jesus was a threat, a danger to be dealt with, a voice to be silenced. But for some, what Jesus said and did meant something good. His words were heard as good news, as "gospel." Their experience of him was redemptive, liberating, empowering. And for some, this experience of Jesus gave meaning to their lives in a way that only something ultimately real and authentic can do, and they gave themselves over to it. These were the first Christians.[1] In Jesus they had seen God. If the quest for the historical Jesus is also to be about the search for God, then we must ask what it was that

---

Parts of this chapter were presented originally as the Calista Olds Lecture in Biblical Studies at The Defiance College in Defiance, Ohio, on October 27, 1994.

1. Our use of this term to describe these earliest followers of Jesus should always be cautious and qualified. One should remember, for example, that all of these early followers were Jewish, as was Jesus himself. None of them had any notion of starting a new religion that would one day stand over against Judaism. Such thinking would not enter into the followership of Jesus until many generations after his death. In using the term "Christian" to describe these early followers of Jesus, I intend to designate persons for whom Jesus became an experience of God. I also intend to suggest that these earliest followers of Jesus were indeed the first "Christians." As I will argue in chapter 6, it did not take a resurrection to call forth such faith in Jesus. For some, it would have happened the day they met Jesus; for others, never at all, in spite of the resurrection proclamation. For a defense of this basic point of view, see Willi Marxsen, "When Did Christian Faith Begin?" pp. 76–95 in *Jesus and the Church,* trans. and ed. Philip E. Devenish (Philadelphia: Trinity Press International, 1992). For Marxsen, "Christian faith began with the event of being moved by Jesus" (ibid., 92).

these first Christians experienced in the company of Jesus that moved them to say that in this person they had come to know what God is really like.

History and Theology

In what follows, I will focus primarily on things Jesus is said to have done; his sayings and parables will be explored more thoroughly in subsequent chapters. But focusing on the so-called "deeds" of Jesus poses some peculiar — some would say intractable — difficulties for the historian. When the Jesus Seminar began its work, it inherited a number of methodological principles from earlier generations of historians in quest of the historical Jesus. But most of those methods were designed to help identify authentic *sayings* of Jesus. When we tried to apply them to things Jesus is said to have done, we soon found that they were not very useful. For example, many sayings of Jesus are attested independently in multiple early Christian sources. Such multiple attestation is usually taken as a sign that a saying is very old, and perhaps goes back to Jesus himself. In dealing with things Jesus is said to have done, we soon found that very few deeds of Jesus were multiply attested. Unless we were to assume that Jesus was a person who talked a lot but did little, we were forced to conclude that there was something about the way early Christians talked about the deeds of Jesus and passed these traditions on that was different from the sayings of Jesus. We did not (and still do not) fully understand these differences. But we knew that the methods of earlier questers were coming up short as we explored this new territory.

Perhaps the best provisional solution to this problem is to say simply that the deeds of Jesus present us with the creative memory of the early church. In the Jesus Seminar, it was seldom that we could assert, even tenuously, the historical accuracy of any particular event or occasion as it is depicted in the gospels, or in fact, that such and such an event occurred at all. But we did notice that certain types of events are depicted with great frequency in the Jesus tradition, and across a variety of sources and forms. Things like healings and exorcisms, cavorting with the unclean and the shamed, conflict with his family — such things began to emerge as "typical" of Jesus in the widespread memory of the early church. Such "typifications"[2] became the basis

---

2. This term was coined by Robert W. Funk and explained in "On Distinguishing Historical from Fictive Narrative," *Forum* 9, nos. 3–4 (1993): 193–98. Funk's note of caution is in order, however. He points out that people might typify things the way they used to be, or as they are, or as we would like them to be, and we do not always distinguish between these things in the telling (196). That is, events narrated as typical of the past may actually represent present

for a general description of the sort of things Jesus probably did, even though the historicity of any single story in the gospels was always hard to demonstrate. It seems, then, that we have inherited from earliest Christianity the creative memory of what people experienced in Jesus' ministry and a collection of stories to illustrate and give form to the memory of that experience. The gospels seldom give us what might be described as a historical event. Rather, we have stories born of memory, impressions of what Jesus was like. The limits of ancient history are considerable, indeed.

Needless to say, then, nothing in this chapter can be said without affixing to it the word "probably." But this is true of most writing of history. The work of the historian can normally offer only probability, not exactitude. History is not science; it belongs in the Humanities building, not Natural Sciences. It can offer no quantifiable data, whose meaning would be self-evident to anyone. There is never even a clear starting point for the historian. History is always somewhat circular in its methods. One looks at the past through the memories of those who experienced it, gathering together the impressions left by events on the lives of people. In the end, the historian must try to render a "reading" of this collective mass of information. She or he must try to assemble it in a way that makes historical sense. She or he must attempt a "reading" of this amorphous collection of evidence that is fair and unprejudiced. But there are no guarantees. There can be no objectivity in history. We are all much too involved in the subject matter of history — human existence itself — to claim objectivity. At best the historian can strive only to be fair, unprejudiced, and self-critical in looking at the past. Certainty always lies beyond the historian's grasp. But this should not be viewed as a loss, a deficiency of history. To the contrary, it is its very nature and strength. For we look to history not out of idle curiosity, but to ask about the relevance of the past for our own present. History does not ask a scientific question, but an existential one. One cannot observe history; one can only encounter it.

For some, this lack of objectivity makes history an inappropriate medium for engaging in theological reflection. For me, it makes it the most appropriate medium. Like history, theology also does not ask a scientific question. To be sure, the age-old longing for certitude of faith, the desire to know beyond a shadow of a doubt the ultimate secrets of the universe, anxiety

---

or future hoped-for realities instead. Thus, one must be on the look-out for typifications that seem incompatible with, or embarrassing to the social location of Christians, and that would be difficult to assimilate into the new way of Christian comportment. In this "debris" of the tradition, we will likely find typifications that describe the gist of what Jesus was about doing (197). This reasoning, of course, bears resemblance to the criterion of distinctiveness, or dissimilarity, typically used in the evaluation of the sayings tradition.

about death and the quest for security, all make it tempting to transform theology into a science. This is the impulse behind the dubious concept of "Creationism," which reduces the Bible to a pseudo-science with a false offer of scientific credibility. But the biblical text itself, a mixture of history and its interpretation, will not allow such an easy escape from the existential question posed to us by both history and theology: the question of meaning. What does human existence mean? The answer to this question is never automatic or self-evident in the way that answers to scientific questions might often be. Answering this question with authenticity is infinitely more difficult than answering any question of science, for it always involves a subjective commitment to seeing the world in a certain way. One cannot calculate the answer to an existential question like a mathematical equation. One must reflect on existential questions. One must ponder them. Answers do not come quickly or automatically. They must be tested in the living of them.

For someone who believes in God, human existence means something because there is a God who gives life its ultimate meaning. To believe in God is to believe in a transcendent reality running through and beyond all things, a fundamental reality in which existence itself is grounded. Faith in God is an act of trusting in this reality and risking a life that is oriented to it. For someone who believes in God, the question of life's meaning must therefore always involve two simultaneous questions posed at once: Who is God? and Who must I become if I choose to give myself over to this God?[3] Finding meaning in life always involves venturing an answer to both of these questions. To be serious about the God question is to ask about that ultimate reality without which life means nothing. Answering it seriously involves moving beyond any abstract ideas about what God is like and giving oneself over to the ultimate reality that is God. That is the risk of faith. When the earliest Christians risked faith in Jesus, they were venturing an answer to this most pressing twofold question: We have found God in the words and deeds of this person, Jesus, and, we really are who he says we are to become. Who was Jesus? And what did he say or do that the earliest Christians experienced as this kind of ultimate reality, a reality to which they could give themselves fully? This is to ask what Jesus *meant* to people. It is the question asked by both history and theology.[4]

---

3. This and the insights to follow are owed to Schubert Ogden, "The Question Christology Answers," 20–40 in idem., *The Point of Christology* (San Francisco: Harper & Row, 1982).

4. The convergence of the interests of theology and history on the question of meaning was one of the insights of proponents of the new quest that created for them the possibility of reopening the quest for Jesus, in spite of the historical difficulties posed by the gospels themselves.

The *Basileia* of God

How did Jesus describe what he was doing? The gospels typically depict him speaking of his activity as the *basileia* of God. Jesus announces the presence of this *basileia;* his parables illustrate this *basileia;* he calls prostitutes, tax collectors, children, and beggars into this *basileia.* In the synoptic gospels this term is used over a hundred times. Jesus is depicted as speaking all the time about the *basileia* of God.[5]

Quite naturally, then, this way of speaking has worked itself into the language of Christian faith. The common way of translating this term into English is to use the word "Kingdom." That is how you will find it in the old King James Version and its descendants, like the Revised Standard Version and its recent revision, the New Revised Standard Version. That translation tradition was very influenced by the olde King's English, in which one speaks of sovereignty using "kingdom." But that translation long outlived the King's English whence it came. It survives today as part of that special antique vocabulary one finds only in the Bible. Now people are beginning to translate it differently, for example, using the neologism "Kindom," removing the androcentrism of the word "king" — and that is right and good. Some people are translating it as "Reign," reverting to a Latin base that is at least less recognizably sexist than the English word "Kingdom." Others are using the word "Rule." Religious terminology always demands this sort of careful attention.

But how would an ancient person listening to Jesus have heard this term *basileia?* When this word appears in a nonbiblical text from the ancient world it is usually translated as "empire." It is a very political term. It is the word ancients used to refer to empires, or more precisely in Jesus' day, *the* empire: Rome. There was only one empire in Jesus' world, and that was Rome. Jesus took this very political term and attached to it the words "of God." This was unusual. As Burton Mack has pointed out, the term "Empire of God" (Kingdom of God), contrary to common assumptions, does not appear very often in the literature of the Roman imperial period. But this is understandable. To speak of "empire" is to speak of Rome. And why speak of an "Empire *of* God," that is, an empire as God would run it, if one does not have something critical to say about the empire as "you know who" runs it.[6] To speak of an

---

See esp. James M. Robinson, *A New Quest of the Historical Jesus,* Studies in Biblical Theology (Naperville, Ill.: Allenson; London: SCM, 1959), 66–72.

5. This term is not limited to the tradition of the synoptic gospels alone, but crops up regularly in Paul's letters, in John, James, Revelation, and in other early Christian literature.

6. For a discussion of the paucity of references to this term in Jewish literature see Burton

Empire of God would have been risky, to say the least. But Jesus chose this very political, very risky concept as the central metaphor for expressing what he was about. Why?

Rome and the World of Jesus

What did Jesus, a peasant from Galilee, know of Rome? Enough. Rome was not a distant, abstract reality to people like Jesus, who lived in its provincial districts. Rome dominated Jesus' world. He lived and died about a century after Rome had taken Palestine by force and made it a province to serve its larger imperial aspirations.[7] In the past, Western European historians have tended to give their cultural ancestors the benefit of the doubt on the question of how they came to control so much. It was, after all, such a gift, the great Roman Peace, the *Pax Romana*. Augustus himself did not blush to boast:

> I extended the frontiers of all the provinces of the Roman people, which has as neighbors races not obedient to our Empire.
>
> I restored peace to all the provinces of Gaul and Spain and to Germany, to all that region washed by the ocean from Gades to the mouth of the Elbe.
>
> Peace, too, I caused to be established in the Alps from the region nearest to the Hadriatic as far as the Tuscan sea. . . .
>
> . . . Two armies were led almost at the same time, one into Ethiopia, the other into that part of Arabia which is called Felix; and large forces of the enemy belonging to both races were killed in battle, and many towns captured. . . .
>
> Egypt I added to the Empire of the Roman people . . . and all of Cyrene. . . .[8]

Mack, *A Myth of Innocence* (Philadelphia: Fortress Press, 1988), 69–74. Mack suggests as a more likely cultural context the ongoing discussion of kingship and rule among Cynic philosophers contemporaneous with Jesus. For the price they paid for their social criticism, see D. R. Dudley, *A History of Cynicism from Diogenes to the 6th Century A.D.* (London: Methuen, 1937), 125–42.

7. The Roman general Pompey entered Jerusalem in 63 B.C.E. after a three-month siege of the city.

8. Excerpted from the *Res Gestae Divi Augusti,* an account of his accomplishments penned by Caesar Augustus himself near the end of his life (Suetonius, *Augustus* 101). A translation of this and other documents relevant to understanding the world of Christian origins is to be found in C. K. Barrett, *The New Testament Background,* rev. ed. (San Francisco: Harper & Row, 1987). For the *Res Gestae* of Augustus see 2–4.

His work did not go unappreciated in verses penned by his pet poet, Horace, and sung by a choir of young men and maidens on the occasion of the Secular Games of 17 B.C.E.:

> If Rome be your handiwork...then do ye, O gods, make teachable our youth and grant them virtuous ways; to the aged give tranquil peace; and to the race of Romulus, riches and offspring, and every glory!
>
> And what the glorious scion of Anchises and Venus [a.k.a. Augustus Caesar], with sacrifice of milk-white steers, entreats of you, that may he obtain, triumphant over the warring foe, but generous to the fallen![9]

More recently, however, scholars like Richard Horsley have begun to cast the Roman *Pax* in a different hue.[10] One need only read a little between the lines of a historian not quite yet entirely co-opted by Rome for a glimpse of how Roman advancement proceeded in a place like Palestine. Josephus, writing more than a century after the fact, provides evidence that Jews had not yet forgotten how, in 43 B.C.E., when the towns of Gophna, Emmaus, Lydda, and Thamma were slow in paying their share of the Judean tribute, Cassius sold all their inhabitants into slavery.[11] Or there was the time when the Roman general, Varus, quelled protests following Herod's death (shortly before the birth of Jesus) by sacking the great cities of Galilee and Samaria. Included among them was Sepphoris, just over the hill from Jesus' native Nazareth. Varus sold its inhabitants into slavery. The protests ended with a public crucifixion of two thousand of the ring leaders.[12] And what became of all those slaves? Rome needed them — for the mines, the great Roman latifundia, the galleys. Rome built its empire on the backs of slaves.[13]

So someone like Jesus would have known about Rome and its great *Pax*, but it may not have looked quite as good to him as it did to Horace. Jesus' sentiments might have been closer to those of Tacitus's fictitious Briton gen-

---

9. From the *Carmen Seculare* of Horace. The Secular Games were held once a century. Horace was commissioned to write this hymn to commemorate the accomplishments of Augustus on this auspicious occasion. The hymn is to be found in Barrett, *New Testament Background*, 6–7.

10. See esp. his *Jesus and the Spiral of Violence* (San Francisco: Harper & Row, 1987).

11. Josephus, *Ant.* xiv.272–75; *War* i.219–20, as noted by Horsley, *Spiral of Violence*, 43.

12. Josephus, *Ant.* xvii.288–95; *War* ii.66–75, as noted by Horsley, *Spiral of Violence*, 43–44.

13. Imperial Rome was a slave economy. The classical historian Moses Finley summarizes: "In the great 'classical' periods, in Athens and other Greek cities from the sixth century B.C. on and in Rome and Italy from early in the third century B.C. to the third century A.D., slavery effectively replaced other forms of dependent labour" (*The Ancient Economy* [Berkeley: University of California Press, 1973], 69). Western European historians have generally allowed apologetical interests to soften the harsher aspects of slave realities in the ancient world. For a more sobering treatment see K. R. Bradley, *Slaves and Masters in the Roman Empire: A Study in Social Control* (New York: Oxford, 1987).

eral, who has just experienced the *Pax Romana* at the end of a Roman lance: "To plunder, butcher, steal, these things they misname empire; they make a desolation and call it peace" (*Agricola* 30).

Rome organized itself into a great hierarchy. Marcus Borg, drawing on the work of the anthropologist Gerhard Lenski, has given an apt description. If one were to depict the shape of Roman society graphically, it might look like an old fashioned oil can, one of those with the long thin spout, turned upside down.[14] At the very tip of that spout — or perhaps hovering just above it — was the emperor. The empire was his to do with as he pleased. This may seem incredible in our own era of government "of the people, by the people, and for the people." But Romans, as with many premodern agrarian cultures, subscribed to a proprietary theory of the state, wherein the state is regarded as a piece of property. The wealth and produce of the empire, at least in theory, belonged to the emperor and those to whom he delegated its benefits and privileges.[15] The emperor controlled the means to life.

Below the emperor, in that gossamer-thin span of spout leading down to the funnel, were his subordinates, "retainers," as anthropologists would call them: religious and military officials, local client kings, significant land holders, large-scale merchants. They benefited directly from the emperor and, in exchange, supported his claim to power. As one reaches the broader part of the funnel, one might find a few more merchants, traders, a small "middle class" who supported those above them. But most people would have fit into that broadening, large open end of the funnel, a vast majority of persons who lived as peasants, that is, at a daily subsistence level. Most people in the empire lived like this — perhaps 80 percent of the population — on the very margins of existence. That is how Rome managed it. Rome's purpose, especially in the provinces, was to suck up as many of a province's resources as it could without provoking it into revolt or killing it off altogether. Rome slowly siphoned the life out of places like Palestine.

This hierarchical Roman order was based on something anthropologists might call a patronage system. A patron (let us say, the emperor) had clients, whom he supported. They, in turn, supported him. But they also had clients,

---

14. Borg's description is to be found in his essay "The Palestinian Background for a Life of Jesus," pp. 37–54 (see pp. 48–49) in Stephen Patterson, John Dominic Crossan, and Marcus Borg, *The Search for Jesus: Modern Scholarship Looks at the Gospels,* ed. Hershel Shanks (Washington, D.C.: Biblical Archaeology Society, 1994). Borg is drawing on Gerhard Lenski's description of agrarian societies in *Power and Privilege* (New York: McGraw-Hill, 1966), 189–296. For a more thorough discussion of the cultural situation of Roman Palestine as it relates to the question of Jesus, see Borg's essay "Jesus and Politics in Contemporary Scholarship," pp. 97–126 in idem., *Jesus in Contemporary Scholarship* (Valley Forge, Pa.: Trinity Press International, 1994).

15. Lenski, *Power and Privilege,* 212–19.

whom they supported, who, in turn, gave them support from below. And so it went, down through the ever widening social pyramid — a kind of giant Amway scheme — with the means to life trickling down the system in a tightly managed quid pro quo system of distribution. John Dominic Crossan describes this system in its totality as the "brokered Empire," wherein the means to life are always carefully brokered from the top down.[16] Such a system, of course, works best for those near its apex. But it works also for those vast crowds of peasants living just at the margins of subsistence. They get just enough — but enough — to live.

But in a patronage system there are always a few — sometimes quite a few — who do not have anything to offer a patron. In the quid pro quo system, they have no *quid* to offer for *quo*. In a patronage system, those who have nothing to offer someone above them gradually fall down through the social pyramid, and eventually out through the cracks in the bottom of the system. Lenski calls these persons "expendables."[17] They are expendable because they have nothing to offer the culture that might be considered of value. These are the beggars and the homeless. These are persons who might do those jobs no one else would do, like tax collecting. These are persons whose person counts for nothing, like prostitutes. With so many people living at the margins of existence, a significant number of expendables was always an inevitability, with persons moving in and out of that status all of the time. Take, for example, the situation of agricultural day laborers. If they are fortunate enough to get a full day's work, then they will receive enough pay to eat for a day. That is what subsistence means. One can earn enough for one day's sustenance, but that is all. There is no savings account put away for a rainy day. When it rains, you beg or you starve. For a peasant living at a subsistence level, expendability is only one day away.

Jesus and Expendables

Where did Jesus fit into this pyramidal system of patronage and brokerage? He did not fit. In the gospels, canonical and noncanonical, and in Paul — in the broad memory and praxis of the early church — Jesus is recalled as living outside the system of brokered power and economy of Rome's Empire. He

---

16. John Dominic Crossan, *The Historical Jesus: The Life of a Mediterranean Jewish Peasant* (San Francisco: HarperCollins, 1991). Crossan chooses this as the subtitle heading his treatment of Mediterranean culture in the time of Jesus (3–88).

17. Lenski, *Power and Privilege*, 281–84.

was an itinerant teacher who scrounged for a living and encouraged others to do so as well. Whether he did this as one who chose to opt out of the system or whether he was himself expendable to it is a matter of dispute, for there is evidence on both sides of the question.

On the one hand, Jesus is depicted in the gospels as inviting people to give up their place in the web of brokerage and become a beggar like him. Consider, for example, Mark's story of the wealthy young man who comes to Jesus asking, "What must I do to inherit eternal life?" (Mark 10:17–22). Initially Jesus gives him the stock answer of his culture: "You know the commandments." But, not wishing to be dismissed so easily, the young man persists until Jesus gives him the *real* answer: "You lack one thing; go, sell all that you own and give it to beggars, and you will have treasure in heaven, and come and follow me." At that, the man turns away, unable to risk removing himself from the security of the web of brokerage and patronage. Originally the story probably ended with something like the saying in Mark 10:23: "How hard it will be for those with riches to come into the Empire of God."[18] This story is not demonstrably historical, but it fits together with enough similar material in the gospel tradition to appear as an accurate typification of Jesus' ways. Jesus is depicted in all four canonical gospels as an itinerant preacher. He invites people to leave gainful activities to become his followers. In Thomas, he advises, "Become itinerants" (Thom 42).[19] And from the apostle Paul's itinerant lifestyle, going from place to place as the Spirit moved him, we can see what is likely the continuation of this practice in the activity of the early church, although increasingly as an exception rather than the rule.[20] The pattern seems clearly to suggest an imperative: If you are in the imperial web of brokerage and patronage, get out of it.

On the other hand, Jesus not only asks people to risk becoming expendable to the Empire, he seems to be constantly in the company of persons who

---

18. The Jesus Seminar designated this saying "pink." It probably originally circulated independently of this story, which was created to give it a context. Bultmann identifies it as an individual logion of Jesus (*The History of the Synoptic Tradition*, trans. John Marsh, rev. ed. [New York: Harper & Row, 1963], 75, 105). Such stories that typify Jesus' behavior may have grown out of particular sayings that richly captured a particular aspect of the ethos surrounding Jesus.

19. The Jesus Seminar was divided on whether Jesus actually said something like this or not. However, it was agreed that Jesus practiced an itinerant lifestyle.

20. This is significant for evaluating itinerancy as a typification of Jesus and his early followers. In the gospels Jesus is depicted as presenting itinerancy as a way of life for virtually anyone who would be his follower. This belongs to what Funk calls the "debris" of the tradition, a detail that is not easily integrated into the typical lifestyle of a Christian. Even in Paul's day, only a few years after Jesus' death, itinerancy was no longer typical, but something practiced only by an exceptional few, like Paul himself. For the gradual decline in itinerancy in the early church see my *The Gospel of Thomas and Jesus* (Sonoma, Calif.: Polebridge, 1993), 171–95.

already are expendable to it, like tax collectors and prostitutes.[21] Jesus most
certainly kept company with known prostitutes.[22] It is difficult to imagine that
an emergent church, seeking at least some amount of respectability from the
world around it, would have created the tradition that Jesus cavorted with
prostitutes and other disreputable types. It is unlikely, then, that the church
can be credited with coining the saying, "Tax collectors and prostitutes go
into the Empire of God before you" (Matt 21:31).[23] It is difficult to imagine
the church even preserving the tradition, unless, of course, this was crucial
to how it had come to understand itself in the followership of Jesus.

Luke has a story that, in this light, appears as an accurate typification of
how Jesus related to prostitutes. In this story (Luke 7:36–50) Jesus is having
dinner at the table of a Pharisee.[24] Luke perhaps sets it up this way to accentuate the purity concerns raised by this story, concerns represented in Luke's
worldview by the Pharisaic party. A woman enters, introduced as a "woman
who was a sinner in this city," which we may take as a circumlocution for
"prostitute."[25] If there is any doubt about this, the unfolding scene removes
it: "standing behind [Jesus] at his feet, weeping, she began to wet his feet
with her tears, wiping them with the hair of her head, and kissed his feet."
Odd as it may seem to modern sensibilities, this business with the tears and
dabbing them up with the hair is a detail drawn from ancient erotica. This is

---

21. The Jesus Seminar was agreed that Jesus associated with "toll collectors and sinners," ate
with them, and was criticized for doing so.

22. For the situation of prostitutes as part of the expendable class, see Luise Schottroff and
Wolfgang Stegemann, *Jesus and the Hope of the Poor;* trans. Matthew J. O'Connell (Maryknoll,
N.Y.: Orbis, 1986), 15.

23. The Fellows of the Jesus Seminar designated this saying "gray," but by the narrowest of
margins. In fact, more Fellows voted this saying red or pink (53 percent) than black or gray. But
because of the high number of black votes (20 percent) the balance was tipped just slightly away
from authenticity.

24. The story is very similar to the story of the woman who anoints Jesus at Bethany (Mark
14:3–9; Matt 26:6–13; John 12:1–8). This has always raised the question, did Luke take the
story from Mark and adapt it to his own purposes (as is the case with most Mark/Luke parallels),
or did he know this story from another source or oral tradition. The differences between the two
stories have led most scholars to the latter conclusion, though one must certainly reckon with
the fact that Luke knew Mark's version of the story, even though he passed over it in favor of
this version from the oral tradition.

25. So Kathleen Corley, *Private Women, Public Meals: Social Conflict in the Synoptic Tradition*
(Peabody, Mass.: Hendrickson, 1993), 124. Corley cites a paper by Delores Osborne as decisive
on this somewhat disputed point: "Women: Sinners and Prostitutes" (paper presented at the SBL
Pacific Coast Region, Long Beach, Calif., April 1987). One should note that only in Luke is she
known as a "sinner." In Mark 14:3–9 she is not a "sinner," but presumably a follower of Jesus.
In John 12:1–8 she is Mary, the sister of Martha (see Luke 10:38–42), who together become
the sisters of Lazarus in this gospel (John 11:19). In later ecclesiastical tradition she becomes
identified with Mary Magdalene, the origin of the spurious notion that *she* was a prostitute.

what impassioned lovers do.[26] She "comes on" to Jesus. This, quite naturally, alarms the host. He says to himself: "If this man were a prophet, he would have known who and what sort of woman this is who is touching him, for she is a sinner." But Jesus does not reject her. Instead he turns to the host and says (I think one may fairly insert a wink here, and perhaps a coy, slightly mocking tone of voice): "Do you see this woman? I came into your house, and you gave me no water for my feet, but she has wet my feet with her tears and wiped them with her hair. You gave me no kiss, but from the time I came in she has not stopped kissing my feet." In a clever turnabout, the unseemly act of a prostitute is received as proper hospitality. She is accepted as she is, doing what she does. Now, Luke's Jesus is no fool. He knows about prostitution, its causes, its hazards, its humiliations. So in the end he says to her, "Your sins are forgiven. . . . Your faith has saved you; go in peace," which means, I think, "You are no longer a prostitute."

This story is probably not strictly historical. It is offered as a typification for how Jesus regarded prostitutes. They are expendable to the Empire, but they are welcome in Jesus' new Empire of God. So are tax collectors. There persists today the common assumption that a tax collector was someone who, far from expendable, enjoyed a comfortable, profitable niche in the Roman imperial system, as would be illustrated by Luke's well-known story of Zacchaeus (Luke 19:1–9). Though not a popular figure (19:7), Zacchaeus is obviously someone with ample access to the means of life. But Luke calls him a "chief tax collector," that is, a tax farmer. He is not the run-of-the-mill collector of tolls and taxes. People like Zacchaeus would typically have engaged subordinates to do the actual work of collecting.[27] Levi, whom Mark depicts as sitting in his toll booth when Jesus comes along and calls him away (Mark 2:14), is such a tax collector. One need only imagine how pleasant a task it would have been to collect Roman tribute from strapped peasants barely making it as it was, to arrive quickly at the profile of such a tax collector. These were persons who could find no other means of making a living. Frequently slaves were purchased for this work. One might guess that they did not last long. In a sense, one might regard "tax collector" as the male equiva-

---

26. See, e.g., the dramatic scene in Xenophon, *An Ephesian Tale*, translated and presented in Moses Hadas, *Three Greek Romances* (Indianapolis: Bobbs-Merrill, 1964), 77. The discussion of the reason for the woman's tears has been considerable, all focusing on the assumption that they must have something to do with remorse, or perhaps joy at having been forgiven (even though this does not come until later in the story). The erotic aspect of the motif has been overlooked, in spite of the fact that, as Corley observes, "the erotic overtones of the story are obvious" (*Private Women, Public Meals*, 125).

27. The picture is sorted out well by Schottroff and Stegemann, *Jesus and the Hope of the Poor,* 7–13.

lent to the female role of "prostitute." Tax collectors and prostitutes are both expendable in the Empire, but they are included first in the Empire of God. We may add to this list lepers, beggars, the blind, those who could not walk or speak, the mentally ill (possessed) — all of them expendables, in whose company we are apt to find Jesus in the gospels. "The last will be first, and the first will be last" (Matt 20:16).[28]

What about Jesus himself? Was he also an expendable? He may have been. There is a tradition — well-known and popular, but poorly attested — that Jesus' was a *tekton*, a "carpenter" (see Mark 6:3). In an industrial culture based on the trading of manufactured goods, such a skill would have made Jesus an artisan, part of a class raised slightly above that of the mere peasant. For this reason, many have uncritically assumed that Jesus was part of the ancient "middle class." However, Jesus did not live in an industrial culture, but the preindustrial, agrarian culture of the ancient world. The basic economic engine in an agrarian culture is the land. Peasants hold land and can therefore participate in the economy. Without the land, they are nothing. In agrarian cultures the artisan class was usually recruited from among those who had been dispossessed of their land. A skill, a craft, a trade was all that stood between them and starvation. In an agrarian culture, artisans generally rank below the peasant class, not above it.[29] So if Jesus was in fact a carpenter, he would have occupied that tenuous narrow band of subsistence hovering just above expendability. On off days, weeks, months, Jesus, like others in his position, would have had to beg for a living.

Jesus knew expendability, he knew expendables, and he invited those who had not fallen out of the Roman system of brokerage and patronage to step out voluntarily and to become part of a new thing, the Empire of God. Why? How did Jesus' words and deeds address the condition of expendability among peasants in provincial Rome? To explore this question we must inquire further into the human experience of expendability. The experience of an expendable person in antiquity included three dimensions, each of which Jesus addressed directly: the experience of being unclean (not clean), the experience of shame (not honor), and the experience of being regarded as sinful (not righteous).

---

28. There are several versions of this saying in the Jesus tradition (see also Luke 13:30; Mark 10:31; and Thom 4:2a). The most dramatic version is found in Matt 20:16 (which probably derives from Q). All other versions of it have been softened, if only a little (e.g., "*some* of the last will be first" [Luke 13:30]; "*many* of the first will be last" [Thom 4:2a]). Only the version in Matt 20:16 was designated "pink" by the Fellows of the Jesus Seminar. All others were "gray." Its broad attestation, its aphoristic brevity and punch, and its coherence with the countercultural ethos surrounding the company of Jesus made its attribution to Jesus plausible.

29. Lenski, *Power and Privilege*, 278–80.

Unclean, Not Clean

Expendables in Jesus' world experienced being unclean, not clean. To be unclean is, in a literal sense, to be dirty.[30] Of course, in human culture the
distinction between the clean and the unclean is far more complicated than
this. Nonetheless, one may perhaps get at this very complicated dynamic by
beginning with dirt. Dirt, according to that well-used old definition, is simply
matter out of place.[31] Dirt in a field is "soil." The same stuff on your face
is... well, "dirt." Food on your plate is appetizing. The very same matter on
your clothes makes them "dirty." Distinctions between what is clean and unclean go to the very basic impulse in every human culture to create order
from chaos. Such distinctions, sometimes functional, sometimes not, create
order and place. They include not only things, but behaviors as well.

Such distinctions are present across all human cultures, but they are not
at all identical. What is clean and unclean can be very culturally specific. For
example, in the United States it is generally considered unclean to eat a cat,
since cats do not belong to the category of things called "food." A cat does not
go on a plate. Cats belong to the "pet" category. Cows, on the other hand, do
belong to the "food" category, and so can be eaten. In other lands, however,
those categories might be reversed. In some parts of India, cows belong to the
category of things called "sacred." To eat one would be a religiously unclean
act, a sacrilege. And I am told, much to my personal revulsion, that there are
places where it is perfectly acceptable to eat a cat. But the revulsion I feel is
culturally specific; it must be inculcated in my upbringing. In this way, observance of the basic distinctions between what is clean and unclean can signal
one's belonging to a social group; failure to observe such codes can indicate
that one does not belong, and so result in ostracizing.

The observance of such distinctions is usually a simple matter; they come
automatically to someone raised and reared in a culture. But they do often
require effort and resources, which, for someone existing at the margins of
culture and economy, may place them out of reach. Such distinctions, after
all, are designed to define the mainstream, to set cultural boundaries. One
who cannot succeed in a culture may not be able to conform to its standards.
Take, for example, the simple matter of clean clothing. It must be washed,

---

30. On the concept of "clean and unclean" and its usefulness in understanding biblical texts,
see Bruce Malina, *The New Testament World: Insights from Cultural Anthropology* (Louisville: John
Knox Press, 1981), 122–52; also L. William Countryman, *Dirt, Greed, and Sex: Sexual Ethics in
the New Testament and Their Implications for Today* (Philadelphia: Fortress Press, 1988), passim.
An earlier study, very influential in this work, is that of Mary Douglas, *Purity and Danger: An
Analysis of the Concepts of Pollution and Taboo* (London: Routledge & Kegan Paul, 1966).

31. Douglas, *Purity and Danger*, 35.

which presumes a place to wash and an extra set of clothes to wear while the other is being laundered. Simple things for most people, but anyone who has ever experienced an urban shelter for the homeless in our own culture knows the problem this poses for expendables. Or consider food. Clean food must be purchased and prepared in a clean way. These are luxuries that the destitute do not have. Expendables are always having to accept matter that is not of their own choosing. Beggars rummage through garbage cans for scraps of food. They beg for what they can get. They wear what they can find. Prostitutes disregard their own desires and accept those of others. To be unclean is to have someone else's stuff on you or in you. To be unclean is to feel violated and dirty.

Finally, in Jesus' culture, as in most, there is an explicit connection between being clean and being holy. In our own highly secular culture it is perhaps a bit more difficult to see this connection. But it was not many years ago that the Saturday night bath was a weekly ritual for many families in preparation for Sunday morning worship. This connection between the clean and the holy is also why most people still dress up to go to church or synagogue.[32] In ancient Israel the connection between the clean and the holy was more explicit. Near the end of Leviticus, where the general rules of purity are laid out, Yahweh says to the people of Israel:

> If you follow my statutes and keep my commandments and observe them faithfully . . . I will look with favor upon you and make you fruitful and multiply you. . . . I will place my dwelling in your midst, and I shall not abhor you. And I will walk among you and be your God, and you shall be my people. (Lev 26:3, 9, 11–12)

To observe the laws of purity was to insure the favor of God's presence in Israel, to reduce the offense of mortal profane life to God so that God would not "abhor" the Israelites and deign to be with them. The concept is illustrated more graphically in a telling passage from Deuteronomy:

> With your equipment you are to include a trowel. When you go to relieve yourself, you are to dig a hole with it and bury your excrement. For the Lord your God travels along with your camp, to save you and to deliver your enemies to you. Therefore, your camp must be holy, so that [God] may not see anything indecent among you and turn away from you. (Deut 23:13–14)

---

32. Douglas maintains that one of the differences between ancient and modern notions about dirt is that ancients related these ideas to religion, while moderns relate them more to hygiene and aesthetics (*Purity and Danger,* 35). As one can see, this may not be such a defining difference after all.

God has standards that should not be offended. This is why any who are rendered unclean must go outside the camp until such time as they may be cleansed. Sometimes this involves only a short period, followed by a ritual cleansing, as with a nocturnal emission, for example (Deut 23:10–11). When the unclean condition has a more permanent or long-term effect, one's ostracizing might last considerably longer, as with leprosy for example:

> Those who have a leprous disease shall wear torn clothes and have messed hair; they shall cover their upper lip and cry out, "Unclean, unclean." And they shall remain unclean as long as they have the disease; they are unclean. They shall live alone and their dwelling shall be outside the camp. (Lev 13:45–46)

The idea is clear: God, like most of us, does not want to be with the unclean. I once attended an urban church where, it was explained to me, the ushers were all fairly stout men so that in the event one of the destitute people who inhabited that neighborhood should come in off the street, he or she could be escorted out of the building. A holy place is a clean place.

Throughout the gospel tradition, Jesus addresses himself to the unclean. It is one of the most common typifications we can identify. Jesus eats with lepers (Mark 14:3). He has conversations with Gentiles (Mark 7:24–30). He welcomes prostitutes into his company (Luke 7:36–50). Jesus and his followers are depicted as habitually eating in an unclean manner. In response to the accusation that Jesus and his disciples do not eat properly, Jesus does not deny the charge, but rather responds:

> there is nothing outside a person that by going in can defile, but the things that come out can defile. . . . Do you not see that whatever goes into a person from outside cannot defile, since it enters not the heart, but the stomach, and goes out into the sewer? (Mark 7:15, 19a)[33]

Mark adds: "Thus he declared all foods clean!" (7:19b), an appropriate remark for Mark's audience, at least some of whom must be Gentiles interested in knowing that Jesus did not condemn eating all their favorite Gentile foods. But the point Jesus makes in the story is really more basic: nothing can defile a person. It is this point that addresses the situation of expendables: their

---

33. The Jesus Seminar designated Mark 7:15 "pink," but 7:19a as "gray," indicating that, though it cannot be traced to Jesus, the saying contains content that may be consistent with what Jesus said. I would designate 7:19 "pink," rather than "gray." Even though it is not quite as well attested as 7:15 (cf. the independent version of this saying in Thom 14), it coheres with 7:15 in content and exhibits the wit and aphoristic style the Jesus Seminar came to associate with Jesus' sayings. For more on this saying in the context of other socially radical sayings in the Jesus tradition, see pp. 100–101.

lives render them unclean. Beggars, lepers, prostitutes, tax collectors — they are all unclean because that is what life has dealt them. Jesus disputes this. It is not what happens to you that defiles. "It is what comes out of a person that defiles. For from within, from the human heart come evil thoughts, fornication, theft, murder, adultery...." Mark supplies the conventional list. But the point is made. The power to be clean lies in the character of a person. "Blessed are those who are clean in their hearts, for they shall see God" (Matt 5:8).[34]

Throughout the synoptic gospels, Jesus seems to be on a virtual crusade against unclean spirits. Mark begins the ministry of Jesus with this story:

> And they went into Capernaum, and immediately on the Sabbath he went into the synagogue and taught.... And immediately there was in the synagogue a person with an unclean spirit. And he cried out and said, "What business do you have with us, Jesus of Nazareth? Have you come to destroy us? I know who you are: the holy one of God." And Jesus reprimanded him and said, "Shut up and come out of him." And the unclean spirit came out of him, convulsing and yelling. (Mark 1:21–26)

This is an apt introduction to a string of stories in which Jesus casts out unclean spirits. Whenever they see him, they fall down and cry out (Mark 3:11). He exorcises an man with an unclean spirit named "Legion" (Mark 5:1–13); he casts out an unclean spirit from the daughter of a Syrophoenecian woman (Mark 7:24–30); he heals a deaf-mute boy by casting out an unclean spirit from him (Mark 9:14–29). The disciples, also, have authority to do this sort of thing (Mark 6:7). And because of this activity, Jesus himself is said to have an unclean spirit (Mark 3:30). Engaging the unclean casts one into their world. He also heals disabilities and diseases that could render one unclean, like leprosy:[35]

> And a leper came to him pleading, and kneeling he said to him: "If you want to, you can make me clean." Moved with pity, he stretched

---

34. The Jesus Seminar was reluctant to assign this saying to Jesus ("black"). To be sure, it is not well attested. It also appears to cohere with the other beatitudes found only in Matthew, which tend to make blessedness a reward for virtue, a very different idea from the original four beatitudes found in both Matthew and Luke (Matt 5:3–4, 6, and 10; Luke 6:20–23). I would rather designate Matt 5:8 (as well as the other Matthean beatitudes) "gray." I am less certain that Jesus would not have said something like this, though I agree that they would be difficult to trace to Jesus.

35. For the various disabilities and blemishes that render one unable to offer sacrifice to God, see Lev 21:16–24.

out his hand and touched him and said, "I do want to. Be clean." And immediately the leprosy left him and he was cleansed. (Mark 1:40–42)

What are we to make of these stories? As a modern person, I do not believe in the existence of spirits and demons. That ancient people did believe in such things helps me to understand the cultural context of these stories and what they mean: Jesus engages in battle the things that render one unclean and outside the company of God and humanity. His ministry meant inclusion for the ostracized. But did Jesus really do such things, or are these simply stories told about Jesus to give form to the memory of his activity of including the unclean? I am undecided. In cultures that believe in demons there are certainly people who are reputed to exorcise them. Jesus could have been such a person.[36] On the other hand, it also belongs to the mythic image of the Son of God that he engages the powers of evil and clears the way for the coming Empire of God. This is Mark's way of thinking about it. His understanding of Jesus' exorcisms presupposes considerable early Christian theological reflection that arose only after Jesus' death. In the end, whether Jesus was a genuine shaman or whether he simply embraced the company of the unclean, the meaning of the memory is the same: in Jesus we have come to know a God who renders impotent the power of dirt to keep the unclean outside the human community.

Shame, Not Honor

Expendable persons experience shame, not honor. Honor and shame are two of the basic anthropological dimensions of ancient life.[37] What is honor; what is shame?

---

36. The Jesus Seminar agreed that Jesus and his disciples would have been seen as exorcists within their own culture. Both his supporters and his detractors seem to agree on at least this. The Seminar also agreed that Jesus was accused of conjuring spirits and being in league with Beelzebul. This things are just too damaging to the reputation of Jesus and the early church to imagine someone creating this as a typification after the fact. For an interpretation of the Jesus tradition that takes seriously his relationship to spiritual realities, see Marcus Borg, *Jesus, A New Vision: Spirit, Culture, and the Life of Discipleship* (San Francisco: Harper & Row, 1987), esp. 25–75. For a cross-cultural view of Jesus' activity as a exorcist, see Crossan, *The Historical Jesus*, 303–53. Crossan makes effective use of the work of Ioan Lewis, *Ecstatic Religion: An Anthropological Study of Spirit Possession and Shamanism*, Penguin Anthropology Library (Baltimore: Penguin Books, 1971).

37. For a helpful discussion of honor and shame in the first-century Mediterranean world of the New Testament, see Malina, *The New Testament World*, 25–50. Malina makes effective use of the work of Julian Pitt-Rivers, *The Fate of Shechem or the Politics of Sex: Essays in the Anthropology of the Mediterranean* (Cambridge: Cambridge University Press, 1977). For the sake of simplicity, shame, in this discussion, is taken as the equivalent of dishonor.

One way of understanding honor and shame is simply to extend into the
social realm the thinking we have already done around distinctions of clean
and unclean. Honor and shame, like distinctions of clean and unclean, have
to do with place. To have honor is to have a place, a role, within which one
is readily recognized by one's peers, a role whose functions one may competently perform. Like matters of clean and unclean, honor and shame have to
do with expectations. One knows what to expect from an honorable person.
Honorable people are clear about their role in life; they know what is expected and do their duty. On the other hand, someone who behaves in a way
that is inappropriate to his or her role, or to society in general, is a shameful
person. Such a person does not behave according to expectations. Their difference is discomfiting. They may even strike one as dangerous. In a peasant
culture with only a minimal social infrastructure, honor and shame are the
forces that give shape to communal life. In the world of rural antiquity there
were no police forces, no lawyers, few courts. In such a culture someone who
steps out of line must be shamed into conformity. Those who prove impervi-
ous to shame and will simply not conform to the expectations of their peers
are regarded as "shameless" and ostracized from the community. In most cultures a set of reliable expectations for various social roles is necessary for the
smooth conduct of social life.

Another way of thinking about honor and shame is to consider how honor
is acquired. Again, one has honor when one has a place in society, a role
within which one is able successfully to function. Acquiring honor involves
three basic steps. First, you must aspire to a role, a place in your culture.
Second, your peers must recognize you in that role. Finally, once you are
recognized in a role, you must now be able successfully to function in that
role. If all of this falls into place, you acquire a grant of honor. However,
if at any point the process breaks down, you are shamed. If, for example,
one aspires to the role of teacher, but no one signs up for the class, one
experiences shame for not having been recognized in the role to which one
has aspired. Or again, if people come, but eventually walk out in frustration
for having learned nothing under one's tutelage, one experiences the shame
of failure.

Shame is a powerful emotion. It has physical as well as psychological dimensions. Shame is not necessarily a moral category. I am not speaking of
guilt, the experience of being ashamed for having done something one knows
to be wrong. Shame is an existential category. It has to do with self-worth,
with one's internal image of oneself, with one's sense of belonging and kinship. Here is an example to which most people can relate and recall the very
visceral aspects of feeling shamed. Remember the first sock-hop you attended

in junior high school? I can recall it well. As I enter the doors to the gym-
nasium I can see my classmates dancing and having fun. I marvel at their
courage and abandon, how they all seem so natural out there on the gym
floor dancing away. I aspire to be one of them, to be a dancer. But doubts
subdue my ambition, so I take my place with the others sitting on the sidelines, not yet ready to take up the challenge. Finally, I summon the courage
to ask the girl sitting next to me if she would like to dance. I am old fashioned. I say, "May I have the *honor?*" May I? Will she recognize my aspirations
to be *her* dance partner, or turn me down and shame me back into my place
on the sidelines? I must carefully calculate this. How popular is she? Can *she*
dance? Successfully negotiating the world of honor and shame requires careful attention to place, abilities, expectations. She agrees to dance with me.
So far, so good. I have "the honor." But challenges arise. My friends issue
cat calls from the sidelines; my honor is in question. I must now successfully
function in the role to which I have aspired. If I cannot, I will be shamed and
perhaps never summon forth the courage to dance again. Fortunately, these
are the 1960s and dancing is not difficult. My honor is retained; shame has
been averted, at least this time. But life is full of such situations. Honor and
shame are ever-present realities of human existence.

Not everyone pays attention to such things. For example, a person who
chooses to disregard the shame of another is called a "fool."[38] Let us imagine
that I am unable to dance, so the partner who has risked a dance with me
decides to cut her losses and flee, leaving me alone, shamed, on the dance
floor. Who will grant me the honor now? Only a fool, who cares little for
her own reputation. If such a person exists, she will appear as a hero to me
and to all of the shamed, but to the rest of the dancers, she will be regarded
as a fool. In the complexities of honor and shame, someone who chooses to
ignore the shame of another is a fool. Or let us imagine that, in spite of the
fact that I have been abandoned on the dance floor, I ignore the shame I feel
and simply continue to dance, incompetently, by myself. People will just shake
their heads and mutter, "Shameless!" In the system of honor and shame, one
who chooses to ignore his or her own shame is called "shameless."[39] Such
persons are beyond the pale; they refuse to recognize honor and shame at
all. Their behavior has become unpredictable, unreliable. They are dangerous
and must be avoided.

Jesus was remembered as a shameless fool. To spend time with expendables
is to be a fool — to refuse to recognize the shame of another. Expendables are

---

38. Malina, *The New Testament World*, 34.
39. Ibid.

by definition shamed. To have honor is to have place, to have a recognized role. This is precisely what expendables do not have. They are expendable to their culture because there is no role in it for them. Beggars must beg with eyes cast down; they are shamed. Prostitutes are worse than shamed — they are "shameless." Forced by their expendability into the sale of their bodies, they must engage repeatedly in behavior against which there are strong societal sanctions and taboos. They must ignore their own shame to survive. One need only recall the story of Jesus and the prostitute from Luke 7 discussed above to see how Jesus was remembered as a "fool," disregarding the shame of another.

There is much opportunity for shame around the issue of marriage and family. In societies strongly oriented to honor and shame, for example, it traditionally falls to the women to guard against shame in the family that might come from extramarital sex. This is why adultery is defined as the sexual violation of a married woman (but not a man) and treated so harshly in the ancient Near East.[40] In conventional texts of John 8 there is found a remarkable story about Jesus and a woman accused of adultery, who is about to be stoned (John 7:53b–8:11). A case for its historicity would be difficult to make, since the origin of this story is impossible to trace. The earliest and most reliable manuscripts of John do not have it. In some early copies of Luke one finds it inserted after Luke 21:38. We do not even know for sure the gospel with which to associate it. It is what is sometimes called a "floating" tradition — something from the oral tradition that pops up in various places, but whose origin is not known. But the memory of Jesus expressed in it is so remarkably countercultural, it must have some claim to authenticity in representing the views of Jesus, even if its claim to historicity is weak.[41]

This story presents us with a classic honor-shame confrontation. The woman in the story is accused of violating her given role (wife) and bringing shame upon her entire extended family. In her patriarchal world, her offense is so severe it warrants complete eradication. She must be stoned, a public, communal form of execution featuring the violent disfigurement of

---

40. Note that sexual relations between a married man and an unmarried, unbetrothed woman are discouraged, but not punishable by law (Mal 2:14–15; Prov 5:15–20), but adultery, i.e., sexual relations between a married or betrothed woman and a man who is not her husband or betrothed, is a capital offense (Lev 20:10; Deut 22:22).

41. As with most cultural codes of the ancient Mediterranean world, early Christians also accepted strong sanctions against adultery (see, e.g., 1 Cor 6:9; Heb 13:4). The leniency of Jesus in this story stands in contrast to ancient Mediterranean society as well as to the practice of the early church. As a typification of the way Jesus would have behaved toward such a person it is therefore difficult to assign to the early church and its practices. That it survives as a typification of Jesus' attitudes seems plausible, even though the provenance of this story remains a mystery.

the offender. But Jesus defends her with a challenge of his own. He challenges the honor of those wishing to eradicate her shame: "Let him who is without sin cast the first stone at her." And in the magical world of Christian storytelling about Jesus, that ends the matter. Her accusers all skulk away, themselves shamed by Jesus' challenge, beginning with the oldest (the most honorable).

This story gives shape to a powerful memory of what Jesus meant to people who experienced shame. Shame is like dirt: it renders one outside the human community and the company of God. Real shame does not come from within (it is not guilt); it comes from without. One must *be* shamed by others. But unlike dirt, it is not so easily washed away. Shame stays with you. No ritual ablutions can nullify its power over a person. It works itself into the image of oneself before others, and there remains as a part of one's personal landscape. In stories like that of the woman caught in adultery, early Christians gave shape to the memory that Jesus refused to recognize shame. No one has the power to shame, to castigate and ostracize one from the human community. The point is the same as with distinctions of clean and unclean. Nothing from outside can render one unclean. Only the things that come from the human heart can render one clean or unclean. So also with shame. One cannot be shamed from without. To be sure, one can feel *a*shamed; one can feel guilt and remorse for things done that should not have been done. That is why many of these stories end with the admonition, "Go and sin no more." But Jesus' insight was that it does not lie within the legitimate power of one human being to shame another, to cast that person out of the company of God and humanity.

There are many illustrations of this principle in the gospels. For example, when the blind man, Bartimaeus, calls out to Jesus from the side of the road and is "shushed" by those around him, Jesus stops the entourage and calls him over (Mark 10:46–52). Or when Martha asks Jesus to castigate Mary for stepping out of her conventional role as a woman, Jesus refuses to do so, but acknowledges her in the new role to which she has aspired: disciple (Luke 10:38–42). This is also the framework within which one ought to understand Jesus' teaching regarding divorce, a traditional act of public shaming in Jesus' culture. He simply disallows it (Mark 10:2–12).[42] In Mark 7 there is a most peculiar story about Jesus and a woman from Syrophoenecia, who asks him

---

42. The Jesus Seminar was reluctant to assign this tradition directly to Jesus ("gray"). However, it is obviously a very early Christian tradition, since it is also found in Q (Matt 5:31–32; Luke 16:18) and in Paul's letters (1 Cor 7:10–11). It is also countercultural in the sense I have spelled out here and consistent with Jesus' views on honor and shame. For these reasons I would designate the tradition on divorce "pink."

to exorcise her demon-possessed daughter. In Mark's story, Jesus responds to her request negatively: "Let the children first be fed, for it is not right to take the children's bread and throw it to the dogs" (7:27). She asks for something she cannot rightfully have, and so he shames her with a well-crafted, ancient Near Eastern insult. But she refuses to accept the shame and retorts, "Yes, Lord; but even the dogs under the table eat the children's crumbs." At this, Jesus repents of his view, capitulates, and grants her request. It is the only story in the New Testament in which Jesus loses an argument, and learns something in the process. Is this the tradition's way of shaping a memory that Jesus received his insights about shame from women?[43]

Jesus not only ignored the shame of others, and so was a "fool"; he also ignored his own shame, and so was "shameless." He did not perform the role to which he was assigned in life. Jesus was a carpenter, an artisan (*tekton*), or so the tradition presents him (Mark 6:3). But we encounter him in the gospels as a teacher, a wandering philosopher who speaks of God, who "preaches." What qualified him for this vocation, this role? He had no training that we know of. As a peasant artisan, formal study would have been unavailable to him. The leisure and training to read and write, to study the traditions of Israel, to practice rhetoric — all of these things would have been lacking in his life. His situation is rather like that of the Cynic philosophers, railed against and ridiculed by the ancient writer Lucian in his biting satire *The Runaways*. Lucian has become fed up with this upstart philosophical movement he sees as dominated by untrained artisans, runaway slaves, and women who have eschewed conventional household duties. What his goddess, Philosophia, says of the Cynics, could well have been said of Jesus and his followers too:

> There is an abominable class of people, for the most part slaves and common laborers, who had nothing to do with me in childhood for lack of leisure time, since they were performing the work of slaves or common laborers, learning such trades as you would expect their type to learn, like cobbling, building, taking care of fuller's tubs, or carding wool. . . . Now, to learn all that is necessary for such a calling would have been a long task, or rather, an impossible one for them. Their

---

43. This is one of the few stories in the gospels that the Jesus Seminar was willing to consider at least somewhat historical ("pink"). His interaction with a woman, and a foreign woman at that, would have been somewhat scandalous in ancient Jewish culture. And even if we might consider the story arising first in a Gentile environment, the fact that Jesus is bested in an exchange of wit and principle makes it somewhat difficult to imagine this as an expression of early Christian piety.

trades, however, were petty and laborious, and barely able to provide them with just enough to live.[44]

Lucian is describing the life of an artisan. For such a person it is simply impossible to develop the skills to become a wandering teacher. He calls the Cynics "shameless," and their effort at *philosophia* "counterfeit." In Lucian's elitist tale of social commentary, Philosophia sends Hermes and Heracles as her henchmen to track down a small band of Cynics: three fugitive slaves and a runaway wife. Their fate is tar and feathers.

In the Gospel of Mark there is a story about Jesus coming to his hometown to preach and heal as he had done elsewhere. But at home it does not go so well. When Jesus begins to teach in his home synagogue, the crowd begins to object:

> "Where did this person get these things he is saying? What is this wisdom given to him? And what are these miracles done by his hand? Isn't this the carpenter,[45] the son of Mary and the brother of James and Joses, Jude and Simon? And are not his sisters right here in front of us?" And they took offense at him. (Mark 6:2–3)

This becomes the occasion for Mark to insert a famous saying of Jesus, "A prophet is not without honor, except in his own country, and among his own relatives, and in his own house" (Mark 6:4).[46] And Mark adds, "He could do no miracles there."

Like other episodes from Jesus' life found in the gospels, we cannot be sure that this one has any claim to historicity. But given what we know about Jesus, it has perfect verisimilitude. The issue here is honor and shame. Jesus aspires to the role of prophet, but his peers, even his family, will not recognize him in that role. They know him too well. They challenge him; they attempt to shame him into accepting his given role among family and kin. But he

---

44. A. M. Harmon, trans. *Lucian*, 8 vols., Loeb Classical Library (Cambridge: Harvard University Press, 1979), 1:69.

45. Other ancient texts read "the son of the carpenter." I have chosen "the carpenter" on the grounds that Mark does not elsewhere show any knowledge of Jesus' father (cf., for example, Mark 3:31–35), and on the text critical principle of *lectio difficilior*, the more difficult reading. As I have just argued, an artisan would have been disqualified from the life of a wandering teacher. But the son of an artisan could perhaps be seen as excelling beyond his familial station.

46. The Jesus Seminar designated this saying "pink." I agree with this judgment. Its triple attestation (see also John 4:44; Thom 31) suggests a very early provenance. It is also very memorable, as its frequent use even today attests. Also of interest is the designation of Jesus here as a "prophet," a claim that predates the more highly developed christological claims of Jesus' later followers. One could even imagine Jesus placing himself in the category of "prophet."

refuses to shrink back from what he has become in his own mind. He is a prophet now. But to the folks back home, he is shameless. And in the end, he dies a death that would seem appropriate to all but those few who chose to accept Jesus as a prophet. Crucifixion was the ultimate act of shaming. Helpless, exposed to the elements, animals, and passersby, staked outside the sacred boundaries of the city walls, the victim of Rome's signature form of execution was literally shamed to death.

Sin, Not Righteousness

Expendables experience sin, or rather, they are regarded as sinful, rather than righteous. With this category we may seem, at least initially, to be on more familiar religious ground: morality. But a closer look at the material reveals that this is not really so. For "sinner," in the ancient world, is not just a moral category; it is a social category as well.

Let us begin with an example from the New Testament to illustrate how the category "sinner" works in relationship to expendability. In the ninth chapter of John, Jesus and the disciples come across a man who was born blind (John 9:1–34). The disciples instinctively ask Jesus: "Who sinned, this man or his parents, that he was born blind?" Notice the automatic connection between the condition of expendability and the assumption that such a person must be deserving of his predicament. One might be tempted to assign this way of thinking to some bizarre and ancient theodicy. But this is to be resisted. In fact, it is the most natural and psychologically necessary solution to the problem of expendability in any culture. What would one have to admit if no particular shortcoming could be ascribed to persons unable to find a place in the social world we have collectively constructed? The answer would be the deeply disturbing realization that there is something morally wrong about a society which is itself incapable of living up to its claim to offer a place for everyone. Moreover, *this* moral shortcoming would be one in which everyone who participates willingly in and benefits from the common social order would be, in greater or lesser degree, culpable. Examples abound from our own modern American social landscape. Women who receive AFDC are not seen as persons for whom there is no place in our economy, but as lazy, dishonest "welfare queens" robbing the rest of us of our hard-earned dollars. Kids who deal in drugs to help support their families are not seen as desperate survivors, but as amoral criminals lusting after the latest designer tennis shoes. The governing assumption in such thinking is that if people operate outside the boundaries of social acceptability, it is not because there is no place for them in the social economy, but because they are somehow deficient in themselves. They are sinners.

This principle can be illustrated in another way from the traditions about Jesus. The following story comes from the Gospel of Mark. Like so many other stories from the synoptic tradition, its historicity cannot be proven. Nonetheless, when one thinks about the potentially damaging nature of this story in a world in which the fledgling church was struggling to rise above the suspicions of its neighbors, it is scarcely possible to account for its presence in the tradition apart from some claim to authenticity as a typification of what Jesus was about.

> And as he passed along the way he saw Levi, the son of Alphaeus, sitting in his tax booth. And he said to him, "Follow me." And he got up and followed him. And it happened that he was having dinner at his house, and many tax collectors and sinners were having dinner with Jesus and his disciples (for there were many who followed him). And the scribes of the Pharisees, when they saw that he was eating with sinners and tax collectors, said to his disciples: "Why does he eat with tax collectors and sinners?" And when Jesus heard this, he said to them, "Those who are well have no need of a physician, but those who are sick. I did not come to call righteous people, but sinners. (Mark 2:14–17)[47]

This story is not isolated in the traditions about Jesus. In Q there is preserved an (apparently) common reproach against Jesus: "Look, a glutton and a drunkard, a friend of tax collectors and sinners" (Luke 7:34b).[48] Notice how in both of these traditions a tandem term is created: "tax collector and sinner." We have already discussed the status of tax collectors among the expendables. This sort of front-lines tax collecting was hazardous work, performed by persons with few other options in an economy to which they were expendable. Now this term is placed alongside another, "sinner," as though they were easily interchangeable. And so they were. Tax collectors were not

---

47. The Jesus Seminar designated the final saying in this story "pink." It also agreed that Jesus participated in table fellowship that would have been considered by some to be unclean and that Jesus occasionally clashed with people over this issue.

48. The Jesus Seminar did not vote on this saying because it is not a saying of Jesus, but of his opponents. One may, however, consider it for historical content. The idea that the early church would have created such a reproach if it had not been current among Jesus' opponents is unlikely. In any event, Mark makes no effort to deny the charge that Jesus ate with tax collectors and sinners, however embarrassing such a reputation might have been. For this reason, I am inclined to think that Jesus did eat with tax collectors and notorious sinners and that the charge of gluttony and drunkenness was grounded in a lifestyle that did not eschew vigorous celebration.

seen as persons doing whatever they could to scrounge up a living, but as traitors, unworthy of the company of respectable people. Joachim Jeremias identified a number of such occupations in the social world of Jesus that suffered under a similar stigma, including shepherds, dung collectors, tanners, peddlers, weavers, bath attendants, gamblers with dice, bandits, and others.[49] Not all of these occupations were despised as notoriously "immoral." Tanners just stank. But all were despised for what they did, scrounging around the edges of Jesus' social world to earn enough to get from day to day. They were all landless expendables.

These are the "sinners" whom Jesus calls into his following. This is clear from how Jesus explains himself at the end of the story: "I did not come to call righteous people, but sinners" (Mark 2:17). There is something missing here, is there not? Luke noticed it, and so adopted Mark's story, but added to the end of this sentence "to repentance" (Luke 5:32). But this changes the meaning of the original story completely. In Mark's version, Jesus does not call sinners "to repentance"; he just calls them. This does not mean that Mark or Mark's Jesus is amoral, for elsewhere he does speak of turning from one's sins (e.g., Mark 1:15; cf. 6:12). Here, however, he is not thinking of "sinner" as a moral category, but a social one. In calling sinners into his following, he recognized the structural nature of expendability in his social world and the illegitimacy of labeling expendables as "sinners" in need of repentance. A tax collector does not need to repent; he just needs land, or a better job. A prostitute does not need better morals; she just needs a legitimate, respectful place to be in the world.

Jesus called sinners. Period. He invited into his company those whose condition rendered them into a category: sinner; unclean; shamed. They all go together in Jesus' world; they are all categories of expendability. Jesus spent his time with sinners, lepers, people with physical disabilities, deaf people, blind people, people who could not walk or talk. He welcomed prostitutes, tax collectors — all manner of expendable people. And he proclaimed for them an empire, the Empire of God, in which the means to life are free and accessible by God's own gracious hand.

---

49. Joachim Jeremias, *Jerusalem in the Time of Jesus* (Philadelphia: Fortress Press, 1969), 303–12; also idem, *New Testament Theology*, vol. 1: *The Proclamation of Jesus* (New York: Charles Scribner's Sons, 1971), 109–13. One must caution, however, against equating, as Jeremias does, the term "sinners" with the *'amme ha-arets,* the "people of the land," or common people. This view is based on a misconstrual of the social landscape of first-century Judaism (see E. P. Sanders, *Jesus and Judaism* [Philadelphia: Fortress Press, 1985], 176–99). Associating with "tax collectors and sinners" did not make Jesus a populist. Rather, he kept company with those who would have offended the propriety even of the common people.

The Unbrokered Empire of God

Crossan calls this the "Brokerless Kingdom."[50] In contrast to Rome's highly brokered empire, the Empire of God is that place where the means to life are offered freely. Jesus was an itinerant pundit, who by his word and deed called into question the structures of his social world that dehumanized and made expendable so many human beings of God's own making. Indeed, he brought these expendables back into the human community. They were no longer unclean; he regarded them as clean. They were no longer shamed; he treated them with honor. They were no longer sinners; he declared them righteous and able to stand in the glorious presence of God. Together they created an empire. Not one in which the means to life are brokered from the top down in a complex hierarchy of quid pro quo transactions, but unbrokered, freely offered, like God's own love to all of God's children.

Crossan has argued that this theology of unbrokered access is symbolized most clearly in Jesus' practice of eating with all manner of folk. Let us return for a moment to that story from the second chapter of Mark, in which Jesus' critics question, "Why does he eat with tax collectors and sinners?" (Mark 2:16b) A moment ago we noticed only the company Jesus kept. Now we should also notice what they are doing: eating together. This memory of Jesus eating with tax collectors and sinners is confirmed and presented in the worst possible light in the Q tradition that contrasts Jesus' "loose" table practices with the ascetic practices of John:

> To what shall I compare the people of this generation, and what are they like? They are like children sitting in the marketplace and calling to one another, "We piped and you did not dance; we wailed and you did not weep." For John the Baptist came eating no bread and drinking no wine, and you say, "He has a demon." The Son of Man has come eating and drinking, and you say, "Look, a drunkard and a glutton, a friend of tax collectors and sinners!" (Luke 7:31–34)[51]

These words are those of Jesus' followers reflecting on the significance of Jesus and his fate. But in so doing, they preserved what must have been a

---

50. Crossan, *The Historical Jesus*, 225ff.

51. Though it could not find a way to trace these words directly to Jesus, the Jesus Seminar agreed that they characterize John and Jesus in a way that is consistent with what we otherwise know of them. Many were troubled, however, by the use of the Son of Man tradition, which (if it is not just a circumlocution for "I" here) bears the christological stamp of the early church. The tradition, which occurs also in Matthew (11:16–19), was designated "gray." This means that even though Jesus probably did not say something like this, it may still contain information of relevance for the historical characterization of Jesus.

common accusation against Jesus and the movement he spawned: "a drunkard and a glutton, a friend of tax collectors and sinners!" It is presented as the
exaggerated and unreasonable and, so, obviously false accusation of the opponents of Jesus. But there must have been an element of truth to the charge.
There are several disputes around the issue of eating played out in the gospel
tradition (see, e.g., Mark 2:18–22; 2:23–28; 7:1–23; and 14:3–9, and their
parallels in Matthew and Luke). One may also point to the considerable reflection in earliest Christianity around meals and meal-time practices, such
as one finds in Paul's letters (see, e.g., Gal 2:11–21; 1 Cor 8–10; 11:27–34;
Rom 14:1–23). All of these examples indicate in one way or another that the
earliest Jesus movement engaged in table fellowship that inspired criticism
and conflict over what, how, and with whom one ought to eat. What is the
issue with eating?[52]

Eating together is a basic human activity, the significance of which can
still be seen today if one thinks for a moment about all that goes into a common dinner invitation. There is always a tinge of anxiety that accompanies
every dinner party. One wonders, will the guests accept my invitation? That
is, will those whom I invite see me in the same way that I see them, as friends
and peers? Eating together is a social activity that establishes group identity
and boundaries. What are the boundaries of a meal? Whom shall I invite?
Will so-and-so get along with so-and-so? Will she want to be seen with him?
A meal is an act of social formation. And what shall I serve? Shall I offer the
president of the corporation macaroni and cheese? What will show her that I
respect and value her company, that I am worthy to be her peer? And what
about next week? Will my invitation be reciprocated, thus reaffirming the
common kinship that I have initiated? Common meals can be social mine-
fields. But once established, the commensality of friends becomes a source of
mutual care, affection, and social nourishment. That is why we risk it.

In the ancient world, eating together was perhaps the most common form
of social formation. Families, friends, associations of various sorts, religious
and ethnic groups, all gathered around their respective tables. The rules, the
etiquette, the menu, the company were all tightly managed, just as they are
today. Gentiles ate with Gentiles; Jews with Jews. Men ate with men; women
with women. Washing preceded eating. Clean hands ate clean food. The host

---

52. A brief discussion of "commensality" in relation to Jesus' activity is found in Crossan, *The
Historical Jesus*, 341–44. Crossan draws effectively on the Claremont dissertation of Lee Klosinski,
The Meals in Mark (Ann Arbor, Mich.: University Microfilms International, 1988). For more on
ancient meal practice see also Dennis E. Smith and Hal E. Taussig, *Many Tables: The Eucharist
in the New Testament and Liturgy Today* (Philadelphia: Trinity Press International; London: SCM,
1990), 21–35, and Corley, *Private Women, Public Meals,* 17–21.

presided, the guests reclined, and the servants served. In the stories about Jesus and his participation in common meals, he is constantly depicted as tweaking these various conventions. He advises that the most highly honored participant ought to prescind from claims to precedence (Luke 14:7–11), and that one's guest list ought not to include one's friends, but the destitute, who could never repay the hospitality (Luke 14:12–14).[53] He and his followers do not wash before eating (Mark 7:1–8; Luke 11:37–41),[54] and Jesus declares that no food has the power to render one unclean (Mark 7:15; cf. Luke 11:41).[55] There are women at table with Jesus, and he does not chase them away (Mark 14:3–9; Luke 7:36–50). He eats with the clean (Luke 7:36; 14:1) and the unclean (Mark 2:15–17; 14:3). And whether Jesus did so or not, many of his earliest followers felt authorized by his teaching to cross ethnic boundaries and to eat with Gentiles (Gal 2:11–14; Acts 10). Jesus seems to have initiated a very peculiar, open practice of table fellowship.

Crossan thinks that the significance of this very central aspect of Jesus' praxis is captured by the parable I introduced at the end of the last chapter, the Great Feast.[56] For emphasis I will repeat it here in its Lukan form:

A person once gave a great banquet, and invited many guests. And when it came time for the banquet, he sent his servant around to the invited guests to say, "Come, for everything is now ready." But they all, one after another, began to make excuses. The first guest said to him, "I've bought a field and must go out to look it over. Please pass along my regrets." And another said, "I've bought five yoke of oxen and must go examine them. Please pass along my regrets." And another said, "I have just gotten married and so cannot come." So the servant went and reported this to his master. Then the householder got angry and said to his servant, "Go out right away into the streets and alleys of the city and bring in the poor, the maimed, the blind, and the lame." And the servant said, "What you have commanded has been done, but there is still more room." So the master said to the servant, "Go out to the highways and hedges and compel people to come in, so that my

---

53. The Jesus Seminar designated the material in Luke 14:11 "gray" and 14:12–14 "black." It coheres well with the general concern exhibited in Luke for the poor and the outcast. It is therefore difficult to separate these sayings from Luke's own hand. Nonetheless, they are consistent with Jesus' own orientation toward the marginal and outcast in his world. Luke obviously understood the point of this in the Jesus tradition and presented it anew in his own day.

54. The Jesus Seminar agreed that Jesus ate with unwashed hands, like most marginal people would have.

55. The Jesus Seminar designated the saying in Mark 7:15 "pink." See p. 71, n. 33 above.

56. Crossan, *The Historical Jesus*, 261–62.

house might be filled. For I tell you, none of those who were invited shall ever taste my banquet." (Luke 14:16b–24)[57]

For the most part, this parable is as close to the version Jesus originally told as we can get, with the exception of one critical element. Almost everyone agrees that Luke seems to entertain a special regard for "the poor." In fact, "the poor, the maimed, the blind, and the lame" in Luke 14:21 echoes a Lukan phrase introduced in the story directly preceding this parable in Luke's gospel (see Luke 14:12–14). Thus, the instruction to "go out right away into the streets and alleys of the city and bring in the poor, the maimed, the blind, and the lame" represents a particularly Lukan way of drawing out the significance of the parable: one should practice charity in one's common meals. Luke's interpretation of this parable is admirable, but very conventional. It restricts the parameters of the parable well within the bounds of social manageability. But if this is to be ascribed to Luke, what is left to the original parable's resolution? "Go out to the highways and hedges and compel people to come in, so that my house might be filled." The peculiar and challenging thing about this parable is just this: the doors to the banquet hall are to be thrown wide open. "Go out to the highways and bring in whomever you might find there." Men and women. Friend and foe. The clean and unclean. Jews and Gentiles. Princes and thieves. Anyone who dares to respond to the invitation may come inside. This is a table without controls, a table without boundaries. It represents a community in which all are welcomed, into which all may come. This is an open table, a table far less manageable and far more threatening than the charitable table of Luke. In fact, as Crossan so succinctly puts it, "Generous almsgiving may even be conscience's last great refuge against the terror of open commensality."[58]

The Basileia *of God*

Now, one might say, "All of this is good teaching." It makes sense, especially to poor people, or to persons who are interested in working for a more open and egalitarian society. But is it more than that? Is it more than good teaching? Is it the Empire *of God*? This is to press beyond the question of social formation and ethics. It is to ask a *theological* question.

---

57. See also Matt 22:2–13 and Thom 64. The Jesus Seminar designated the Lukan and Thomean versions of this parable "pink," the Matthean version "gray."

58. Crossan, *The Historical Jesus*, 341.

Willi Marxsen liked to remind us that not everyone who heard Jesus and experienced him first hand had the same reaction.[59] Some said, "This guy is a nut!" Others said, "This is good teaching. Admirable. Interesting." But others said, "In this person's words and deeds I have experienced God's very own presence in my life." Some people gathered around Jesus' open table and said, "Whoa! I'm never going to do that again. Eating with the unclean — that's just not what God-fearing people do." Others said, "Now that was interesting. Perhaps I'll try it again sometime." But others said, "Around that table I experienced something I would claim as nothing less than the very love and acceptance of God. It is God who calls us to such tables. The words I heard from Jesus were the Word of God." Is this good teaching, or does this activity unveil the fundamental principle of the universe? At such tables do we discover the very ground of all being? That is what early Christians risked believing: that what they learned from Jesus and experienced in his presence was not just a good teaching or way of life, an ethic — though it was all of these. Rather, it was an expression of who they would claim God to be. To them, Jesus was a sign-act of who God is. It is God who offers everyone the means to life, unbrokered, freely given as a gift. Jesus' unbrokered Empire is the Empire *of God*. This is what those who chose to follow Jesus experienced as good news, "gospel." The unbrokered Empire of God is the gospel of Jesus.

But is Jesus' unbrokered Empire of God really good news? History, of course, cannot tell us this. It can tell us only that some people did experience it that way and chose to give themselves over to that reality as a life-transforming vocation. History can tell us what Jesus said and did, within limits. It can even tell us what the followers of Jesus, or later interpreters of Jesus, like Paul or the gospel writers, believed was the real significance of what he said and did. But history cannot tell us if any of this is true. It cannot tell us what we ought to believe. It cannot compel us to risk, as early Christians did, the claim that in Jesus they had come to know who God is. Faith is always a claim, a risk to believe. Historical research cannot minimize that risk, nor should it try. But historical research can clarify the nature of the risk one is asked to take in embracing Jesus' words and deeds as "gospel." To ask about the historical Jesus is to ask just what it was that the earliest Christians were confessing when they risked the claim that in Jesus they had come to know God. Was it good news? Is there gospel in the words and deeds of Jesus? This is the risk and the claim that Christian faith invites one to make.

---

59. Willi Marxsen, "Jesus Has Many Names," pp. 1–15 (esp. 1–6) in idem, *Jesus and the Church*, trans. Philip Devenish (Philadelphia: Trinity Press International, 1992).

Chapter 3

The Empire in a Word

On the Radical Wisdom of Jesus

---

*There was a danger of our thrusting ourselves between
people and the gospels, and refusing to leave the individual
alone with the sayings of Jesus.*

*There was a danger that we should offer them a
Jesus who was too small, because we had forced Him
into conformity with our human standards and human
psychology. To see that, one need only read the Lives of
Jesus written since the [eighteen] sixties, and notice what
they have made of the great imperious sayings of the Lord,
how they have weakened down His imperative world-
contemning demands upon individuals, that he might not
come into conflict with our ethical ideals, and might tune
His denial of the world to our acceptance of it. Many
of the greatest sayings are found lying in a corner like
explosive shells from which the charges have been removed.
No small portion of elemental religious power needed
to be drawn off from his sayings to prevent them from
conflicting with our system of religious world-acceptance.
We have made Jesus hold another language with our time
from that which he really held.*

— ALBERT SCHWEITZER, *The Quest of the Historical Jesus* (1906)

89

The Countercultural Wisdom of Jesus

Among the earliest Christian writings concerning Jesus are simple collections of sayings attributed to him, his collected wisdom. Jesus was remembered for, among other things, what he said. Early collections of sayings, such as Q,[1] represent the efforts of Jesus' followers to gather together the sayings, parables, and witticisms of their teacher, not for sheer memory's sake, but in order that they might continue in the tradition of their master, repeating what he had said as new occasions arose in which the wit and wisdom of so great a sage as Jesus might prove useful. In the collected wisdom of Jesus we find some of the earliest memories of Jesus that shaped the course his followers would take after his death. Yet, even with these simple sayings we are dealing with a memory of Jesus, not his recorded voice. But in these sayings we approach as close as we can to the original impression he made on people.

Jesus was a sage, a very clever person with a gift for coining memorable aphorisms and creating illustrative narratives. His sayings and stories had a remarkable ability to stir the thoughts of those who heard them. Scholars of the early Christian sayings tradition like to distinguish between proverbs and aphorisms in the corpus of things attributed to Jesus.[2] Proverbs are short, pithy sayings which seem to encapsulate common wisdom that is self-evident to anyone who is reasonably clear of thought. Here is a good example of a proverbial saying attributed to Jesus: "A blind person should not lead a blind person, otherwise both might fall into a pit" (Matt 15:14; Luke 6:39 [Q]; Thom 34).[3] It is straightforward, self-evident, and

---

1. Q is discussed in chapter 1, pp. 20–21.

2. The following discussion of aphorisms draws from the work of John Dominic Crossan, *In Fragments: The Aphorisms of Jesus* (San Francisco: Harper & Row, 1983), 3–36.

3. The Jesus Seminar designated this saying "gray" in each of its versions. I would agree with this assessment. In this case the Seminar's designation means that it is so common that any teacher could have said this, and thus, Jesus could have too. But the blend with common wisdom is so complete that it would be impossible to identify this as Jesus' voice as distinct from any other. I am undecided about whether one should attribute this sort of thing to Jesus or not.

applicable in a myriad of situations. It is typical proverbial wisdom. Jesus is credited with many such common sayings, even though he did not create them all. The self-evident nature of this material makes it the stuff of common currency.

More distinctive of the wit and wisdom associated with Jesus is another sort of saying, the aphorism. Very much like the proverb, an aphorism, too, has that same short, pithy quality, a kind of clever punch that makes its point quickly. Here is a good example of an aphoristic saying attributed to Jesus: "Foxes have their holes, birds their nests, but a person has no place to lay his/her head and rest" (Matt 8:20; Luke 9:58 [Q]; Thom 86).[4] Like the proverb, the aphorism is also derived from keen observation of the world around the sage. But unlike the proverb, the wisdom of the aphorism is not self-evident. It makes an unusual observation, pointing out something incongruous, or, as in this case, ironic. Its claim to truth comes as a jarring reality. Like the proverb, it is difficult to deny, yet, unlike the proverb, it is also difficult to accept. Later in the development of the Jesus tradition this saying would be used to ground the itinerant lifestyle of Jesus' early followers.[5] But originally, it was probably a wry observation about the incongruity of human homelessness that was all too common in Jesus' world. Jesus is credited with many such aphorisms, which together present a vision of the world that is countercultural and critical of conventional assumptions about the world and what is involved in living life meaningfully.

The gathering of sayings into collections such as Q was not a neutral activity in the ancient world. It was generally associated with the intellectual and spiritual activity of cultivating wisdom. The collection of the insights of a sage in antiquity was a cross-cultural phenomenon. In Greece and Rome, in Egypt, further east in the regions of Persia, as well as in the Jewish culture of Palestine, it was a common practice to compile the collective wisdom of the sages.[6] The questions posed by this ancient wisdom tradition were basic: What is the world like? Who are we? How does one live life meaningfully? On the whole, this ancient wisdom tradition tends to be

---

Jesus probably did utter such "bromides" from time to time, but such things do not add much to our knowledge of him.

4. The Jesus Seminar designated this saying "pink" in each of its versions. I would agree with this assessment. It will be discussed below in the context of a number of sayings having to do with homelessness.

5. So argues Gerd Theissen, *Sociology of Palestinian Christianity* (Philadelphia: Fortress Press, 1978), 10.

6. The cross-cultural practice of collecting words of wisdom in the ancient world is documented by John S. Kloppenborg, *The Formation of Q: Trajectories in Ancient Wisdom Collections* (Philadelphia: Fortress Press, 1987), 263–316.

rather conservative. The scribal activity involved in the cultivation of wisdom usually found sponsorship under the aegis of a king and was carried
on in a court context. Such venues did not encourage innovation and dissent. The status quo was reinforced. Traditional sources of authority, such
as that of a parent, were invoked as both a literary convention and a social
ideology.

When one examines the wisdom associated with Jesus against this cultural
backdrop, the peculiarity of the Jesus tradition becomes clear. While the tradition of Jesus' sayings takes the form of collected wisdom, the content of
this tradition belies the typical conservatism normally found in such collections. Jesus' wisdom, far from conservative, lays relentless and constant siege
to the conventions of ancient life. The Jesus movement received no official
sponsorship. To the contrary, the insight offered by Jesus and his followers
undermined the official view of the world from the bottom up. The wisdom
of Jesus is countercultural wisdom.[7]

But while Jesus and his followers did not find a home in the court of a
king, such as Herod, they did speak often about a kingdom, a reign, an "empire" — the Empire of God. Why speak of an Empire *of God?* What is the
point? As I have already indicated in the last chapter, to speak thus is to
invite comparison, to suggest "this is what it would be like if God were to
rule." Implicit in the rhetoric of Jesus is a critique of *the* empire, Rome and
its subsidiary minions, like Herod. Imperial Rome is a far cry from the ideal
empire over which God would rule. Small wonder, then, that the term "Empire of God" is not a very common one in the discourse of the ancient world.
One finds it occasionally in the dissident wisdom of Hellenistic Judaism, or
perhaps in the speeches of cantankerous Cynic philosophers, the burr in the
side of imperial Rome.[8] In the collected wisdom of Jesus one finds it all the
time. It is one of the keys that unlocks the very character and intent of the
sayings tradition. Jesus did not intend simply to offer a set of teachings that
would enrich the lives of his followers. He meant to offer a thoroughgoing,
theologically based critique of his culture.

---

7. For further discussion of the peculiar character of early Christian wisdom, see Stephen J.
Patterson, "Wisdom in Q and Thomas," pp. 187–221 (esp. 198–207) in Leo G. Perdue, Bernard
Brandon Scott, and William Johnston Wiseman, eds., In Search of Wisdom: Essays in Memory of
John G. Gammie (Louisville: Westminster/John Knox Press, 1993).

8. For the Cynic and popular philosophical use of this term see Burton Mack, A Myth of
Innocence (Philadelphia: Fortress Press, 1988), 69–74. For their role in public social criticism,
and the price they paid for it, see D. R. Dudley, A History of Cynicism from Diogenes to the 6th
Century A.D. (London: Methuen, 1937), 125–42.

The Empire Is *Now*

When Jesus used the term "Empire of God" he was, to be sure, speaking in idealistic terms, but not necessarily in transcendental terms. The empire of which he spoke was not an other-worldly realm, a place far removed from the everyday reality of common life. Jesus spoke, rather, of the Empire of God as here, now, arriving, already breaking in on the world as he knew it. Mark's gospel remembers Jesus opening his public life with the declaration: "The time has come, the Empire of God is at hand! Repent and believe in the gospel" (Mark 1:15).[9] This reminiscence has at least a kernel of historicity. It coheres with a number of other sayings from the earliest layers of the tradition which speak of the Empire of God as imminent, indeed, already present. In Q and Thomas one finds this saying, for example:

> When you see a cloud rising in the west, you say at once, "A shower is coming"; and so it happens. . . . You know how to read the appearance of the earth and sky; but you do not know how to read the present moment (Luke 12:54–56; Matt 16:2–3 [Q]; Thom 91).[10]

The Empire of God is a looming reality, something which Jesus sees already on the horizon. His own role in bringing it to fruition is an active one. So he says,

> I have cast fire upon the world, and see, I am guarding it until it blazes. (Thom 10; Luke 12:49 [Q])[11]

---

9. The Jesus Seminar designated this saying "black." As it is, situated in Mark's gospel, it is difficult not to interpret it in an apocalyptic context. Over the course of its deliberations, the majority of Fellows in the Jesus Seminar came to reject the notion that Jesus was an apocalyptic prophet heralding the end of the age. For this reason, the saying was not thought to come historically from Jesus, but from the early church, which did embrace an apocalyptic worldview. My own view is that the sense of imminence and urgency one finds in this saying does echo something of the voice of Jesus, as I will argue presently; thus, I would designate it "gray," indicating that although it probably does not go back to Jesus himself, the saying nonetheless contains elements consistent with his ideas.

10. The Jesus Seminar designated this saying "gray," indicating that although it probably does not go back to Jesus, the saying nonetheless contains elements consistent with his ideas. Again, the presumed apocalypticism of the saying probably prevented the Seminar from assigning the saying to Jesus. However, the Thomas version of the saying shows that it need not be understood in an apocalyptic sense. It simply speaks of the urgency of the times. For this reason, I would designate the saying "pink," rather than "gray." Its multiple attestation in Q and Thomas indicates that it is at least of early provenance in the tradition. Its brief, aphoristic quality, together with its ironic tone and culturally critical attitude make it memorable and coherent with many other such sayings attested early in the Jesus tradition. My best judgment is that some form of it probably does go back to Jesus.

11. The Jesus Seminar designated the Thomas version of this saying "pink," but the Lukan version "gray." I agree with this assessment and so cite it in its Thomas form. The Lukan version,

There is an impatience in these sayings, a yearning for what could already be if only he and those around him had the wherewithal to make it a reality. In this well-known saying from Luke and Thomas, the potential quality of the Empire of God becomes clear. The Thomas version reads:

> The Empire of God will not come by waiting for it. It will not be a matter of saying here it is or there it is. Rather the Empire of the Father is spread out upon the earth, and people do not see it (Thom 113; par. Luke 17:20–21).[12]

The Empire of God is already, potentially here. It demands a decision for or against the new reality that is presenting itself in the impatient activity of the Jesus movement. The following proverbs may have come into the tradition as an expression of this call for decision:

> No one sews a piece of unshrunk cloth on an old garment; if she does, the patch tears away from it, and a worse tear is made. And no one puts new wine into old wineskins; if he does, the wine will burst the skins, and the wine is lost, and so are the skins; but new wine is for fresh skins. (Mark 2:21–22; Thom 47:3–5)[13]

> No one can serve two masters; for either he will hate the one and love the other, or she will be devoted to one and despise the other. You cannot serve both God and mammon. (Luke 16:13; Matt 6:24 [Q]; Thom 47:2)[14]

The Empire of God is here, already breaking in on the present world, challenging old loyalties, and demanding a decision for or against the new reality. But what was the new reality for which the Jesus movement was agitating? What could they see that drew them toward this new horizon?

---

taken originally from Q, has been recast into the form of an "I have come" saying, which may presume the later christological claim that Jesus was a messenger from heaven. The Thomas version does not presume this.

12. The Jesus Seminar designated this saying "pink" in both its versions. I would agree with that assessment. There is a related saying in Thom 3; I will deal with that saying later in the chapter.

13. The Jesus Seminar was torn in its judgment about this pair of proverbial sayings. The first was designated "gray" and the second "pink" in both the Mark and Thomas versions of the tradition. Many Fellows were reluctant to ascribe common wisdom to Jesus, since such sayings would not be distinctive of him, even if he did utter such truisms from time to time, like every ancient teacher. On the other hand, these two sayings fit well with the other sayings discussed here that express an urgency and necessity for making a decision about the things Jesus says and does. For this reason, I would designate both of them "pink."

14. The Jesus Seminar wavered on these sayings, again, because they are proverbial and common. On final consideration, however, they were given a "pink" designation, with which I would concur.

The Radical Empire of God

The Reversal of Common Values

Throughout the tradition of Jesus' sayings we find a common thread binding it all together: a social radicalism that calls into question common assumptions about how people ought to order their lives. In a very old saying that found its way into three independent early Christian sources, this questioning attitude comes to clear, crisp expression:

> Whoever seeks to gain one's life will lose it, but whoever loses one's life will keep it. (Luke 17:33; Matt 10:39 [Q]; Mark 8:35; John 12:25)[15]

Here Jesus understands something very basic about human existence. We tend to take our cues from the social world in which we are constantly immersed. Our social world has all the answers we need to life's most pressing questions: Who am I? What shall I do with my life? What shall I value? Whom shall I value? One's social world can lay out a script for human existence, provide one with an identity and an agenda. The world can script your life, if you let it. It assigns each one of us a role, a role defined in terms of the social conventions within which we agree to live. We know what the expectations are for each role. We know our lines. We know where we should be, with whom we are to speak, where we are to stand. In this saying Jesus calls upon his followers to give up their lives, to give up the script, and to receive the new life that is offered in the Empire of God. To give up the script — that is the point.

But how can one possibly do this? How can one give up that script, that plan, that way of life which holds so much in store for us? How could one mortgage the future for such an unknown thing as the Empire of God? As naturally as such questions come to us, the earliest followers of Jesus were less likely to have asked them with the same sense of urgency and angst. As we have already seen in the last chapter, Jesus drew his followers from the extreme margins of ancient society. The unclean, the outcast, the beggar, the prostitute — these were the people among whom Jesus spent his days. He was one of them. He and they were cultural expendables. They fell through the cracks of ancient society. Their roles in the script, if written at all, were nothing to cling to. "The last will be first, and the first will be last" (Matt

---

15. The Jesus Seminar assigned the version of this saying found in Luke 17:33 a "pink" designation, but all other versions a "gray" or "black." The latter each includes a self-referential comment ("for my sake" / "for my sake and the gospel's") reflecting the church's devotion to Jesus. The Q version of the saying (Luke 17:33) does not reflect this later development, and so is probably the more original form. I have cited this version.

20:16; Luke 13:30 [Q]; Mark 10:31; Thom 4:2a).[16] This aphorism is good news to the last, but it is bad news for the first. Jesus moved among the last, the least, the marginalized of his world, and declared the advent of a new Empire of God in which their roles would take new shape. Are you a beggar in this script?

> Blessed are the beggars, for yours is the Empire of God. (Luke 6:20b; Matt 5:3 [Q]; Thom 54)[17]

Are you hungry in this script?

> Blessed are those who hunger, for you shall be satisfied. (Luke 6:21a; Matt 5:6 [Q]; Thom 69:2)[18]

Are you sad and depressed in this script?

> Blessed are those who cry, for you will laugh. (Luke 6:21b; Matt 5:4 [Q])[19]

Are you hated and treated unfairly in this script?

> Blessed are you when people hate and exclude you and revile and slan-der you. Rejoice and be glad, for your reward is great in heaven. For just so did they treat the prophets who were before you. (Luke 6:22–23; Matt 5:11–12 [Q]; Thom 68)[20]

---

16. The most dramatic version of this saying is found in Matthew 20:16, which comes from Q. All other versions of it have been softened, if only a little ("*some* of the last will be first" [Luke 13:30]; "*many* of the first will be last" [Thom 4:2a]). Only the version in Matt 20:16 was designated "pink" all others were "gray." I would concur with this view, and so cite it in this Matthean form.

17. Luke and Thomas repeat this saying in roughly this form. Both were originally designated "red" by the Jesus Seminar, but later reassigned to "pink." In some form, this version comes from Jesus. The better-known version from Matthew's Sermon on the Mount (Matt 5:3) has been spiritualized ("Blessed are the poor *in spirit*...") in a distinctly Matthean way, and so was considered less likely to have been coined by Jesus.

18. The Jesus Seminar designated the Lukan version of this saying, which comes from Q, as "red." The less literal Matthean version ("hunger and thirst for justice") was designated "pink." The Thomas version is difficult to translate. By one reading, it sounds very similar to Luke 6:21a. By another translation it reads: "Blessed are those who hunger, that the belly of one in want might be filled." The Jesus Seminar also designated this version "pink." I have cited the "red" version from Luke. However, here is an instance where one could easily imagine Jesus uttering different versions of a saying on different occasions.

19. The Jesus Seminar designated Luke's version of this saying "red," Matthew's "pink." I have cited it as it might have occurred in Q, their source. In any event, it originally comes from Jesus.

20. The Jesus Seminar designated each of the extant versions of this saying "gray," meaning that, though in their present forms they do not go back to Jesus, there are elements in them that are consistent with his thought. I have included the saying in this spirit by omitting those

Jesus proclaimed the advent of a new Empire of God in which the world's values are rendered impotent and unimportant. Instead, Jesus lifted up those who were victims of those values and placed them in the center of the new Empire. He said:

> Everyone who exalts oneself will be humbled, and whoever humbles oneself will be exalted. (Matt 23:12; Luke 14:11; 18:14b [Q])[21]

The Wisdom of Jesus is first and foremost about the reversal of common values. The Empire of God calls for a reordering of human life and relationships that places those who are valued least in the world at the very center.

Purity and Piety

The topic of Jesus and the religious practices of his day is a difficult one for Christians to address with any sense of fairness. For centuries, Christians have dealt with Judaism only as a caricature, as a system of legalistic piety, whose unreasonable demands could never be observed, and so would inevitably lead to hypocrisy. This view, nurtured in part by a (mis-)reading of the apostle Paul and in part by reading Matthew 23 as a general critique of Judaism, must be recognized for the pernicious distortion that it is. These are the roots of Christian anti-Semitism, and they cannot go unchallenged.[22] Still, throughout the Jesus tradition there runs a steady stream of critique of

aspects of the extant versions that suggest a later provenance. Though we cannot know Jesus' exact words in this case, in my view Jesus probably said something like this. It is attested very early (in both Q and Thomas) and is quite consistent with the other blessings discussed above. For an argument for the historicity of all four of these beatitudes see Crossan, *The Historical Jesus: The Life of a Mediterranean Jewish Peasant* (San Francisco: HarperCollins, 1991), 270–74.

21. The Jesus Seminar designated this saying "gray," probably because it is common wisdom. The principle is often advocated in Jewish and Christian tradition without reference to Jesus (Prov 11:2; Ps 18:27; Luke 1:51–52; Jas 4:6; 1 Pet 5:5). Here, in my view, is an example in which the criterion of distinctiveness fails when it is used negatively, that is, to argue against authenticity (for an explanation of how distinctiveness might be used legitimately as a positive criterion, see Appendix 1B). Based on the strong tradition of reversal present in the Jesus tradition, it is quite likely that Jesus would have said something like this. One must suppose, after all, that Jesus did learn something from his religious tradition and that the early church did indeed learn some things from him. I would designate this saying "pink."

22. The observations of E. P. Sanders in *Jesus and Judaism* (Philadelphia: Fortress Press, 1985), 174–211, are particularly pertinent here. However, his own treatment of Jesus and observance of the Jewish law (245–69) is inadequate. He dismisses out of hand the idea that Jesus' views of different aspects of Torah observance might have shown variation, on the grounds that everyone would have regarded all parts of the law as equally binding (247). This position is too rigid and cannot account for differences in attitude about the "great tradition" that prevail among different classes and in different complex situations that would naturally arise in a multicultural setting such as first-century Palestine. It is unlikely, for example, that a marginal peasant from Galilee would have held the same view of Torah as a later, rabbinically trained student of the law.

religious practices. We must therefore venture an attempt to understand this aspect of Jesus' teaching, however dangerous the subject may be.

The criticism of religious practice we find in the Jesus tradition focuses on issues of purity and piety. These concepts are related. Both have to do with structuring one's relationship with God. Neither are unique to Judaism; they are common elements in the religious life of all cultures.

From earliest times, the people of Israel cultivated a strong sense of ordering life according to the will of God. The Hebrew epic is, in many ways, all about this. The Levitical laws were not thought of as acts of human legislation. They were received as the divinely ordained way of structuring life. To live in the presence of God meant steadfastly observing the ways of life that are acceptable to God. A breach in that order — a violation of God's Torah — required separation from God until such time as proper order could be restored. Sins, violations of the ordering system of laws, required atonement. But it was not just sin — a moral violation of the divine order — that required atonement. Any breach, any disordering of the divine order of things could produce a situation of uncleanness or impurity, requiring some restorative act to set things aright once more. So, for example, a woman is rendered unclean by the unorderable chaos of childbirth. As a result, she must be separated from contact with holy objects or places until a period of time has passed and she has given an offering to the priest to make atonement. When order is thus restored, she is considered clean once more (Leviticus 12). Whether some or any of these regulations have hygienic or other such origins is not really the point. The point is one's acceptability in the presence of God. To be pure is to be acceptable to God, and therefore eligible to belong to the people who dwell in the presence of God.

In Jesus' day the issue of purity had become an important one, forced to the forefront by the situation of foreign rule. Israel was occupied by Roman forces during this period; Hellenistic culture had been making inroads into the Palestinian landscape for centuries. Many Jews felt that their culture, their very identity as a people of God was under siege. Some, such as those who withdrew into the desert at Qumran, chose isolation as the answer to the polluting influence of the pagan presence. In their desert compound, they could practice daily ritual ablutions as a way of maintaining the state of purity necessary to a proper relationship with God. Others, such as the Pharisees, sought ways of maintaining Torah observance in spite of the presence of foreign influence. As new situations arose in this multicultural environment, they worked out the implications for Torah observance so that Jews engaged in a normal life could still maintain a state of purity. Under the pressures of occupation, the maintenance of purity through Torah observance became a way of preserving a Jewish sense of identity and belonging in the face of cultural and political dissolution.[23]

But as we have already seen in the last chapter, maintaining a state of purity is most problematic for persons living at the margins of society. Let us take the example of food rules. Every culture has ideas about what is acceptable to eat and what is not. There are also ideas about food preparation and consumption are equally sacred. One eats clean foods in a clean way. For most people, such rules do not pose problems. Clean foods are to be had in the marketplace; their proper preparation is usually provided for in an ordinary home. But Jesus did not restrict his relationships to "normal people." He moved on the margins of his world. He cavorted with beggars and drifters, with prostitutes, the hungry, the homeless. Beggars must eat what they are offered or whatever they can scrounge from the trash heap. Drifters have little opportunity to "clean up" for dinner. Among the expendables, to be unclean is a veritable condition of life.

In the Gospel of Mark there is a story that illustrates this problem quite well. The story itself is probably Mark's, but in it he uses a saying of Jesus that is quite old and probably authentic. Mark's story presents it in an authentic way:

> Now when the Pharisees came together to him, with some of the scribes who had come from Jerusalem, they saw that some of his disciples ate with defiled, that is unwashed, hands. (For the Pharisees and all the Jews do not eat unless they wash their hands, observing the traditions of the elders; and they do not eat anything from the marketplace unless they have washed it; and there are many other traditions which they observe, the washing of cups and pots and bronze vessels). And the Pharisees and the scribes asked him, "Why do your disciples not live according to the tradition of the elders, but eat with hands defiled?" (Mark 7:1–5)

At this point in the story Mark places on the lips of Jesus a highly polemical indictment of Pharisaic practice (7:6–13).[24] This probably has more to do with Mark's disputes with Pharisees in his own day than with anything Jesus thought or said. But at the end of this long diatribe he includes the brief saying that probably goes back to Jesus himself:

---

23. For an up-to-date general introduction to the Essenes, Pharisees, and other groups in early Judaism, see Frederick J. Murphy, *The Religious World of Jesus: An Introduction to Second Temple Judaism* (Nashville: Abingdon, 1991), 187–245.

24. The Jesus Seminar designated this material "black." I would agree with this assessment.

And he called the people to him again and said to them, "Hear me
all of you and understand: there is nothing outside a person, which,
by going in, can render one unclean; rather, it is what comes out of a
person that renders one unclean." (Mark 7:14–15)[25]

This quite pragmatic attitude toward the law grows out of the very circumstances of life lived on the margins of subsistence. It is not a general
indictment of Judaism, or even the law.[26] To read it as such would be to mis-
understand the role of the law in ancient Judaism. In Jewish thought, the
Torah is a gift from God, not a burden to be borne. Its purpose is to create
a relationship with God. But what of those who do not observe the statutes
of the law, not because they will not, but because they *cannot?* What if circumstances render one unable to procure clean food, or to prepare it cleanly?
What if one is simply too poor to afford what it takes to stay clean? Are the
dirty and the shamed to be excluded from the community in which God's
presence is desired? Jesus' insight about God was that God loves and cares
for persons regardless of whether they are able to maintain a state of purity
or not. It is an insight that is utterly consistent with that strain of prophetic
Jewish thought that declares God's special interest in the fate of the poor,
and harsh judgment against any social order that disregards the needs of the
destitute.[27]

One can see from this that Jesus' attitude toward the law was not exactly
that of the apostle Paul, with whom we have come to associate the rejection of the Jewish law much more than with Jesus. Paul, in attempting to
build Christian communities in which Gentiles could live in full acceptance,

---

25. The Jesus Seminar designated this saying "pink," an assessment with which I would agree.
It is also found independently in Thom 14:5, so we know that Mark did not create this saying. Then who did? It is certainly distinctive, countercultural, and memorable. It is also clever,
which some members of the Jesus Seminar thought was part of Jesus' success as a teacher, and
a little off-color (considering the things that render one unclean when they come out of the
body: excrement, semen, menstrual blood, etc.). If one thinks of an off-color Jesus as slightly
embarrassing to an early church struggling for acceptability, this too may count for authenticity.

26. As Rudolf Bultmann pointed out many years ago (*Jesus and the Word,* trans. Louise Pettibone Smith and Erminie Huntress Lantero [New York: Charles Scribner's Son's, 1958], 61–64),
Jesus, like most Jews of his day, simply accepted the validity of the law. This is not to say, however, that he did not come into conflict with its original meaning or conventional interpretation.
"For the essential fact about a teacher is not his acceptance of an authoritative mass of tradition,
but the way in which he interprets it" (ibid., 64).

27. Note that the concern here is not with the *'amme ha-arets,* or "people of the land,"
common people or ordinary peasants. As Sanders rightly indicates, such persons would have
maintained an appropriate sense of purity, even though not attaining to the highly refined standards cultivated among the *haberim,* an elite group which practiced the strictest observance of
purity in table fellowship (*Jesus and Judaism,* 188–99). Jesus' concern is with the destitute, the
expendables of his world, for whom all normal proprieties could not be assumed.

argued that observance of the Jewish law should not be made a prerequisite for belonging. In this sense Paul argued that for Christians the law was no longer valid. Jesus did not argue that the law is no longer valid. Rather, his view seems consistently to presuppose that the law is a gift from God. When its observance becomes not a gift but a burden, it can no longer serve to shape that relationship with the God whose nature is compassionate love. The principle is illustrated by another story in Mark, again probably fictive, which makes use of a very early saying of Jesus that is probably historical:

> And it happened that he was going through the grain fields on the Sabbath; and as they made their way his disciples began to pluck heads of grain. And the Pharisees said to him, "Look, why are they doing what is not lawful on the Sabbath?" And he said to them, "Have you never read what David did, when he was in need and hungry, both he and those who were with him, how he entered the house of God, when Abiathar was high priest and ate the bread of the Presence, which it is unlawful to eat for any but the priests, and how he gave it also to those who were with him?" And he said to them, "The Sabbath was made for people, not people for the Sabbath. So the Son of Man[28] is lord even of the Sabbath." (Mark 2:23–28)[29]

This remarkable story poses the question as clearly as can be imagined. The trade-off is obvious: meeting basic human need (hunger), or observing the law. The saying, which comes at the very end, renders any such trade-off completely absurd: the law itself was created for humanity's sake. If the law is a gift from a God whose fundamental nature is compassionate love, it would simply not make sense to place observance of the law before human need. This is exactly the view one would expect from someone who spent his days with tax collectors, sinners, prostitutes, and homeless beggars.

---

28. In Mark's rendering of this saying, "Son of Man" should probably be taken as a title referring to Jesus. In Mark, Jesus' authority is constantly at issue. But this expression can have a less pointed, nontitular meaning as well: "person." This was probably the meaning in the original saying of Jesus. Since the Sabbath was made for people, people should naturally rule over its observance (so Rudolf Bultmann, *History of the Synoptic Tradition*, trans. John Marsh, rev. ed. [New York: Harper & Row, 1963], 16–17).

29. The Jesus Seminar designated the saying in vv. 27–28 as "pink," but regarded the set-up for it in vv. 23–26 as Markan. I would concur with this assessment. The saying itself is brief, aphoristic, and memorable. It also has that countercultural edge that coheres so well with the sayings we are discussing. The set-up, on the other hand, has a secondary, literary feel. The Pharisees are Mark's stereotypical enemies sent to hound Jesus throughout Galilee, and the reference to the story of David in 1 Sam 21:1–7 is a bit too complex to imagine as a piece of oral tradition passed down from Jesus.

Jesus probably offered this sort of pragmatic critique of various pious practices. In so doing, however, he did not dismiss these practices as such. As
with the law, the issue was not whether acts of piety, such as prayer, fasting,
or the giving of alms, are in themselves either good or bad. Like most Jews
of his day, Jesus would have assumed that all of these things are good.[30] The
issue is whether one can engage in such practices with integrity. This is clear
from two sayings regarding Sabbath observance, which survived long after the
Jesus tradition had been taken into Gentile lands where Sabbath observance
would no longer have been an issue. Each is attested only once, but their ad-
ventitious character in the later period suggests that they nonetheless come
from an early stage in the tradition, perhaps even from Jesus himself. The
first comes from the Gospel of Thomas:

> If you do not observe the Sabbath as a Sabbath, you will not see the
> Father. (Thom 27:2)[31]

The second is a little-known saying that is found at Luke 6:5 in one important early manuscript, *Codex Bezae Cantabrigiensis*. It is one of those "orphan
sayings" that finds its way into a manuscript tradition, but whose origin is not
known. It was probably passed down orally until a scribe included it in *Codex
Bezae* or one of its ancestors. The saying comes as part of a brief anecdote:

> That day [Jesus] saw someone working on the Sabbath and said to him,
> "Sir, if you know what you are doing, you have my blessing. But if you
> do not, you are accursed and nothing but a lawbreaker.[32]

If this little story correctly represents Jesus' views, he apparently did not
reject the practice of piety altogether. Rather, the issue for Jesus was integrity.
The purpose of piety is to give expression to one's relationship with God.
Pious practice should therefore be done in such a way that this relationship

---

30. In the Gospel of Thomas the critique of piety seems to have evolved several steps further;
here popular piety is condemned outright: "If you fast you will give rise to sin for yourselves;
and if you pray, you will be condemned; and if you give alms, you will do harm to your spirits"
(Thom 14:1–3). The Jesus Seminar did not consider this as representative of Jesus' own view.

31. The Jesus Seminar, in my view, did not assess this saying correctly. It was considered
together with Thom 27:1, as though the two sayings were an inseparable pair. But they are not;
each can stand on its own. Thom 27:1 speaks in terms that are very Thomean: "If you do not fast
from the world, you will not find the [the Father's] Empire." The Seminar correctly designated
this saying "black." The saying on observing the Sabbath, however, does not so clearly offer a
Thomean perspective. Its call for consistency and integrity are consistent with the other sayings
we are considering in this section, and so must be said to contain at least a remnant of Jesus'
sentiments about the matter. I would designate it "gray" and include it as a reminiscence.

32. The Jesus Seminar did not consider this saying in its deliberations. As with Thom 27:2, I
would designate it "gray," indicating that, though the saying cannot with confidence be assigned
to Jesus, it presents material that is consistent with Jesus' own ideas.

is expressed adequately, reflecting both the compassionate loving character of God on the one hand, and the transformative effect of knowing such a God on the other. This is what we see in Jesus' own piety. He is not depicted in the gospels as engaging in such practices very often. But there is a very old prayer tradition that has come down to us in the gospels and elsewhere[33] known as the Lord's Prayer. Its best-known form is to be found in Matt 6:9–13. Matthew includes it in a series of (mainly Matthean) instructions concerning piety (6:1–24) in the central section of the Sermon on the Mount. But it also occurs in Luke 11:2–4, and so was likely passed along to Matthew from the source he and Luke share in common, Q. The Q version of the prayer probably read something like this:

> Father, let your name be revered; let your Empire come. Give us today enough bread for the day. Forgive our debts, to the extent that we have forgiven those indebted to us. And do not lead us into trial.

This simple prayer, though less elaborate than the later versions we are accustomed to repeating, is probably as close to Jesus' original views on prayer as we can get.[34] It is focused on the relationship between God and persons in the followership of Jesus. It opens with an address, naming God as the patriarch of the new family constituted by those who follow Jesus. The significance of this form of address is not primarily its intimacy,[35] but rather its placing of each person in the community under the authority and patronage of God alone. There is to be no patriarch who stands over and above others in the new Empire of God; all stand equally under God's immediate care.[36] Next follows a plea that all they have come to know about God might be made real in their midst, that God's Empire might truly come. Then comes a request for basic needs in the life of a peasant (bread, debt relief), together

---

33. See also *Didache* 8:2.

34. The Jesus Seminar did not think the Lord's Prayer was created by Jesus himself. It was skeptical that Jesus would have taken steps to establish a liturgical life for a church that would not emerge until after his death. Nonetheless, it agreed that the content of individual petitions in the prayer is consistent with the views of Jesus. The address as "Father," reverence for God's name, the coming of God's Empire, the request for bread, and forgiveness of debts were all designated "pink" by the Seminar. The final petition was designated "gray," on the suggestion that this appeal for deliverance might be more at home in the early church's experience of persecution. However, it seems to me that the considerable trouble Jesus got into during his own lifetime is reason enough to consider this petition relevant for his experience as well. I would designate it "pink," along with the other petitions.

35. See James Barr, "Abba Isn't Daddy," *Journal of Theological Studies* n.s. 39 (1988): 28–47.

36. This is the significance of calling God "father." So Elisabeth Schüssler Fiorenza, *In Memory of Her* (New York: Crossroad, 1988), 150–51, following F. Belo, *A Materialist Reading of the Gospel of Mark* (Maryknoll, N.Y.: Orbis, 1981), 324, n. 110. For further discussion, see below, pp. 111–12, 116–17.

with a pledge to participate in meeting the needs of others. Finally, it closes with one last plea that God should spare them from any unnecessary trial. It is an acknowledgment of weakness and a recognition that life is hard enough as it is. Whether Jesus actually coined the prayer as it appeared in Q, or whether the church later collected these petitions as reflective of Jesus' own prayers, it represents adequately the ideas about piety we see ascribed to Jesus throughout the tradition. The Lord's Prayer expresses both the gracious love of God, a God who gives bread, not a stone (Matt 7:9 [Q]),[37] and the response of those who have been transformed by the experience of this God, who long for God's Empire even as they already participate in it.

The Economy of God's Empire

There are, of course, economic implications to be drawn from this new Empire of reversed values. If common wisdom exhorts one to frugality and prudent investment, not so in the wisdom of Jesus. He said:

> If you have money, do not lend it at interest, but give it to one from whom you will not get it back. (Thom 95)[38]

The following saying expresses sentiments that are entirely coherent with this way of thinking. Thus, it may well come from Jesus, even though it is attested only in the Gospel of Thomas:

> Whoever finds the world and becomes rich, let that one renounce the world. (Thom 110)[39]

This latter saying underscores that "economics" has to do with more than simply the exchange of currency. It has to do fundamentally with how the world is ordered. Our word "economics" is built on two Greek words: *oikos* ("house" or "household") and *nomos* ("law"). It means, literally, the "house

---

37. The Jesus Seminar designated this saying "pink." I would agree with this assessment, since it coheres so well with the Lord's Prayer material.

38. The Jesus Seminar designated this saying "pink." There is another version of it in Matthew (5:42) and Luke (6:30), which comes from Q. It read something like this: "Give to anyone who begs from you, and do not refuse anyone who wants to borrow from you." The first clause was close enough to Thom 95 to warrant a "pink" designation as well. But the second clause appears to soften the intention of the more original Thomas version. "Borrowing" assumes that whatever is offered will be returned. Generosity is admirable, but a step back from total divestiture.

39. World renunciation could be seen as a call to an anti-worldly asceticism, something much in keeping with the Thomas tradition. That, together with the fact that this saying is found only in Thomas, led most Fellows of the Jesus Seminar to designate it "black." But it need not be read in terms of asceticism. Read economically, its coherence with the other sayings discussed here leads me to a "gray" vote, indicating that, though the saying itself is not easily traced to Jesus, it contains sentiments consistent with his own views.

rules," that is, the way one structures the human domain such that the means for life may be dispersed to those who need them. Such sayings do not simply decry the love of money and the amassing of wealth (even though this is basic). They call into question the economics of a culture. To "find the world," to discover its secrets, how it works and how it can work for you, to become successful at the game as it is conventionally played — all this is what Jesus asks his followers to renounce. Jesus calls upon his followers to give up on the "house rules" and to find another way to secure the means for life.

There is a tradition in Matthew's Sermon on the Mount (Matt 6:25–33), which is also found in Luke (12:22–31). It thus goes back to Q. Its well-ordered, tightly composed structure, and the fact of an independent version of it in Thom 36, suggest that it predates Q, perhaps an early sermonette that circulated in the earliest years of the Jesus movement as a kind of summary of Jesus' "economic" wisdom. In it Jesus is heard to say:

> Therefore I tell you, do not be anxious about your life, what you shall eat, or about your body, what you shall wear. Is not life more than food and the body more than clothing? Consider the ravens, they neither sow nor reap, nor gather a harvest into barns, and yet God feeds them. Are you not more valuable than birds? And which of you by worrying can add a minute to your life? And why worry about clothing? Consider the lilies, how they grow. They neither toil nor spin, and yet, I tell you that even Solomon in all his glory was not decked out like one of these flowers. But if God so clothes the grass of the field, which is alive today and tomorrow thrown into the fire, how much more will he clothe you, you of little faith. So do not worry, saying, "What will we eat?" or "What will we drink?" or "What will we wear?" For the whole world seeks these things, and your Father knows that you need them too. Rather, seek first his Empire, and all these things will be yours as well.[40]

It is often assumed that this little speech is about waiting passively for God to provide all of life's necessities. But that is not exactly what it says. In fact, to assume this is to overlook perhaps the most important part of the speech.[41] Its final line makes a kind of "pie-in-the-sky" theology impossible

---

40. The main body of this speech was designated "pink" by the Jesus Seminar. However, it was inclined to regard the final two sentences as additions made by the early church ("black"). I disagree with this assessment. In my view, the sense of the entire speech turns on the last sentence (as I will argue presently). For the speech to make sense as a speech of Jesus, this material must also be included. I would designate the whole thing "pink," if not "red."

41. Cf. the remarks of Hans Dieter Betz on Matt 6:33 (*Essays on the Sermon on the Mount* [Philadelphia: Fortress Press, 1985], 114–15; also *The Sermon on the Mount*, Hermeneia [Min-

here: "Rather, seek first his Empire. . . . " At the very climax of the speech
a program is implied. To "seek his Empire" means to order life in such a
way that the Empire of God becomes a reality. If one does this, or rather,
if a *community* does this, the necessities of life will all fall into place. God
would not ask one to live in such a way that this would not be the case
("your Father knows that you need these things"). "Seek *first* his Empire,
and all these things will be yours as well." Jesus' words speak about ordering
human relationships in such a way that no one is expendable and all have
unbrokered access to the means for life.

Become Wanderers

The little we know about the earliest followers of Jesus suggests that they took
these things seriously. Gerd Theissen has argued, for example, that they did
indeed divest themselves of possessions and wander the countryside, relying
for support upon others sympathetic to their cause. They did this in imitation
of Jesus, who was himself a homeless wanderer.[42] Whether this was by choice
or by necessity is a question deserving of greater attention.[43] It is not clear,
for example, whether the familiar saying contrasting the homelessness of the
"Son of Man" with the at-home-ness of foxes and birds (Matt 8:20; Luke 9:58
[Q]; Thom 86)[44] is an ironic lament or the basic philosophy of a program.
Whether it began as such or not, in any event the homelessness of Jesus and
his followers became a way of life in which they found meaning. This is clear
from such sayings as Thom 42, perhaps the shortest, most direct saying in
the entire Jesus tradition: "Jesus said, 'Become wanderers.' "[45] Homelessness

---

neapolis: Fortress Press, 1995], 481–84). They may be taken as instructive for Matthew's source,
Q, as well.

42. Theissen, *Sociology of Palestinian Christianity*, 8–16.

43. In the last chapter I argued that Jesus, like other artisans, would have moved in and
out of the "expendable" class of beggars and drifters. He keeps company with such folk because
he is one of them. Schottroff and Stegemann, on the other hand, suggest that Jesus and his
followers did not originally belong to this class of people, but "voluntarily placed themselves on
the bottom rung of the social ladder" (*Jesus and the Hope of the Poor*, trans. Matthew J. O'Connell
[Maryknoll, N.Y.: Orbis, 1986], 46). Theissen does not understand the role of the wandering
radical as entirely voluntary, but as a charismatic calling over which one might have little control
(*Sociology of Palestinian Christianity*, 8). On the other hand, understood sociologically, it is a
response to economic, ecological, political, and cultural factors (31–95). In this sense, wandering
radicalism is to be understood as a (fringe) religious response to various social pressures. Jesus
and his followers exercised a radical religious option in response to the pressures of their lives.

44. The Jesus Seminar designated this saying "pink." It has good, early multiple attestation
and is memorable as a short, aphoristic lament filled with irony.

45. The Jesus Seminar was evenly divided on this saying. The voting resulted in a .50
weighted average, meaning that the vote was split right down the middle. I was among those

has become more than a condition of expendability. It is now a matter of imperative importance for a life freed for faithful trust in God's new Empire.[46]

In Matthew and Luke — and so in Q before them — there is imagined a scene in which Jesus sends out seventy of his followers with instructions on how they are to comport themselves. The scene itself may or may not be historical,[47] but it makes use of sayings of Jesus in a narrative framework that explains what the followers of Jesus believed they had been commissioned by Jesus to do. The Q scene is best preserved in Luke 10:1–12:

> After this the Lord sent out seventy others, and sent them on ahead of him, two by two, into every town and place where he himself was about to come. And he said to them, "The harvest is great, but the laborers are few. Pray, therefore, to the Lord of the harvest to send out workers into his harvest. Go your way. Behold, I send you out as lambs in the midst of wolves. Carry no purse, no bag, no sandals. And greet no one on the road. Whatever house you enter, say first, 'Peace to this house!' And if a child of peace is there, your peace will rest upon them. But if not, it will return to you. And stay in the same house, eating and drinking what they provide, for laborers deserve their wages. Do not move from house to house. Whenever you enter a town and they receive you, eat what is set before you; heal the sick in it and say to them, 'The Empire of God has come near to you.' But whenever you enter a town and they do not receive you, go into the streets and say, 'Even the dust of your town that clings to our feet, we wipe off against you; but know this, that the Empire of God has come near.' I tell you, it will be more tolerable on that day for Sodom than for that town."[48]

who would have assigned a "pink" vote to this saying. At the very least, its coherence with the rest of the itinerancy tradition means that it contains material consistent with Jesus' own views.

46. For the meaning of this saying and the considerable debate it has occasioned, see Stephen J. Patterson, *The Gospel of Thomas and Jesus* (Sonoma, Calif.: Polebridge Press, 1993), 128–31.

47. Problematic for the historian is the "mission" indicated in the scene. Did Jesus himself initiate such a mission to spread the movement he started, or did such a missionary consciousness first arise with the church? In its favor is the early, independent multiple attestation it enjoys at the earliest stratum of the Jesus tradition. The Q version is preserved best in Luke 10:1–12. But there is a Markan version of this scene as well, the Sending Out of the Twelve (Mark 6:7–11), which Luke incorporates elsewhere (Luke 9:1–5). Matthew appears to have blended together the Markan and Q versions of the scene in Matt 10:1–16, creating one single mission speech. This is a typical Matthean editorial technique.

48. Just how much of this speech comes from Jesus is highly debated. The opening lines were too suggestive of early Christian missionary activity for the Jesus Seminar to consider them traceable to Jesus himself ("black"). The Jesus Seminar also assigned the closing lines to the early church and its mission ("heal the sick ... shake off the dust ... the Empire has come near ... more tolerable for Sodom ... " all "black"). The heart of the speech was seen as closer to the voice of

Crossan has emphasized that embedded in this scene is information that is vital to understanding the way of life embraced by Jesus' followers and the program behind it.[49] First, notice that these itinerants are to go forth dramatically unequipped: no purse, no bag, no sandals. In contrast to the peripatetic philosophers who roamed the roads of the ancient world, the followers of Jesus are not to practice the self-reliant resourcefulness that would make them independent of all the vicissitudes of fate and social intercourse. They are, rather, to render themselves radically dependent upon those who, perchance, might take them in. At the heart of the program is the necessity of human relationship. Without this, nothing can happen.

Second, this relationship is to be characterized by a mutuality of shared resources. For their part, the followers of Jesus are to care for the sick and bring into reality the Empire of God in that place: "heal the sick in [that place] and say to them, 'The Empire of God has come near to you.'" They cannot just talk about the Empire of God. They must enact it by reaching across the boundaries of clean and unclean to touch the sick, to care[50] for them, and to bring them into the wholeness of the new community. For their part, those who take in the wanderers are to feed them. They are to open the family table to these outsiders. The centrality of the table and shared food as a symbol of community and sustaining, nurturing relationship is a cross-cultural human reality that is with us still today. From the formal dinner party to the church potluck, our willingness to feed one another is a profound enactment of desired relationship and community.[51]

The itinerancy of the Jesus movement was more than a countercultural spurning of conventional lifestyles. It was a symbolic departure from the

---

Jesus, but only "stay in the same house, eating and drinking what they provide," and "whenever you enter a town and they receive you, eat what is set before you" received a "pink" designation; the rest was "gray." I am not convinced of this dissected result. The very heart of the speech (10:8–9) is found also in the Gospel of Thomas: "When you go into any region and walk about in the countryside, when people take you in, eat what they serve you and care for the sick among them (Thom 14:4). This tradition is also reflected in 1 Cor 10:27. It is therefore among the earliest and best attested items in the Jesus tradition. It should be "red." The final warnings of doom (10:10–12) cohere not with Jesus' teaching (compare "Love your enemies...," for example), but with the turn to apocalyptic judgment that is now associated with the later stages of the Q tradition. I agree that they should be "black." So should the opening missionary sayings in 10:2–3. The rest of the speech (10:4–9), however, coheres quite well with the central core. It should all be regarded as deriving in some sense from Jesus ("pink").

49. Crossan, *The Historical Jesus*, 332–48.

50. The Greek word conventionally translated "heal" in this text is *therapeuo*, which has the broad general meaning to give care to the sick. Thus, to insist on "healing" as the goal of this interaction may be to raise the stakes beyond what the saying itself would warrant. It may be enough to care, even if you cannot always heal.

51. For more on the significance of table sharing, see the discussion in the last chapter, pp. 83–86.

isolation of human marginalization and expendability with all of its accouterments: shame, defilement, hunger, loneliness. The followers of Jesus forced the issue of community and threw themselves into relationships of mutual care and nurture as the proper enactment of the Empire of God in their own lives and those of the persons they encountered. As homeless beggars they created an "at-home-ness" with anyone willing to take them in and embrace the new reality of the Empire of God.

Who Is My Family?

And yet the itinerant life was an unusual life, and disruptive. The life of a peasant in antiquity was normally lived out on a local scale. Much has been made of the achievements of Rome — the great Roman *Pax* — the great "peace" that made travel possible, and with it, commerce. But for most persons these realities were remote. The horizon of the peasant's world was normally but a few day's walk. One grew up in the village of one's father. And, barring the forced displacement of war or economic disaster, one lived one's life in the context of home and family. One worked the family fields, or, lacking in land, assisted the family in eking out its subsistence living by plying a menial trade. All hands were necessary to provide enough for the family's daily needs. The agrarian culture of Roman antiquity afforded the peasant a subsistence living, but no more.

The Jesus movement called people away from this life to become mendicant beggars. It could not have a been popular movement from the point of view of those left behind. Aside from the hardships imposed on the family, which must now get by without the labor of one of its adult members, one must reckon with the generally conservative ethos that prevails in peasant culture.[52] One cannot expect that a local ne'er-do-well would find ready acceptance in the role of itinerant philosopher among his or her family and peers. In the last chapter we discussed briefly a scene from the Gospel of Mark, which depicts Jesus' attempt to bring the movement to Nazareth, Jesus' own presumed hometown (Mark 6:1–6). The scene is realistic, if not strictly historical. His friends and neighbors are incredulous. Though they hear his words of wisdom and see his "powers" (this much is Mark), they cannot set aside the fact of his inauspicious life among them as a carpenter,[53] his normal mother, his ordinary brothers and sisters. And so, Mark says quite plausibly,

---

52. Theissen, *Sociology of Palestinian Christianity*, 11–12.
53. Some ancient versions of Mark 6:3 read "the son of the carpenter."

"They were offended by him." Here Mark takes the opportunity to insert a saying of Jesus known also to John and Thomas — and so quite old:

> A prophet is not without honor, except in his own country, and among his own relatives, and in his own house. (Mark 6:4; see also John 4:44; Thom 31:1)[54]

This is the general context in which one must understand some of the most difficult aphorisms in the whole corpus of Jesus' sayings. These are the so-called "hard sayings" that invite men and women to leave their families of origin behind and enter into the followership of Jesus. The following such saying is found in Q and the Gospel of Thomas. I cite it in its Thomas form, which is likely the closest to the original saying of Jesus:

> Whoever does not hate one's father and mother cannot become my disciple. And whoever does not hate one's brothers and sisters and take up the cross in my way will not be worthy of me. (Thom 55; see also Thom 101:1–2; Matt 10:37; Luke 14:26 [Q])[55]

It would be difficult to overstate the importance of family as the basic social unit in an ancient agrarian culture. To understand its importance, one must first banish from all consideration any modern notions of identity based on the self as an individual. In addition to its importance as the basic economic unit, the family was first and foremost the source of one's very identity. One's father and one's lineage determined one's identity within the local community. And within the family, one's place relative to other members — to siblings, to older and younger adults — determined one's place within the

---

54. The Jesus Seminar designated this saying "pink." I agree with this judgment. Its triple attestation suggests a very early provenance. It is also very memorable, as its frequent use even today attests. Also of interest is the designation of Jesus here as a "prophet," a claim that predates the more highly developed christological claims of Jesus' later followers. One could even imagine Jesus placing himself in the category of "prophet."

55. The Jesus Seminar designated Thom 55 "gray," Matt 10:37 "gray," and Luke 14:26 "pink." But this is mistaken in my view. The Thomas version of this saying envisions a young person leaving his or her family of origin. The split is generational (cf. Matt 10:34–36; Luke 12:51–53 [Q]; Thom 16). This is the likeliest scenario for imagining entry into the itinerant Jesus movement. In the Matthean and Lukan renderings of the Q saying, additional family members are added to the scenario, so that one must now imagine not just sons and daughters leaving home, but husbands leaving wives and parents leaving children to fend for themselves. This is no doubt part of the hyperbole that, ultimately, leads to hating "even one's own life" (Luke 14:26b), and so takes this very difficult saying out of the realm of realistic expectations, forcing a nonliteral, hortatory interpretation. This assessment of the tradition, of course, hinges on the assumption that Jesus did not encourage men to abandon their wives and children (Luke 14:26) or mothers and fathers to abandon their children (Matt 10:37). This would not be consistent with Jesus' sayings about valuing children (Mark 10:14b) and his prohibition against divorce (Mark 10:11–12).

complex hierarchies of position and privilege. One's identity was both familial and communal. Jesus realized that the script one receives within the context of family life could be one of the most powerful forces of human definition, for good or for ill. One could experience in family life a sense of acceptance and love. But in the strongly hierarchical structure of the ancient family, one could also experience most profoundly there a sense of loss, of dehumanization. Jesus' view of family was not an idealized one. He realized that family is also the place where love is lost, where betrayal is most painful, where abuse most humiliating. We know almost nothing about Jesus' own family life, but a memory imbedded in the tradition retains at least a glimpse of Jesus' own struggle with his family. According to the Gospel of Mark, upon hearing about his great following, Jesus' family tried to restrain him because people were beginning to say that he was "beside himself," i.e., mentally disturbed (Mark 3:21).[56]

Among those who, like Jesus, could not find in family an acceptable place to work out a life and future, Jesus created a community of followers that could function as a kind of surrogate family. Later in his gospel, Mark records this anecdote about Jesus and his family, found also in the Gospel of Thomas. It must have circulated very early on:

> And his mother and his brothers came and stood outside [where Jesus was speaking] and sent to him, calling him outside. And a crowd was sitting around him. And they said to him, "Your mother and your brothers are outside asking for you." And he answered, "Who are my mother and my brothers?" And looking around at those who were sitting around him, he said, "Here are my mother and my brothers! Whoever does the will of God is my brother, and sister, and mother." (Mark 3:31–35; see also Thom 99)[57]

The followers of Jesus are a family, a new family constituted by its devotion to the understanding of God proffered by Jesus. But this new family is an odd one by ancient standards. Elisabeth Schüssler Fiorenza has noticed that

---

56. I would regard most of these indications of tension between Jesus and his family as accurate typifications of what his relationship with them was like. After all, after Jesus' death his family seems to have been taken warmly into the Jesus movement, with James becoming a leader in the Jerusalem community and Mary receiving new respect and admiration that only grew with the passage of time. Thus, it is unlikely that the church would have created this tradition. It must be left over from the earlier period, when Jesus actually did come into conflict with his family.

57. The Jesus Seminar considered only the final saying as deriving from Jesus. The independent version of it in Thom 99 was designated "pink." The Seminar was evenly divided on the Markan version of the saying; in the end it was designated "gray," owing to slight editorial changes effected by Mark in building it into this story.

in naming the members of his new family — brother, sister, mother — Jesus has left out the most significant member, structurally speaking, of the ancient family: the father.[58] Ancient Jewish kinship structures were organized patrilineally. Families were ordered hierarchically under a patriarch. One's identity, one's belonging, one's lineage was dependent upon having a father. But in this new family of Jesus there is no father, no patriarch. Schüssler Fiorenza suggests that in the absence of patriarchy, a new possibility was created for an egalitarian community of equals. As I have already indicated in discussing the Lord's Prayer above, the early Christian practice of addressing God as "Abba," or "Father," was probably related to this pattern of community organization. With God as the head of this newly redefined and reconstituted family, Schüssler Fiorenza argues, there could be no patriarch, no single "head" to whom all others would defer. Indeed, even after two or three generations of Christian community formation, the Gospel of Matthew still presented God as "father" in precisely this way. In a section devoted to the critique of religious leaders, Matthew's Jesus instructs:

> You are not to be called rabbi, for you have one teacher, and you are all brothers [and sisters]. And call no man your father on earth, for you have but one father, the heavenly father. Neither be called masters, for you have one master, the Christ. The one who is greatest among you shall be your servant; those who exalt themselves will be humbled, and those who humble themselves will be exalted. (Matt 23:8–12)

This egalitarian community formation based on the concept of God as "father" may go back to the earliest days of the Jesus movement.

The Theology of Jesus

Jesus did not speak simply of a *just* Empire or a *wise* ruler. He spoke, rather, of an Empire *of* God. That is, when he spoke ideally about how life ought to be ordered, about how human relationships ought to work, he spoke about these things *theologically*. Jesus had a visionary understanding of who God is. Out of that understanding he developed an idea about how life could be lived in faithfulness to that God. Who was the God of Jesus? What was Jesus' own theology?

It is striking to notice how seldom this question is posed in the literature about Jesus. In the older literature it is supplanted by the question of Jesus'

---

58. Schüssler Fiorenza, *In Memory of Her*, 146–47.

own self-understanding, his "messianic consciousness," or the nature of his own unique relationship with God. But these are not questions of theology. They have to do, rather, with Christology, a subject which — so most historians today would agree — was not a question for Jesus himself. It was the early church that supplied this interest, as it reflected on the theological significance of what it had experienced in the words and deeds of Jesus. However, that Jesus probably did not have a Christology does not mean that he did not have a theology. Insofar as he chose to speak about just rule as the Empire *of God*, we must assume that he did indeed have a theology of sorts.

It was not by accident, however, that the early church eventually gave expression to this implicit theology using christological categories, speaking of Jesus using terms like "Messiah," "Lord," "Savior," "Son of God," and other such epithets suggesting that in Jesus' words and deeds people had experienced God in a decisive way. For while Jesus spoke of what it was like to live in the just Empire of God, he does not seem to have said much about God in any abstract or speculative sense. He did not entertain theological discussion, such as one finds in Plato, Aristotle, Philo, or even the rabbis. Nor was it his habit to take on the persona of the ancient prophets of old, speaking in a "spirit of the Lord." He spoke of the Empire of God as present. He made pronouncements about the implications of its presumed reality. He illustrated its character in parables. And he probably lived in a way that embodied what he was talking about. In sum, in Jesus' words and deeds many people experienced the Empire of God as present. That is how people could later speak of Jesus as a divine epiphany. To speak of Jesus as the son of God was not to falsify the claims of Jesus or to deliberately inflate them beyond the scope of what Jesus himself would have intended. This is simply how people, in retrospect, could say they had experienced Jesus.

So the question of Jesus' theology must not be concerned first with the titles ascribed to Jesus, nor with the special relationship Jesus is said to have had with God, nor with any other of the church's expressions of its faith. These christological expressions have to do with early Christians' *response* to Jesus and the experience of God they claimed to have had in his words and deeds. To ask about Jesus' own theology is to ask first about the experience itself, not the response to it. What is the character of God that comes to expression in Jesus' words and deeds? What did Jesus believe to be true about God that led him to speak of God's Empire in the way that he did? Once we have answered this question, then it is possible to see how the insights Jesus had about God were refracted christologically into the early church's confessional statements about Jesus himself.

In speaking of God's Empire as a present reality, already potentially present, Jesus gave expression to the idea that God is not remote, but directly involved in the lives of ordinary people, a part of human history. Refracted christologically, this basic idea became the doctrine of the incarnation in the confessions of the early church. Jesus himself would not have spoken thus about himself; he did not claim to be God incarnate.[59] But he did declare the presence of the Empire of God. This is the origin of the basic Christian conviction that God is present in the human condition. This is the meaning of the incarnation.

In speaking of God's Empire as that place in which human values are reversed, in which those who are expendable to the regnum status quo become the center of attention, an Empire which belongs to beggars, Jesus gave expression to the idea that God is no respecter of human values and judgments about the relative worth of people. A human being has only one value to God, an ultimate value. To God there are no expendables. This is also the theological point implicit in Jesus' critique of purity and piety. No one is unclean to God; there is no one unfit for the presence of God. God's love embraces all, as they are, even prostitutes, tax collectors, sinners. In the theology of Paul, this basic insight emerged as the concept of grace, the idea that God loves humanity as a gift, without regard to any human attempt to become more acceptable to God. There is nothing one need do in order to be loved by God. When one realizes this, the result is a human transformation that Paul described as freedom from sin, and empowerment to embrace a new way of life grounded in love and care for others (Romans 6).

This idea that the experience of God is transformative and leads to new acts of love directed toward others is basic to Jesus' own understanding of piety: "Forgive our debts just as we have forgiven the debts of others." The third petition of the Lord's prayer (Matt 6:12||Luke 11:4a) is not a conditional formulation (even though Matt 6:14 would later bend the tradition in that direction, as though God's grace were conditional upon acts of virtue). The subtle use of hos ["just as"] in formulating the third petition indicates that one simply cannot experience the love of God apart from acting out of its reality in one's relationships with others. This is why the followers of

---

59. In fact, Jesus may have explicitly objected to any such close associations of himself with God. In Mark 10:18 Jesus responds to someone who addresses him as "good teacher" with the words: "Why do you call me 'good?' No one is good but God alone." The Jesus Seminar designated these words "gray," because they are so bound up with the introduction to a story most Fellows did not consider to be historical. I have difficulty, however, seeing these words as purely Markan. Mark is certainly no opponent to christological assertion (cf., e.g., Mark 9:7). They may come from an earlier memory of Jesus' own sense of piety. This, of course, stands in utter contrast to the Gospel of John's frequent identification of Jesus with God. This high-blown Christology reflects a much later and much further developed Christian theological situation.

Jesus could assume that Jesus, like many other Jews of his day, would have regarded Deut 6:4–5 and Lev 19:18 as the ideal summation of the Jewish law. The following anecdote appears in Mark:

> One of the scribes approached when he heard [Jesus and his opponents] arguing, and because he saw how well Jesus answered them, he asked him, "Of all the commandments, which is the most important?"
>
> Jesus answered, "The first is, "Hear, O Israel, the Lord your God is one Lord, and you are to love the Lord your God with all your heart and all your soul and all your mind and all your strength." The second is this: "You are to love your neighbor as yourself." There is no other commandment that is more important than these. (Mark 12:29–31)

If Jesus actually uttered these words, he was repeating a common Jewish understanding of the law. But this lack of distinctiveness does not make them any less authentic as the proper Jewish expression of Jesus' piety.[60] The Jewish God whom the earliest Christians had come to know in Jesus as gracious love called for a dual response: love for God and love for neighbor. They are, in a sense, two sides of the same coin: the appropriate response to a God of unstinting, all embracing love. But Jesus took the concept a step further. If God's love is unstinting, boundless, then the proper response to that God must also be unstinting and boundless. Thus, one is called upon to love and care not only for one's neighbors, but one's enemies as well (Matt 5:44; Luke 6:27, 35a [Q]).[61] Even one who attacks you violently can be confronted with such unstinting, patient love (Matt 5:39–41; Luke 6:29).[62]

The idea that God calls persons into relationships of radical love and mutual care is implicit in Jesus' words about economy. Exploitative relationships,

---

60. Because these words are not distinctive it is difficult to identify them as coming historically from Jesus. This is the weakness of "distinctiveness" as a historical criterion. It prevents us from seeing Jesus as part of the crowd. But who Jesus was and what he said was no doubt influenced by "the crowd." It is as important to see this as it is to see Jesus' distinctiveness. The Jesus Seminar designated these words "gray," indicating that, though they cannot easily be traced to Jesus, they might have content that is consistent with his ideas. I would go a step further and designate them "pink."

61. The Jesus Seminar designated "red" the basic saying "Love your enemies." But it drew back from assigning all of the related material that Matthew and Luke associate with it to Jesus (Matt 5:44b–48; Luke 6:27–28, 32–36). Yet it seems to me that if this whole tradition is properly summed up by Matt 5:48 (the Jesus Seminar did designate this "pink"), then all of this material must be said to hold content that is consistent with Jesus' ideas about God: "To sum up, you are to be perfect just as your heavenly Father is perfect." This way of putting it bears the marks of Matthew's hand, but the point, viz., to emulate God's graciousness in one's own life, probably comes from Jesus.

62. "Turn the other cheek...Go an extra mile" received a rare "red" vote from the Jesus Seminar.

such as the lending of money at interest, are rejected in favor of seeking the Empire of God, in which the basic needs of food and clothing are met for all. It is also implicit in the lifestyle embraced by the followers of Jesus, as expressed in Q's instructions for itinerant missionaries. Announcing the arrival of God's Empire means caring for the sick where you find them and accepting the hospitality of those who receive you. Life proceeds on the assumption of mutual care, radical dependency, relationships of support. As the history of the early church unfolded, this radically itinerant lifestyle gradually gave way to more settled modes of existence. But the idea that God's Empire means living in relationships of mutual care found new expression in the communal ecclesiology advanced by Luke. His vision of what the church ought to be is found in Acts 4:32–35:

> And the community of those who believed was of one heart and mind, and no one said that any of the things which they possessed was their own, but they held all things in common. And with great power the apostles gave their witness to the resurrection of the Lord Jesus, and there was great grace upon all of them. There was not a needy person among them, for whoever among them had lands or houses sold them and brought the proceeds from the sale and placed it at the apostles' feet; and it was given out to anyone who had need.

One seldom associates this story with Jesus, but it is clear that the early church did see this radically communal practice as directly related to him. Notice how Luke places in the center of this account a reference to the apostolic witness to the resurrection of Jesus. Why the close tie between the resurrection proclamation and the creation of communities of mutual care? To say that God had raised Jesus from the dead was to say that God had vindicated him, validated his claims about the Empire of God. What people experienced in Jesus' words and deeds was not just an encounter with a God who loves them, but also a call to form communities in which the experience of love and care would be institutionalized. In the resurrection proclamation the early church expressed its faith that this experience was indeed an *authentic* experience of God; God really does gather people into such communities.

Finally, Jesus called those around him his new "family." He also addressed God as "father," thus creating the idea that those who gathered around him might experience God as one who welcomes persons into God's own family. One should not overly sentimentalize this aspect of Jesus' theology. Jesus' address of God as "Abba" has sometimes been taken as a sign of Jesus' own uniquely intimate relationship with God. But this practice was not unique to

Jesus. Paul shows that in the early Christian movement it was common for anyone to address God in this way:

> For all who are led by the Spirit of God are sons [and daughters] of God. For you did not receive the spirit of slavery to live again in fear, but you received the spirit of sonship, in which we cry out, "Abba, Father!" The Spirit itself testifies together with our spirit that we are children of God. And if we are children, we are also heirs, heirs of God and co-heirs with Christ, provided that we suffer with him in order that we might also be glorified with him. (Rom 8:14–17)[63]

For Paul, it is not the intimacy of one's relationship with God that is signaled by addressing God as "Abba," but rather the familial nature of the relationship, a familial relationship to God in which the followers of Jesus share equally with Jesus himself. Indeed, intimacy may not have been a chief characteristic of ancient family life. It signals, rather, belonging to something that rescues one from human marginality (here, slavery) to share in a new life with the promise of a future (heirs). To experience God as Father is to experience oneself as valued, a member of God's own family.

In the Gospel of Thomas, saying 3, there is a tradition that gives eloquent expression to this understanding of God. It is probably a much developed version of the saying of Jesus found in its more original form in Luke 17:20– 21 and Thomas 113. But in this more developed form, the implicit theology of the tradition is made more explicit. The first part of this saying makes use of an old wisdom motif, the futile quest for God in the remote regions of the cosmos, to introduce the concept of God's presence close at hand:

> Jesus said, "If your leaders say to you, 'Look, the Empire is in heaven,' then the birds of heaven will get there before you. If they say to you, 'It is in the sea,' then the fish of the sea will get there before you. Rather, the Empire (of God) is inside of you and it is outside of you."

This much simply restates the concept behind Luke 17:21: The Empire of God is within (or among) you. But then Thomas continues:

> When you know yourselves, then you will be known, and you will understand that you are children of the living Father. But if you do not know yourselves, then you dwell in poverty, and you are poverty.

It is doubtful that Jesus himself was responsible for these exact words.[64] But in them, those who learned of Jesus from the Thomas tradition were saying

---

63. See also Gal 4:1–7.
64. The Jesus Seminar designated the first half of Thom 3 "gray" and the second half "black."

something quite true about the meaning of Jesus' words. In Jesus' words, those who found themselves at the margins of human existence discovered that in spite of the world's great capacity to shame, to declare unclean, to regard as expendable, they were nonetheless included in the family of God. Their value was not determined by their tenuous status within the world, within whose system of brokered value they might have been regarded as quite superfluous. Their value was determined by their status as true "children of the living Father." To God they were not expendable. To encounter the God who comes to expression in the words of Jesus is to discover oneself as valued ultimately by God, an heir to the promises of God.

What people experienced in Jesus was a word of love, acceptance, belonging, and value. Jesus spoke about God in just these terms. So when people heard his words and believed them to be true, their experience became not just that of a remarkable teacher. They experienced his words as the Word of God. This was the beginning of the Christian understanding of who God is. It began with the theology of Jesus himself.

Chapter 4

The Empire in Story

On the Parables of Jesus

Every fury on earth has been absorbed in time, as art, or
as religion, or as authority in one form or another. The
deadliest blow the enemy of the human soul can strike is
to do fury honor. Swift, Blake, Beethoven, Christ, Joyce,
Kafka, name me a one who has not been thus castrated.
Official acceptance is the one mistakable symptom that
salvation is beaten again, and is the one surest sign of fatal
misunderstanding, and is the kiss of Judas. . . .

Performance, in which the whole fate and terror rests,
is another matter.

— JAMES AGEE, Let Us Now Praise Famous Men (1939)

Perhaps no other form of speaking has come to be associated with Jesus of Nazareth more than the parable. Jesus was a masterful storyteller; the parables he used frequently to illustrate what he meant by "the Empire of God" are master works of narrative precision and insight. For this reason, the parables of Jesus have always been an object of intense interest and study. Some of the best minds to turn their attention to theology have occupied themselves with these gems in the tradition. The effort has not been in vain.

What Is a Parable?

A generation ago Robert W. Funk began what has become a classic essay in parables interpretation by referring to the work of a scholar who wrote a generation before him, C. H. Dodd. There is still no better way to introduce the whole matter of how modern scholarship has come to understand parables than by treading in such competent footsteps. From Dodd we have an eloquent definition; from Funk, a programmatic parsing of its crucial elements:

> At its simplest the parable is
>
> 1. a metaphor or simile
>
> 2. drawn from nature or common life,
>
> 3. arresting the hearer by its vividness or strangeness, and
>
> 4. leaving the mind in sufficient doubt about its precise application to tease it into active thought.[1]

Dodd's definition offers a design for exploring the nature of Jesus' parables. Each part of it deserves a closer look.

---

1. The definition comes from C. H. Dodd, *The Parables of the Kingdom* (New York: Charles Scribner's Sons, 1961; original, 1935), 5. Funk made use of it in "The Parable as Metaphor," pp. 133–62 (see p. 133) in his *Language, Hermeneutic, and the Word of God: The Problem of Language in the New Testament and Contemporary Theology* (New York: Harper & Row, 1966).

A Parable Is a Metaphor

This is the first, and perhaps most important element of Dodd's classic definition: "A parable is a metaphor or simile." Most modern parables scholarship begins with the proposition that Jesus used parables to illustrate metaphorically what he was trying to say. His parables answer the question, "What is the Empire of God like?" with "It is like . . . " or "What do you mean by that?" with "Let me tell you a story that will illustrate what I mean." This is the language of simile and metaphor. It is plain language, yet richly evocative in its comparative function. Dodd said of Jesus' parables: "They are the natural expression of a mind that sees truth in concrete pictures rather than conceives it in abstractions."[2] Parables use "concrete pictures" to work on the imagination.

The parables of Jesus have not always been regarded in just this way. This is because the gospels themselves sometimes use the parables to function differently. For example, for much of the church's history, church leaders and theologians have treated the parables as cryptic allegories, coding each element in the story to a hidden referent. The real meaning of the parable is thus concealed to all but those who hold the key that unlocks the code. The Gospel of Mark itself introduces this use of the parables with the following theory:

> And [Jesus] said to [the disciples], "To you has been given the secret of the reign of God, but for those outside, everything is in parables; so that they may see but not know, and hear but not understand, lest they should turn and be forgiven." (Mark 4:11–12)

However effective this technique might have been for adapting the parables for use in new situations, it was probably not the intention of someone who once said, "Preach from your housetops . . . ," to offer his greatest insights only in secret code. This bit of common sense we owe to Adolf Jülicher, a German theologian who produced his comprehensive two-volume study of the parables around the turn of the century.[3] In his careful analysis of the parables, Jülicher was able to demonstrate that the allegorization of parables was in each instance a secondary procedure that did not originate with Jesus himself.

A good illustration of this is Mark's allegorization of the parable of the Sower (Mark 4:3–8 [the parable itself]; 4:14–20 [Mark's allegorical inter-

---

2. Dodd, *The Parables of the Kingdom*, 5.
3. Adolf Jülicher, *Die Gleichnisreden Jesu*, 2 vols. (Tübingen: Mohr (Siebeck), 1910). Unfortunately, Jülicher's work has never been translated into English.

pretation]). On a first reading, Mark's allegory seems to offer a seamless, effective presentation of the parable's true meaning. The seed that is sown is the word of Jesus, the soil the audience who receives it (4:14–15). But as the allegory proceeds its consistency begins to break down. With the second group of seeds (4:16–17), it seems as though it is now the sprouting seeds, not the soil, who comprise the audience. In the next movement (4:18–19), the interpretation becomes quite confusing. Now the seeds are those who hear the word (v. 18), but the sprouted seeds are the word itself (v. 19). In the final movement, the confusion resolves itself in contradiction: the seeds are now clearly those who hear the word, not the word itself (4:20). All of this is not to insist that Mark's allegory is totally without effect. On an initial hearing one might rightly agree that preaching is like sowing. Sometimes it takes, sometimes it does not. This is true enough. But on a closer reading, the awkwardness of the allegory suggests that this was not part of the parable's original design.

Another strategy for interpreting the parables of Jesus has been to see in them great examples of moral behavior. This was Jülicher's tack, but it also finds its roots in the gospels' own use of Jesus' parables. Perhaps the best-known example of this is the so-called parable of the Good Samaritan (Luke 10:30–35). This is one moral lesson we have all learned well. Everyone knows what a "Good Samaritan" is. Hospitals, nursing homes, crisis hot lines, counseling centers — all bear the name of this consummate helper. And that is how Luke intends one to hear this story. Would that more had listened to his counsel: "Go and do likewise" (Luke 10:37). But as edifying and helpful as this legacy has been, does it belong originally to the parable itself? Probably not.

This conclusion, offered first by Robert W. Funk in an essay that marks another turning point in the history of parables interpretation,[4] is also based on a careful reading of the text. Luke's use of the Good Samaritan is, on the face of it, artificial. He uses it to complete a story originally found in Mark, which does not include this parable (cf. Mark 12:28–31). In that original story, Jesus and a scribe come to an agreement that the greatest commandment is to "love the Lord your God with all your heart, and with all your soul, and with all your might," and that the second greatest is to "love your neighbor as yourself" (Mark 12:30–31). They then part amicably. But Luke, unsatisfied with this ending, has the interlocutor (now a lawyer) continue his line of questioning. "And who is my neighbor?" he asks. He wants clarifica-

---

4. Funk, *Language, Hermeneutic, and the Word of God,* 199–222. Some of Funk's insights were published already in "How Do You Read? (Luke 10:25–37)," *Interpretation* 18 (1964): 56–61.

tion: to whom shall I show love? Then follows the story of the Samaritan. On a first reading, the point is clear: one is to show love to whomever needs it. This is the point that Luke intends. It is a good point, and easy to understand. But it is secondary. Luke has clearly tacked it on to Mark's original story. And, as might be expected with second-hand use, the fit is not exact. Notice how the story does not really answer the question posed by the lawyer. The lawyer has asked about someone to whom he should show love. But the Samaritan is not an example of such a person. He is not the object of love, but one who himself demonstrates love. Luke recognizes this awkwardness, and so has Jesus rephrase the lawyer's original question at the end of the story: "Which of these three proved to be a neighbor *to* the one who fell among robbers?" The question is no longer "Who is my neighbor?" but "How shall *I be* a neighbor?" In the end, the parable works as an example story, but only with adjustment and strain.

But did Jesus use it as such? Probably not. Notice also how the example of the Good Samaritan depends on the willingness of the audience to identify with the Samaritan and to take him as an example. This might have been natural enough for Luke's Gentile audience, as it is for us today. But this would not have been the case with Jesus' *Jewish* audience. The enmity between Jews and Samaritans in Jesus' time is proverbial. To assume that Jews would have naturally identified with the Samaritan in the story is absurd. Rather, without the Lukan framework our attention is drawn to another character, the one person who is present throughout the story, who is left undescribed, a universal body into which anyone can slip to experience the story. This, of course, is the victim. This is the character with whom Jesus' original audience would have identified. But to see the story from this angle, as a Jew, as a victim, waiting for help, and receiving it finally from the one person from whom you would never receive anything willingly, the Samaritan — that is another kind of story altogether. It is a parable.

So what is a parable? It is not an allegory; nor is it an example story. A parable uses the language and strategy of metaphor. Metaphoric language is poetic language; it conveys what plain, discursive prose cannot. This does not mean that Jesus should be imagined as a kind of ancient Allen Ginsberg, sporting a goatee and beret, sitting behind the microphone in a basement coffee house. He was simply a good storyteller. Yet one should not down-play the creativity displayed in some of Jesus' parables. He was a *good* storyteller. He knew how to use language skillfully to introduce people to his vision of reality. The storyteller's use of language warrants deeper consideration if we are to understand more clearly what Jesus was doing in creating parables.

We owe much of what we can appreciate about the poetic dimensions of Jesus' use of language to Amos Niven Wilder.[5] The brother of famed playwright Thornton Wilder, this gifted interpreter of scripture used a brilliant career at the University of Chicago, and later at Harvard, to impress on exegetes trained in the classical historical-critical disciplines the need to attend to the literary dimensions of the texts of the Bible as well. He considered it almost an occupational hazard of New Testament scholars to develop a tin ear to the beauty and poetry of these texts, even while smoking out every tiny historical reference, every linguistic nuance. Wilder knew that in these texts, as with all creative acts, the whole is more than the sum of its parts. Most interpreters of Jesus' parables had come to see this at least in part, when they rejected the allegorical reading of parables, with its propensity to attach individual meaning and significance to each detail in the story. But how to step back and read these parabolic metaphors as wholes — this we owe in large measure to Wilder and those who followed his lead in exploring Jesus' use of language.

Wilder himself was indebted to a theological movement that flourished in the United States and Germany in the 1950s and '60s. This movement, known in the United States as "the New Hermeneutic," took language to be the central problem of theological inquiry.[6] His focusing of the problem in this way was indebted to the later work of the German existentialist philosopher Martin Heidegger.[7] Heidegger believed that language is the unique expression of human beings and that, as such, it bears in itself the power to disclose the meaning of human existence. This was the key to the New Hermeneutic's approach to theology. Language has the power to create world. Anyone who has listened to a great poet or storyteller knows this to be true. In the poet's images are disclosed verities of human existence uniquely available to the soul that is sensitive to the poet's words. The gifted storyteller or novelist has the power to create worlds in which human events unfold,

---

5. Wilder's most influential work on this score is *The Language of the Gospel: Early Christian Rhetoric* (New York: Harper & Row, 1964), subsequently republished as *Early Christian Rhetoric: The Language of the Gospel* (Cambridge: Harvard University Press, 1971).

6. For a discussion of the New Hermeneutic, see James M. Robinson, "Hermeneutic since Barth," pp. 1–77 in James M. Robinson and John B. Cobb, Jr., eds., *The New Hermeneutic,* New Frontiers in Theology II (New York: Harper & Row, 1964). Other essays in this volume by Gerhard Ebeling, Ernst Fuchs, John Dillenberger, Robert W. Funk, Amos Wilder, and John Cobb are also helpful.

7. The "Later Heidegger" and his influence on Continental theology is discussed by James M. Robinson in "The German Discussion of the Later Heidegger," pp. 3–76 in James M. Robinson and John B. Cobb, Jr., eds., *The Later Heidegger and Theology,* New Frontiers in Theology I (New York: Harper & Row, 1963).

revealing truths about life, recognizable in one's own experience, and yet left inarticulate without the story's assistance. In the parables, Jesus used language to create a world in which his vision of reality[8] could be played out in events conjured up in the imagination. As such, Jesus' parables were not just signs pointing to some other reality (allegory, example story). As true metaphors, they bear in themselves Jesus' vision of reality. They demonstrate it, make it tangible, taking advantage of the power of language and imagination. Through the parable, Wilder writes,

> the hearer not only learns about that reality, he participates in it. He is invaded by it. Here lies the power and fatefulness of art. Jesus' speech had the character not just of instruction and ideas but of compelling imagination, of spell, of mythical shock and transformation.[9]

The Good Samaritan, the Prodigal Son, the Great Feast, the Tenants — in all of these stories Jesus uses language to create world, the new and strange world of the Empire of God.

This means that parables are more apt to work at the level of human experience rather than of ideas and abstract propositions. Parables take advantage of a different way of knowing, an experientially based knowing, different from that based on abstract, propositional thinking. Metaphor, insofar as it involves an act of imagining reality, stands closer in character to "event" than to "abstraction."[10] In his parables, Jesus brought the reign of God into language. He created a world, a "language event," in which the reality of the reign of God could be experienced through the power of imagination.[11] Such is the power of metaphor.

---

8. Compare the insight of Charles Hedrick, *Parables as Poetic Fictions: The Creative Voice of Jesus* (Peabody, Mass.: Hendrickson, 1994), who understands Jesus' parables as "poetic fictions." Hedrick writes: "the fictions of Jesus are occasional partial 'descriptions' of his 'world,' his view of reality. Each story is related to the whole of the collected stories, as each is also related to an inaccessible complete narrative construct of Jesus' view of the world" (32). This seems to me quite consistent with the New Hermeneutic's understanding of how language functions in the parables. However, Hedrick offers this description of parables as an alternative to understanding them as referencing the Empire of God. But if Jesus used the Empire of God as the rhetorical device for speaking of his vision of reality (the world, if God were ruling), then such a distinction is not warranted.

9. Wilder, *The Language of the Gospel*, 92.

10. Funk, *Language, Hermeneutic, and the Word of God*, 143.

11. The concept of parable as a "language event" derives from the work of Ernst Fuchs, one of the early proponents of the New Hermeneutic. The most pertinent of his works in English is *Studies in the Historical Jesus* (Naperville, Ill.: Allenson, 1964).

Parables Use What Is Common

This is the second important element in Dodd's definition: "drawn from nature or common life." The metaphors Jesus used were generally drawn from
the common experience of those to whom he spoke. They came from the
world of Galilee, a world of villages and small urban enclaves, of agriculture,
of tenants and landlords, of fishers, shepherds, and laborers. The imaginary
events he created were typical — even stereotypical of that world. Disputes
about the rent, dangerous journeys, surprise discoveries — all of this would
have been familiar ground to the imagination of a Galilean peasant. This
"common" quality of Jesus' parables warrants reflection.

Strategically speaking, this is a good tactic. The commonness of the
metaphor makes it easily accessible. By using such common scenes and
stereotypical characters, Jesus was able quickly to draw the hearer into the
world he was constructing. It is efficient — that is, for the ancient hearer,
someone with a vast store of immediate knowledge of the world of ancient
Galilee. This, of course, is not at all true for modern interpreters of Jesus'
parables. We must work to familiarize ourselves with that strange world, or
we will miss important aspects of the parable. This is one of the most challenging aspects of the interpretation of Jesus' parables: that which made Jesus'
parables accessible and utterly relevant to common folk of his day is precisely
that which often makes them opaque and mystifying to us. Little things, like
the amount paid a day laborer for a day's work, or the common reputation
of shepherds, or the attitude of Jews toward Samaritans — these are essential
to understanding Jesus' parables, but they are often the most difficult things
for modern readers to discover. They belong to the common knowledge and
lore of ancient Galilee, much of which has simply been lost to us. Modern
intuition and sensibilities are of no help here. Research into the customs of
antiquity is the only answer, and an imperfect one at that.[12]

But the commonness of Jesus' metaphors has a further significance as well.
In using typical, easily recognizable scenes as the field within which to play
out the Empire of God, Jesus was suggesting that God encounters people in
the concrete everydayness of their lives. The transcendent is immanent. The
Empire of God is — or could be — a present reality already breaking into

---

12. In the history of parables research, there are many helpful volumes that seek to fill in
the cultural world in which the parables of Jesus originally made sense. One of the most helpful
studies is that of Joachim Jeremias, *The Parables of Jesus*, 2d ed. (New York: Charles Scribner's
Sons, 1972), a book originally published in German in 1947, but updated and revised in at least
ten editions. The most recent, thorough, and up-to-date treatment of this dimension of parables
research is that of Bernard Brandon Scott, *Hear, Then, the Parable: A Commentary on the Parables
of Jesus* (Minneapolis: Fortress Press, 1989).

the world as we have constructed it. It is relevant. Funk quotes Wilder with approval on this point: "Jesus, without saying so, by his very way of presenting man, shows that for him man's destiny is at stake in his ordinary creaturely existence, domestic, economic, social."[13] Jesus' parables engage persons in the midst of their world, but challenge them to see that familiar world in a new way. But that brings us to yet another aspect of Dodd's definition.

Parables Can Be Arresting

This is the third element of Dodd's definition: "Arresting the hearer by its vividness or strangeness." Even though Jesus used common situations and characters or the most familiar of objects in his parables, in the end, his use of them was far from common. These are strange stories, odd, even disorienting at times. And the more one ponders them, the odder they become. As Funk so deftly puts it, "The world of the parable is like Alice's looking-glass world: all is familiar, yet all is strange, and the one illuminates the other."[14]

They usually do not start out strange, however. One sees this especially in parables that are extended narratives. As the story begins, all is familiar, all is normal, and everything appears as one would expect it to be. Let us return to the Good Samaritan for a moment to illustrate the point. Jesus begins with a common scene and a typical scenario. "A person was traveling from Jerusalem to Jericho ... " That road from Jerusalem to Jericho was a well-known road, and notoriously dangerous by reputation. And what happens next? "And he was waylaid by robbers, stripped, beaten, and left for dead." This is just what the hearer expects; we were just waiting for it to happen. Such typicalities have the effect of drawing the hearer into the story *with certain expectations.* We know the place; we know the scenario; we know how it will end. The story continues: "a priest ... and a Levite came to that place, but passed by on the other side." If a priest or a Levite will not stop (they never do!), surely a common, ordinary Israelite will come along and save the day. This is what Jesus' original audience would have guessed. But then a hated Samaritan shows up. Now what? All bets are off. Expectant anticipation is replaced by anxiety and chaos. Will the Samaritan stop? What will he do if he does? We no longer know how the story will end.

This is typical of the way Jesus' parables work.[15] They begin with a com-

---

13. Funk, *Language, Hermeneutic, and the Word of God,* 155, citing Wilder, *The Language of the Gospel,* 82.

14. Funk, *Language, Hermeneutic, and the Word of God,* 160.

15. See Funk, *Language, Hermeneutic, and the Word of God,* 158–61.

mon slice of life, one which carries with it a host of expectations. But as the parable unfolds, the familiar world of experience and expectation is replaced as the parable begins to take twists and turns that the hearer could not anticipate. The world we thought we knew is not the world being played out in our imaginations after all. That old, familiar world has been replaced by a new and strange one. As expectations fail, a gap opens up. And in that gap there is room for a new way of thinking about reality to move into our imagination.

John Dominic Crossan has explored this aspect of parabolic speech in his masterful treatise *The Dark Interval*.[16] In this brief book, Crossan lays out what he calls a "taxonomy of story." He takes seriously the insight of the New Hermeneutic that language has the ability to create world. But he tries to be more specific about how that process works and to what end. One type of world-creating story we might call "myth." Myth, says Crossan, drawing on the insights of the famed French anthropologist Claude Lévi-Strauss,[17] has as its basic function the reconciliation of incongruities and problematic aspects of our reality. Myth smooths out the wrinkles in our construction of the world. For example, in the United States we live by the ideal of equality: "We hold these truths to be self-evident: that all men are created equal." And yet, in actuality our social world is marked by dramatic inequalities. How shall these incongruous realities be reconciled? We have in our cultural lore a common myth that manifests itself in a myriad of Horatio Alger–type stories, of how a poor lad with nothing works hard and eventually succeeds. The myth works the problem out in narrative form. The incongruity of inequality in the land of equality is smoothed out, made tenable by the myth that hard work yields success. Of course, deep down we all know that the world is much more complicated and troubling than this. But we all love a happy ending. That is the function of myth. Myth creates world — or at least a world we can live with.

On the opposite end of the spectrum in Crossan's taxonomy of story lies "parable." If myth constructs a narrative around the incongruities in our world such as to reconcile them and make them tolerable, parable does the opposite. It takes the world as we have constructed it and finds the incongruities, exposes them, even accentuates them such that the limits of our world are made apparent. Its assumptions are challenged. Its underpinnings

---

16. John Dominic Crossan, *The Dark Interval: Towards a Theology of Story* (Sonoma, Calif.: Polebridge Press, 1988). This work was published originally in 1975 (Niles, Ill.: Argus Communications).

17. Crossan draws particularly on Lévi-Strauss's basic work, *Structural Anthropology* (Garden City, N.Y.: Doubleday & Co., 1967).

are attacked. Parables do this by playing with the hearer's expectations. They begin with the world of familiar roles and patterns, but as the story proceeds, expectations are thwarted, the familiar is undermined. The narrative fixes nothing and breaks up everything. If myth creates world, parable destroys world. Arresting indeed.

Parables Make You Think

Here is the fourth and perhaps most difficult part of Dodd's definition to grasp and accept: "leaving the mind in sufficient doubt about its precise application to tease it into active thought." When read properly, Jesus' parables can be deeply troubling. They call into question the basic assumptions of ancient life, many of which are still part of our worldview today. They are challenging. And yet they do not always resolve all the questions they raise. They are open-ended. They provoke thought.

One of the reasons Jesus' parables are so troubling is that they seldom offer any single, concrete answer to the questions they raise. They are seldom reducible to a single idea, a proposition, a moral.[18] There is an open-ended quality about them. This can be troubling in a world where many assume that religious faith is about finding answers to life's most difficult questions. This was not Jesus' approach. In the parables he is often content to point out that there *are* troubling questions to be raised about how humanity orders itself and that our failure to recognize such questions is precisely that which prevents us from realizing a transcendent quality to life. We fail to raise questions because we fail to see the limits of our construction of reality. We are unable to see the flaws in the way we have imagined the world. Jesus' parables call that construction of reality into question and undermine it to the point of collapse. And at that point of dissolution, when the parable begins to turn away from our expectations and carry us into the unknown, there, at the limit of our worldview, we encounter the beyond, the transcendent.[19] The parable brings us to the brink of decision: to turn away from the unknown beyond and flee back into the world of familiar comfort, or to cross over and risk falling into the unknown realm of the transcendent, where fa-

---

18. See Funk, *Language, Hermeneutic, and the Word of God,* 148–52.

19. This is the "dark interval" to which Crossan refers. It is that moment when the old world of familiar assumptions falls away, leaving a void, that space where new imaginings may begin to form.

miliar markers are scarce, and we must reorient ourselves by venturing a new way of thinking.[20]

This last point deserves underscoring: Jesus' parables lead one into a new way of thinking. They do not bring one to a final point of meaning — a new set of rules to be followed, a moral to the story. This is not to say that there is no meaning to a parable, no point to its telling, no purpose in it. It is just that the meaning of a parable does not take the form of final principles to be derived from it. Its meaning is directional; it points one in a new direction that must be thought through.[21]

This particular aspect of parables becomes clearer if one recalls the New Hermeneutic's concept of "language event." Parables are events. They can be experienced as events. But how does one attach meaning to an event? What did the assassination of John F. Kennedy mean? What has the bombing of a federal building in Oklahoma City meant? These were events, profoundly troubling ones. And no two persons in our culture experienced them exactly alike. We all bring complex personal and corporate histories to such events. Their meaning emerges only as we think through their implications in light of everything else we know about the world of human existence and begin to live differently as a result of what we have experienced.

Jesus' parables are carefully crafted language events in which one en-counters another world, the world of God's Empire. What will the result of that encounter be? Some of those who heard Jesus tell these stories just turned away shaking their heads. Such preposterous tales are the product of a perverted view of the world, they said. Others found them interesting and provocative, and resolved to listen again sometime. But others were drawn into the world of Jesus' parables and never came out. They could never see

---

20. Wilder, *The Language of the Gospel*, 82–83; Funk, *Language, Hermeneutic, and the Word of God*, 144–45. The idea that parables bring one to a point of decision was one of the contribu-tions of the New Hermeneutic to the American discussion of parables. Wilder (83) quotes Ernst Fuchs positively on this score: "Without question, it is from within this sphere of community and family living that Jesus speaks. It is from this life that he takes illustrations for his parables.... But all that is not just scenery, not just 'material' for a poet.... Jesus is not just using the details of this world as a springboard, but means precisely this 'world.'... Jesus calls for faith and therefore decision. This decision places the man who responds on the side of God and the marvelous di-vine work in hand (Matt 17:20). But: what the hearer now does, he does in the same area of daily life that Jesus evokes so vividly and plastically in his sayings and parables" (from "Das Neue Testament und das hermeneutische Problem," *Zeitschrift für Theologie und Kirche* 58 [1961]: 211).

21. Cf. Funk, *Language, Hermeneutic, and the Word of God*, 133–36. Crossan worked with this basic insight to develop an approach to parables that emphasizes their "polyvalency," that is, their ability to combine with various human experiences to create meaning. See esp. his *Cliffs of Fall* (New York: Seabury Press, 1980); *Finding Is the First Act: Trove Folktales and Jesus' Treasure Parable*, Semeia Supplements (Philadelphia: Fortress; Missoula, Mont.: Scholars Press, 1979); and *Raid on the Articulate: Cosmic Eschatology in Jesus and Borges* (New York: Harper & Row, 1976).

the world in the same way again, but were drawn forward to think through life and existence on new terms, to try to live in the Empire of God.

Recovering the Parables of Jesus

The parables, as we have them in the gospels, are not preserved in the way that Jesus originally spoke them. There are many reasons for this. For example, the gospels are written in Greek. Jesus himself may not have always spoken in Greek. It is possible that in the countryside many people still spoke some form of Aramaic, the *lingua franca* of this region before the Greeks, and later the Romans, imposed Greek and Latin as the common languages of public life and commerce. Jesus may have originally told some of his stories in Aramaic, in which case their original words are lost forever. Or, Jesus may have told the same parable on different occasions in slightly different ways. A good storyteller never tells the tale twice in the same way. Which, then, is the original?

But more important than these reasons, there is the tremendous problem of how the parables of Jesus were preserved by the church. Long after the end of Jesus' public career, his followers continued to repeat the stories he had told in many different settings and on various occasions. And with the shifting demands of each occasion, the stories were changed. There is nothing inherently wrong with this. After all, a story told in the same way, but under different circumstances, may not mean the same thing at all. Interpretation was always a necessary component of the Jesus tradition as the followers of Jesus continued to use his sayings and parables in new times and new places. This is what our gospels are: attempts to render the Jesus tradition faithfully in particular times and places. The church, of course, is still interested in these canonical renderings of the parables. But if Christian faith is to bear any relation to Jesus of Nazareth, then we ought also to have at least some interest in the parables as Jesus created them. The question is, how can we recover something of the original parables of Jesus from the tradition that has so changed and transformed them? This is a classic question of New Testament scholarship.

In the abstract, this problem may seem almost intractable. Here, no less than in other areas of the Jesus tradition, we are dealing with the active memory of the early church. But when one looks at specific instances, the clouds begin to part to reveal distinct possibilities within reasonable limits. The gospel writers are not always subtle in their interpretive techniques. Let us return to the example of the Sower (Mark 4:3–8). Mark's use of this parable as an allegory is clear from his addition of a specifically allegorical interpretation (4:14–20). Working backward from this interpretation, it is possible also to see ways in which Mark has edited the parable to accommodate it more to his interpretation. Crossan has noticed,[22] for example, that Mark's treatment of the fate of the second batch of seed is long, convoluted, and awkward:

> Other seed fell on rocky ground, where it had little soil. And it sprang up immediately, because it had no depth of soil. But when the sun came out it was scorched, and since it had no roots, it withered. (Mark 4:5–6)

There is too much here. Little soil, no roots, withering — this would be enough. But Mark also includes rapid germination and a scorching sun. This piling on of images soon makes sense, however, as one reaches Mark's allegorical interpretation. The immediate germination becomes the shallow exuberance of the undercommitted; the scorching sun becomes the trials and tribulations that lead to a speedy retreat. Mark has told the parable in such a way that anticipates the interpretation he intends to give it. These suspicions are confirmed when we compare Mark's version of the Sower to another, independent version of it found in the Gospel of Thomas (Thom 9). In the Thomas version of the parable, the fate of the second batch is described simply, as we might have expected:

> Other seeds fell on rock, and did not take root in the soil, and so did not produce heads of grain.

With close attention to detail, and a little common sense, we can usually arrive at a version of the parable that is closer to Jesus' original story than what we have in any particular gospel. Having multiple independent versions of the parable also helps a great deal. By comparing independent versions of the same parable we can often arrive at the basic form of the story that is very close to the original. But in the end, we will never recover Jesus' exact words. We must be content with recovering the gist, or basic lines, of Jesus' original story.

Over time, scholars of the Jesus tradition have studied these problems using a method of analysis called form criticism.[23] Form criticism asks about

---

22. John Dominic Crossan, "The Seed Parables of Jesus," *Journal of Biblical Literature* 92 (1973): 147–48.

23. The two classic works on form criticism to which scholars still refer regularly are Rudolf Bultmann, *History of the Synoptic Tradition*; trans. John Marsh (New York: Harper & Row, 1963 [German original published in 1921], and Martin Dibelius, *From Tradition to Gospel*, trans. Bertram Woolf (New York: Charles Scribner's Sons, 1971 [German original published in 1919]).

the typical forms in which the Jesus tradition was passed along orally in the period of Christian origins, when texts were rare and talk abundant. It also looks at the typical settings in the life of the early church (*Sitz im Leben*) in which these typical forms had their usefulness and origin. In this way, the development of the tradition could be traced as it was adapted to new situations in the life of the early church. The form critics also gave attention to the changes wrought in the tradition to see whether any general tendencies could be detected. This subdiscipline of form criticism is called tradition history.[24]

One of the outstanding scholars in the study of the tradition history of the parables was Joachim Jeremias. His study *The Parables of Jesus* has become a classic in parables interpretation, passing through many editions and revisions since its initial publication in 1947.[25] In this book Jeremias devoted almost a hundred pages to the tradition history of the parables, identifying at least ten ways in which they were typically altered in the course of their transmission at the hands of the early church.[26] Jeremias's ten principles are still worth noting as we prepare to look at Jesus' parables afresh. His "principles of transformation" are as follows:

1. The Translation of the Parables into Greek. We have already noted this in passing. Today, scholars are less sure that Jesus always spoke in Aramaic. Most people in his culture would have been bilingual, many using Greek as their primary language. Still, Jesus probably spoke in Aramaic some of the time.

2. Representational Changes. As the parables were used in different cultural settings, some of the original figures, known in Galilee, but not necessarily elsewhere, would have been altered to more familiar local images.

3. Embellishment. Any good storyteller practices this with a flare.

4. Influence of Old Testament and Folk-Story Themes. Christians frequently turned to their sacred scriptures, the Hebrew Bible, to help them interpret the tradition surrounding Jesus. The less formal authority of folk tales also exercised an influence.

---

24. An updating and assessment of the early views of Dibelius and Bultmann on tradition history is offered by E. P. Sanders, *The Tendencies of the Synoptic Tradition,* Society for New Testament Studies Monograph Series 9 (Cambridge: Cambridge University Press, 1969).

25. See p. 126, n. 12 above.

26. *The Parables of Jesus,* 23–114.

5. The Change of Audience. Across the gospel tradition one can observe this already. A parable addressed to opponents in Mark may, in Matthew, be addressed to the disciples. Such changes can alter the meaning of the parable dramatically. Each time the parable was told, its audience had to be taken into account.

6. The Hortatory Use of the Parables by the Church. Jesus' parables about the Empire of God were often used as examples of and exhortation to good behavior.

7. The Influence of the Church's Situation. With the passage of time, the church encountered new situations, problems, and questions. The parables were often used to address these new situations as they arose. For example, after his death, many of his followers expected Jesus to return very soon. When that did not happen, Christians used pieces of the tradition, including some of Jesus' parables, to try to explain the delay. Similarly, they retooled parables to encourage missionary activity or to establish leadership roles and structures in the early church.

8. Allegorization. The church used allegory to tie a parable to a particular situation by assigning very specific meaning to each piece of the parable. Such "over-coding"[27] of the parables is to be resisted. Rather, their metaphoric quality invites one to step back and view them as wholes, allowing each parable to have its effect as an unfolding event.

9. Collection and Conflation of Parables. Like Jesus' sayings, so too were his parables collected and used. Sometimes placing parables together can affect their meaning, as one parable becomes suggestive for the reading of another.

10. The Setting. Just as the presumed audience can make a difference in how one hears a parable, so also its presumed setting — the situation within which it was told — can make a difference. The gospel writers all place the parables in some situation in Jesus' life. But these settings are largely fictive; we cannot presume that this or that parable was actually told by Jesus under the circumstances described in one of the gospels. All presumptions about the original setting of a parable should be avoided.

Using these insights about the development of the tradition, Jeremias reconstructed what he thought was the original gist of each of the parables

---

27. Scott (*Hear, Then, the Parable,* 58) takes this phrase from Umberto Eco, *Semiotics and the Philosophy of Language* (Bloomington: Indiana University Press, 1984), 144–56.

of Jesus. Others have followed in his steps, sometimes in agreement with his results, sometimes with new proposals. Most recently Bernard Brandon Scott has produced a magisterial study of the parables, which, like those of Jülicher, Dodd, and Jeremias, is destined to become a landmark in parables scholarship. Scott uses the insights of Jeremias and other form critics to recover what he calls the "originating structure" of each parable.[28] This term recognizes that, though the original words of Jesus' parables may be lost, by comparing different versions of a parable and using form-critical analysis we can at least arrive at the original structure of what Jesus actually said.

In his parables Jesus used the power of language, story, and imagination to invite those who heard him into a new way of constructing human life and relationships. Life is what you make of it. Jesus understood this. Reality is not the stable playing field one might easily assume it to be, based on the concrete objects with which we fill it. It is very much a product of human imagination. We give life its shape and meaning through our assumptions and our active construal of events. In his parables, Jesus invited people to construe life in a new way. He called this new way the Empire of God.

It Is Not What You Expected

Big things sometimes come in small packages. Some of Jesus' parables are like that. A few words wrapped around a simple image, they appear small, harmless, and relatively inconsequential. But they are like grenades. That is how Albert Schweitzer described his favorite, but often neglected, sayings of Jesus: "explosive shells from which the charges have been removed." That is how I would describe two little, well-known parables of Jesus. They happen also to be two of the most securely historical items in the whole of the Jesus tradition. The Jesus Seminar designated both of the them "red." They are a good place to begin.

The first is a simple little parable — a simile, really — that goes something like this:

> The Empire of God is like leaven, which a woman took and hid in three
> measures of flour, until it was all leavened.[29]

---

28. Scott, Hear, Then, the Parable, 18–19. The concept is drawn from John Dominic Crossan (Cliffs of Fall, 27), who speaks of recovering a parable's ipsissima structura. Scott, more than anyone else, has consistently offered an "originating structure" for each of the parables he treats. His work was especially helpful in the material that follows in this chapter.

29. There are three versions of this parable in the Jesus tradition: Luke 13:20–21; Matt 13:33b; and Thom 96:1–2. The first two, which derive from Q, were designated "red" by the

This seems innocent enough. "A little leaven leavens the whole lump." Or is it "One bad apple spoils the whole bunch"? Is this a good thing or a bad thing, leaven? To the ancient Jewish ear it was foremost an *unclean* thing. It was the one thing banned from the house during the highest of holy days in ancient Israel, Passover (Ex 12:15). This is probably why early Christians could use the image of leaven quite naturally as a metaphor for corruption. "Clean out the old leaven that you might become fresh dough, as you really are unleavened," says Paul to the Corinthians (1 Cor 5:7). Mark's Jesus cautions the disciples, "Take care, beware the leaven of the Pharisees and the leaven of Herod" (Mark 8:15). Or it may be that leaven — which is, after all, mold — was almost universally regarded as a symbol of decay in the ancient Mediterranean world. "In the view of all antiquity, Semitic and non-Semitic, panary fermentation represented a process of corruption and putrefaction in the mass of dough."[30]

So maybe this is not such a good thing, this Empire that is like leaven. What will it do if it gets into our dough? Will it corrupt? Is it unholy? Unhealthy? Unclean? Perhaps that is why the woman in this little simile "hides" the leaven in the flour. What if she were to get caught? Would she be punished for her subversion? And this is no small amount of flour, either. "Three measures." That's about fifty pounds![31] The Thomas version of this parable says that she then "made it into large loaves" (Thom 96:2b). But this is jumping ahead. There will be large loaves soon enough. Imagine the surprise when the baker mixes up a batch of dough with this leaven-laced flour, and the mass begins to rise! Fifty pounds of rising flour-become-dough could get out of hand very quickly. The Empire of God is not what you expected. But, large loaves — how bad can that be?

Jesus also said that the Empire of God is like . . . *a grain of mustard seed, which a man took and sowed in his garden. And it grew and became a great shrub, so that the birds of the sky come and make nests in its branches.*[32]

Jesus Seminar. The third, from Thomas, was designated "pink." Jesus could have repeated any one of these versions, or something very similar. I have given the parable more or less as it would have appeared in Q.

30. A. Kennedy, "Leaven," *Encyclopaedia Biblica* (London: Adam and Charles Black, 1902), 2754, as cited by Scott, *Hear, Then, the Parable*, 324.

31. Jeremias, *The Parables of Jesus*, 147.

32. There are four versions of this parable in the tradition: Matt 13:31b–32; Luke 13:19; Mark 4:31–32; and Thom 20:2. The first three are closely related. Matthew and Luke used Mark's version, but also made use of a second version from Q. All three of these were designated "pink" by the Jesus Seminar. The fourth version, from Thomas, was designated "red." Jesus could have uttered it in any of these forms. I have cited it here in its originating structure, as reconstructed by Scott, *Hear, Then, the Parable*, 379.

This brief simile, too, seems innocent enough at first: an example of small things becoming large, of shelter and home. As an image of the Empire of God it speaks a hopeful word about growth and future potential. But to an ancient Jewish ear like that of Jesus, it might not have sounded quite so natural. It is not just any seed that is sown. It is a mustard seed. In the world of Jesus, one is not supposed to do that — sow mustard in a garden. It belongs to the class of seed-bearing plants. It does not belong in the vegetable patch. To sow it there would be unclean.[33] Now, such distinctions were not arbitrary. Mustard can be somewhat of a nuisance. It germinates quickly and sows its seeds. Pliny said of mustard, "Once it has been sown, it is scarcely possible to get the place rid of it."[34] It is not just a seed. Mustard is a weed.[35] That is the Empire of God of which Jesus speaks: a pesky weed.

At least it is powerful and large, this weedy Empire of God. This miraculous little seed grows up to become a large shrub. But just how big is a shrub (*lachanon*), anyway? This sort of shrub, mustard, comes in varieties ranging in size from two to six feet.[36] This is not bad, but hardly what one would hope for when speaking of the Empire *of God*. Jesus teases his audience with this parable. In the last line ("the birds of the sky can make nests in its branches") he invokes an image of Empire encountered in various places in the Hebrew epic. Trees with great, powerful, nurturing branches are proverbial symbols of the great empires of old.[37] One can just begin to imagine the Empire of God stretching forth its great and powerful branches, like the great cedars of Lebanon, offering strength and shelter to all who gather under its boughs. But then one remembers: he is not talking about a tree, but a shrub, and a weedy shrub at that. Jesus mocks power with this ironic gesture.

So Jesus likens the Empire of God to a weedy shrub, planted where it ought not to be. It is not the big and powerful realm you expected. But at least it is tenacious. It will not be going away soon. There is a feisty hope in this parable, a determination to hang on, even if they try to rid the place of you. Mustard does have its good qualities. And there is more to its good side than mere tenacity. Pliny, this time commenting on mustard's usefulness, turned to Pythagoras for a remarkable accounting:

33. For a discussion, see Scott, *Hear, Then, the Parable*, 381–83. That the original parable spoke of sowing the seed in a "garden," see Scott, ibid., 374–76.

34. Pliny, *Natural History* 29.54.170 (as cited by Scott, *Hear, Then, the Parable*, 380).

35. Douglas Oakman, *Jesus and the Economic Questions of His Day*, Studies in the Bible and Early Christianity 8 (Lewiston, N.Y., and Queenston, Ont.: Edwin Mellen Press, 1986), 127.

36. See Irene and Walter Jacob, "Flora," *The Anchor Bible Dictionary* (Garden City, N.Y.: Doubleday, 1992), 2:812.

37. See, e.g., Dan 4:12; Eze 17:23; 31:5–6.

Pythagoras judged it to be the chief of those plants whose pungent properties reach a high level, since no other penetrates further into the nostrils and brain. Pounded it is applied with vinegar to the bites of serpents and scorpion stings. It counteracts the poisons of fungi. For phlegm it is kept in the mouth until it melts, or is used as a gargle with hydromel. For toothache it is chewed.... It is very beneficial for all stomach troubles.... It clears the senses, and by the sneezing caused by it, the head; it relaxes the bowels; it promotes menstruation and urine.[38]

Now *that* is a useful plant![39] The Empire of God may not be what you expected, but it is not without its qualities. It clears the head, penetrates the brain. It is good against all poisonous foes. It clears the throat, restores your voice. Calms your troubled soul. Clears the senses. Cleans you out. Mustard may not be what you want in the garden, but for an empire of the unclean, the shamed, the expendable, tax collectors, prostitutes and sinners, it may be just what the doctor ordered.

This Is Not the Empire of God

In all three synoptic gospels and in Thomas there is found a parable about an absentee landlord and his rebellious tenants. Some form of it probably goes back to Jesus.[40] By comparing the various versions of it in Mark (12:1–11), Matthew (21:33–43), Luke (20:9–18), and Thomas (Saying 65), and taking into account the peculiar interests of each of these gospel writers, we might surmise that Jesus himself usually told this story something like this:[41]

> There once was a man who owned a vineyard, who leased it out to tenants. When the time came, he sent one of his servants to collect what was due him from the vineyard. But the tenants seized him and beat him up, and sent him away empty-handed. So he sent another servant, and this one, too, they

---

38. Pliny, *Natural History* 20.87.236–37 (as cited by Scott, *Hear, Then, the Parable,* 380).

39. One might ponder whether Jesus knew all of this about mustard. This would be difficult to know. One might presume that Pythagoras knew what he knew from local folk knowledge about such things. As one with a reputation for healing, it is not unlikely that Jesus could have been aware of the value of certain medicinal plants.

40. The Jesus Seminar designated the version in Thom 65 "pink," and all other versions "gray" or "black," owing to the considerable redactional work done by the synoptic evangelists on their versions, respectively. These secondary features will be discussed presently en route to the parable's most plausible originating structure.

41. The following reconstruction adheres closely to Scott's originating structure (Scott, *Hear, Then, the Parable,* 237).

beat up and sent away empty-handed. So the owner decided to send his son,
saying, "Perhaps they will respect my son." But when the tenants saw that it
was the son they said, "This is the heir to the vineyard! If we kill him, the
vineyard will be ours!" So they seized him and killed him.

In this basic telling of the story, one will mark the absence of several
features from the individual biblical versions, each of which transforms the
parable into an allegory having to do with the death of Jesus. For example,
Mark's version includes a description of the vineyard (Mark 12:1b) drawn
straight from the opening lines of Isaiah's famous "Song of the Vineyard" (Is
5:1–2) a poem about unruly Jerusalem. For Mark, the vineyard is Jerusalem,
the place where Jesus was killed, and where in his day the great Jewish War
would culminate in the razing of the city and the slaughter of its inhabitants.
And it is not just any son who is sent to the vineyard, but the "beloved son,"
a clear reference in Markan parlance to Jesus (cf. Mark 1:11; 9:7). For Mark,
the reason for the destruction of Jerusalem was this city's rejection of Jesus.
This is made clear by his conclusion to the story. Rather than ending with the
death of the son, Mark's allegory continues with the vengeance of the landlord: "What will the owner of the vineyard do? He will come and destroy the
tenants, and give the vineyard to others" (Mark 12:9). For Mark, Jerusalem's
destruction was the work of God, vengeance for its treatment of Jesus. The
"others" referred to in this verse are, no doubt, the Gentile Christians who
are just now coming into Mark's church. For further effect, Mark (or someone[42]) has attached Ps 118:22 directly to the parable, so as to leave no doubt
that the story is really about the rejection of Jesus, not tenants and landlords.

Matthew adds his own flare to Mark's version, which he used as a source.
He creates two groups of servants from Mark's original three solo envoys
(Matt 21:34–36). He probably sees these as Jesus' predecessors, the former
and later prophets, who, like Jesus, were persecuted in Jerusalem (cf. Matt
23:24). Luke, too, adds his own special touches. For example, his concern
over the long delay of Jesus' second coming is reflected in Luke 20:9, where
the owner of the vineyard departs to another country "for a long time."
And finally, Thomas saw his own special interests in the story and crafted

---

42. It is a peculiarity of the tradition that in both Mark and Thomas (Thom 66) Ps 118:22
(23) is transmitted in close proximity to this parable. While most scholars agree that it was not
originally part of the parable (see Charles Carlston, *Parables of the Triple Tradition* [Philadelphia:
Fortress Press, 1975], 180), the psalm passage apparently was circulated widely in connection
with this parable. Crossan (*In Parables: The Challenge of the Historical Jesus* [Sonoma, Calif.: Polebridge, 1992], 90–91) has argued that in Thomas one sees something like the first stage of
this process, where the psalm accompanies the parable, but as a distinct saying. This is allegory
in its nascent stage. Mark represents a later stage in the process, where the psalm has been
incorporated fully into the telling of the parable.

it accordingly. In Gnosticism, the ability of the redeemed to recognize the re-
deemer is an important theme. This may explain the rumination of the owner
in Thomas's version after the rejection of the first servant: "Perhaps they did
not recognize him." All of these additions are secondary to the original parable and are typical of the sort of allegorical interpretation common among
ancient Christians and their contemporaries.[43]

By seeing through these layers of interpretive patina we can catch a
glimpse of the original parabolic metaphor created by Jesus himself: a simple
story about landlords and tenants. But what does it mean? It is my opinion
that not all of Jesus' parables were designed to reveal Jesus' vision of how
life would be if only it were lived consistently with God's rule. Some of his
parables do not reveal the Empire of God at all. Rather, they reveal the *world*
as it really is. If Jesus was visionary in his thinking about God's rule, he was
just as *realistic* in his thinking about the world. This is a parable about the
world — the world as it really is when we dare to peek behind the carefully
erected mythic facade designed to protect our sensibilities from its brutalities.
The striking thing about this parable is how predictable, and yet surprising
and disturbing its outcome is. Its characters all behave on cue, following reasonable expectations for the roles they are assigned in life. But in the end, no
one wins. The last word belongs to death.

Consider the owner of the vineyard. Does he act inappropriately? He is
the owner, after all. He has a deal with the tenants; he only follows through
with it. He sends his servants to collect his due. They are his to send. He
sends his son, who is honored to represent his father on family business. But
in spite of his normal good and acceptable intentions, in the end, he loses
everything: his servants, the vineyard, his son.

And what of the tenants? One must remember their plight. Scores of families lost their ancestral lands during the period of Roman rule in Palestine.
Caught in the vice of double taxation, owing both to Jerusalem and to Rome,
they were forced to sell the source of their livelihood, their birthright, the
sign of divine blessing in the great Hebrew epic, the land.[44] Tenants were dispossessed peasants. Was their situation fair? Had they not the right to seize

---

43. A more detailed discussion of these secondary features is to be found in Scott, *Hear, Then,
the Parable,* 238–45.

44. On the economic pressures on Jewish peasants in the first century, see Gerd Theissen,
Sociology of Early Palestinian Christianity (Philadelphia: Fortress Press, 1978), 39–45 (for taxes
and tax-debt see esp. 42–43). More recently William Arnal has sketched out the situation with
respect to loans and foreclosure in provincial Rome more clearly. He concludes from the papy-
rological evidence that "foreclosure was a major motivation behind lending" ("The Rhetoric of
Marginality: Apocalypticism, Gnosticism, and Sayings Gospels," *Harvard Theological Review* 88
[1995]: 486; see 485–89 for his full discussion).

the opportunity when it presented itself, to slay the enemy and take back their due? The idea of killing for land should not seem repulsive to anyone familiar with the American myth of origins, or the story of Caanan's conquest, for that matter. And yet, will these ragtag tenants really win in the end? Can they hold the land they have seized? I doubt it. Their jubilation will soon turn to dread, as they wait for the other shoe to fall. If Mark's ending were not so clearly allegorical, we might well see it as an appropriately realistic end to the drama.

And what about the son? His behavior is completely honorable. His future awaits him. He is the heir. He has so much to look forward to, so much to anticipate, so much to plan for. He is a good son. His father gives him a task, and he does his best. But where does his honor leave him in the end? He is dead, cast outside the vineyard to rot in shame.

So what did Jesus mean by telling such a glum and violent tale? This is not the Empire of God. We labor under the illusion that the world as we have constructed it is a just and fair place. One need only play by the rules, accept your assigned role, and everything will work out fine. But it is an illusion, a myth. We think — hope — that it works, but it does not. Jesus lived among persons for whom the world never worked. He knew that the justice and fairness of the workaday world was an illusion. This nihilistic parable exposes it as such. In it, no one errs. No one behaves in a way that is inconsistent with conventional expectations. And yet, no one wins. Can a world so radically hierarchical in its assumptions as to accept without question the existence of landlords and tenants and slaves ever really offer more than this? Jesus' parables were not just visionary glimpses of the Empire of God. They represent an all-out offensive against the world as it was/is conventionally conceived. Before the Empire of God can capture the imagination and become a reality, the old world of conventional assumptions must first be undermined to the point of collapse.[45]

---

45. For a similar reading of the parable of the Tenants see William Herzog, *Parables as Subversive Speech: Jesus as Pedagogue of the Oppressed* (Louisville: Westminster/John Knox, 1994), 98–113. Herzog describes this and other parables which expose injustice in the world in terms provided by Paulo Freire. They are "first-level codifications," designed to "unmask the world of oppression" (Herzog, *Parables as Subversive Speech*, 77). Herzog, who takes Mark's version of the parable as his point of departure, sees this parable as a first-level codification of the unjust and violent system of tenant farming. The point of the story comes at the end, when the tenants are crushed (Mark 12:9a). Herzog thinks that other of Jesus' parables might be read similarly, as "first-level codifications." They include the parables of the Talents (Matt 25:14–30; Luke 19:11–27), the Unmerciful Servant (Matt 18:23–35), and the Laborers in the Vineyard (Matt 20:1–15). The suggestion has merit, although I would not consider the last of these such a parable, as will become clear below. And there may be other parables that function similarly to undermine the order of things in the world without necessarily offering a positive vision for something new.

It's Not What You Earn

Jesus was not always so dour, even on the subject of vineyard workers. Matthew has another vineyard parable that also may well come from Jesus (Matt 20:1–15).[46] It has to do not with tenant farmers, but persons occupying the next rung down on the social ladder, one step closer to expendability. This story is about day laborers. Like tenants, they would have been dispossessed peasants, but without a permanent agreement for work. You might find them at crossroads or in the marketplace, waiting to pick up a day's wages on the fly. They were excess labor in the agrarian economy. The story probably went something like this:

> The Empire of God is like when a land holder went out early one morning to hire workers for his vineyard. The ones he found he agreed to pay one denarius per day, and then sent them into his vineyard. And he went out again about the third hour of the day and saw other workers standing around without work. So he said to those: "You go into the vineyard too, and I'll pay you whatever is just." So off they went. And again he went out at the sixth hour and the ninth, and did the same. And at about the eleventh hour he went out and found others standing around. So he asked them, "Why have you been standing around here idle all day?" They said to him, "Because no one has hired us!" So he said to them, "You go into the vineyard too." And when evening came, the owner of the vineyard said to his supervisor, "Call in the laborers and pay them their wages." And when those hired in the eleventh hour came, they received one denarius. So when those who had been hired first came, they thought they would receive more. But they each also received one denarius. So they began to grumble against the owner, saying, "Those you hired last worked only one hour, yet you have made them equal to us, who have borne the burden of the day and the scorching heat." But he said to one of them, "Friend, am I treating you unjustly? Did you not agree with me for a denarius?"

Now, initially one might wonder whether Jesus told such a parable at all. After all, it is found only in Matthew. And one might easily see it as an allegory for persons who had come to Christian faith late in the movement

Among them I would include the parable of the Rich Fool (Luke 12:16b–20; Thom 63 [the Jesus Seminar: "pink"]), and the parable of the Unjust Judge (Luke 18:2–5 [the Jesus Seminar: "pink"]).

46. The Jesus Seminar designated this parable "red," even though it is attested only in Matthew. Lack of multiple attestation cannot be used to eliminate something from consideration as coming from Jesus. The capriciousness of the tradition does not allow one to make such assumptions. I will discuss presently why I do not think that Matthew created this story.

(Matthew wrote some fifty to sixty years after Jesus' death), or perhaps late in life,[47] or perhaps even late in the history of salvation.[48] But if this is how some early Christians understood it, Matthew did not. He uses it in his story of Jesus' final trip to Jerusalem (Matt 19:1–20:28). In this section of his gospel, Matthew presents Jesus as reassuring his disciples that, though they may seem to count for nothing now, when it is all over they will be exonerated. It is they who, in the end, will "sit on the twelve thrones, judging the twelve tribes of Israel" (Matt 19:28). Matthew uses the story of the Rich Young Man (19:19–30), a story which he knew from Mark (10:17–31), to contrast the weakness of the rich man with the strength of the disciples. Matthew, like Mark, then concludes the story with the saying: "So many that are first will be last, and the last first." Matthew includes our parable at just this point. He thinks of it as another illustration of how the last will be first and the first last. Just to underscore the point, he includes this saying one more time at the conclusion of the parable (20:16).

But the fit is awkward. The story is not really about a last/first, first/last *reversal*. It is about the last and first being treated *equally*. Perhaps one could see Matthew's point if one worked it out on an hourly rate, or some such logic. But it is an awkward fit. Matthew did not create this story to fill a gap here. He knew it from the tradition and used it, with modification. His adaptation is for the most part clear. I have already mentioned the addition of Matt 20:16. Matthew probably also added 20:8c ("beginning with the last, up to the first") in order to heighten the last/first theme. Matt 20:15 is also most likely a Matthean addition to the story. It reads literally: "Is your eye evil because I am good?" This good/evil contrast is a frequent Matthean motif. And 20:14 — at least the last half of this verse — only sets up 20:15. It is probably also Matthean. We are left with the story, more or less, as I have told it above. If you need an ending, you might add to the owner's words, "Take what is yours and go" (Matt 20:14a). I prefer to leave it open-ended.[49]

Parables are best when they leave you with a question. This one leaves you slack-jawed. "Friend, am I treating you unjustly? Did you not agree with me for a denarius?" What kind of trick question is that? Of course they agreed for a denarius, but that does not make the owner fair in his treatment of the workers. Work is work; a worker is a worker. A worker who does much work

---

47. This is Origen's interpretation (*Commentaris secundum Matthaeum* 13.1342–46).

48. Irenaeus (*Adversus Haereses* IV, xxxvi, 7) and Augustine (*Sermones* XXXVII) both understood it in this way.

49. Again, for a more detailed and documented treatment of these critical issues, see Scott, *Hear, Then, the Parable*, 284–87.

should get much pay; one who does a little work should get a little pay. That is the way the world works, if it is fair. But is "fair" the same as "just"?

This parable catches us in our assumptions. That is intentional. Notice how the wages of the later workers are never agreed to ahead of time. "I'll pay you whatever is just." We are left to assume. The calculations begin immediately. Remember, these workers are dispossessed peasants. They are not the unemployed living off their savings. Peasants live at a subsistence level: a day's wage is enough to eat for a day. A denarius just about covers that. But what about a fraction thereof? The calculations involve not "how much we'll make," but "how hungry we'll be." Not so hungry, now that they are hired, even at the eleventh hour, but hungry all the same. In the workaday world, grace is measured by degrees. But what is fair is fair, after all.

But then the dénouement begins. The storyteller skillfully builds the drama. Not the first, but the last hired are paid first. What will they receive? Half a denarius? A quadran? A lepton? Less? Landowners were not known for their fairness at the end of the day, even if one had an agreement to begin with. Excess labor did not have much leverage. They may have already made their first mistake by running off to the fields without even negotiating.[50] But they are paid a denarius. Well, that is a surprise. How nice! Now *that* is a good landowner. There will be fewer hungry peasants in the village tonight. But how nice? The calculations begin anew. If those who came in the eleventh hour received a denarius, then first hour workers ought to receive at least twelve. Twelve denarii! In a subsistence economy, *that* is a fortune. The expectations! The excitement! The disappointment: "But they each also received one denarius." "No fair!" the cry goes up. And rightly so. And then this crazy logic: "Did you not agree with me for a denarius?"

What does a human being have a right to expect from life? Fairness? Hardly. What is fair depends on the rules by which we agree to play, and whether in fact the rules are followed. A day's wage for a day's work. You're

---

50. One recalls the world of the excess laborer in Steinbeck's *Grapes of Wrath*. So also in the ancient world of Palestine. See F. Gryglewicz, "The Gospel of the Overworked Workers," *Catholic Biblical Quarterly* 19 (1957): 190–98. On the other side, J. Duncan Derrett ("Workers in the Vineyard: A Parable of Jesus," *Journal of Jewish Studies* 25 [1974]: 64–91) constructs a complicated scenario in which all the workers are actually owed the same amount at the end of the day, and are thus treated fairly. But Derrett's scenario is too complicated and carries with it assumptions that are suspect. One is that day laborers value their leisure and must be induced to work. Another is that customs like the *po el batel* (a kind of customary minimum wage) would have been observed scrupulously by landowners. And finally, if it is the intention of the storyteller to present a situation that is fair, why does he include the grumbling of the workers who are paid last? Derrett's reading of the parable is allegorical: the owner is God, the late workers are Christians, the early workers Jews. I am suspicious of this reading: a just God treats Christians fairly, while Jews grumble over their misperceived mistreatment.

paid what you're worth. If you don't work, you don't eat. It all seems fair enough. But it never really works. The rules are not consistently applied. Does everyone really work a day for a day's wage? And what are you worth? And how do you eat when there is no work? This parable is about work, worth, and eating. If one still labors under the illusion that the workaday world is a fair and just way of making sure that all have the basic means to life, then this story will be deeply disturbing. It is unfair. But more than that, if taken seriously, it deeply undermines the quid pro quo system of human relationships that govern even our economy. Who among those workers will show up the next morning at the first hour? Everyone gets the same, regardless of how much they work. Will anyone show up at all?

But what if we define the question differently: In the Empire of God, what does a human being have the right to expect? A denarius a day. That is, enough to eat on for one day. You get what you need — what everyone needs — no more, no less.[51] In the Empire of God, it's not what a person earns, but what a person needs that is that person's due. Is that, *could* that be the basis for an economy? Yes, but only if one is willing to reimagine radically the basis for human relationships. Jesus imagined an Empire of God in which the basis for human relationships would be the mutual assurance that all would have what they needed, not what they could earn. Human worth is a given. It does not depend on one's ability to offer something of value to someone else, to secure one's own existence in the rough-and-tumble world of brokerage and competition. In the Empire of God, the means to life are offered to all freely, as a gift, regardless of what has been earned.

The Table Is Open

Freely, as a gift. Is it possible, really, to imagine life lived out on such terms? How would one have to think for this idea about God's will for human existence to begin to make sense? It would involve not just the chaotic overturning of our basic assumptions about the distribution of resources. It would involve examining our basic assumptions about life together — community. Jesus created a parable that challenged his hearers to do just that. I have

---

51. This is all said, of course, from the perspective of a peasant existence, for whom subsistence is the standard. If we might correctly assume that Jesus was himself a peasant, or an artisan struggling just below the level of normal peasant life, a denarius a day would indeed represent what is needful. This is not to say that Jesus was right about this. Subsistence does not meet every need. Our own imagined possibilities for meeting human need must not be limited by this perspective.

dealt with it in passing earlier in this volume. I return to it now because it involves something so central and basic in the formation of human community: table sharing. The parable, as Jesus told it, probably went something like this:[52]

> A person once gave a banquet and invited guests. When the time came for the banquet, he sent his servant out to summon the guests. And he came to the first guest and said, "Come, for the banquet is ready." But he replied, "I have just bought a field and must go to inspect it. Please, have me excused from the banquet." So he went to another and said, "Come, for the banquet is ready." But he replied, "I have just bought a yoke of oxen and must go to examine them. Please, have me excused from the banquet." And to a third he went and said, "Come, for the banquet is ready." But he said, "I have just gotten married, so I cannot come." So the servant returned home and reported to his master that all those whom he had invited had asked to be excused. And the master said to his servant: "Go out to the streets, and whomever you find there, bring them in to eat."

This parable had a rich interpretive history in the early church. Matthew (22:1–14) and Luke (14:14–25) knew the parable from their common source, Q. But they each made use of it differently. Matthew's hand was the heaviest in reshaping the story. To him, the parable suggested itself as an allegory for the history of salvation. In his version the banquet has become a wedding banquet (22:2), an oft-invoked metaphor for the coming salvation. The unfortunate guests, now cast as murderous rebels (22:6) reminiscent of the evil tenants of Matt 21:33–41, are punished by the host, a king, who destroys them and burns their city (22:7). This last detail is probably a reference to the destruction of Jerusalem, which has by now been integrated into Matthew's grand scheme of history. But when new guests are brought in off the streets, a new problem surfaces as the story continues to mirror concerns in Matthew's own Christian community: sorting out the good from the bad, the faithful from the unfaithful. The king must now sort through the guests. When he finds one without a wedding garment (that none of the guests brought in off the streets would have had such a garment is a logical point lost in the interpretive zeal of the evangelist), he is "bound hand and foot, and cast into the outer darkness," where "people will weep and gnash their teeth" (22:13).

---

52. This version is close to Scott's originating version in *Hear, Then, the Parable*, 161. It is closest in form to the version found in Luke 14:16b–24 and Thom 64, both of which the Jesus Seminar designated "pink." Matthew's version (22:2–13), which shows considerable Matthean redaction, was designated "gray." The secondary details of these versions will be discussed presently.

These last phrases are typical Matthean references to the final judgment. And so the story comes to a puzzling end, which makes sense only if one remembers that to Matthew, the story is not a story, but a highly coded allegory for what has come to pass and what will come to pass in the history of salvation.

The story as I have recreated it above is closer to the version we find in Luke and the Gospel of Thomas. Thomas added to the parable a kind of moral to the story: "Businessmen and merchants will not enter the places of my Father." With this in mind one can more easily see why Thomas adds a fourth excuse to his version — "I have some claims against some merchants..." In Thomas the reluctant guests are all business and merchant types. Otherwise, it must be fairly close to the original. Luke's version confirms this. His adjustments are minor. He introduces the story with 14:15:

> When one of those sitting at table with him heard this, he said to him, "Blessed is the one who shall eat bread in the Empire of God!" But he said...

This makes it a story about the heavenly banquet to be celebrated when Jesus finally returns (Luke is consistently concerned with the delay of the second coming). And at the end of the story he adds to the substitute guests "the poor and maimed and blind and lame" (14:21). This would not have been out of character for Jesus himself, but this particular formulation is so Lukan that it is hard not to see his own concern with charity for the poor shining through here. Take these secondary elements away, and you have a simple story: a banquet; three guests, three excuses; and a surprising ending.[53]

Anyone who has given a dinner party understands the basic human dimensions of this story. Giving a dinner party is risky business. On the surface, it is a fairly straightforward proposition. One gathers a few friends together for a meal, there is pleasant conversation, and a good time is had by all. But beneath the surface there are dangerous currents and crosscurrents. Let us take the guest list, for example. Whom do you invite? Naturally, one's peers. But who are they? How far up the social food chain might I reach with an invitation before I risk being turned down — being shamed and "put in my place"? And how far down do I reach without risking an association that will compromise my own place and position in the community? And whom can I risk putting at the same table? Will they all get along? Will they see one another as peers? We all know the rules of table fellowship: like eat with like.[54]

---

53. Again, see Scott, *Hear, Then, the Parable,* 162–66, for a more thorough treatment of all these issues.

54. For more on ancient customs around table fellowship, see chapter 2, p. 84.

Now, this parable is a social nightmare. What if one gave a party and nobody came? Was it just a bad night? Did I misjudge my place? Is there a conspiracy out there that I am only now beginning to see? Have I any friends at all? The embarrassment and the shame should be palpable. In the event of such a social disaster, most people would lock the front door, close the blinds, take the phone off the hook, and retreat under the covers for the rest of the weekend in the hope that no one would notice that they had suddenly become the community pariah. This is a classic transaction in honor and shame. When the householder asked, "May I have the honor of your presence at my table?" everyone said, "No." He has been shamed and now must live with the consequences.

But in this story of shame, a surprising thing happens. The shamed refuses to accept his shame. The servant does not even have time to pause before he is sent back out on the street, and this time without a guest list. It is as though the householder has said, "If I do not have any peers, anyone who will deign to share my table with me, then I'll throw open the doors and commune with anyone who wishes to call me friend." The social food chain disappears. His honor, his shame — none of it matters. The food is free, and so is the company. Hospitality is not a transaction. Community is not economy.

That is a very different way of thinking about community. Jesus likened the Empire of God to an open table, around which all might gather, to which all are invited. His idea that in the Empire of God the means to life are offered freely, without requirement, was grounded in a new idea about community: that relationships themselves are not to be brokered. Jesus called people into a new experience of community that was itself offered freely, without requirement.

You Need Your Enemy

But how far does community extend? Are there any limits to what one should tolerate in the community of God? This is the subject of another parable, the Samaritan. It occurs only in Luke (10:30–35), but Luke did not create it. In fact, so far as we can tell, Luke has not been very creative in his treatment of it at all. His version is probably as close to the original as we can hope to get for now.[55] He tells it like this:

A man was going down from Jerusalem to Jericho, and he fell among robbers, who stripped him and beat him, and left him half dead. Now by chance, a

---

55. The Jesus Seminar designated it "red." For details, see the discussion to follow.

priest was going down that road, and when he saw him, he passed by on the other side. So also a Levite, when he came to the place and saw him, he passed by on the other side. But then a Samaritan, as he journeyed, came to where he was. And when he saw him, he had compassion. And he went over to him and bound up his wounds, pouring on oil and wine. Then he set him on his own animal and took him to an inn, and took care of him there. And the next day he took out two denarii and gave them to the innkeeper, saying, "Take care of him, and whatever more you spend, I will reimburse you when I come back.

Earlier in this chapter I discussed the Samaritan at some length.[56] It is the best-known instance of a parable that is used in the gospels as a moral example story. But as I pointed out then, a parable is not an example story. And Luke's attempt to use this one as an example for neighborliness, while effective in its own way, shows the strain of secondary adaptation. It does not answer the question posed by Luke's lawyer, "Who is my neighbor?" Rather, it speaks of being a neighbor, like the Samaritan. The Samaritan exemplifies neighborliness, a move that is possible in Luke's Gentile world, but not very likely in Jesus' Jewish world. Luke's point ("Go and do likewise") is widely appreciated. It is noble. But it is not parabolic. To appreciate this parable as a parable, we must begin by forgetting Luke for the moment.

This parable is foremost a story. It uses language to create a world and an event through which anyone who hears it might experience Jesus' distinctive view of reality. But how does one experience an event that is really only a story? What are the points of entry through which the hearer might pass into this world? To really experience the story, one must locate oneself within it, not as a casual observer, but as a participant. In this case, there are many different points of entry for the hearer. Each new character provides an opening. But with whom would a Jewish peasant naturally identify in this story? Certainly not the Samaritan. As we have discussed above, it is quite unlikely that Jesus' Jewish audience would have naturally or eagerly seen a Samaritan as exemplary. The priest? Perhaps a few, but not most. The priest's station in life is too far removed from that of the common peasant to allow easy entry here. The Levite? Again, a few, but not most. The hearer's invitation into the story is offered primarily through the "man going down from Jerusalem to Jericho." He is a nondescript person. He could be any one — any one of us. He is the focal point of the story, around whom the plot unfolds. He, alone, is present from the beginning of the story to its end. And his vulnerable po-

---

56. See pp. 122–23 above.

sition draws empathy. We find ourselves rooting for him, hoping for a rescue. He's our man.[57]

But this is a different focus from that to which we are accustomed with this story. Seen from the point of view of the victim, its significance unfolds quite differently indeed. As we enter the story, we are confronted with a convention: the road from Jerusalem to Jericho. It is a notorious way, leading out through a desert of crevasses and gullies, prime cover for bandits and thieves.[58] Our empathies are aroused, as are our fears. This is an ambush waiting to happen. And so it does. Our man is attacked and left for dead. The plot is laid. How will he — we — get out of this dangerous predicament? From the point of view of the victim in the ditch, how will the story look as it unfolds around us?

In a few quick scenes the tension builds. Stereotypes and clichés are used to fix our expectations in assumed realities. The stereotypes are ancient — and modern. The hypocritical clergy, too busy to be bothered with the real problems of real people, are present in the priest. In accord with the anti-clerical prejudices among the common folk,[59] he passes by on the other side. And so too the Levite. He's a wanna-be priest, too good for common company. He passes by as well, as we expect.[60] A priest and a Levite. . . . There is a pattern developing here. The attentive in Jesus' audience would have heard a cliché taking shape. "Priest" and "Levite" are the first two members of a common triad: "a priest, a Levite, and an Israelite." One might hear it in a formulation to stand for "all Israel," or perhaps in a joke, sounding something

---

57. The idea that the original audience of Jesus would likely have identified with the victim, not the Samaritan, derives from Robert W. Funk's reading of the parable in *Language, Hermeneutic, and the Word of God*, 210–16, and later in "The Good Samaritan as Metaphor," pp. 74–81 in John Dominic Crossan, ed., *Semeia 2: The Good Samaritan* (Missoula, Mont.: Scholars Press, 1974), later published in Robert W. Funk, *Parables and Presence* (Philadelphia: Fortress Press, 1982), 29–34. The interpretation that follows is based on Funk's reading of the parable. His work on the Good Samaritan marks a turning point in parables interpretation, from understanding them as moral example stories to understanding them as true metaphors.

58. So Jeremias, *The Parables of Jesus*, 203.

59. For the anticlericalism among ancient peasants see Funk, "The Good Samaritan as Metaphor," 78; and esp. Scott, *Hear, Then, the Parable*, 196–97, and notes 39–42.

60. Many interpreters have asked "Why did they pass by?" But this question is misdirected. The question is more correctly, "Why does the storyteller have them pass by?" Derrett asks the first question, and answers it by pointing to purity concerns. In his view, they would have been completely justified in their avoidance of the man in the ditch (*Law in the New Testament* [London: Darton, Longman, & Todd, 1970], 212–14). Whether purity would have in fact been at issue in such a case (likely not; see Scott, *Hear, Then, the Parable*, 195–96), such reasoning ignores the role of these figures in the story. They are not presented as positive, justified characters. They are straw figures against which to study alternatives. If one asks the second question ("Why does the storyteller have them pass by?") the answer is clear: they are stereotypes, figures presented to capture the anticlericalism of the peasant audience.

like "a Catholic priest, an Episcopalian vicar, and a Baptist minister all get to heaven. And when they meet St. Peter...." The sappy plot unfolds from there. In our ancient cliché, the third member, an Israelite, stands for the common person.[61] By using this old saw, the storyteller draws us into the trap of our own expectations. We all know who is coming next. The next person around that corner will be a good old Israelite, a common person. He will save the day. She will get us out of this jam. Priests and Levites — well, you know the type. But have no fear, an Israelite must be just around the bend!

But then it happens. It is not an Israelite, our friend, who appears, but a Samaritan, our enemy. The plot thickens as the questioning begins. What will happen now? Will he see us? Will he stop? What is he doing here in the first place? Will he help us, or finish us off? We hope he will pass by on the other side and let us be. Samaritans are unclean. They are dangerous. They are not to be trusted. They are not to be touched. Our best hope is that he won't even notice us here in the ditch. After all, an Israelite is on the way.

But the Samaritan sees us. He stops. He comes over. The pulse quickens. Our naked body trembles. A bad day just got worse. He bends down; we stiffen. And then... he binds up our wounds. He pours on oil and wine. The sting of the care is too much to take, almost. He lifts us out of the ditch and onto his beast — the beast of a Samaritan. Our ride out of here will not be clean. He brings us to an inn. What will they think of us here? Will they know that we are Jewish? Will they think we are Samaritan? What have we become?

What are the limits of human community? How far was Jesus willing to go to redefine the basis for belonging and relationship? Jews and Samaritans were mortal foes. This is more than the cliché it has become. In Jesus' world it was a bitter human reality. So what does it mean when a hated, feared Samaritan saves the day? Does it mean that the Empire of God is that place where we find ourselves in a relationship with someone with whom we would never be caught dead? Does it mean that the Empire of God happens when we realize that we need our enemy just to survive? Does it mean that the Empire of God is experienced when we find help and relief from someone from whom we have no right to expect it? Does it mean that in the Empire of God those things which give identity and mark community boundaries no longer stand in the way of human care, and we are lost in one human identity? The parable of the Samaritan is an experience, not an example.

---

61. For the cliché-like nature of the triad see Scott, *Hear, Then, the Parable*, 198. Also I. Abrahams, *Studies in Pharisaism and the Gospels*, Library of Biblical Studies (New York: Ktav, 1967; orig. published in 1917), 35–36; and A. Mattill, "Good Samaritan and the Purpose of Luke-Acts: Halévy Reconsidered," *Encounter* 33 (1972): 367.

No one can say exactly what an experience means, or whether its power is enough to transform and transport one into another worldview. But this is what it reaches for. An afternoon with a Samaritan could change your life.

The Shameless Empire

Jesus challenged the human boundaries that divide one group from another. But the brokenness of human relationships does not always manifest itself along the lines of ethnic division. Sometimes there is a brokenness that manifests itself within groups, within nations, within tribes, even within families. The following well-known story addresses the latter:

> There was a man who had two sons. And the younger of them said to his father, "Father, give to me the share of the property that belongs to me." So he divided his livelihood between them. Not many days later the younger son gathered up all his property and went away to a distant country. There he squandered his property in loose living. And when he had spent everything, a severe famine arose in that country, and he began to come up short. So he went and attached himself to one of the citizens of that country, who sent him out to the fields to feed the swine. And he would gladly have eaten the pods that the swine were eating, but no one gave him anything. But when he came to his senses he said, "How many of my father's hired servants have enough bread to eat and then some, but I am dying of hunger here. I will get up and go back to my father and say to him, 'Father, I have sinned against heaven and in your sight. I am no longer worthy to be called your son. Treat me as one of your servants.'" And he got up and returned to his father.
>
> But while he was still a long way off, his father caught sight of him and was deeply moved. He ran out to him, embraced him, and kissed him. And the son said to him, "Father, I have sinned against heaven and in your sight. I am no longer worthy to be called your son...." But the father said to his servants, "Quickly, bring out the best robe and put it on him, and put a signet ring on his hand, and put sandals on his feet. And bring the fatted calf and slaughter it. Let us feast and celebrate, for this son of mine was dead and has come back to life." And they began to celebrate.
>
> Meanwhile, the older son was out in the field. And as he got closer to the house he heard music and dancing. And he called over one of the servants and asked him what this was all about. And he said to him, "Your brother has come home and your father has slaughtered the fatted calf, because he has gotten him back safe and sound." But he was angry and would not go

in. So his father came out and began to plead with him. But he answered his father, "Look, all these years I have served you. I never once disobeyed any of your orders. But you have never ever provided me with even a kid goat that I might celebrate with my friends. But when this son of yours showed up, who has squandered your livelihood on prostitutes, you killed for him the fatted calf!" And he said to him, "Child, you are always with me. Everything that is mine is yours. But it was appropriate that we celebrate and rejoice, for this brother of yours was dead and has come back to life."

Not everyone agrees that this is an original parable of Jesus. First, it is found only in Luke (15:11–32) and is full of Lukan turns of phrase. It could be a Lukan composition. Furthermore, it fits very well with the leitmotif established by Luke at the opening of chapter 15. It illustrates Jesus' motives in eating with tax collectors and sinners.[62] Others have argued that Luke created only the final episode. The older son, they argue, is a stand-in for the Pharisees who criticize Jesus at the beginning of the chapter.[63]

But these arguments do not persuade me. The linguistic evidence is mixed. There are some Lukanisms in the parable, but there are many non-Lukan turns of phrase as well (Semitisms, for example), too many to suppose that this is a purely Lukan composition. Rather, one must more reasonably conclude that Luke has told this story in his style, but not created it from whole cloth.[64] As for the way this story fits into Luke's overall scheme, one must say that the fit is not very snug. Luke repeatedly emphasizes the joy expressed over sinners who *repent* (note his interpretive spin on the Lost Sheep [15:7] and the Lost Coin [15:10], even though neither of these parables is really about repentance, but finding something that has been lost). But repentance is not emphasized in the Prodigal Son. To be sure, the prodigal rehearses a repentance speech, but the father preempts its delivery in his overwhelming joy at seeing his son once again (15:20–24; cf. 15:18–19, where the full speech is given). And if the story is really about repentance, then why conclude the

---

62. Luise Schottroff, "Das Gelichnis vom verlorenen Sohn," *Zeitschrift für Theologie und Kirche* 68 (1971): 27–52.

63. E. Schweizer, "Zur Frage der Lukasquellen, Analyse von Luk 15, 11–32," *Theologische Zeitschrift* 4 (1948): 469–71; idem, "Antwort an Joachim Jeremias, S. 228–231," *Theologische Zeitschrift* 5 (1949): 231–33; James Sanders, "Tradition and Redaction in Luke xv.11–32," *New Testament Studies* 15 (1969): 433–38. On the other side, see Jeremias, who argues for the integrity of the parable as a whole in "Zum Gleichnis vom verlorenen Sohn," *Theologische Zeitschrift* 5 (1949): 228–31; also Bernard Brandon Scott, "The Prodigal Son: A Structuralist Interpretation," in *Society of Biblical Literature Seminar Papers (1975)* (Missoula, Mont.: Scholars Press, 1975): 186–89.

64. Carlston summarizes the evidence in "Reminiscence and Redaction in Luke 15:11–32," *Journal of Biblical Literature* 94 (1975): 368–83. His conclusion, adopted here, is given on p. 383.

story with an episode about the older son's resistance and not the joyous reunion itself? Was it a dig at the Pharisees represented in 15:2? Perhaps, but
the application proves difficult. In Luke's scheme, Judaism is ultimately rejected, but not so the older son. "All that is mine is yours" he is promised
(15:31).[65] It works, but only with strain. As with many other parables, Luke
made use of the Prodigal Son to illustrate a point. But the awkward fit shows
that this use was secondary.

What, then, did the pre-Lukan version of the parable look like? Without any other sources or versions at our disposal, it is difficult to say. We
will never be able to disengage it fully from the way Luke tells it. In telling
the parable as I have above, I have stayed close to Luke's version, omitting
only the two references to the lost being found (15:24b and 15:32b), which
I assume Luke added in order to create more continuity between this story
and the other two he has assembled in Luke 15. Beyond that, we are stuck
with Luke. But, as will become clear, even after years of oral transmission and
Lukan editing, it still bears the marks of the clever, parabolic storytelling that
was so characteristic of Jesus.[66]

Many interpreters have thought about this parable primarily in terms of
sin and repentance. In a sense this is correct. That is, after all, how Luke
uses it. But if this were all that it is about, one could simply conclude the
parable with the joyous reunion of father and son. Repentance is followed
by grace. End of story. But that is not the end of the story. And the end is
built into the beginning of the story: "A man had *two* sons." This parable is
about more than sin and repentance. It is about what happens when someone
does something wrong, realizes it, and then wants to be taken back in. The
final episode is just as important as the first two. In it there is concealed a
wrenching decision.

Let us begin with the younger son. His behavior is, well ... shameful. I use
that term in the technical sense here. As we begin to read the parable, it
may be helpful to recall the basic structures of honor and shame discussed in
chapter 2. Remember, to have a grant of honor, one must (1) aspire to a certain role in one's culture, one's social world, (2) be recognized in that role by
others, one's peers, and (3) be able to function successfully in that role. If at
any point the system breaks down, honor gives way to shame. If one's aspirations are not recognized, shame is the result. Failure to function competently
in the role to which one has aspired, likewise, results in shame. Remember,
too, that shame is contagious. It spreads to anyone daring to associate with

---

65. Scott, *Hear, Then, the Parable*, 105, n. 24; contra Sanders, "Tradition and Redaction," 438.
66. The Jesus Seminar designated this parable "red."

the shamed. And one more thing about shame. In the social hierarchy of human relationships, shame may be conveyed from the top down, or across, from peer to peer, but never from the bottom up. For example, it is easy for a parent to shame a child. Or siblings might shame one another. But it is nigh unto impossible for a child to shame a parent. The ability to shame someone, to deny someone honor, depends on possessing the power and authority to pass judgment on another and to define that person in a social role. Children are seldom granted this kind of power and authority over their parents. Remember the fifth commandment: "Honor thy father and thy mother."[67]

In this story the younger son knows what he is doing when he asks for his share of the inheritance. He wants to be regarded as a responsible — honorable — householder, like the other adults in his culture. He knows the rules, the expectations, the requirements. He knows the role to which he aspires. So does his father. It is up to his father to recognize his son's aspiration or not, to grant him this honor or to deny it. And he does grant it. But not without some consternation. The father wants to be a good — honorable — father. He does not want to make any big mistakes that would call into question his ability to function well in his role, that of father. Is he a father or a fool? His honor is also on the line.[68]

It does not take long for the storyteller to establish the plot. "Not many days later...." One might say, our young anti-hero wastes no time in getting into trouble. In but a few days he abandons the family and manages to squander his entire inheritance on "loose living." He has aspired to a role, and his father has recognized those aspirations. But now he is unable to function successfully in his new role. And so he brings shame upon himself, and, by the way, his father too. Neither has handled this matter of inheritance successfully. The son has blown all his money. The father foolishly trusted him. In the eyes of their peers, both are shamed.

It gets worse before it gets better. "And a severe famine arose in that country...." In tough times, fools suffer. By conventional wisdom, the foolish boy gets what he deserves. He tries to right himself, to work out of it, but shame has him caught for the moment in a downward spiral. He hires himself out to a pig farmer. He sets his sights low. He has a new aspiration: swineherd. In a Jewish context this is no aspiration at all. It is an unclean profession. It lies beyond the realm of acceptable roles altogether. But he does not care.

---

67. Cf. Bruce Malina, *The New Testament World: Insights from Cultural Anthropology* (Louisville: John Knox Press, 1981), 36: a challenge to one's honor may be effected only by one who is a perceived equal. Persons of inferior social standing may not shame a superior; they simply haven't the social strength.

68. See Scott, *Hear, Then, the Parable*, 109–11.

He has become shameless.[69] Unbelievably, it gets even worse: "And he would gladly have eaten the pods that the swine were eating...." He has fallen even lower than the swine. He aspires to swinehood. And there he sits, brooding.

At this point he gets an idea. "I will get up and go back to my father and say to him, 'Father, I have sinned against heaven and in your sight. I am no longer worthy to be called your son. Treat me as one of your servants." He aims low. He now aspires to the role of "servant," not "son." But "servant" is considerably above where he is now. He will need a speech, and so he plans one. It includes an admission of guilt, of shame, and a new aspiration. He practices it once through, and off he goes. He is shamed. He is unclean. But hope springs eternal. After all, when last he checked, his father was a fool.[70] And so begins the dénouement.

The scene shifts to the road home, the final bend, the last anticipatory steps. What will he find when he gets home? Will they know him? Will they acknowledge him? Will he be punished, or shunned altogether? Can one who brings shame and ruin upon the entire family expect more? And then something surprising happens. His father catches sight of him and he is overjoyed. Can this be his son, who was given up for dead? He runs to embrace him, and, prepared for just this moment, the prodigal son begins his speech: "I have sinned against heaven and in your sight. I am no longer worthy to be called your son...." But his words are interrupted, overwhelmed, drowned out by the joyous commotion. Before he can utter a single word more his arms slip into a robe, and a ring slips onto his finger — probably a signet, the sign and seal of his family's honor. Let the celebration begin! Father is a bigger fool than he thought.

Enter the older son. He is not a fool. All his life he has behaved honorably. He always follows orders; he never fails to do the right thing. This is important to him, and his family. His honor establishes a relationship, a rapport in the community that is key to participating in the agrarian economy of barter and handshake. When he says he'll pay next week, he pays next week. But now his father's other son has returned. *His* word means nothing. He has no honor. He is shamed and beyond — he is shameless. What will it mean to take him back into the family? Shame is not so easily shed. One cannot

---

69. Recall, a shameless person is one who has ceased to regard all conventions of honorable behavior at all. Malina's description is most apt here: "the honorable person is one who knows how to and can maintain his or her social boundaries in the intersection of power, sexual status, and respect for others, including God. The shameless person is one who does not observe social boundaries. The fool is one who takes a shameless person seriously" (*The New Testament World*, 34).

70. Recall Malina: "The fool is one who takes a shameless person seriously" (*The New Testament World*, 34).

simply declare the slate clean and assume that the whole world will go along. The prodigal's shame may infect the whole family.[71] No wonder he refuses to go in. He is not stubborn. He simply isn't a fool.

But his father insists; he begs him to come in. He asks for the honor of his presence. He asks for his *honor*. Now what should the elder son do? If he goes in and participates in this shameless display of welcoming and restoration, he will share in the shame of it all. There will be no one left in this family with even half a name. But what if he refuses, will not go in, and thus denies his father the honor of his presence? Does not the Lord say, "Honor thy father and thy mother?" Would this not itself be a shameful act? Can you shame your father without bringing shame upon yourself? He is in a lose/lose situation. If he goes in he is shamed by association. If he stays out he is shamed by his own dishonorable behavior toward his father. He is out of good options, cleverly backed into a narrative corner from which there is no escape. No one ultimately wins in the honor/shame game. At best, the wins are temporary, and they come with a price.

The parable does not tell us how the story is resolved. It ends with a question hanging in the air: will he go in? It is the question of whether or not one should accept the rules of the game as they are given to us and play out our options, bad as they are, or try to imagine a different game altogether. Jesus' parables hold up the world of conventional wisdom to close scrutiny so that we can see what it really is, unmasked in its failure to deliver what it promises. But that world is not all there is. In the collapse of confidence that comes with honest scrutiny, a space is opened up for making new assumptions about life and human relationships, for imagining new realities out of which to act. The older son has assumed, as anyone would, that life is about honor, about finding a role and functioning successfully in it. Honor is about carving out a space for oneself in the world, and defending that space with all one's might. The problem is, life gets messy. Sooner or later we find ourselves in a situation that messes up the life we have built, threatens our reputation, jeopardizes our standing in the community of our peers. And so we must choose. Shall we play by the rules of honor and shame and defend our turf against all threats, whether from friend or foe? Shall we try to hold on to what we have achieved under a set of rules we all agreed on, or shall we risk opting for another set of rules altogether?

The older son does have another option. He can forget about honor and shame and go in and enjoy the relationship that is to be had with his only

---

71. Note the degree to which honor is collective and attached to family name. See Malina, *The New Testament World*, 33–34.

brother. He can decide that the basis for our life together is not to be honor, position, place, or peer. The basis for real life together is, in actuality, love, care, and reconciliation. These things are foundational in the Empire of God. But to embrace them always means leaving old priorities behind.

Rearranging Priorities

In the Gospel of Matthew there is a cluster of three parables (Matt 13:44–50) that Matthew includes in a larger assembly of parables we know as Matthew 13. They are the parables of The Treasure (13:44), The Pearl (13:45–46), and The Fisher (13:47–50). Matthew did not create these parables; they are all known from the independent parallel tradition found in the Gospel of Thomas (Sayings 109, 76, and 8). Their appearance in isolation from one another in Thomas shows that they probably circulated independently in some early Christian circles. But their clustering in Matthew gives us an interesting clue to their history and interpretation. Let me explain.

The first of the three was probably told more or less in the way that Matthew tells it (13:44). The Thomas version appears less original, conforming to a rather common tale in Jewish literature, in which someone sells a field in ignorance, only to learn later that the new owner has discovered hidden treasure in it.[72] In Thomas's version of The Treasure (Thom 109), the one who finds the treasure becomes a lender of money, something despised in Thomas and in ancient Jewish culture generally (cf. Thom 65). It is a story of finding, followed by corruption. Corruption by the world is a theme in Thomas, picked up in fact in the very next saying: "Let one who has found the world and become wealthy renounce the world" (Thom 110). In his hands the parable has been radically altered for a new situation and purpose. But originally, it probably went more or less like this:[73]

The Empire of God is like a treasure hidden in a field, which someone found and then covered it up again. Then, in his joy, he goes and sells everything to buy that field.

---

72. The closest parallels are in *Midrash Rabba* on Song of Songs (4.12.1) and *Mekilta de-Rabbi Ishmael* on Ex 14:5. See John Dominic Crossan, *Finding Is the First Act: Trove Folktales and Jesus' Treasure Parable,* Semeia Supplements (Philadelphia: Fortress; Missoula, Mont.: Scholars Press, 1979), 65–67. L. Cerfaux noticed the similarities already in "Les paraboles du royaume dans l'évangile de Thomas," *Muséon* 70 (1957): 314.

73. The Jesus Seminar designated both Matt 13:44 and Thom 109 "pink." In the case of Thom 109, I disagree, for the reasons stated above. I concur with the judgment about Matthew.

The next one is virtually the same in both Matthew (13:45–46) and Thomas (Saying 76). Matthew probably changed the main character into a pearl merchant, thus making his behavior more explicable. In Thomas he is just a merchant. A merchant who sells his entire consignment of merchandise to buy a pearl for himself is odd (but parabolic, as we shall see). Matthew makes him less odd: naturally, he is a *pearl* merchant.[74] But in another respect Thomas adds his own flair: he calls the merchant "shrewd," or "wise," a nod to the abiding quest for wisdom in Thomas. Thomas also adds another traditional saying to the end: "You also seek his unfailing and enduring treasure, where no moth comes to devour and no worm destroys." Without this added dressing, the parable probably went this way:[75]

The Empire of God is like a merchant with a consignment of merchandise, who found a pearl. So he sold all the merchandise and bought the pearl for himself.

Then comes the third parable in the cluster. The Matthean (13:47–50) and Thomas (Saying 8) versions of The Fisher are very different. Matthew's is not really about a fisher, but a net, which is pulled up full of fish. The fisher then sorts out the good from the bad. Matthew then adds this interpretation:

So it will be at the close of the age. The angels will come out and separate the evil from the righteous and throw them into the furnace of fire; there people will weep and gnash their teeth. (Matt 13:49–50)

This "weeping and gnashing of teeth" is very typical Matthean talk.[76] In fact, he is focused in this part of his gospel on the final judgment (see especially his interpretation of the parable of the Wheat and the Weeds in 13:24–30). His parable of the Fisher meshes perfectly with this theme. As with the Wheat and the Weeds, in the end, there must be a sorting out of the good from the bad. But Thomas's version of this parable does not have this structure. In fact, it follows the same pattern as the parable of the Treasure and the parable of the Pearl. In it, a fisher pulls up a net full of fish. There he finds one beautiful, large fish, and so lets all the other fish go. He is just like the field hand who finds the treasure or the merchant who finds the pearl. Like them, he gives up everything for the one precious thing he finds. Originally, it probably went as follows:[77]

---

74. Jeremias notes this in *The Parables of Jesus*, 199.

75. The Jesus Seminar designated both versions of The Pearl "pink."

76. Cf. Matt 8:12; 13:42; 22:13; 24:51; 25:30.

77. The Jesus Seminar designated both the Thomas and Matthean versions of this parable "black." This, in my view, was a mistake. In considering this parable the Seminar focused its

> *The Empire of God is like a fisher, who cast his net into the sea and pulled
> it up full of fish. But among them he found one beautiful[78] fish. So he threw
> all the others back, and chose the one fish without difficulty.*

We should rather call it the parable of the Fish.

Here is a trio of parables: the Treasure, the Pearl, and the Fish. Matthew
probably found them as a group, but only altered the last of the three to illustrate his vision of the final judgment. The other two were tagalongs from the
tradition. Originally, they were collected and circulated as a group because
of their common structure and theme. In each of them we find a person
going about a daily routine. It is business as usual. A field hand works a
field. A merchant plies his trade. A fisher fishes. Just another day in a workaday world. But then something remarkable happens. The field hand turns up
buried treasure. The merchant finds a gem. The fisher nets a trophy. But
what happens next, in each, is rather odd. If one fails to pay close attention,
their strangeness, and their point, might be missed.

Let us take the case of the Treasure. The finder's course seems reasonable,
if a little underhanded, as a means of securing the treasure. But there is a
hitch. According to rabbinical law, if the treasure is in disarray and can be
presumed to have no obvious owner, the find belongs to the finder. However,
if the thing looks like it has an owner, then the finder's claim cannot be
asserted. In this case, the owner of the field would possess it.[79] Which leaves
us with this quandary: "If the treasure belongs to the finder, buying the land
is unnecessary. But if the treasure does not belong to the finder, buying the
land is unjust."[80] What shall we presume? Either way, the excitement and
desperation of the finder is underscored. He is willing to sell all, cash in his
life, to take no chances and go for broke all at the same time — whatever it
takes to get that one treasured thing.

And what of the merchant who finds a pearl? Notice what he does to
obtain it: he sells all his merchandise. Notice also that he does not intend
to sell the pearl — he is not a *pearl* merchant. He buys it *for himself*. In the

---

attention on the Matthean version. It was dissuaded from considering it as a parable of Jesus
because of its patently allegorical features and the way it gives expression to Matthew's vexation
over the apocalyptic end times. In this deliberation, Thom 8 did not really receive separate
consideration; nor were its similarities to the other two parables in this trio noticed. I would
designate the Thomas version of the Fisher "pink," on analogy with these other two.

78. In the Thomas version itself the fish appears as a beautiful "large" fish. This "largeness"
motif appears elsewhere in Thomas's parables (cf. Thom 96: the Leaven, and Thom 107: the Lost
Sheep), and so may hold some esoteric significance for the Thomaean redactor. Accordingly, I
have omitted it from this hypothetical originating version.

79. See Scott, *Hear, Then, the Parable*, 398–99, for a summary of the evidence.

80. Crossan, *Finding Is the First Act*, 91 (as cited by Scott, *Hear, Then, the Parable*, 399).

end, he has the pearl. But how will he now make a living? You can't eat a pearl. You can't sleep in a pearl. You can't wear a pearl. He is also a fool. He liquidates his livelihood in a rush to buy the pearl of his dreams.

And finally there is the fisher. He is not fishing for sport. A beautiful fish is a beautiful thing, but in the end, a fish is still food. And this brings us to the real problem: he throws all the other fish away to possess that one prize fish. But why? Why discard those perfectly good fish just to possess the beautiful one. He, too, is carried away in his joy, and so scraps a perfectly good catch to possess the object of his joy.

All of these fools have one thing in common: they are willing to scrap the workaday rules of their workaday lives and make a break for it. They give up everything to lunge after something so precious, so wonderful, so beautiful, that they are willing to risk everything for it. Their lives are moving along with utter normalcy when suddenly they are confronted with something so compelling that it forces them to make a choice between old priorities and something new. They go for it!

Choosing the Empire of God

In the memory of the early church, Jesus presented people with just this kind of choice. He asked people to make a decision, to choose between a life lived out under the rules and assumptions that form the unquestioned fabric of social intercourse and another life, one that requires stepping up to the limits of the world as it has been collectively imagined and daring to venture across the limit into another realm, the Empire of God. He presented people with a choice, an ultimate choice. There is a story in the Gospel of Mark that, although it is probably not historical, still adequately typifies the sort of decision forced by Jesus in his parabolic preaching:

And as he was heading out on the road someone ran up and knelt down in front of him and asked, "Good teacher, what must I do to inherit eternal life?" But Jesus said to him, "Why do you call me good? No one is good except the one God. Do you know the commandments: Do not kill; do not commit adultery; do not steal; do not lie; do not commit fraud; honor your father and mother?" And he said to him, "Teacher, all these commandments I have observed from my youth." But when Jesus looked him in the eye, he loved him, and so he said to him, "You lack one thing. Go! Sell all you have and give the proceeds to the poor, and you will have treasure in heaven. Then come and follow me." But he was stunned by what he said, and went away dejected, for he was a person with many possessions. (Mark 10:17–22)

The field hand, the merchant, the fisher — they all give up their lives in a risk to grasp something more precious. This is the essence and challenge of parable. In Jesus' parables, as in his sayings and aphorisms, we encounter a new set of assumptions about life, a new way of ordering life and relationships, a new way of imagining human existence. It is a new world coming into existence in story. The question is, as the parable brings us to the edge of the world as we have always imagined it, as the solid ground we thought would firmly support us to the end begins to give way to the undermining activity of Jesus' words, will we have the courage to step forward into the free-fall risk of what lies ahead, or will we scramble back to *terra firma?* The person in Mark's story cannot do it. The stakes are too high. He is too heavily invested in the world as it is. He retreats in the face of the unknown, the unsecured, the chaotic, and settles back into a familiar life. The Empire has worked quite well for him. He has no interest in an Empire of God.

Jesus used parables to bring into existence the Empire of God. This new Empire was not about morality. The commandments, though not rejected, are not the heart of the matter either. The Empire of God is about re-imagining life on new terms. In his parables, Jesus forces one to look at the world squarely, without illusion, and to see it for what it really is. It is our world, not God's. It works for some people some of the time. But ultimately it does not work, because it cannot reflect an ultimate reality whose nature is love. Jesus challenged those around him to re-create the world, to reconstruct human life and relationships in a way that would reflect and embody that ultimate reality. That is what the Empire of God is, or would be, if one were to choose to risk it.

Chapter 5

The Empire of God Is Now

On Jesus and the End of the World

The life of Christ is not an exhibition of overruling power. Its glory is for those who can discern it, and not for the world. Its power lies in its absence of force. It has the decisiveness of a supreme ideal, and that is why the history of the world divides at this point in time. . . .

If the modern world is to find God, it must do so through love and not through fear.

— ALFRED NORTH WHITEHEAD,
Religion in the Making (1926)

Jesus and the End of the World

For almost a century New Testament scholarship has been united around at least one proposition: the beginnings of New Testament theology are rooted in thinking that is thoroughly eschatological. Eschatology comes from the Greek words *eschatos*, which means "last," and *logia*, which means "speech." Eschatology is literally "talk about last things." In theology, eschatology has come to be associated with the doctrine of the end times, when, according to traditional church doctrine, God will bring history and the world as we know it to an end. But it can also have a more general meaning. Eschatology can also refer to any decisive moment when former ways and older ideas give way to something new. When New Testament scholars use it to speak of Christian origins they are usually using it in the first sense: beliefs about the impending end of the world, the eschaton.

Eschatology became a buzz word in New Testament theology at around the turn of the century, when it was realized that Jesus' preaching, as it is presented in three of the four canonical gospels (Matthew, Mark, and Luke), is very much concerned with "last" things — that is, the end of the world. In the Gospel of Mark, Jesus predicts that God will intervene to bring history to a violent and cataclysmic end and that this catastrophic event is to happen very soon:

> But in those days, after the tribulation, the sun will be darkened, and the moon will not offer its glow, and the stars will fall from the sky, and the powers of heaven will be shaken. Then shall they see the Son of Man coming in the clouds with great power and glory. Then shall he send out the angels and gather the elect from the four winds, from the farthest reaches of heaven and earth....
>
> Truly, I say to you, this generation shall not pass away before all these things come to pass. (Mark 13:24–27, 30)

A version of this chapter appeared originally as "The End of Apocalypse: Rethinking the Eschatological Jesus," *Theology Today* 52, no. 1 (1995): 29–48.

The problem, of course, is that these things did not happen. Generations came and went, but history carried on, leaving Christian theology with a very difficult dilemma: what shall we do with eschatology?

Over the years New Testament historians and theologians have struggled through debate after heated debate about Jesus' eschatological preaching. What does it mean? Should one take Jesus' apocalypticism literally? If so, should we assume that he was simply off on the timing and prepare ourselves for imminent tribulation? If such a course of action seems too rash and out of step with a twentieth-century worldview, might Jesus' apocalyptic preaching be seen as nonetheless valuable, and therefore worth translating, let us say, using existentialist categories? Might we embrace the idea of being eschato-logical, of embracing new beginnings and breaks with the past, without being apocalyptic in any literal sense? Or is apocalypticism only peripheral and inci-dental to Jesus' preaching, or perhaps not even part of his original preaching at all? Generally speaking this last option has been out of the question. For the apocalypticism of Jesus is such a potentially embarrassing thing, so scan-dalous to the post-Enlightenment intellect of the twentieth century that its acceptance has long been considered a test of scholarly objectivity; anyone who would reject this hypothesis is viewed by his or her peers as a hopeless romantic, unable or unwilling to accept the scandalous reality that Jesus did not think like us.

But in spite of all this, New Testament scholarship is once again involved in a lively discussion of this issue: did Jesus in fact believe that history was coming to a rapid, apocalyptic end? Amid protestations from theologians and exegetes alike, a growing number of New Testament scholars is beginning to read the evidence in a way that calls this once assured result of criti-cal scholarship into question. To understand the nature of this debate and its significance for theology it is necessary to begin with the origins of the apocalyptic hypothesis itself.

The Origins of the Apocalyptic Hypothesis

1992 marked the centennial anniversary of the publication of Johannes Weiss's revolutionary book, *Jesus' Proclamation of the Kingdom of God*.[1] In this brief but important monograph Weiss argued that the new empire of which the historical Jesus actually spoke was to be an apocalyptic event, that

---

1. Johannes Weiss, *Jesus' Proclamation of the Kingdom of God*; trans. Richard Hiers and David Holland (Philadelphia: Fortress Press, 1971 [German original published in 1892]).

is, one which God would usher in through the agency of an emissary, the Son of Man, whose return, flying in on clouds of glory, would be marked by great violence, tribulation, struggle, and ultimately judgment for all. This is, after all, how Mark 13 (and Matthew 24 and Luke 21, following Mark) presents the matter. Paul, too, thinks of the arrival of the Empire of God in apocalyptic terms:

> The day of the Lord will come like a thief in the night. When people say, "There is peace and security," then sudden destruction will come upon them as travail comes upon a woman with child, and there will be no escape. (1 Thess 5:2–3)

As self-evident as such a reading of the sources has seemed in recent years, it was not so self-evident in 1892. Historical inquiry into the cultural milieu into which Jesus was born and within which he preached was still a relatively young field in the late nineteenth century. It was philosophical analysis, not history, that served as the interpretive key to understanding the scriptures. Theologians such as Albrecht Ritschl, for example, were at work transforming the ethical idealism of Immanuel Kant into the full flowering of liberal theology. It was Ritschl, one may recall, who spoke of Jesus' reign of God as "a fellowship of moral attitude and moral properties extending through the whole range of human relationships."[2] Naturally, when Johannes Weiss, the young, still wet-behind-the-ears student of Ritschl, appeared on the scene arguing that what Jesus actually preached about was an apocalyptic event that would bring the world to a violent and cataclysmic end, he did not receive much of a hearing. The German idealism of the nineteenth century was above all else optimistic about the future; the Jesus of Weiss would have been utterly irrelevant to its credo.

Weiss would not find popular acceptance until after the year 1906, when Schweitzer published the book that would establish him as one of his generation's great biblical scholars: *The Quest of the Historical Jesus*. This book, perhaps the most often cited work in New Testament scholarship, is also probably the most thoroughly misunderstood. It is often said that Schweitzer showed — by reviewing and then debunking all previous attempts at a historical reconstruction of Jesus' life — how futile and self-serving any attempt would ultimately be. This is not what Schweitzer intended to show at all. Rather, his criticism was aimed against scholars of the nineteenth century whose analysis was grounded in the theology and ideology of liberalism rather

---

2. *The Christian Doctrine of Justification and Reconciliation*, trans. H. R. Mackintosh and A. B. Macauley (Edinburgh: T. & T. Clark, 1902 [German original published in 1883]), 285.

than genuine historical analysis. In Schweitzer's view, Ritschl's Jesus was "a figure designed by rationalism, endowed with life by liberalism, and clothed by modern theology in a historical garb."[3] Schweitzer was not critical of historical research per se. To the contrary, he had very definite ideas about what historical research could tell us about Jesus: he was as Weiss had described him — an apocalyptic preacher convinced that the end of history was near.

While the acceptance of Schweitzer's work was not universal, it did find a receptive audience (especially in Europe) and ultimately won the day for Weiss's view of Jesus. From our own vantage point today, we may look back upon the ninety-some odd years since the publication of Schweitzer's work and say that the apocalyptic hypothesis has been the dominant paradigm for understanding Jesus for most of the twentieth century. But why was Schweitzer able to succeed in 1906 where Weiss had failed in 1892? The answer is simple: times changed. The optimism of the nineteenth century had by 1906 almost completely evaporated with the increasing political instability that characterized Europe in the years leading up to World War I. In its place there arose a profound sense of dread and uncertainty as an increasingly dark future loomed ever larger on the horizon. The mood is captured most poignantly in the autobiography of Sir Edward Grey, who, on the eve of World War I, recalls having uttered to a close friend words that would be used repeatedly to capture the spirit of times: "The lamps are going out all over Europe; we shall not see them lit again in our lifetime."[4] In the midst of the cultural optimism of 1892, Weiss's apocalyptic Jesus was a scandal; in the atmosphere of cultural pessimism that was just beginning to come to expression in 1906, this apocalyptic Jesus was just what the doctor ordered.

This state of affairs in Western culture has not altered itself much over the course of this century. This has been true especially in Europe. The devastation of two World Wars, the economic instability and collapse which fueled the fires of discontent, the specter of the Holocaust which hangs over the European psyche as a constant reminder of humanity's potential to social pathology and unfathomable evil, and finally the nuclear age, in which Central Europe was held hostage between two super powers, a kind of buffer zone within which the horrors of a limited nuclear war would convince the antagonists to pull back before destroying the entire planet — all of these factors have given twentieth-century European culture a profound sense of pessimism about culture and the future. If anyone could recall during the

---

3. Albert Schweitzer, *The Quest of the Historical Jesus*, trans. W. Montgomery, 2d ed. (London: Adam and Charles Black, 1911) [German original published in 1906]), 396.

4. Viscount Grey of Fallodon, *Twenty-Five Years* (New York: Frederick A. Stokes Co., 1925), 2:20.

very latest developments in European history having caught at least a glimmer of hope for the future, it has since been quashed once again with the emergence of such ominous and heinous phenomena as "ethnic cleansing."

In North America this cultural trend was delayed for the first half of this century. With the exception of the 1930s, North American culture during this period was oriented toward progress and hope in the future. While the tragedy of two World Wars was felt here as well, it was not experienced with the intensity and sense of loss that characterized Europe. Here no cities were destroyed, no cultural treasures lost, no crowds of refugees roamed streets of rubble in search of relatives lost to the ravages of war. Instead, our streets were filled with ticker-tape. News reels and Hollywood combined to create a romance of war, and the victories served to bolster the self-confidence of North American culture at levels never before experienced. As might be expected, the apocalyptic Jesus of Weiss and Schweitzer did not make much of an impact here at that time. Instead, Walter Rauschenbusch's Social Gospel — the North American version of liberal theology — exercised the greatest influence on the quest for the historical Jesus among North American scholars, led by the Chicago School of Shirley Jackson Case and Shailer Mathews. Here Rauschenbusch's call for "Christianizing the Social Order" still made sense in an atmosphere of undiminished hope for what might be achieved in human culture.[5]

But by the 1950s the cultural pessimism which began with the political collapse of Europe and the catastrophe of two World Wars eventually began to wash up onto the victorious, self-confident, can-do shores of North America as well, as we faced the psychologically debilitating realities of the Cold War, the threat of nuclear or environmental disaster, and the social upheaval of the 1960s. Americans, too, began to experience the cultural malaise that had held its grip on Europe for the first half of the century. This change in attitude is expressed perhaps most eloquently by Reinhold Niebuhr in his 1952 essay *The Irony of American History:*

> Could there be a clearer tragic dilemma than that which faces our civilization? Though confident of its virtue, it must hold atomic bombs ready for use so as to prevent a possible world conflagration.... Our dreams of a pure virtue are dissolved in a situation in which it is possible to exercise the virtue of responsibility toward a community of nations only by courting the prospective guilt of the atomic bomb.... Our dreams of moving the whole of human history under the control of the human will are ironically refuted by the fact that no

---

5. Walter Rauschenbusch, *Christianizing the Social Order* (New York: Macmillan, 1912).

group of idealists can easily move the pattern of history toward the desired goal of peace and justice. The recalcitrant forces in the historical drama have a power and persistence beyond our reckoning.[6]

What Niebuhr, as a member of that generation which created the nuclear age, saw as a tragic and bitter irony has become for the present generation an existential presupposition. For Generation X, the bomb is just one small part of a cultural legacy of courting disaster and mortgaging the future that is simply a fact of life. The result has been a pessimism about culture and its future, pervasive throughout Western society, that has not gone unnoticed in the annals of philosophical history. The great historian of Western thought W. T. Jones has written about our age:

> Students of contemporary culture have characterized this century in various ways — for instance, as the age of anxiety, the aspirin age, the nuclear age, the age of one-dimensional man, the postindustrial age; but nobody, unless a candidate for political office at some political convention, has called this a happy age.... The rise of dictatorships, two world wars, genocide, the deterioration of the environment, and the Vietnam war have all had a share in undermining the old beliefs in progress, in rationality, and in people's capacity to control their own destiny and improve their lot.[7]

Jones may thus speak of a "collapse of confidence" in Western thought. Is it any wonder that, as in European theology during the first half of this century, so also in North America since the 1950s, the optimistic strains of the Social Gospel and its liberal Jesus have gradually given way to the assumption that Jesus preached an apocalyptic eschatology? For the moment, the theological future belonged to those who would attempt responsibly to interpret this apocalypticism theologically: Barth, Bultmann, Niebuhr, Moltmann (not to mention the less thoughtful Fundamentalist harbingers of doom — Lindsay, Graham, Falwell — who have regrettably become icons in American popular religion). The apocalyptic Jesus of Johannes Weiss found his home among us. No longer a stranger, his pessimism about the future gave expression to the profound pessimism that characterized our own cultural psychology.

---

6. Reinhold Niebuhr, *The Irony of American History* (New York: Charles Scribner's Sons, 1952), 1–3.

7. W. T. Jones, *A History of Western Philosophy*, 5 vols., 2d ed. rev., vol. 5: *The Twentieth Century to Wittgenstein and Sartre* (San Diego: Harcourt, Brace, Jovanovich, 1975), 2.

The Collapse of the Consensus

But nothing lasts forever, even the hard-won results of methodologically con-
scientious historical research. New data that does not fit the old paradigm,
data generated from new discoveries or new methods and insights into the old
subject matter, gradually accumulates to reach a critical mass beyond which
the old paradigm is exposed as no longer adequate. I believe that the latest
phase of research into the history of the gospel tradition has produced too
many results that do not fit the apocalyptic paradigm of Johannes Weiss. This
is reflected in much recent scholarship on Jesus. In 1986 Marcus Borg ventured "A Temperate Case for a Non-Eschatological Jesus,"[8] a case which he
built more elaborately in *Jesus, A New Vision*, issued the following year.[9] In
1991 John Dominic Crossan published his magisterial study of Jesus, *The Historical Jesus*,[10] followed by a popular rendition in 1994, *Jesus: A Revolutionary
Biography*.[11] Far from Weiss's apocalyptic prophet of the end times, Crossan's
Jesus is a radically countercultural social critic, who proclaimed immediate
access to an unbrokered reign of God for persons marginalized from the conventional means to humane living. And, of course, there is the work of the
Jesus Seminar itself. Throughout the four canonical and one noncanonical
gospels covered in their report,[12] one will find no apocalyptic sayings printed
in red.

But these recent results, now the subject of vigorous debate,[13] do not
come as a surprise to most specialists. For several years the old consensus
has been falling apart as the century of the apocalyptic Jesus came to a quiet,
almost unnoticed close. In the 1980s two polls of New Testament scholars
specializing in the study of the historical Jesus indicated that already holes
were developing in the ranks of the once lock-step scholarly consensus that

---

8. *Forum* 2, no. 3 (1986): 81–102; reprinted in Borg, *Jesus in Contemporary Scholarship* (Valley
Forge, Pa.: Trinity Press International, 1994), 47–68.

9. *Jesus, A New Vision: Spirit, Culture, and the Life of Discipleship* (San Francisco: Harper &
Row, 1987).

10. *The Historical Jesus: The Life of a Mediterranean Jewish Peasant* (San Francisco: HarperSan-
Francisco, 1991).

11. *Jesus: A Revolutionary Biography* (San Francisco: HarperSanFrancisco, 1994).

12. *The Five Gospels: The Search for the Authentic Words of Jesus* (New York: Macmillan, 1993).

13. Most notably, E. P. Sanders, *The Historical Figure of Jesus* (Harmondsworth: Penguin,
1993), a popularizing rendition of his earlier critically acclaimed work, *Jesus and Judaism*
(Philadelphia: Fortress Press, 1985). Sanders continues to maintain that Jesus was thoroughly
apocalyptic in his worldview. See also the shrill defense of the older position by Howard Clark
Kee, "A Century of Quests for the Culturally Compatible Jesus," *Theology Today* 52, no. 1 (April
1995): 17–28, and of Sanders's former student Paula Fredriksen, "What You See Is What You
Get: Context and Content in Current Research on the Historical Jesus," *Theology Today* 52, no. 1
(April 1995): 75–97.

Weiss's apocalyptic Jesus was the best historical construct. When posed the question: "Do you think Jesus expected the end of the world in his generation, i.e., in the lifetime of at least some of his contemporaries?" two-thirds of those responding from the Historical Jesus Section of the Society of Biblical Literature replied "no."[14] A similar poll of participants in the Jesus Seminar revealed that they too rejected Weiss's view, by a 3 to 1 majority.[15] James M. Robinson, in assessing the state of the quest thirty years after the appearance of his watershed chronicle of the new quest, can speak now of a paradigm shift in the way scholars are thinking about the historical Jesus.[16] It can no longer be assumed that Jesus was an apocalyptic prophet. What has called for such a complete about-face away from the old consensus?

The old consensus, while holding a certain cultural appeal, was in fact based upon a consensus among the sources themselves. The earliest of the canonical gospels, Mark, presents Jesus as thoroughly steeped in and motivated by Jewish apocalyptic. But Mark is not alone in presenting Jesus in this way. The second source used by Matthew and Luke, the sayings gospel referred to as "Q," also understands Jesus as a prophet of apocalyptic judgment. This was especially important, for Q is the earliest identifiable document in the gospel tradition. Finally, Paul, who authored our earliest New Testament writings, also understood Christian faith as grounded in an apocalyptic view of history, his utopian communities of the Spirit anticipating proleptically the imminent arrival of the Empire of God. But this consensus began to falter in the face of historical-critical research. New developments on a number of fronts combined to undermine the older view.

Q and Early Christian Wisdom

First, thirty years of research on "Q" has begun to produce a new consensus about this document. Beginning with the work of the German scholar Dieter Lührmann, and more recently in the research of North Americans Arland Jacobson and John Kloppenborg,[17] it has become increasingly clear that Q was

---

14. Borg, "A Temperate Case," 98–99.

15. James R. Butts, "Probing the Polling: Jesus Seminar Results on the Kingdom Sayings," *Forum* 3, no. 1 (1987): 110. This survey repeats that of Marcus Borg, who polled the Jesus Seminar on this issue in 1985 ("Temperate Case," 98–99). Then, just over half of those who responded to Borg's survey rejected Weiss's hypothesis. Thus, the 1986 poll shows a significant and rapid movement away from the old consensus.

16. In a paper delivered at the 1990 International SBL meeting in Vienna.

17. Dieter Lührmann, *Die Redaktion der Logienquelle* (Neukirchen-Vluyn: Neukirchener Verlag, 1969); Arland Jacobson, *The First Gospel: An Introduction to Q* (Sonoma, Calif.: Polebridge, 1992); John S. Kloppenborg, *The Formation of Q: Trajectories in Ancient Wisdom Collections*, Studies in Antiquity and Christianity (Philadelphia: Fortress Press, 1987).

not originally an apocalyptic document at all, but — to take the widely accepted view of Kloppenborg — a collection of wisdom speeches, such as one
finds in Luke's Sermon on the Plain (Luke 6:20–49||Matt 5:3–12, 38–48;
7:1–5; 12:33–35; 7:15–20, 21–27) or the speech On Cares (Luke 12:22–
32||Matt 6:25–34). The Q apocalypse (Luke 17:22–37||Matt 24:23–28,
37–42), as well as the sayings of judgment aimed against "this generation"
scattered throughout the document, affixed like barnacles to this earlier stratum of wisdom speeches, belong to a later edition of Q. They represent a
moment of frustration in the history of the Q community itself, when it realized that the wisdom of Jesus was not having as great an impact as it had
originally hoped.

The relatively obscure and technical work of Kloppenborg and others
working today on the problem of Q is very important for two reasons. First,
the fact that the Q tradition is not ultimately rooted in apocalypticism means
that the once apparent unanimity of the early sources around this point is
no more. Moreover, it is Q, the *earliest* source we have for the preaching
of Jesus, that has broken ranks. That leaves Paul and Mark as the remain-
ing early witnesses to an apocalyptic understanding of Jesus. But Paul seldom
makes use of sayings or other traditions from the teaching of Jesus; thus, it
is not at all clear that Paul's apocalypticism developed directly out of Jesus'
own preaching. It may have simply been the only framework within which
Paul, a Pharisee, could have understood something like the resurrection of
Jesus. For Paul, as for other Pharisees, resurrection was a sign of the end
times. As for Mark, his apocalyptic outlook need not have come from Jesus.
He wrote many years after Paul and Q and may have stood under their influence. Moreover, his experience of the violence of the Jewish War, which,
after all, was in fact bringing his world to an end, would have been enough
to draw him to such an understanding of Jesus.

The Gospel of Thomas

While scholars of the synoptic tradition were working on the problem of Q,
another development appeared on the scene that would serve to confirm the
general tendencies of the synoptic tradition identified by Kloppenborg and
others: the Gospel of Thomas. It will be recalled from the discussion in chapter 1 that the Gospel of Thomas is not a gospel like those with which we are
familiar in the canonical tradition. Unlike those gospels, it does not purport
to say anything about the life of Jesus; rather, it is simply a collection of Jesus'
sayings. It is in this respect quite comparable to Q, which itself contains very
little narrative. Its chief importance for the present discussion, however, lies

in its content: of the 114 sayings ascribed to Jesus in the Gospel of Thomas, more than half have parallels in the synoptic tradition, including parallels to both Q and Mark. Furthermore, these sayings in Thomas do not derive from the synoptic gospels themselves, but rather from the same oral traditions available to the synoptic evangelists and their sources.[18] This means that we now have in Thomas a critical tool with which to better understand the development of the synoptic tradition itself. Those attributes which Thomas and the synoptic tradition share are more likely to have come from an early point in the development of the Jesus tradition, perhaps even Jesus himself. Conversely, those things which are not shared, but isolated to one or another of these developing trajectories are less likely to have early roots.

The Thomas and synoptic trajectories do share much in common. Both contain parables — especially parables of the Empire of God, in which worldly values and expectations are turned topsy turvy. Both speak of the reign of God as present, and spread out "among you" (Thom 3 and 113). Almost all of Luke's Sermon on the Plain is found at some point in Thomas, including the beatitudes: "Blessed are the poor" (Thom 54), "the hungry" (Thom 69:2), and "the persecuted" (Thom 68). Portions of the speech On Cares are found in Thomas (Thom 36). And there are a host of wisdom sayings found in both trajectories. Whatever this common tradition has to tell us about the preaching of Jesus, there is one element profoundly absent from it: apocalypticism. Most of Thomas's parallels to Q are to Kloppenborg's early wisdom stratum in Q (Q^1). There are a few parallels to sayings from the later apocalyptic stratum (Q^2), but where there are parallels to Q^2, in each case tradition-historical analysis shows that the Q saying has been secondarily "apocalypticized." This is also true of Thomas-Mark parallels. When Mark's version of a saying or parable is framed to reflect apocalyptic concerns, such framing can without exception be shown to be secondary.[19] Thus, what the study of Q had already suggested about the relatively late tendency of the synoptic tradition to develop in the direction of apocalyptic is confirmed by comparative analysis with the Gospel of Thomas. The earliest identifiable stratum of the Jesus

18. So I have argued in The Gospel of Thomas and Jesus (Sonoma, Calif.: Polebridge, 1993), 9–110. This view of Thomas is followed by most North American scholars. European scholarship tends not to regard Thomas as an independent tradition. For a review of the extensive discussion of the relationship between Thomas and the synoptic gospels, see Stephen J. Patterson, "The Gospel of Thomas and the Synoptic Tradition: A Forschungsberichte and Critique," Forum 8, nos. 1–2 (1992): 45–97.

19. Patterson, The Gospel of Thomas and Jesus, 217–41; see also idem, "Wisdom in Q and Thomas," in Leo G. Purdue, Bernard Brandon Scott, and William Johnston Wiseman, eds., In Search of Wisdom: Essays in Memory of John G. Gammie (Louisville: Westminster/John Knox Press, 1993), 187–221.

tradition is not apocalyptic. It is therefore becoming less and less likely that Jesus himself preached an apocalyptic message.[20]

But advances in the study of Q and Thomas have not been the sole factors in turning the tide against the apocalyptic hypothesis of Weiss and Schweitzer. Other developments in New Testament scholarship have been preparing the way for such a shift for quite some time.

The Post-Bultmannian Movement

One of these may be identified as emerging from within the ranks of neo-Orthodox theology itself, whose main spokespersons, Rudolf Bultmann and Karl Barth, essentially embraced the hypothesis of Weiss and Schweitzer and undertook to transform apocalypticism into a theologically relevant modern paradigm. But the next generation of scholars, especially those who had studied with Bultmann, began to question the data which necessitated this procedure. In an essay published in 1957, Bultmann's former student Philipp Vielhauer noticed that in the gospels the apocalyptic Son of Man figure is not found in the same context as talk about the reign of God. This, Vielhauer argued, was because these two concepts did not naturally belong together in contemporary Jewish thought. The Son of Man figure belongs to speculation concerning a future ideal age ushered in by God's emissary; the phrase "reign of God" expresses the living hope that God reigns (now!). Since Vielhauer presumed that the reign of God was at the center of Jesus' preaching, the Son of Man sayings naturally fell under suspicion. This suspicion is confirmed in Vielhauer's systematic tradition-historical treatment of all the Son of Man sayings in the gospels, with the result that all except one (Matt 24:37–39 — here the question remains open) are judged to be products of later Christian interpretation, not sayings of Jesus himself.[21]

Soon thereafter another of Bultmann's students endorsed Vielhauer's position. Also in 1957 Hans Conzelmann published an article in which he argued that insofar as Jesus associates the reign of God with his own person and preaching, he excludes any futuristic/temporal aspect from the concept. Rather, Jesus' proclamation of the reign of God functioned existentially as a call to decision to accept or reject its reality. Consequently, there is no room

---

20. In his recent work, *The Historical Jesus* (San Francisco: HarperCollins, 1991), John Dominic Crossan takes as his starting point this earliest identifiable stratum. His is the first study to take seriously the implications of recent research on the Gospel of Thomas, research in which Crossan himself has played a significant role.

21. Philipp Vielhauer, "Gottesreich und Menschensohn in der Verkündigung Jesu," in W. Schneemelcher, *Festschrift für Günther Dehn* (Neukirchen, Kreis Moers: Buchhandlung des Erziehungsvereins, 1957), 51–79, esp. 77 and 56–71.

for a future intermediary figure such as the apocalyptic Son of Man.[22] This position was also adopted by perhaps the best known of Bultmann's students, Ernst Käsemann. Käsemann cast Vielhauer's basic position in terms of Jesus' relationship to John the Baptist:

> The fact of the matter is surely that while Jesus did take his start from the apocalyptically determined message of John the Baptist, yet his own preaching was not constitutively stamped by apocalyptic but proclaimed the immediate nearness of God. I am convinced that the man who took this step cannot have awaited the coming Son of man, the restoration of the twelve tribes in the messianic kingdom, and therewith the dawn of the parousia, as the means of experiencing the nearness of God.[23]

Thus, among the students of Rudolf Bultmann the Weiss/Schweitzer hypothesis that Jesus spoke of a future apocalyptic reign of God was given up in favor of the idea that in his preaching Jesus proclaimed a reign of God that was already in some sense present.

The American Discussion of Parables

Another older development that prepared the way for the current paradigm shift came about in the area of parables research, discussed in the previous chapter. Crucial to the shift away from the apocalyptic hypothesis were those developments associated with American parables scholarship in the 1960s and '70s. The American discussion of parables, it will be recalled, began with the work of Amos Wilder. The brother of famed playwright Thorton Wilder, he would naturally, perhaps, bring a family sensitivity to literary critical matters to bear on the study of the New Testament. Wilder explored the parables of Jesus as metaphors. A true metaphor, Wilder argued, is more than a sign, a point of comparison. Rather, as a narrative, an extended metaphor creates for the listener a world whose reality unfolds in his or her imagination. In spinning extended metaphors for the reign of God, Jesus draws the listener into the reality that is created in the telling of it so that he or she actually becomes a participant in it. Thus, through Jesus' parables the listener does not simply hear about the reign of God; rather, it becomes a reality to be experienced, to shock, to transform.[24]

---

22. Hans Conzelmann, "Gegenwart und Zukunft in der synoptischen Tradition," *Zeitschrift für Theologie und Kirche* 54 (1957): esp. 281–88.

23. Ernst Käsemann, "The Beginnings of Christian Theology," in R. W. Funk, ed., *Journal for Theology and the Church*, vol. 6: *Apocalypticism* (New York: Herder and Herder, 1969), 39–40.

24. Amos Wilder, *Early Christian Rhetoric: The Language of the Gospel*, rev. ed. (Cambridge: Harvard University Press, 1971), 84.

This understanding of parable as a metaphoric creation of the reign of God is important for the work of two other American parables scholars: Robert W. Funk and John Dominic Crossan, persons now at the center of the new discussion of the historical Jesus. In an essay now considered to be a watershed in the modern study of parables, Funk contrasts the parable, as metaphor, to a simple simile in which A is said to be like B. While a simile is illustrative of an object that is already known, a metaphor has the ability to create something new, using language to call into being an imaginative reality heretofore not experienced and still unknown. In this sense parables have the capacity to occasion the revelation of something new — the Empire of God. In Jesus' parables this is accomplished by using something common, something from the everyday world of Jesus and his listeners as the basic subject matter of the parable. But as the narrative unfolds, something surprising and unconventional always happens, thwarting the listener's expectations and creating an alternative reality to that of his or her common experience. The parable thus becomes a "language event,"

> in which the hearer has to choose between two worlds. If he elects the parabolic world, he is invited to dispose himself to concrete reality as it is ordered in the parable, and venture, without benefit of landmark but on the parable's authority, into the future.[25]

The idea that a parable is a language event in which the reign of God is encountered by the listener is central also to the work of Crossan. Crossan emphasizes the extent to which language gives shape to a person's perception of the world, especially through the stories we tell. Recall how Crossan explores this function of language in laying out a kind of "taxonomy of story." At one end of a spectrum of world-shaping stories lies "myth." Myth is a story we tell to help make sense out of life, to reconcile all of the intolerable incongruities we all know to exist in our world, but which we would rather not contemplate. In this way myth has the function of establishing and legitimating our social world. Parable, on the other hand, does the opposite. Rather than smoothing over the contradictions in our world, parable tends to undermine the world-creating script provided by myth and to accentuate or even create contradictions and tensions. If language, through myth, creates world, language, through parable, has the ability to destroy world. "Parables," writes Crossan,

> are stories which shatter the deep structure of our accepted world and thereby render clear and evident to us the relativity of story itself. They

---

25. Funk, *Language, Hermeneutic, and the Word of God* (New York: Harper & Row, 1966), 162.

remove our defenses and make us vulnerable to God. It is only in such experiences that God can touch us, and only in such moments does the Kingdom of God arrive.[26]

For Crossan, Funk, and Wilder, parables are key to understanding how it is that Jesus can authentically speak of the Empire of God as present: it becomes a reality in the very preaching of Jesus itself. It encounters the listener insofar as he or she allows the parabolic event to deconstruct the world as he or she has constructed it: as the conventional world of meaning(-lessness) is shattered by the parable, the Empire of God comes breaking in. In parable, the Empire of God is at hand.

So the newest phase of research on Q and the Gospel of Thomas, calling into question the apocalyptic hypothesis, did not emerge in a vacuum. For many years now New Testament scholarship has been chipping away at the apocalyptic paradigm. Through the post-Bultmannian discussion of the Empire of God as present, not future, and the newer American discussion of parables as language events in which the Empire of God becomes a present reality, New Testament scholars have become accustomed to entertaining a view of the Empire of God that is not apocalyptic. The realization that the earliest phase of the Jesus tradition was not apocalyptically oriented simply served to confirm this view of the reign of God in the preaching of Jesus. The convergence of these various lines of research is what convinces me that we are now arriving at a new consensus position about the reign of God: Jesus did not conceive of it as a future, apocalyptic event, but as a present reality to be experienced as breaking in upon the present world of human existence.

The Legacy of Apocalyptic Theology

What will the collapse of the apocalyptic hypothesis mean for Christian theology? Can Christian theology get along without apocalyptic eschatology?

Of course, the historian's research showing that Jesus did not himself think of the reign of God in terms of imminent apocalyptic scenarios does not mean that theology, especially biblical theology, can be done with such matters. After all, much of the New Testament is still oriented to an apocalypticism that emerges already in the letters of Paul and in the earliest canonical gospel, Mark. New Testament theology must still face the uncomfortable fact that apocalyptic thinking shaped the way many early Christians came to see

---

26. *The Dark Interval: Towards a Theology of Story* (Sonoma, Calif.: Polebridge, 1988 [originally published in 1975]), 100.

Jesus as somehow significant for their own future. More work, such as that which has been done on Revelation by Adela Yarbro-Collins[27] and Elisabeth Schüssler Fiorenza,[28] which explores how apocalypticism functions as cathartic and ennobling for persons pushed to the margins of an oppressive society, needs to be done with respect to Paul and the synoptic gospels as well. It may be that in certain culturally specific circumstances apocalypticism indeed provides an apt language for giving expression to Christian hope.[29] At the same time, Christian theology must take seriously the ultimate failure of all such scenarios. For they are all scenarios of *imminent* catastrophe. It will not do to salvage them by simply delaying their arrival into an indefinite future. Ultimately we must realize that God will not, perhaps *cannot*, rectify injustice through the violence and power of apocalypse.

But quite apart from our assessment of how apocalypticism functions in early Christianity, we must also turn our attention to how apocalypticism has functioned in our own culture. Even though the historian's work may not dislodge apocalyptic eschatology from Christian theology altogether, it may open enough space to question the apocalyptic focus of so much of modern Christian theology and to consider anew the basic theological issues that confront the church, and more broadly the cultural dilemmas to which theology must ultimately direct itself.

In raising such questions we must recognize at the outset that the apocalyptic paradigm itself was not without positive cultural significance at a critical juncture in Western history. For example, when Niebuhr wrote that the ethical demands made by Jesus will be possible "only when God transmutes the present chaos of this world into its final unity," that the reign of God "is in fact always coming but never here,"[30] he intended to call American culture into a stance of self-criticism. This is no less true today.

But the apocalyptic paradigm can also have its own debilitating and self-serving tendencies. The repeated assertion that God's decisive activity in the world belongs to the future and that until God decides to act we must be content to live in an imperfect world can lead to complacency about the problems we face as a culture. In the face of such a temporal-theological dual-

---

27. *Crisis and Catharsis: The Power of the Apocalypse* (Philadelphia: Fortress Press, 1984).

28. "Redemption as Liberation: Rev. 1:5–6 and 5:9–10," *Catholic Biblical Quarterly* 36 (1974): 220–32.

29. Richard Horsley (*Jesus and the Spiral of Violence* [San Francisco: Harper & Row, 1987], esp. 121–45) speaks of this function of apocalyptic in the preaching of Jesus himself. Horsley embraces the older view that Jesus was an apocalyptic prophet, but describes carefully the social, political, and psychological function of apocalyptic within a resistance movement.

30. Reinhold Niebuhr, *Interpretation of Christian Ethics* (New York: Harper & Brothers, 1935), 58.

ism, in which the present is given over to an imperfect humanity while the future is placed exclusively in God's exclusive hands, one can also conclude that any present, human attempt at reform is ultimately futile. Moreover, it is unnecessary, for the security of God's intervention in the future means that ultimately humanity will not have to deal with its current problems anyway. The idea of a father God, who arrives just in time to save his unruly children from their own inevitable foolishness, can be an unhealthy starting point, both theologically and culturally. Finally, the fact that most biblical apocalyptic scenarios feature violence has had a particularly ominous effect on how we imagine solutions to problems we think we are able to handle. The massive use of force and violence with almost god-like efficiency during the Gulf War was nothing less than apocalyptic for those on the receiving end of that onslaught. One must also wonder at the long-term effect such an overwhelming use of power will have on the human psyche. The power of apocalypse is no longer imaginable solely as God's domain. We, too, have the power to bring cultures, civilizations, even history itself to an end. Whatever its virtues might have been in calling Western culture into a stance of greater self-criticism in the first part of this century, in our own time the apocalyptic paradigm has taken its toll.

To remove the apocalyptic paradigm from the center of theology might mean that the temporal-theological dualism which claims the present for the imperfect, inevitably flawed realm of human activity, while relegating the future to the transcendent realm of God's absolute sovereignty, would have to be abandoned. In fact, perhaps what is called for initially is a therapeutic theological reversal in which the present is relinquished to the divine purpose of justice and peace, while humanity claims as its own responsibility the future, whose inhabitability will be determined by the extent to which we are willing to take up the task of giving it an inhabitable shape. No more can the apocalyptic hope for a better world created at God's sole initiative, a hope that continually recedes into the future, allow us to breathe a complacent sigh about the massive cultural problems that face us as a society as we pray for Christ's swift return. Liberation theologians have long tried to convince European and North American theologians from traditionally empowered groups of how self-serving this theological paradigm has been: waiting is easy if you already have everything, and there is nothing for which you must wait. Now historical criticism has formed a new alliance with liberation theology and offered new grounds for calling this dominant paradigm into question.

But what will replace it? And how will any new paradigm avoid the pitfalls on the one hand of an uncritical acceptance of Western bourgeois culture as the culmination of God's hope for human existence, and on the other hand

of a purely apocalyptic theology, with its unending deference to the future
as the transcendent realm of God's activity? Is there a Christian theology
that allows one to be optimistic about realizing in human history a level of
justice and peace that would make the Kingdom of God more than a mere
cipher for Christian idealism, while at the same time retaining the capacity
for self-critical evaluation of culture?

Theology without Apocalyptic

At the end of the nineteenth century there seemed to be but two choices for
Western theology: the moral theology of liberalism or the radically world-
negating theology of apocalyptic. Over time, the latter carried the day
because the latest critical thinking about Jesus, together with the powerful
forces of cultural change, lay in its favor. Yet another shift in the critical
consensus will again call for a theological adjustment. But the choices today
will not be the same as those of a hundred years ago. A new consensus that
Jesus was not an apocalyptic prophet will not necessarily mean a return to
nineteenth-century liberalism. On the contrary, in my view there are crucial
elements in the latest phase of Jesus scholarship that point in quite another
direction. Each has to do with a concept most scholars still agree in placing
at the center of Jesus' preaching: the Empire of God.

As we have seen in chapter 2, when Jesus spoke of the arrival of a new
"empire," he was not using language unfamiliar to those around him. The
term he used, *basileia*, conventionally rendered "kingdom," was a very common political term. When Jesus used it he would have been very conscious of
the fact that it had another primary referent. This was the term that Rome
used to describe itself. When we encounter it in ancient secular texts or
in inscriptions from the period, we always translate it "empire." There was
only one empire in the Mediterranean basin in the first century: the Roman
Empire.

The Roman Empire saturated every aspect of life. From the seven hills of
its opulent capital to the dusty roads of its servile provinces, Rome spread
its peace to all the world: the *Pax Romana*. Jesus would have known this
peace early in life. About the time Jesus was beginning life in Nazareth,
recall, Rome sent its general, Varus, into Galilee to quell protests over the
prospects of yet another Rome-appointed client ruler from the notorious
house of Herod. Just over the hill from Nazareth he razed the city of Sepphoris and sold its inhabitants into slavery. In Judea he burned Emmaus to

the ground and crucified two thousand for their part in the protests.[31] All in a day's work. Jesus encountered this peace again at the end of his life, when he too became its victim, one of thousands, who died on a Roman cross.

Helmut Koester has recently warned that any credible treatment of the historical Jesus must begin with and take seriously the fact that Jesus died as a victim of the Roman *Pax*.[32] His death was not an accident. To be sure, it was not likely observed as the world-transforming event Christians would later proclaim it to be. But neither was it a mere accident on the stage of history, an unfortunate incident in a world filled with random violence. Jesus was arrested and tried in a Roman court, convicted of sedition against the Roman state, and executed in a manner typical of the way Rome dealt with its enemies. Why? We do not have to imagine an unspoken political or military agenda or secret ties to Zealots to account for Jesus' fate. It was enough that Jesus dared to speak of a new Empire, an Empire *of God*. To speak thus is to say that there may be something amiss in the Empire we now have. Indeed, to speak of an Empire that belongs to beggars, the hungry, the depressed, the persecuted,[33] an Empire in which the first are last and the last first,[34] in which the abundance of God's creation is offered freely to all, would have been to challenge imperial priorities and offer Empire precisely to those expendables left out of Rome's concept of *Pax*. In daring to speak of Empire, Jesus joined a line of philosophers, Cynics, and prophets who questioned the authenticity of the Roman *Pax*, and he paid for it with his life.[35]

Jesus saw clearly the pain and brutality of the world in which he lived and dared to construct in word and deed a new world coming into being. In this sense Jesus' preaching may be said to have an eschatological dimension, even though it was not apocalyptic. This is not mere special pleading or a vain attempt to rescue the visionary aspects of eschatology without the offense of apocalyptic. Apocalyptic was but one form of eschatology in the ancient world. In the violent and catastrophic days of the Jewish war it was this form of eschatology that Mark deemed most appropriate to giving expression to Christian hope. But before Mark, before Q, or even Paul, there was Jesus and his eschatological vision of the Empire of God. The deeply

---

31. Josephus, *War* ii.66–75; *Ant.* xvii.288–95.

32. Helmut Koester, "Jesus the Victim," *Journal of Biblical Literature* 111 (1992): 3–15.

33. I am referring, of course, to the four beatitudes in Luke's Sermon on the Plain (Luke 6:20b–23). I have discussed their historicity in chapter 3, p. 96.

34. I am referring to the saying familiar from Mark 10:31. It is found also in Matt 19:30; 20:16; Luke 13:30; and Thom 4:2. Of these various versions the Jesus Seminar attributed Matt 20:16 and the Greek version of Thom 4:2 found in POxy 654 to the historical Jesus. I have discussed this saying's historicity in chapter 3, p. 95.

35. I will deal more extensively with the death of Jesus in the next chapter.

political overtones of this terminology suggest another primary frame of reference for understanding his words: the political eschatology proffered by Rome
throughout the lands of its conquest. Rome, too, spread the "good news" of
a new, universal Empire, of which there would be no end; it was penned by
such great court poets as Horace and Virgil and inscribed on its monuments
throughout the ancient world. They too could speak of a "savior," a "Son of
God" born to save the world and bring about this new Empire and to rule as
its "Lord."[36] This savior was Augustus.

It is no accident that the earliest Christians took over this vocabulary
and made it their own in the years following Jesus' death. This was a hostile
takeover: the polemical intent of the parallelism cannot be missed.[37] They
understood that Jesus had been the victim of Roman eschatology and that
this was no accident. Jesus' eschatological vision had offered a radically different alternative to Roman eschatology. The difference might be described
effectively in any number of ways. Crossan's efforts at such a description are
particularly apt:[38] Rome offered a "brokered Empire," in which the means to
life were tightly controlled as they passed down the chain of brokered relationships, patrons and their clients engaged in an uneven, but functional,
quid pro quo, until at long last the final few droplets of sustenance might drip
through to the bottom of the heap. Jesus, by contrast, began at the bottom,
with the expendables: the beggars, the prostitutes, the blind and disabled,
offering them a "brokerless" Empire, in which the means to life are offered
freely, without condition, around a table open to the unclean, the dispossessed, the shut out. This was another sort of empire, the Empire of God. Its
radical reversal of priorities and values means that it cannot easily be merged
with a political and social order which still presupposes that the means to
life must be brokered. Jesus did not advocate a kind of moral fine tuning
that would eventually perfect human society. He offered a radically different
notion of how to order human life.

There is one more difference between these alternative views of Empire.
One empire was already here, the other was not. Or was it? The Roman
Empire was surely present. Its reality was not in question. Roman eschatol-
ogy was *realized* eschatology.[39] For a Jewish peasant in the first century this

---

36. The language of the imperial cult is documented in Adolf Deissmann's classic work,
Light from the Ancient East, trans. Lionel R. M. Strachan from the 4th (1923) German edition,
New York: George H. Doran, 1927), 338–78. Koester provides a succinct summary of Roman
eschatology in "Jesus the Victim," 10–13.

37. Deissmann suggests that this Christian mimicking of official imperial language constitutes
a "polemical parallelism" (*Light from the Ancient East,* 342–43).

38. *The Historical Jesus.*

39. Koester, "Jesus the Victim," 10–13.

would have been abundantly clear. But what about Jesus' unbrokered Empire of God? Jesus proclaimed its presence, but not in the same self-confident way that Rome could assert its Empire. Jesus could proclaim the presence of his unbrokered Empire only in a qualified sense. This qualified presence finds expression in the saying of Jesus attested in Luke 17:20b–21:[40]

> The Empire of God is not coming with signs to be observed; nor will they say, "Lo, here it is!" or "There!" for behold, the Empire of God is in the midst of you.

Its twin in the Gospel of Thomas (Thom 113) reads similarly:

> His disciples said to him, "When will the Empire come?" "It will not come by watching for it. It will not be said, 'Behold, here' or 'Behold, there.' Rather, the Empire of the Father is spread out upon the earth, and people do not see it."

Here the Empire of God is not offered as a future apocalyptic reality upon which one must continually wait. But neither is it a fully present realized eschatology. Its essence may be described only as *potential*. This notion of the Empire of God is the same that comes to expression in the parables of Jesus. In the parables the Empire of God becomes a reality for those who hear only insofar as they enter into the narrative of the parable, giving themselves over to its reality and experiencing the new verities of human existence disclosed therein. In the parables one finds a world that looks ever so much like the cultural world of common orientation, and yet as the parabolic narrative unfolds one finds that world systematically subverted and deconstructed. As this familiar world crashes in on itself new space is created for the Empire of God. But all of this has permanent existence only as potential: only as persons choose the parabolic experience as that reality out of which they shall live does the Empire of God become real and realized. In the preaching of Jesus the Empire of God is neither future nor assuredly present; it exists as a potential to be actualized in the decision to live out of its audaciously presumed reality.

Jesus' preaching about the Empire of God offers an alternative view of the future that is quite different from the options left to us at the end of the last century. Jesus' view of the future was not an apocalyptic one, in which God would intervene with violence to overthrow God's enemies or ours. Regardless of how evil our enemies have appeared to be, God has not, and

---

40. The Jesus Seminar designated this saying "pink." I have discussed this saying as a saying of Jesus in chapter 3, p. 94. For an older argument for its authenticity see N. Perrin, *Rediscovering the Teaching of Jesus* (New York: Harper & Row; London: SCM, 1967), 68–74.

probably will not destroy them in the manner of our dreams and fantasies. On the other hand, Jesus' daring to speak of Empire, calling into question Rome's Empire and eventually becoming its victim, should caution us against any form of realized eschatology that presumes our golden age has arrived. For Jesus preached an Empire of God whose presence was not guaranteed, and perhaps could not ever be. It depends on one's decision to live out of its reality in an act of faithfulness. But in precisely this sense Christian theology must still be thought of as fundamentally eschatological. It is indeed about bringing something to an end and beginning something new. In the preaching of Jesus the person of faith receives an invitation to embody new beginnings in his or her very existence, to assert the present reality of the Empire of God, and to live it from potential into actuality. The Empire as "eschaton," as "end," means the end of life lived out of the realities of sin, injustice, violence, shame, and pain. But it also has an "end" — that is, a goal. It is not a distant goal, or one so remote that one must despair of ever reaching it. The Empire of God is reached day in and day out, in the very everyday decisions one makes to live faithfully to God.

Chapter 6

The Death of Jesus the Jew

On the Hope and Tragedy That Unites and Divides Us

---

*The Jews are the blood relatives, the cousins and brothers
of our Lord; if his flesh and blood could be boasted of, the
Jews belong to Jesus Christ much more than we do. Hence
I beg my dear Papists to call me a Jew, when they are tired
of calling me a heretic.*

— MARTIN LUTHER,
Dass Jesus Christus ein geborener Jude sei (1523)

*What then shall we Christians do with this damned,
rejected race of Jews? Since they live among us and we
know about their lying and blasphemy and cursing, we
cannot tolerate them if we do not wish to share in their
lies, curses, and blasphemy....*

*First, their synagogues ... should be set on fire, and
whatever does not burn up should be covered over with
dirt so that no one may ever see a cinder or stone of it....*

*Secondly, their homes should likewise be broken down
and destroyed. For they perpetrate the same things there
that they do in their synagogues. For this reason they ought
to be put under one roof or in a stable, like gypsies, in
order that they may realize that they are not masters in
our land, as they boast, but miserable captives....*

185

Thirdly, they should be deprived of their prayer books and Talmuds in which such idolatry, lies, cursing, and blasphemy are taught.

Fourthly, their rabbis must be forbidden under threat of death to teach any more.

Fifthly, passport and traveling privileges should be absolutely forbidden to the Jews. For they have no business in the rural districts since they are not nobles, nor officials, nor merchants, nor the like. Let them stay at home. . . .

Sixthly, they ought to be stopped from usury. All their cash and valuables of silver and gold ought to be taken from them. For this reason, as said before, everything that they possess they stole and robbed from us through their usury, for they have no other means of support. . . .

Seventhly, let the young and strong Jews and Jewesses be given the flail, the ax, the hoe, the spade, the distaff, and spindle, and let them earn their bread by the sweat of their noses as is enjoined upon Adam's children. . . .

To sum up, dear princes and nobles who have Jews in your domains, if this advice of mine does not suit you, then find a better one so that you may all be free of this insufferable devilish burden — the Jews.

— MARTIN LUTHER,
Gegen die Juden und ihre Lügen (1542)

The Legacy of Christian Anti-Semitism

The passages offered at the beginning of this chapter, both penned by the sixteenth-century reformer of Christianity Martin Luther, are emblematic of the paradoxical relationship that has existed between Christians and Jews for almost two millennia. It is a relationship that is characterized by both hope and tragedy. The hope, that Jews and Christians might live as close cousins, appreciating one another for the beauty of our closely related religious traditions, stems from the fact that our Christian roots are Jewish roots. Jesus was Jewish. This means that all we Christians profess to know about God must be credited at some level to Jewish life and culture. This, of course, is not to say that Jesus was in no way peculiar, that his voice was not a distinctive voice within his culture. But the fact that Jesus' voice was a distinctive voice does not make it any less a *Jewish* voice. Can it be doubted that the whole long, violent history of Jewish-Christian relations in the West might have been much different if we Christians had simply remembered the fact that our savior was Jewish? Remembering this, and honoring the culture and people of Jesus, would certainly not have made Christians any less Christian, but more.

But this brings us all too quickly to the tragic side of our relationship, about which there is far more to be said than of the hopeful side. The tragedy begins, like the hope, with the fact that Jesus was Jewish, as were most of those earliest Christians to whom we owe our distinctive Christian scriptural tradition. Christianity began as a Jewish messianic movement. Most of Christian scripture was produced during this early period, when Christians were arguing with other Jews about Judaism and Jewish concepts, about how to read the Jewish scriptures in light of recent events in their common history, and about whether and in what sense Jesus might be seen as the Jewish Messiah. These struggles can be seen in texts like the Gospel of Matthew or the Gospel of John, where the Christian (but still Jewish) voice of dissent over against the dominant streams of Jewish culture reaches almost fever pitch. In this debate, not even all Christians could agree with one another, as the arguments the apostle Paul is seen to have with his more traditionally Jew-

187

ish opponents in the Jerusalem church clearly demonstrate.[1] Very early on, Christian leaders decided that this contest could not end in a draw. Christians and Jews could not agree to disagree. Near the end of the first century, the author of the Epistle of Barnabas, a Christian who was very much caught up in this struggle for the legacy of Judaism, wrote to his Christian audience:

> Take heed to yourselves now, and do not become like some, heaping up your sins by saying that the covenant is both theirs and ours. It is ours. Yes, they lost it once and for all in this way, when Moses had just received it. For the scripture says, "And Moses was on the mountain fasting for forty days and forty nights, and he received the covenant from the Lord, tablets of stone, written by the finger of the hand of the Lord." But by turning to idols they lost it. For thus says the Lord, "Moses, Moses, go down at once, for your people, whom you brought forth out of the land of Egypt, have violated the law." And Moses understood and threw the two tablets from his hands. And so their covenant was broken, in order that the covenant of Jesus the beloved might be sealed in our hearts, in hope of his faithfulness (Barnabas IV.6–8).[2]

Even as Barnabas was writing these words, Christianity was changing from a mixed Jewish-Gentile movement to a predominantly Gentile phenomenon. The Jewish War some years earlier had left the Jerusalem church decimated, and the larger church with fewer and fewer Jewish members. At the same time, Pauline Christianity had opened the doors for Gentiles to come into the church. Within a relatively short period of time, Christianity would cease to understand itself as Jewish in any meaningful sense, and instead become a new Gentile religion. But this new Gentile church still held on to that early scriptural legacy of Paul, Matthew, John, and the like. Now their words, the frustrated arguments of a minority Christian-Jewish voice awash in a hostile Jewish majority, could be appropriated by Gentile Christians and joined to a long-standing Gentile tradition of anti-Jewish rhetoric. This development would prove ominous. It is one thing, after all, for the writer of Matthew, a member of a tiny, powerless, heretical Jewish sect, frustrated that its messianic claims had not been accepted by the vast majority of Jews — it is one thing

---

1. This is seen most clearly in Galatians 2, where Paul describes an argument he had with certain leaders in the Jerusalem church, including James and Peter, over whether Gentiles had to be circumcised in order to become Christian, and whether it was appropriate for Christian Jews to eat with Gentiles. This conflict, however, marks a theme running through many of Paul's letters.

2. Based on the text of Barnabas edited by Kirsopp Lake in *The Apostolic Fathers* (Cambridge: Harvard University Press, 1912), 350.

for him to say of that majority culture "The blood of Jesus be upon [you] and [your] children" (Matt 27:25). It is quite another thing for a Gentile to say this about Jews in general. Christianity and postbiblical Judaism have a common history. They began life as two siblings fighting over the approval of their common Jewish parent, each claiming to be the legitimate heir. Then Christianity married into another family, the Gentile family. Forgetting our family ties, but not our rivalrous roots, our family enmity now became deadly, and the history of Christian anti-Semitism is the long and tragic result.

Perhaps nothing has been more crucial to the life-blood of Christian anti-Semitism than the charge that the Jews killed Jesus. This persistent theme in early Christian diatribe against Judaism probably received its most enduring form in the influential work of Augustine (354–430). Like most learned Christians of his day, Augustine read the Jewish scriptures allegorically and typologically. Their stories were not to be read literally, but as cryptic messages, whose real significance could be seen only through the eyes of Christian faith. In his reply to the Manichaean teacher, Faustus, Augustine interpreted the story of Cain and Abel (Gen 4:1–16) typologically, such that Cain's murder of Abel becomes the model for understanding the Jewish role in the death of Jesus, and the subsequent fate of the Jewish people in a world that would become increasingly Christian. Here Augustine likens Abel's acceptable sacrifice to Christian faith and Abel's rejected sacrifice to traditional Judaism:[3]

> As Cain's sacrifice of the fruit of the ground is rejected, while Abel's sacrifice of his sheep and the fat thereof is accepted, so the faith of the New Testament praising God in the harmless service of grace is preferred to the earthly observances of the Old Testament....

As in the story, jealousy leads to homicide, so also Augustine's typology proceeds to the theme of murder:

> Abel, the younger brother, is killed by the elder brother; Christ, the head of the younger people, is killed by the elder people of the Jews. Abel dies in the field; Christ dies on Calvary.... Then God says to Cain, "What hast thou done? The voice of thy brother's blood crieth unto me from the ground." So the voice of God in the Holy Scriptures accuses the Jews.

---

3. The following passages are drawn from Philip Schaff, ed., *Nicene and Post-Nicene Fathers of the Christian Church*, vol. 4: *St Augustine: The Writings against the Manichaeans and the Donatists* (Edinburgh: T. & T. Clark; Grand Rapids: Eerdmans, 1988; orig. published 1887), 186–88.

Augustine's interpretation of what happens next establishes a theme in Christian anti-Jewish theology that would persist unchallenged well into the modern era: the curse of the wandering Jew. As God curses Cain with the words: "When you till the ground, it shall no longer yield to you its strength; you shall be a fugitive and a wanderer on the earth," Augustine divines,

> Here no one can fail to see that in every land where the Jews are scattered they mourn for the loss of their kingdom, and are in terrified subjection to the immensely superior number of Christians. "My case is worse, if Thou drivest me out this day from the face of the earth; and it shall be that everyone that findeth me shall slay me." Here he groans indeed in terror, lest after losing his earthly possession he should suffer the death of the body.

But at this point Augustine follows the story, warning that just as Cain is protected by the words "whosoever shall kill Cain, vengeance shall be taken on him sevenfold," so also the Jews are not to be slain for their crime. Rather,

> the continued preservation of the Jews will be a proof to believing Christians of the subjection merited by those who, in the pride of their kingdom, put the Lord to death.

Here are all the classic elements of Christian anti-Jewish theology: the contrast between the "earthly Old Testament" and the more spiritual "harmless" grace of the New Testament; at the same time, however, a supersessionist reading of certain Old Testament passages; and most importantly, the charge that the Jews are responsible for the death of Jesus and must therefore pay the price for this crime through continual suffering. Over the centuries, this way of thinking about the Jews became so natural to Christian theologians that it almost became unrecognizable as anti-Semitic. It was not an aberration born of hate, but simply the truth. No one will doubt, for example, the sincerity of Dietrich Bonhoeffer, who gave his very life in the struggle against Hitler's anti-Semitic regime. Yet listen to the arguments Bonhoeffer uses in opposing Hitler's Aryan clauses, which restricted the ability of Jews to hold state office, regardless of their religious affiliation. Bonhoeffer argued that Jews ought to be considered free from such laws if they were to convert to Christianity:

> The church of Christ has never lost sight of the fact that the "chosen people," who nailed the redeemer of the world to the cross, must bear the curse for its action through a long history of suffering. "Jews are the poorest people among all nations upon earth, they are tossed to and

fro, they are scattered here and there in all lands, they have no certain place where they could remain safely and must always be afraid that they will be driven out..." (Luther, *Table Talk*). But the history of the suffering of this people, loved and punished by God, stands under the sign of the final homecoming of the people of Israel to its God. And this homecoming happens in the conversion of Israel to Christ.... The conversion of Israel, that is to be the end of the people's period of suffering.[4]

It may seem shocking to hear such clearly anti-Semitic ideas coming from one of the saints in the crusade against anti-Semitism. But such was the low level of awareness of this problem in Christian theology prior to World War II. Bonhoeffer invokes the name of Luther for his cause. So did those who opposed Bonhoeffer. In the Nuremberg trials, Julius Streicher, an early proponent of Hitler's policy of genocide, used Luther's tract *Gegen die Juden und ihre Lügen* in his defense.[5] To understand the role that this theological tradition has played in our history, it is important to see that it was indeed used on both sides of the Jewish question, by both villains and heroes. Anti-Semitism in Christian theology is not an aberration, a fringe tradition promulgated only by radical anti-Semites. It has operated for most of Christian history at the level of common assumption. Almost everyone has assumed its validity. From our vantage point in history — and only because of that vantage point, not any superior courage or wisdom — we can now begin to see how misguided this theological tradition is. We can now see that it derives from prejudice and feelings of superiority. It derives from the desire to be right, absolutely and infallibly right in the competitive marketplace of religious ideas. It derives from a history of enmity that has little to do with Jesus and much to do with the historic, hostile relationship between Jews and Gentiles. And it derives from a decision on the part of Gentile Christians to read the texts of those first Christian generations, the gospels, as though they were history. This is where those who would search for the historical Jesus have a moral imperative to enter into this discussion. What does it mean that Jesus was Jewish? Did Jesus reject Judaism? Did the Jews reject Jesus? Were the Jews really responsible for Jesus' death? What can historical research tell us about these common flash points in anti-Jewish Christian theology?

---

4. Dietrich Bonhoeffer, *No Rusty Swords: Letters, Lectures and Notes, 1928–36*, ed. Edwin H. Robertson, trans. Edwin H. Robertson and John Bowden (New York: Harper & Row, 1965), 226.

5. Clark M. Williamson, *Has God Rejected His People? Anti-Judaism in the Christian Church* (Nashville: Abingdon, 1982), 101.

Did Jesus Reject Judaism?

It is commonly assumed that Christianity's break with Judaism was inevitable because Jesus himself rejected Judaism. But this way of thinking about Jesus' relationship to the Jewish culture of the first century, Jesus' own culture, is erroneous on several levels.

First, it assumes that there was something in Jesus' day called Judaism. There was not. There were, of course, the religious practices of Jewish people living in the Mediterranean basin in the first century, some of which would have been very familiar to Jesus. But to speak of "Judaism" in the modern sense of this term is to speak of a religion as a distinct arena of life standing alongside other arenas, such as social life or politics. It is questionable whether one may speak of "religion" at all in this way when discussing the ancient world, or any culture other than the modern Western cultures that are descended from Europe. Ancient people would not have thought of religious life as something distinct from social or political life. For an ancient Jewish person like Jesus, there would have been no concept of the separation of church and state. This seems obvious enough. Yet how often have modern people asserted that Jesus was not a political figure, but a religious figure whose critique was focused on matters of faith, not politics? But the very division of life into religious and political spheres is a modern, Western, and particularly American cultural innovation.[6]

A good illustration of how misleading such categories can be when thinking about Jesus is the way many people regard Jesus' action in the Temple of Jerusalem, the so-called "cleansing" of the Temple (Mark 11:15–17, and pars.). It is often assumed that with this action Jesus intended to clean out the Temple, rid it of corruption, and in this way "reform" the Judaism of his day.[7] But the Temple of Jerusalem was not just the center of ancient Jewish religious life. It had always been the symbolic and actual center of Jewish political life as well. Even in Jesus' day, when Palestinian politics were dominated by the forces of Roman imperialism, the Temple continued to be the center of political life. During the first half of the first century the Jewish

---

6. This insight from the history of religions is brought to bear on the problem of understanding Jesus' relationship to his culture by Richard A. Horsley in a number of publications. See his *Jesus and the Spiral of Violence* (San Francisco: Harper & Row, 1987), 151–55; and his essay "The Death of Jesus," in Bruce Chilton and Craig A. Evans, eds., *Studying the Historical Jesus: Evaluations of the State of Current Research* (Leiden, New York, London: Brill, 1994), 397. For a more general discussion of the point see Wilfred Cantwell Smith, *The Meaning and End of Religion* (New York: Harper & Row, 1978).

7. On this position and its untenability see E. P. Sanders, *Jesus and Judaism* (Philadelphia: Fortress Press, 1985), 61–71.

high priest was customarily appointed by the Roman prefect of Judea or by the imperial legate stationed in Syria.[8] This, in fact, was the typical *modus operandi* of imperial Rome. Rome often left local political and religious institutions intact, but co-opted these indigenous forms of leadership, usually centered in large urban places like Jerusalem. It was through local institutions like the Temple that Rome exercised its power over provincial regions. In Jesus' day the Jerusalem Temple had become part of the imperial apparatus.[9] In such a climate Jesus' action in the Temple cannot be seen as a simple gesture of religious reform. It was nothing less than a symbolic *destruction* of a highly symbolic religio-political institution.[10] Jesus' own words about the Temple confirm this understanding of his action. There is a very old and widely attested saying in the Jesus tradition that addresses the Temple itself. Mark sets this saying in a scene in which Jesus addresses the disciples shortly after his action against the Temple. He utters it as they are coming out of the Temple the next day. Jesus says:

> Do you see these great buildings? There will not be left here one stone upon another, that will not be thrown down. (Mark 13:2)

Mark's setting is artificial, designed to relate Jesus' words and his action on the previous day to the destruction that did eventually come upon Jerusalem and the Temple many years later, during the Jewish War (see Mark 13:3–37). But this saying was probably originally related to the Temple act in some way. In a closely related tradition, Jesus claims that it is he who will topple those stones. This second tradition comes up in Mark a few chapters later, in Jesus'

---

8. See Josephus, *Ant.* xviii.34–35.

9. For a discussion of the complex social, political, and religious place of the Temple in first-century Jewish culture and popular opposition to it see Gerd Theissen, "Jesus' Temple Prophecy: Prophecy in the Tension between Town and Country," in his *Social Reality and the Early Christians: Theology, Ethics, and the World of the New Testament*, trans. Margaret Kohl (Minneapolis: Fortress Press, 1992), 94–114. Theissen stresses that the tension between urban areas, like Jerusalem, and outlying places, like Galilee, must be taken into account when assessing the full impact of Jesus' action in the Temple.

10. There is a developing wide agreement both that Jesus' action in the Temple is historical and that it denoted the symbolic destruction of the Temple, not its reform. The larger context in which such an act is to be understood is still a matter of disagreement. Sanders (*Jesus and Judaism*, 71–119) regards it as stemming from Jesus' pursuit of Jewish restoration theology, in which the present Temple would be destroyed and rebuilt in the coming new age. Horsley also sees Jesus' action as rooted in apocalyptic theology, but thinks that Jesus' symbolic destruction of the Temple was an attack on its concrete political role in mediating Roman oppression to the Jewish people. After its destruction, he finds it hard to imagine Jesus and his followers looking forward to a newly restored Temple (*Jesus and the Spiral of Violence*, 286–300). Crossan agrees with Horsley's basic approach, but would not assume an apocalyptic theological framework for Jesus' action (*Who Killed Jesus?* 37–65).

trial before the Sanhedrin, in the form of an accusation for which Jesus must be punished:

> We heard him say, "I will destroy this temple that is made with hands, and in three days I will build another not made with hands." (14:58)[11]

We shall return to this charge, and the Temple act, presently. But for now it is enough to underscore that Jesus' action in the Temple did not constitute a religious critique of Judaism. It was the symbolic destruction of an institution that, for many Jews like Jesus, represented the infiltration and domination of Israel by an oppressive, foreign power.

It is true that Jesus was a person who saw much wrong in his culture and criticized things that he could not abide. But all too often, Christians have chosen to see Jesus' cultural critique as a critique of Judaism, and not a critique of things which, in reality, might be found in many cultures. For example, his critique of purity should not be understood as a specific attack on Judaism's purity codes. For the most part, Jesus simply assumes the validity of Jewish religious traditions and practices, as any Jew with reverence for God would.[12] However, he did object to the exiling of persons from the human

---

11. This is probably not the earliest version of this saying. In my view, the version found in Thomas 71, though fragmentary, is probably the most original surviving form of the saying: "I will destroy this house, and no one will be able to build it [. . .]." This version, like the saying in Mark 13:2, speaks of the Temple's total destruction and is thus quite consistent with Jesus' action in the Temple. There is no mention of rebuilding it "after three days." This feature, which is found also in John's version (John 2:19), probably reflects the post-Easter setting of the church, which soon attached an allegorical meaning to this saying when Jesus' predictions/hopes did not materialize. As John writes: "Actually he was talking about the Temple of his body. After he had been raised from the dead, his disciples recalled that he had said this and believed the scripture and the prediction Jesus had made" (John 2:21–22).

The Jesus Seminar did not consider any of these sayings to be historical. It was sharply divided over Mark 13:2; the voting placed it exactly on the edge between "gray" and "pink." In my view, the saying coheres so closely with the Temple action that it must have some claim to historicity. It was less divided over Mark 14:48 and its parallels, including Thom 71. The prophetic quality of the saying, together with the obvious reference to Jesus' resurrection made many Fellows skeptical, and rightly so. But prophetic sayings need not always be understood as predictive, but may function simply as extreme critique. And Thom 71 indicates that there may have been a form of this saying that did not make reference to Jesus' resurrection. As such, one might well imagine Jesus saying something like this in reference to the Temple.

12. There are many examples to illustrate this in the gospels. For example, when Jesus heals a leper in Mark 1:40–45, he charges him to "show yourself to a priest, and offer for your cleansing what Moses commanded, as a proof to the people" (Mark 1:44). That early followers of Jesus could disagree over basic issues like whether to observe kosher food rules or to require circumcision of Gentiles wishing to become Christians shows that Jesus himself could not have been programmatically opposed to purity codes per se. However, as I have argued above (see pp. 71–73), Jesus did critique some aspects of purity customs. Paula Fredriksen's dismissive rebuttal of Marcus Borg and N. T. Wright (see her "What You See Is What You Get: Context and Content in Current Research on the Historical Jesus," Theology Today 52, no. 1 [1995]: 86–91), while

community on the basis of traditional taboos, such as the popular abhorrence of leprosy. But such dehumanizing taboos and practices are to be found in most cultures. In our own day, persons with HIV fall under the same sort of ostracism. Jesus would have objected to this modern sense of maintaining purity just as much as he objected to its ancient equivalents. Jesus, of course, made many such criticisms within the specific context of his own ancient Jewish culture. But one misses the point entirely if one assumes that his critique was of Judaism and not of the way human beings tend to treat one another in many cultures, including our own modern, American majority *Christian* culture.

At the same time, just as there is a tendency among Christians to see Jesus' criticisms of the world around him as his rejection of Judaism, there is also a tendency to regard his positive insights about God, and the human priorities that result from these insights, as unique and very uncharacteristic of Judaism in general. But this also is not very accurate. Taking, again, the example of Jesus' critique of popular piety, it must be remembered that this is a very old and well-respected tradition among the fabled prophets of Judaism. It was Hosea who said, "I desire steadfast love and not sacrifice, the knowledge of God, rather than burnt offerings" (Hos 6:6). Jesus himself may have sung at some point the words of the psalmist, "The sacrifice acceptable to God is a broken spirit; a broken and contrite heart, O God, thou wilt not despise" (Ps 51:17).[13] Even more rooted in Jesus' Jewish heritage was his regard for the poor and marginal. Here the relevant material from the sages, prophets, and singers of ancient Judaism is far too abundant even to begin recitation. When Jesus declares that the Empire of God belongs to the poor and destitute (Luke 6:20b) he is siding with the best of his culture's insights about God's special regard for the poor and against the dominant view running through virtually every human culture, especially our own late twentieth-century view, that the poor are least of all blessed of God. Indeed, we assume that their problems are their own, the result of the sins of sloth and irresponsibility. It is amazing how close our Jesus stands to the great Jewish theologians of old and how distant his commitments are from the cultural norms that have come to pass for "Christian" values in our own time.

---

perhaps helpful in pointing out excesses, does not adequately account for those places where Jesus does in fact criticize certain purity codes.

13. And one should not, by the way, assume that this poetic embrace of the values of love, knowledge, and contrition meant that literal sacrifices in the Temple were to be rejected.

Did the Jews Reject Jesus?

If Jesus did not reject Judaism, did the Jews then reject Jesus? It is often said by Christians, for example, that the Jews expected a certain kind of Messiah, a military leader who would overthrow the powers of domination and oppression. But Jesus came as another kind of Messiah, a peaceful, nonviolent Messiah, who left the Jews disappointed and bitter. So they turned on him and had him crucified. This view is reinforced by the way the gospels depict Jesus' final days in Jerusalem, wherein the crowd, after welcoming Jesus into the city with wild enthusiasm, later turns on him and asks for his crucifixion.

This common view is filled with assumptions that cannot be sustained in light of historical critical analysis. First, the idea that (all) the Jews were waiting in expectation of a Messiah is probably not very accurate. Nor is it a valid assumption that the views of those who did entertain some form of messianic expectation would have been in any sense uniform. Jewish messianic expectations during the time of Jesus would probably have been much less widespread and more diverse than most Christians today imagine them.[14] The construct of "Jewish messianic expectation," when construed as monolithic and militaristic, can only be seen as a Christian straw man over against which Jesus stands out as the peace-loving alternative. This distortion also forgets that Jesus may not always have been such a pacifist. After all, there is a very early tradition that portrays Jesus in terms quite contrary to this characterization: "Do not think that I have come to bring peace on earth; I have not come to bring peace, but a sword."[15]

---

14. So Marinus de Jonge, "The Use of the Word 'Anointed' in the Time of Jesus," *Novum Testamentum* 8 (1966): 132–48. More recently see the collection of essays edited by Jacob Neusner, William Scott Green, and Ernest Frerichs, *Judaisms and Their Messiahs at the Turn of the Christian Era* (Cambridge: Cambridge University Press, 1987), esp. the essays by Green and Burton Mack. See also R. A. Horsley, " 'Messianic' Figures and Movements in First-Century Palestine," pp. 276–95 in James H. Charlesworth, ed., *The Messiah: Developments in Earliest Judaism and Christianity* (Minneapolis: Fortress Press, 1992), and John J. Collins, *The Scepter and the Star: The Messiahs of the Dead Sea Scrolls and Other Ancient Literature* (New York: Doubleday, 1995). Horsley and Collins note the relative paucity of messianic interest in first-century Judaism generally speaking. For the diversity of Judaism in general in this period, see Morton Smith, "Palestinian Judaism in the First Century," in Moshe Davis, ed., *Israel: Its Role in Civilization* (New York: Harper & Row, 1956), 67–81; also Gary Porton, "Diversity in Post-Biblical Judaism," in Robert A. Kraft and George W. E. Nickelsburg, eds., *Early Judaism and Its Modern Interpreters* (Atlanta: Scholars Press, 1986), 57–80.

15. This saying is found independently in both Thomas (Thom 16) and Q (Luke 12:51; Matt 10:34). The Jesus Seminar designated this saying "black," but this is perhaps too negative a view about its historicity. In its present form, using the common "I have come" formulation, it probably does not come from Jesus. Nevertheless, its sentiments may be consistent with something Jesus did say (for a full discussion of the issue, see Stephen J. Patterson, "Fire and Dissension: Ipsissima Vox Jesu in Q 12:49, 51–53?" *Forum* 5, no. 2 [1989]: 121–38). Conflict with home

Another assumption that history may throw some doubt upon is the very idea that Jesus claimed to be the Messiah in the first place. Only once in the entire gospel tradition does Jesus actually claim to be the Messiah (Mark 14:62), but this is probably not historical.[16] There are, of course, various places where others make messianic claims on Jesus' behalf; this is indeed the perspective of the gospel writers themselves. Mark, for example, proclaims in his opening lines that this is "the beginning of the gospel of Jesus *Christ.*" But this only begs the question of whether Jesus would have seen himself in this role.

A particularly instructive instance of how one finds such messianic claims in the gospels is Peter's famous confession at Caesarea-Philippi. When asked, "But who do you say that I am?" Peter replies, "You are the Christ." Then Mark adds, mysteriously: "And [Jesus] charged them to tell no one about him" (Mark 8:29–30). This last remark enjoining the disciples to silence is a well-known motif that passes throughout the Gospel of Mark. Why the secrecy about Jesus' messianic identity? Some have argued that this has historical roots, that Jesus wished to keep his messianic status a secret to avoid drawing to himself the political and martial attributes that typically accompany ancient Jewish messianic conceptions. But we have already noted how problematic it would be to try to depoliticize Jesus in accordance with modern notions about distinctly sacred and secular realms. Moreover, though, there is no evidence at all in the gospel tradition to suggest that Jesus or early Christians consciously tried to redefine the concept of the Messiah.

A more likely explanation of the Markan messianic secret has to do with the history and development of messianic ideas within the early Christian movement. In Rom 1:3–4 the apostle Paul uses what was probably a very old formulation of the Christian gospel to address the church at Rome:

---

and family is a frequent topic of discussion in the Jesus tradition (see chapter 3, pp. 109–112 for discussion). And if, as most would argue today, the Temple incident has some claim to historicity (see below), one would have to concede that Jesus was not always calm and irenic.

16. In response to the high priest's question, "Are you the Messiah?" Jesus responds "I am; and you will see the Son of Man seated at the right hand of power, and coming with the clouds of heaven." The Jesus Seminar designated these words "black." I would agree with that judgment. First, if one may even assume that the scene itself has any claim to historicity (doubtful: see p. 200, n. 22 below), it is unlikely that these words were remembered by someone and passed along to a follower of Jesus. In the scene itself, no followers of Jesus are present. Furthermore, Matthew and Luke do not follow Mark in presenting this as Jesus' answer (see Matt 26:64; Luke 22:67b), but portray Jesus as more evasive. This is more in character with Jesus' responses throughout the trial scenes and may come from a source available to them other than Mark. Finally, these words are strongly reminiscent of Mark 13:26, from Mark's apocalypse. Mark may have fashioned this response to capitalize on Mark's apocalyptic scenario, which includes the destruction of Jerusalem for its sins against Jesus.

The gospel concerning his Son, who was descended from David according to the flesh and *designated* Son of God in power according to the spirit of holiness *by his resurrection from the dead.*

Notice the italicized words. They indicate that in this tradition Jesus was not recognized as the Son of God (here understood as a messianic title) until he was designated so *after* his resurrection from the dead. This is similar to the idea conveyed in the early Christian hymn Paul cites in Phil 2:6–11. In this hymn Jesus' titles all follow upon his exaltation after his death.[17] This observation has led many to the conclusion that the earliest followers of Jesus did not regard him as the Messiah during his own lifetime, because Jesus did not so regard himself. Only later, in view of all that had happened to Jesus, and all that his followers had experienced after his death, did they begin to speak of Jesus as the Christ. This is why the tradition is devoid of any sayings in which Jesus identifies himself as the Messiah.[18]

But there soon developed many stories — Jesus' baptism, the Temptation in the Wilderness, numerous miracle stories, and the like — in which Jesus is depicted as the Son of God or Messiah. It would be easy for newcomers to assume, on the basis of these stories, that Jesus was a glorious figure, a god-man striding through life to ultimate triumph. But Mark knew that this is not the way it was, and so created the motif of the messianic secret. In Mark, Jesus' real identity is not to be revealed until after his death on the cross. In this way Mark made sure that his readers would realize that in spite of all the wonderful, fantastic stories about Jesus, in reality no one knew who Jesus was in his own lifetime. Any tendencies to triumphalism must be tempered with the reality of the crucifixion.[19]

---

17. A similar idea is attributed to Peter in Acts 2:36. In comparison to other New Testament views, in which Jesus' christological status begins in secret at his baptism (Mark 1:9–11) or even at the beginning of time (John 1:1–18), this view is probably older.

18. This insight is one of the lasting contributions of William Wrede's book *The Messianic Secret* (London and Cambridge: James Clarke; Greenwood, S.C.: Attic Press, 1971; German original published in 1901). Others before him held similar views, however. Julius Wellhausen argued that Jesus claimed to be the Messiah only at the very end of his life. Johannes Weiss and H. J. Holtzmann held similar views, as noted by J. C. O'Niell, *Who Did Jesus Think He Was?* (Leiden: E. J. Brill, 1995), 8–10.

19. Wrede was the first to propose that the Markan "messianic secret" was the result of a conflict between an older view that Jesus did not become the Messiah until after his resurrection and a subsequent view that he was the Messiah already in his lifetime. According to Wrede, Mark smoothed out this conflict by portraying Jesus as the Messiah in his lifetime, but making a secret of this fact. Hans Conzelmann altered this view slightly by ascribing to Mark greater intention in creating the secrecy motif ("Present and Future in the Synoptic Tradition," *Journal for Theology and the Church* 5 [1968]: 42–44). In his view, Mark uses this motif to tone down the

The problem of the messianic secret, together with the early Christian confessional traditions, in which Jesus' messianic status is conferred only after his death (Rom 1:3–4; Phil 2:6–11; Acts 2:36), are what led the majority of Fellows in the Jesus Seminar to join a long tradition of scholarship in reaching the conclusion that Jesus probably did not claim to be the Messiah.[20] This, like many other confessional claims about Jesus, arose first in the period after his death as a way of proclaiming the real significance Christians claimed to see in Jesus. Thus, it is probably not correct to say that the Jewish people rejected Jesus on the basis of his claim to be the Messiah. Jesus probably did not make such a claim.

Leaving the question of messianic expectations and Jesus' own messianic identity aside, then, is it not still true that Jesus was never accepted by the Jews in the same way that he was accepted by Christians? In a sense, of course, this is true. Jesus was never a popular figure among first-century Jews. But why? First, most Jews living in Jesus' day would never have heard of him. He was, after all, a relatively minor figure in his own lifetime. It was half a century or more before his following reached sufficient size to warrant the notice of any more than a few thousand souls in a vast sea of ancient humanity. But even if Jesus could have somehow been an overnight media sensation, heard and seen by all, it is not likely that he ever would have become a very popular figure. Why? Because of what he said and did. He was an unusual person. His words were often harsh and difficult. How many people could really accept the invitation to leave home and family, to "hate one's father and mother," to abandon one's very life to accept the tenuous life offered in the Empire of God? How many people could really accept the injunction to "love your enemies, do good to those who hate you"? Not many, just as there are not many today who can really accept these things — Jews, Christians, or others. These are simply difficult things to accept. But this in no way justifies the idea that the Jews rejected Jesus. For there were some — at least a few — who did hear him and accept his words as truth. And all of these remarkable people were Jewish.

---

extravagant claims being made for Jesus' great works demonstrating his divine status. Mark, according to Conzelmann, wants to underscore that though Jesus was the Messiah, this was not at all obvious until after his death and resurrection. For a thorough discussion of the Markan "messianic secret," see Christopher Tuckett, ed., *The Messianic Secret*, Issues in Religion and Theology 1 (Philadelphia: Fortress; London: SCM, 1983), esp. Tuckett's "Introduction: The Problem of the Messianic Secret," 1–28.

20. For the modern period, Wrede's basic position has been articulated in its most persuasive and influential way by Rudolf Bultmann in his *Theology of the New Testament* (New York: Scribner's, 1951), 1:26–32.

Did the Jews Kill Jesus?

What are we to make, then, of the gospel accounts of Jesus' final days in Jerusalem, of the familiar Palm Sunday scene of Jesus' triumphal entry into the city amid shouts of joy and acclamation, and of the subsequent hostility of the crowd calling for Jesus to be crucified?[21] On the face of it, these accounts do not make for very good history. The Triumphal Entry is excellent literary theater, quite appropriate to the Christian view of the real significance of this climactic moment. But the scenario itself is not very plausible as actual history. That throngs would have even noticed an obscure Galilean riding into the city on a donkey, a common scene, after all, stretches reasonable credulity. And the trials of Jesus are notoriously fraught with historical difficulties that are not easily resolved.[22] However, that the scenes themselves offer no opportunity for the followers of Jesus to have witnessed any of these events first hand is enough to call into question the historicity of any of their details. And that final scene of mass betrayal, wherein the Jewish crowd declares its preference for Barabbas the criminal to Jesus the innocent victim, appears to have no basis in fact whatsoever. Aside from the gospels themselves, there is no evidence that Pilate or any other Roman governor in Palestine practiced such a tradition of releasing a prisoner at festive times.[23] This, too, must be regarded as literary theater, not history.

---

21. For a critical review of scholarship on the final days and death of Jesus, see Richard A. Horsley, "The Death of Jesus." Two major studies too recent for inclusion in Horsley's review are Raymond Brown's *The Death of the Messiah* (New York: Doubleday, 1994), and John Dominic Crossan's book-length critique of Brown's work, *Who Killed Jesus?* (San Francisco: HarperCollins, 1996).

22. See especially Paul Winter, *On the Trial of Jesus*, 2d ed., rev. and ed. T. A. Burkill and Geza Vermes (New York and Berlin: De Gruyter, 1974). Winter's work built on the earlier work of Hans Lietzmann, "Der Prozess Jesu," *Sitzungsberichte der Preussischen Akademie der Wissenschaften in Berlin* 14 (1931): 313–22. Lietzmann and Winter were particularly adamant that the trial before the Sanhedrin is not historical and is part of the anti-Jewish program operative in all the canonical gospels at this point. More recently Crossan (*Who Killed Jesus?* 82–111) has argued similarly using evidence from the Gospel of Peter, against the more positive evaluation of Brown (*Death of the Messiah*, 328–547). If there was a trial before the Sandehrin, could it have been held at night, as Mark 15:1 (and pars.) and John 18:28 imply, or on the eve of the Passover? According to the Mishna (Sanhedrin 4.1) this would have been forbidden in Jewish custom. The Mishna also requires that witnesses for the accused be brought forward (Sanhedrin 4.1); in the gospels' accounts no witnesses for Jesus are produced. According to the same Mishnaic code, any unanimous decision (see Mark 14:64) is to be nullified, to guard against a kangaroo court. And could the Sanhedrin execute someone or not (see John 18:31)? This is itself a much disputed question.

23. Winter, *Trial of Jesus*, 131–34. Some have argued (most recently Brown, *Death of the Messiah*, 814–20) that what the gospels report is a single instance of amnesty, not a custom. This, however, approaches the realm of special pleading for the historicity of the accounts.

All of this is to say, as we have said many times already, that these accounts, like all gospel stories, must be read first as narratives created in
particular times and places to speak to the needs of early Christian communities, not as literal history. What were the issues faced by the earliest
Christians in the wake of Jesus' death by crucifixion? The first and most obvious is the fact that they had begun to worship a person who was regarded
by most of the world around them as a criminal, rightfully tried and executed
by the authorities. Second, the fact that he was executed by crucifixion posed
its own peculiar difficulties. Crucifixion was a form of punishment reserved
for lower-class persons accused of sedition against the Roman order.[24] Such
beginnings would have had obvious implications for Roman officials wonder-
ing how to regard this new Jewish messianic movement. This issue would
have been complicated by the subsequent history of the Jewish people as a
whole, which came increasingly into conflict with Rome. In such an atmosphere, Jews accused of sedition, like Jesus, and their followers were above all
not to be trusted. And finally, there was the fact that Christians and other
Jews disagreed over the real significance of Jesus. For Christians he was the
Messiah; for other Jews he was not.

As Christians began to retell the story of Jesus' death to themselves and to
others, these concerns were ever at the fore. They wished to show that Jesus
was not in fact guilty of any crime and that he had been executed unjustly.
They wished to show that even Pilate, the Roman authority in charge, could
see that Jesus was innocent and posed no real threat to Rome. And they
wanted to show that the real problem lay not with Jesus, nor with Rome, but
with those Jews who had rejected Jesus, preferring instead the violent path of
a rebel, like Barabbas, to the way of Jesus.

Let us begin with the problem of Jesus' innocence. For most of his contemporaries, Jesus was obviously guilty of the crime of sedition. But to his
followers he was not. Rather, he was wrongly accused, unfairly tried, and
unjustly executed. For the followers of Jesus, all of them Jews familiar with
their ancient traditions, this was not an unfamiliar story. The Psalms, especially the Psalms of lamentation, continually give voice to the victim of
injustice, wrongly accused, betrayed, mocked, and forsaken. For many years
scholars who have studied the gospel accounts of Jesus' final days have noticed how much the Psalms (especially Psalm 22) supply the details for these

---

24. For the Roman nature of the punishment see Winter, *Trial of Jesus*, 90–96. For further
discussion, see Horsley, "The Death of Jesus," 409–13; also Martin Hengel, *Crucifixion in the
Ancient World and the Folly of the Message of the Cross* (Philadelphia: Fortress Press; London:
SCM, 1977).

scenes.[25] The authorities conspire to kill him (Mark 14:1, pars.; see Pss 31:4; 35:4; 38:12; 71:10). He is betrayed by his friends around a table (Mark 14:18, pars.; see Ps 41:9). In Gethsemane, in a scene no one could have witnessed, Jesus' own words are supplied by the psalmist: "My soul is full of sorrow . . ." (Mark 14:34, pars.; see Pss 42:6, 11; 43:5). At his trial false witnesses testify against him (Mark 14:56–59, pars.; see Pss 27:12; 35:11; 109:2), yet he stands silent before his accusers (Mark 14:61; 15:5, pars.; see Pss 38:14–16; 39:9). On the cross, Jesus' garments are divided (Mark 15:24, pars.; see Ps 22:18). He is mocked by passersby (Mark 15:29, pars.; see Pss 22:7; 109:25). He feels forsaken and so utters the first line of Psalm 22: "My God, my God, why hast thou forsaken me" (Mark 15:34, pars.; see Ps 22:1). Near the end, he is given vinegar to drink (Mark 15:36, pars.; see Ps 69:21). All of this is not mere coincidence. Nor is it the description of a great cosmic plan, ordained in scripture and fulfilled in Jesus. It is the skillful work of a Christian exegete, using the sacred traditions of Israel to give expression to his or her deepest convictions about the real significance of Jesus' death: he was not a criminal, guilty as charged, but an innocent victim like those who sing in the ancient psalms of Israel.[26]

It was just such a process that also produced the opening scene of the passion narrative, the Triumphal Entry. This time, however, it is not the Psalms that are invoked, but the prophets, specifically, an oracle from Zechariah:

> Rejoice greatly, O daughter of Zion!
> Shout aloud, O daughter of Jerusalem!
> Lo, your king comes to you;
>   triumphant and victorious is he,
> humble and riding on an ass,
>   on a colt, the foal of an ass. (Zech 9:9)

Mark opens the scene on the Mount of Olives (11:1), where, according to the prophet, God was to appear (Zech 14:14), or where, according to Josephus, the Messiah was expected to come in the latter days (*Ant.* xx.169). Then Jesus orders the colt, one "on which no one has ever sat" (11:2). The reader can see all of this unfolding in careful orchestration. As Jesus rides

---

25. The most influential early study is that of Barnabas Lindars, *New Testament Apologetic: The Doctrinal Significance of the Old Testament Quotations* (Philadelphia: Westminster, 1961), 75–137.

26. Early studies, like that of Lindars, assumed that the accounts were basically historical, but embellished with details from the psalms and elsewhere. More recently, the historicity of the accounts has been questioned in view of their narrative conformity to a literary type, or genre, from Jewish literature, the story of the Persecuted Righteous One. See especially George W. E. Nickelsburg, "The Genre and Function of the Markan Passion Narrative," *Harvard Theological Review* 73 (1980): 153–84.

into the city, the "daughters of Jerusalem" (in Mark simply "many") begin to shout their acclamation: "Hosanna! Blessed is the one who comes in the name of the Lord," words drawn, of course, from the Psalms (Ps 118:25–26). They are drawn from the traditional Passover Hallel (Pss 113–18), and are words that might have been sung by any pilgrim entering the city at Passover. But somehow the crowd sees that there is more to this pilgrim, and so continues the cheer: "Blessed is the kingdom [basileia] of our father David that is coming. Hosanna in the highest." The pilgrims' song becomes a welcome paean for the Messiah. But how could the crowd know this about Jesus, that he was the Messiah? Does every man on a colt remind them of Zechariah? How could they know that this was a colt "on which no one has ever sat"? How could they know that this little entourage had begun on the Mount of Olives? How could they know all of the things that the reader needs to have noted along the way in order to make this the royal arrival that Mark intends it to be? They could not, and yet they provide its theme music. History or musical theater? Rodgers and Hammerstein could not have orchestrated it better. This was the way early Christians used scripture to say what they had come to believe was really true about Jesus: he did not arrive in Jerusalem as a criminal, but as a king. This poetic use of scripture is certainly legitimate. It is how we use scripture even today to help us interpret events unfolding around us. But we should never pretend that the results of such acts of interpretation are history.

We now encounter two further concerns of early Christians in the wake of Jesus' death. Songs of a new empire (basileia) were not a welcome sound in the ears of Romans. Was Jesus a threat to the Empire? Were his followers? After all, he was crucified — no ordinary death. Crucifixion was a mode of torture reserved for peasant rebels. Its slow, agonizing manner of bringing on death was particularly effective at demonstrating what Roman officials wanted everyone to know about the inevitable fate of would-be revolutionaries. It was used with great frequency in Palestine, so that, presumably, everyone knew of its significance.[27] So was Jesus a rebel? The other concern has to do with the Jewish attitude toward Jesus. If he entered Jerusalem as the promised Messiah, how is it that so very few Jews came to acknowledge this as true? These two issues are complicated by the fact that within a generation after Jesus' death, the Jewish people would be spiraling toward a violent revolution against Rome. This is the setting within which accounts of Jesus' trial must be considered.

---

27. For example, about the time Jesus was born, Varus, the Roman legate at Antioch, quashed a mass rebellion against further Herodian rule by crucifying two thousand of the insurrectionists at one time (Josephus, War ii.66–75; Ant. xvii.288–95).

In the story of Jesus' trial, the Roman role is filled, of course, by Pilate. It is he, who, through the narrative, must address the concerns of Romans about this new movement. The Jewish role is filled by the Jewish officials, on the one hand, and the Jewish crowd on the other. It is they who again, through the narrative, must address the question of the Jewish response to Jesus. All of these figures — Pilate, the Jewish officials, and the crowd — are historical figures. But their real-life historicity should not be confused with the *roles* they play as characters in this narrative drama, the purpose of which was to work out the issues facing the Christian community in the years following Jesus' death.

Pilate's role in the drama is transparently simple. In spite of the fact that Jesus has just symbolically destroyed the Temple, the center of religious and political life in Jerusalem, which would have been understood as an affront to both Jewish and Roman authority; in spite of the fact that he has come to Jerusalem proclaiming the advent of a new empire, implying, of course, that the current Empire might leave something to be desired; and in spite of the fact that Jesus has done all of these things during Passover, the annual celebration of Israel's delivery from Egyptian bondage, the symbolism of which could hardly have been missed — in spite of all this, Pilate evidently harbors no suspicions about Jesus whatsoever and regards him as an innocent victim. He appears vaguely dissatisfied with the chief priests' accusations (Mark 15:2–5). He tries to release Jesus, but the crowd, agitated against Jesus by the chief priests, will not hear of it (Mark 15:6–11). He questions the crowd's demand for a crucifixion, saying, "Well, what has he done wrong?" (Mark 15:14). In the end, he orders Jesus crucified just to please the mob (Mark 15:15). His attitude toward Jesus is ambivalent at worst, benign at best. He clearly does not regard him as a threat to the Empire. If there is any doubt about this, Matthew tries to clear it up once and for all by washing Pilate's hands of the affair, literally (Matt 27:24). Luke also avoids any ambivalence by giving Pilate a few more lines, addressed to the "chief priests, the rulers, and the people":

> You brought me this man as one who was leading the people astray, and after examining him before you, behold, I did not find this man guilty of any of your charges against him. . . . I will therefore punish and release him. (Luke 23:14, 16)

But in the end he relents, as in Mark, at the insistence of the throng, and allows him to be crucified. In John it is the same. Pilate seeks to release Jesus, but eventually buckles under pressure from the Jews who have arrested him (John 18:28–19:16).

Historically, all of this would be rather unlikely. Pilate has plenty of reasons to be wary of Jesus, and yet he is swayed by the crowd. Pilate...swayed by the crowd?! As Crossan has recently so aptly put it, brutal crowd control was one of Pilate's specialties.[28] But this is not history. It is narrative intended to address the question of whether Romans ought to be concerned about Jesus and his followers. The answer is clearly, "no." If Pilate was not concerned, why should anyone else be? Jesus was innocent; so are Christians; even Pilate could see that. As Jews, Christians, and Romans all spiraled toward the Jewish war in the latter half of the first century, it was probably important for Christians to say that, even if it was not true. Jesus *was* a threat to the Empire, and Pilate was probably smart enough to realize that.

But what about the Jews? How shall we explain their role in these stories? There were two issues concerning Jews, Christians, and Romans brewing in the latter half of the first century. One, of course, had to do with Jews and Christians. The former had rejected the latter's claims about Jesus. The second had to do with Jews and Romans. Recall that their mutual relations were in steady decline throughout the first century, until, in the 60s, all-out war would break out. The Jews would lose this struggle for independence from Rome and in the process see their holy city, Jerusalem — the holy city also of Christians — destroyed. Both of these issues are addressed through the role of "the Jews" in the stories around Jesus' death.

In these narratives we come to some of the most tragic literature in the history of Jewish-Christian relations. For in them we find the Christian claim that it was the Jews who were really responsible for the death of Jesus. It is at the insistence of the Jews that Pilate finally gives in and has Jesus crucified. We have already seen how historically implausible this is. The idea that Pilate would have seen no threat in Jesus is not very likely. Nor is the notion that Pilate would have bent to the will of a Jewish mob against his own better judgment. Moreover, the scenario in which the Jews ask for Jesus' crucifixion involves a supposed custom for which there is no evidence: the so-called *privilegium paschal* (the privilege of amnesty granted to a single prisoner during Passover, referred to in Mark 15:6 and John 18:39–40).[29] In this well-known scene, Pilate asks the Jews whom he should release, Jesus or Barabbas? They choose Barabbas over Jesus. Barabbas is a rebel "who had committed murder in the insurrection" (Mark 15:7).[30] That Pilate would have released such a

---

28. *Who Killed Jesus?* 111.

29. See n. 23 above.

30. That Barabbas was in fact a historical figure has itself been questioned. The name is quite peculiar. Literally, it means "son of the father." Is Barabbas the literary alter ego of Jesus created by Mark or some other early Christian? Abba is also a very common name; Bar Abba might

character during the volatile time of Passover, especially at the insistence of a Jewish mob(!), is not very likely. And so we are reminded once more that this is not history, but narrative designed to address issues facing the Christian community.

What is accomplished in this scene with respect to the issues facing the church in the first century? First, it establishes an etiology, a point of origin for the Jewish rejection of the church's claims about Jesus. They rejected him from the very beginning. Jewish opposition to Christianity is rooted, by this account, in Jewish opposition to Jesus himself. Like their Jesus, an innocent victim of the Jewish mob, the church now suffers the fate of the innocent victim. In John, where the plot against Jesus is inspired when Jesus makes certain claims about himself (see John 5:18), this is most clear. Jesus' conflict with the Jews mirrors exactly the conflict Christians are having in John's day with the synagogue (see esp. 9:22; 12:42; and 16:2).[31] But in Mark and the synoptic gospels the function of the story of the Jewish mob is just as evident. Just as the church struggles to convince the Jews of Jesus' real identity, so also Jesus tries to convince them in the text. But he fails. A psalm is appropriated to give expression to the disappointment Christians felt about this:

> The very stone which the builders rejected
>   has become the head of the corner;
> This is the Lord's doing,
>   and it is marvelous in their eyes.
>   (Ps 118:22–23; see Mark 12:10, pars.)

But in Mark (followed by Matthew and Luke), where the Barabbas episode plays a role, there seems to be an additional message. In the Barabbas story, the Jews choose Barabbas, the murderous insurrectionist, over Jesus, the peaceful, innocent victim. This is more than mere irony. In this scenario there is veiled recrimination. It begins earlier in the story, when the narrative first begins to get serious about the Jews' rejection of Jesus. If we back up to Mark, chapter 12, we find Jesus telling a story to the Jewish leaders in Jerusalem (Mark 12:1–12; the setting is provided by 11:27). This story was originally a parable, told by Jesus in another time and place. But now it has been allegorized to fit into Mark's final complex scenario.[32] In this allegorized version of

---

have sounded something like "Joe Smith." Is Barabbas, then, a symbolic "anyone," whose literary function is to suggest that the Jews would have chosen anyone, even a rebel, instead of Jesus?

31. This is the widely held historical-critical view of John presented by J. Louis Martyn, *History and Theology in the Fourth Gospel*, 2d ed., rev. (Nashville: Abingdon, 1979).

32. For the details on how Mark has allegorized the parable see Bernard Brandon Scott, *Hear, Then, the Parable* (Minneapolis: Fortress Press, 1989), 238–41; see also chapter 4, pp. 138–39.

the parable, the vineyard has become Jerusalem, the evil, murderous tenants the Jews, and the murdered son Jesus. Now, remember when Mark is writing. There is a war on. Jerusalem itself may be under siege, or even destroyed. In this setting Mark transforms the parable of the Tenants into an allegory for how it was that Jerusalem came to be in such dire straits. The Jews, the evil tenants, had rejected Jesus, the son. And to make sure that everyone gets this point, Mark adds these words at the end of the story: "What will the owner of the vineyard do? He will come and destroy the tenants, and give the vineyard to others" (Mark 12:9). Because the Jewish leaders in Jerusalem rejected Jesus, Jerusalem will be lost, says Mark. As Mark's telling of the parable concludes, we soon see that this is woven into the Jewish plot to have Jesus arrested and crucified (Mark 12:12). This plot, which began in 11:18, where Jesus angers the chief priests and scribes with his criticism of the Temple, comes to fruition a few chapters later when these same leaders incite the Jewish mob to ask for the release of Barabbas, the insurrectionist, rather than Jesus. Here is the recrimination. As Mark writes, Jerusalem is being lost. And why? Because the Jews refused to listen to Jesus, and in the end chose Barabbas, the murderous insurrectionist, over Jesus, the Prince of Peace.

It is important for Christians to see all of this in its proper context. These stories are not historical. They come from a time when the followers of Jesus were still a tiny sect within Jewish life and culture. It was a time of war, conflict, and suffering on all sides. Within that conflict, what we hear today as a Christian voice in our gospels was in fact a tiny minority voice critical of an overwhelming majority. They were saying that none of this would have happened if the Jewish people, their own people, had only listened to Jesus. Perhaps they were right. Perhaps they were not; perhaps conflict with Rome would have broken out much sooner had this been the case. In any event, hindsight is always 20/20. And lest one get carried away by the perfection of the vision, we must always remember that it did not really happen that way. The Jews did not kill Jesus. Pilate did not wash his hands. A crowd of Jews did not say in unison, "His blood be upon us and upon our children."

What did really happen? Most of the details of Jesus' final days will never be known to us; most of what we would like to know is lost in time. We can only make educated guesses about what really happened. We know that Jesus spoke of a new empire, the Empire of God. We know that such a word would not have been well-received by those whose stake in *the* Empire was greatest. We can guess that Jesus did come to Jerusalem, and very likely it was at Passover. And we can guess that once there, he did not change his mind about things. He, like other pilgrims, probably visited the Temple, and saw in it what other Jews of his station would have seen: the seat of power.

It was the locus of imperial co-optation. Through it flowed taxes and tribute. And yet it was also to him, as to other Jews, a holy place, the symbol of God's presence with the people of Israel. This irony may have struck a sour chord with him. Here, more clearly than anywhere, he would have experienced the frustrating incongruity between the Empire that cynically brokered power and privilege to the elite of the elite, and his vision of the brokerless Empire of God. That he criticized the Temple and did something that demonstrated his dismay is very likely.[33] This in itself would have been enough to get Jesus arrested. First to notice him would have been the priestly officials — although it could just as well have been a Roman centurion watching the crowd for signs of trouble. Jesus was eventually crucified by Roman authorities.[34] If this is so, we can well imagine that there was a trial — as much of a trial as any angry peasant idealist could be expected to receive. If Jesus *could* still speak, one can guess that he spoke then as on other occasions of his new Empire of God. And so he was executed for political sedition under a placard reading "King of the Jews," a serious accusation couched in irony.[35]

Lessons Learned?

The death of Jesus was a shocking event for the followers of Jesus, an event filled with pathos and trauma. As such it soon became a seminal event, a watershed over which would pass generations of Christian experience and reflection. For early Christians engaged in continuing Jesus' struggle against the Empire and its values, his death became a martyr's death worthy of imitation. Like Jesus, they were called to die as martyrs faithful to the cause of the Empire of God. For the unclean and marginalized who continued to be a part of the Jesus movement, his spilled blood became the atoning sacrifice that cleansed them, washed them "whiter than snow." But the interpretation of Jesus' death has not always been benignly applied. Many have been called to

---

33. This seems to be the one thing that almost everyone can agree upon. See, for example, Sanders, *Jesus and Judaism*, 61–76; Crossan, *The Historical Jesus*, 355–60; Horsley, *Jesus and the Spiral of Violence*, 292–300; Marcus Borg, *Jesus, A New Vision* (San Francisco: Harper & Row, 1987), 174–76. For a contrary view, however, see Robert J. Miller, "Historical Method and the Deeds of Jesus: The Test Case of the Temple Destruction," *Forum* 8, nos. 1–2 (1992): 5–30.

34. This much is assured by Tacitus, *Annals* 15.44, and Josephus, *Ant.* xviii.63 (see chapter 1, pp. 15–16 above).

35. I have already noted that crucifixion was a form of execution reserved for seditious, lower-class challengers to Roman authority. The charge "king of the Jews" is also political in nature, and suggests sedition. On the historicity of the placard on the cross, see Horsley, "The Death of Jesus," 413–14.

die in the name of Jesus, but for causes far less than his. And atonement the-ology has found other homes, not among the unclean and marginalized, but among the well-off and prominent seeking absolution from sin without having to bear the consequences. In the narratives we have just studied, Jesus' death became an occasion for finger-pointing and recrimination that has proven to be most unfortunate for Christian history. When mixed with subsequent de-velopments in the unfolding history of the church, these stories became the main ingredient in a volatile mixture of Christian anti-Semitism. We cannot read them today without taking into account this tragic history.

Historically, Jesus was killed at the hands of Roman imperial forces. To be sure, there were Jewish officials in Jerusalem who would have played a role in his demise. But they, too, were part of the imperial system, a system that was ultimately not Jewish, but Gentile. Yet, in our stories of Jesus' death, the Gentile players are exonerated, while the Jewish players receive all the fault. Moreover, the scope of Jewish involvement is expanded to include not just a few leaders, but a whole crowd of Jews assembled from all over the Jewish world for the Passover celebration in Jerusalem. We can understand how this happened. Christians, who still would have thought of themselves as Jews, were angry with their cousins for having rejected the one whom they regarded as the true Messiah. Jesus, in their view, was as much the victim of those who should have accepted him, but didn't, as he was the victim of Pilate. At the same time, these Christians wanted to avoid antagonizing the Gentile world of Rome, in which they would, like everyone else, soon have to make their way. So Pilate gets off the hook. He washes his hands of the whole affair.

All of this might have turned out to be quite harmless had Christianity remained a Jewish sectarian movement. But it did not. By the end of the first century the trickle of Gentiles seeping into the church from the very be-ginning had become a flood. Very soon Christianity would become a Gentile religion, not a Jewish sect. Jesus would become one of us, not one of them. No longer really a Jew, he became *our* savior and entered the Gentile world of Christianity. This set the stage for these passion narratives to work per-versity in the heart of Christianity. For Jesus, the Jewish victim of a Gentile empire, now became Jesus, the Christian victim of a Jewish mob. This is the origin of Christian anti-Semitism. This subtle shift made it possible for Gen-tile Christians to see Jews as the source and cause of all their problems, to assert that in spite of what may appear to be true on the surface, in fact it is we Christians who are the victims of the Jews. This sort of scapegoating has ever been at the center of anti-Semitism. The passion narratives could aid and abet this prevarication when they were removed from their origin in an internecine Jewish struggle and claimed for a Gentile church, eager to prove its religious and moral superiority over Judaism. These narratives, with their accusations against the Jewish mob, could now be joined to a history of Gentile anti-Semitism, giving it a new religious vigor. One wonders, given all that has transpired between Christians and Jews over the two millennia since Jesus' death, whether Christians can ever safely use these narratives again.

If this is to be possible at all, it will have to be with a very keen sense of history and perspective. Jesus was killed by an imperial juggernaut into which almost everyone was swept up in great enthusiasm. His death had nothing to do with the struggle between Judaism and Christianity. It had to do with the struggle between those who have power and those who do not; between those who enjoy easy access to food, clothing, housing, and various of life's pleasures and those who must make do without almost everything; between those who live at the center of things and those who exist at the margins. Jesus offered a word of criticism, shot like an arrow from outside the city wall into the heart of his culture. His word hit home, and it stung. For that he was killed. The meaning of Jesus' death is to be found in this struggle, not in the struggle of Christianity to triumph over Judaism. His death can become an event that "saves us from aimlessness and sin" whenever we understand it as a call to stand against unprincipled power and to enact a word of love for those who experience well-being least in our own culture. In his book *Galilean Journey*, Virgilio Elizondo writes of the significance of Jesus' final days in Jerusalem in a way that reflects the struggle that engulfed Jesus:

> If the liberating way of Jesus had stopped in Galilee, we would be forced to agree with the critics of Christianity who claim that religion is but the opium of the masses. But Jesus did not stop there. He made it known in no uncertain terms that he *had* to go to Jerusalem....
>
> In our times, and in all times, Christ has to go his way to Jerusalem. Again he has to face the structures of oppression in today's world. As his Galilean followers were called to go with him, so today his follow-ers are likewise called to go with him and in him to the Jerusalems of today's world. God chooses disciples not just to make them feel good, but for a mission. "I have chosen you to go out and bear much fruit" (John 15:16). To accept God's election is not a passive privilege, but an active mission. It is a call to be prophetic in both deeds and words. It is a call to live a new alternative in the world and to invite others to this new way.[36]

---

36. Virgilio Elizondo, *Galilean Journey: The Mexican-American Promise* (Maryknoll, N.Y.: Orbis, 1983), 104.

Chapter 7

Was Jesus Right?

On the Meaning of Resurrection

Instead of taking men's freedom from them, Thou didst make it greater than ever! Didst Thou forget that man prefers peace, and even death, to freedom of choice in the knowledge of good and evil? Nothing is more seductive for man than his freedom of conscience, but nothing is a greater cause of suffering. And behold, instead of giving a firm foundation for setting the conscience of man at rest forever, Thou didst choose all that is exceptional, vague, and enigmatic; Thou didst choose what was utterly beyond the strength of men, acting as though thou didst not love them at all — Thou, who didst come to give Thy life for them! Instead of taking possession of men's freedom, Thou didst increase it, and burdened the spiritual kingdom of mankind with its sufferings forever. Thou didst desire man's free love, that he should follow Thee freely, enticed and taken captive by Thee. . . . But didst Thou not know he would at last reject even Thy image and Thy truth, if he is weighed down by the fearful burden of free choice? They will cry aloud at last that the truth is not in Thee, for they could not have been left in greater confusion and suffering than Thou has caused, laying upon them so many cares and unanswerable problems.

So that in truth, Thou didst Thyself lay the foundation for the destruction of Thy kingdom, and no one is more to blame for it. Yet what was offered Thee? There are three powers, three powers alone, able to conquer and hold captive forever the conscience of these impotent rebels for their happiness — those forces are miracle, mystery and authority. . . .

And so we have corrected Thy work and have founded it upon miracles, mystery and authority. And men rejoiced that they were again like sheep, and that terrible gift that had brought them such suffering, was, at last, lifted from their hearts.

— FYODOR DOSTOEVSKY,
The Grand Inquisitor (1880)

The Resurrection Question

Why did early Christians first come to say that God had raised Jesus from the dead? For many a Christian believer, the answer to this question seems so obvious that it renders the question itself ridiculous, or, to some, even blasphemous. According to the gospel accounts, Christians encountered Jesus shortly after his death, saw that he was same Jesus they had known before, and so became convinced, as anyone would, that he had arisen from the grave. This view assumes that the gospels are historical reports of what actually happened, a view that is held with comforting confidence by many Christians today.

But the historian of early Christianity cannot take so comforting a view. The contradictions inherent in the reports themselves are enough to trouble even the casual reader. For example, who discovered the empty tomb where Jesus had been laid? Was it Mary Magdalene (John), Mary Magdalene and another Mary (Matthew), Mary Magdalene, Mary the mother of James, and Salome (Mark), or Mary Magdalene, Johanna, Mary the mother of James, and certain unnamed "others" (Luke)? And did she (they) report what she (they) had found (Matthew, Luke, John) or not (Mark)?[1] After the resurrection, did Jesus appear to the disciples (Matthew, Luke, John) or not (Mark)? And if he did appear to them, was it in Galilee (Matthew) or in Jerusalem (Luke, John).[2] And in the end, did Jesus ascend into heaven (Luke) or not (Matthew, John)? These and many other inconsistencies have been noted many times since the Deist Hermann Samuel Reimarus first catalogued them in the eighteenth century.[3] Reimarus is pretty sobering reading if you have

---

This chapter was first offered as a paper to the Jesus Seminar, meeting in Santa Rosa, Calif., on March 3, 1995.

1. Note that most scholars believe that Mark originally ended with 16:8; 16:9–15 are late and come from another hand.

2. Note that John 21 is considered by most scholars to be a late addition to the original text of John. Even, so, if John 21 is included, the appearance by the Sea of Tiberius is not at all similar to the mountaintop appearance in Matthew.

3. *Reimarus: Fragments*, ed. Charles H. Talbert, trans. Ralph S. Fraser (Philadelphia: For-

never seriously considered how well the gospels would stand up in court under the normal rules of evidence. On the particular matter of the resurrection, the four gospels agree on almost nothing. Even so, these evidential problems pale when compared to the even larger metaphysical, or just plain *physical*, problems such as the fate of Jesus' body after it was resuscitated and restored to life. What became of it when he ascended? Is it still here somewhere? Did it go up into space and disintegrate in the outer reaches of the atmosphere?

In mentioning these things, I do not mean to mock those who believe in the literal truth of all they read in the gospels. I only mean to point out why historical critical scholars of the Bible have maintained for more than a century that the gospels are not history, and in fact were never intended to be read as such. Among such scholars there are many, like myself, who are confessing Christians. There are even some, like myself, who still believe in the resurrection.

The resurrection narratives at the end of the gospels are of little historical value. They do have value in their own right, but that value must be measured within the context and self-ordered design in which each is presented to us. They derive from the second or third Christian generation, thirty-five to seventy-five years after the death of Jesus. In terms of the history of the resurrection tradition, they all represent relatively late developments in Christian thinking about the resurrection. If we are to look at the earlier stages of this tradition, even the earliest stages, we must look elsewhere, to the apostle Paul, the first Christian voice we hear in the New Testament. Fortunately, however, Paul was not living in a vacuum, creating *ex nihilo* everything he said and did on behalf of his fledgling churches. He knows and makes use of earlier traditions: early hymns, prayers, sayings of Jesus. In 1 Corinthians 15 he makes use of what appear to be the earliest Christian traditions about the death and resurrection of Jesus. If we want to know how it was that the earliest Christians first began to say "God has raised Jesus from the dead," it is here that we must begin.

The Limits of Historical Investigation

The text in question is 1 Cor 15:3–8. This complex of older traditions and Pauline commentary reads as follows:

---

tress Press, 1970), 153–97. Reimarus's "Fragmenta" were originally published posthumously and anonymously in 1774–78.

3For I delivered to you as of first importance what I also received:
   That Christ died for our sins, in accordance with the scriptures;
   4That he was buried;
   That he was raised on the third day, in accordance with
      the scriptures.
   5And that he appeared to Cephas, then to the Twelve;
   6Then he appeared to more than 500 brothers at one time
      (most of whom are still alive, though some have died);
   7Then he appeared to James and all the apostles.
8Last of all, as to one untimely born, he appeared to me.

Not every aspect of these verses is available for historical analysis. It is important at the outset to acknowledge both the limits and the possibilities in this approach. First the limits.

Paul presents this material not as history, but as preaching (vv. 1–3a). This does not mean that he thinks these things did not really happen; he simply realizes that he cannot prove that they are historically true. They may only be believed or rejected. In the end his only recourse is to say "so we preached and so you believed" (v. 11). The statements themselves reflect this insofar as they come to us in creedal form, as is widely recognized. Their content also necessitates an acknowledgment of historical limitations. The use of passive verbs in these formulations, as is also widely recognized, reflects the *passivum divinum*, that is, the use of the passive voice to avoid making direct reference to God.[4] This is common in ancient Jewish literature. Paul asserts that it is God who has raised Jesus from the dead and who has made him to appear to various persons. So Paul here means to speak, in part, about transcendent realities, things done by God. The historian cannot assess truth claims made about the transcendent realm.

On the other hand, Paul here speaks, in part, of very human things. These provide possibilities for the historian. First, he is reporting things that people have said. The historian can ask who said them, when they said them, and why. Second, Paul speaks here of things which God has done *to real people*: Peter, James, Paul himself, and less concretely the "Twelve," the "apostles," and five hundred or more other unnamed persons. The historian

---

4. "He was raised" (*egegertai*) in v. 4b and "he appeared" (*ophthe*) in vv. 5–8 both translate passive verbs in the original Greek. The second of these verbs is difficult to translate. *Ophthe* is the third person aorist passive form of *horao*, meaning "to see." So it could mean simply "he was seen." But when in the LXX it is used with a dative object, as it is here, it customarily represents a visionary, theophanic experience. In formulating the sentence in this way, its author seems to place Jesus' appearances alongside those of Yahweh to Moses, the prophets and the like, suggesting that God is the somehow involved in this action as well.

might ask whether these persons had actual experiences which they took to
be postresurrection appearances of Jesus. I will pose each of these questions
in turn.

Jesus Was Raised...

Two Distinct Traditions

It is commonly noted that 1 Cor 15:3–8 contains pre-Pauline creedal formulations that were repeated some time before Paul uses them here. There
is little dispute that vv. 3–4 are traditional and pre-Pauline. Some, however,
argue that this creedal statement also included v. 5a. On vv. 5–7 the field
is divided. Many maintain that Paul has collected this information himself,
others that it, too, is traditional, with the exception of Paul's own comment
in v. 6b. Verse 8 is Paul's own statement about his experience, and so is not
traditional.[5] My own view is that vv. 3–4 are an early creedal statement.
It consists of a series of formulaic clauses, each introduced with the con-
junction *hoti* ("that").[6] That each is punctuated by the phrase "according to
the scriptures," indicates that this is an exegetical tradition, surprisingly early
though it may be. Already before the middle of the first century followers of
Jesus have been searching the scriptures in order to come to terms with Jesus'
death. Verses 5–7 (less v. 6b) are also traditional. This is shown, again, by
the formulaic repetition of the adverb *epeita/eita* ("then") and the verb *ophthe*
("he appeared"). Together they form a separate "appearance" tradition.[7] This

---

5. For a review of the discussion see Reginald Fuller, *The Formation of the Resurrection Narratives* (Philadelphia: Fortress Press, 1971), 9–14; also Paul Hoffmann, "Auferstehung Jesu Christi:
II/1. Neues Testament," *Theologische Realenzyklopädie* 1, 491.

6. So Jean Héring, *The First Epistle of St. Paul to the Corinthians* (London: Epworth, 1962),
158. However, he does not agree that vv. 5–7 are also traditional (see below).

7. For vv. 5–7 as a separate "appearance" tradition see Fuller, *Formation*, 13–14 and 15–49
passim, following U. Wilckens, "Der Ursprung der Überlieferung der Erscheinungen des Auferstandenen," 56–95, in W. Joest and W. Pannenberg, eds., *Dogmen und Denkstrukturen*, Festschrift
E. Schlink (Göttingen: Vandenhoeck & Ruprecht, 1963); also *Die Missionsreden der Apostelge-
schichte* (Neukirchen: Neukirchener Verlag, 1960), 74–80. In my view, v. 5 in its entirety belongs
to this second tradition. The use of *ophthe* ("*he appeared*") clearly ties these three verses together;
Paul himself has probably added *hoti* at the beginning of v. 5 to provide a smooth transition between the two traditions he uses here. That a final appearance clause would not be necessary to
fill out the death, burial, resurrection sequence in vv. 3–4 is shown by the pre-Pauline tradition
in Phil 2:6–11, which proceeds directly from death to exaltation, with no mention of appearances whatsoever. The idea that v. 5a *must* be included with the tradition in vv. 3–4 is perhaps
connected with the assumption that it was the appearances that gave rise to the resurrection
proclamation in the first place. In what follows I intend to challenge this assumption. But one
can see already in vv. 3–4 that this is not the case. The claims made in these verses are not

second tradition is not exegetical, but experiential: its claims are based on experiences persons are said to have had of the risen Jesus.

However one reconstructs the pre-Pauline formulae, it is enough to recognize that there are two different types of assertions here that should not be conflated too facilely. This is underscored by the divergent forms in vv. 3–4 and 5–7 and the resulting likelihood that they come originally from two different and distinct creedal formulae. Their content is also different and distinct. The first set of formulae makes statements about the death and resurrection of Jesus; the second set makes statements about Jesus appearing to people after his death. These are not the same thing and they need not necessarily be connected. In fact, in the Pauline letters they are *not* normally connected. For example, in Romans 6, perhaps Paul's most developed statement on the significance of Jesus' death and resurrection, there is no talk of appearances to Paul or to anyone else. Or alternatively, when Paul refers to his own "appearance" experience (1 Cor 9:1; Gal 1:15–16) he does not relate it to the resurrection. Its significance is in relation to his commission to preach, not as a proof for the resurrection of Jesus. Finally, the two sets of formulae are grounded differently. The first represents an exegetical tradition ("according to the scriptures"). The second does not, but, presumably, is grounded in experiences people are said to have had. For the moment, I will confine myself to the first set of formulae, the resurrection tradition.

The Resurrection Tradition

That the death and resurrection statements reflect a distinct confessional tradition, at least among the Pauline churches, is demonstrated by the repeated appearance of a two-member formula throughout the Pauline letters.[8] Paul makes use of it in Gal 2:19–20; Rom 6:3–4; 7:4; and 14:9. It occurs in its simplest form in 1 Thess 4:14: "we believe that Jesus died and arose." But a still more basic form is also found throughout the Pauline corpus, one which focuses only on the resurrection itself. It appears in various versions, including (1) a participial construction (Rom 4:24; 8:11a, b; 2 Cor 4:14; Gal 1:1), describing God as "the one who raised him [Jesus] from the dead..."; (2) a simple finite construction (Rom 10:9; 1 Cor 6:14; 15:15): "God raised him [Jesus] from the dead"; and (3) a relative construction ·modifying Jesus

---

grounded in experiences of the risen Jesus, but in scripture and the work of exegesis ("according to the scriptures").

8. For a summary of the form-critical discussion see Hoffmann, "Auferstehung Jesu Christi," 483–85.

(1 Thess 1:10): "whom he [God] raised from the dead." All three of these forms share the following set of common elements:

1. the use of *egeiro* ("to raise") with God as the subject or implied actor;

2. the expression *ek nekron* ("from the dead");

3. the use of the simple name "Jesus."[9]

From this form-critical analysis one can see that in its simplest form, the resurrection tradition is very primitive. This is shown by its explicit *theological* rather than *christological* focus. The actor is always God; Jesus (never referred to as "Christ" in this tradition) is the recipient of divine action. The idea that God would intervene to vindicate a faithful, yet unjustly killed martyr is an old and well-rehearsed idea in Jewish tradition.[10] Such a statement would have been possible on the day Jesus was executed, presupposing nothing more than the idea that a righteous person had been killed.

The Origin of the Resurrection Tradition

This brings us to the question of the origin of the resurrection tradition. Why did early Christians first say something like "God raised Jesus from the dead"?

The most obvious answer might be that they had heard stories about the resurrection. But, as many have observed, it is a peculiar thing about the early Christian tradition that, with the possible exception of the patently late story in Gos Pet 10:38–11:43, there is not a single account of the resurrection in all of early Christian literature. With the entombment of Jesus on one side and the empty tomb and postresurrection appearances on the other, the resurrection itself stands as a black hole in the middle of the tradition. It is simply never described. Leaving aside any theological point to be made from this, historically we can say with confidence that such stories were clearly not the basis of the early Christian claim that God had raised Jesus from the dead, because, so far as we know, there are none.

What we do have, of course, are appearance stories in abundance, from which the resurrection might have been inferred. But, as I have already noted in passing, the appearance and resurrection traditions are not usually presented in tandem. In this respect 1 Cor 15:3–8 is a bit misleading in its explicit use of the appearance tradition to reinforce belief in the resurrection. Paul does this under the extraordinary circumstance of needing to present

---

9. For a summary of the form-critical discussion see ibid., 479–80.
10. See the discussion below.

an overwhelming argument for the resurrection of Jesus, and then only in the service of his larger aim to convince the Corinthians of his belief in the general resurrection of the dead. And even here Paul shows that such an argument is precariously constructed when he reverts to the only real basis for his claim in v. 11: "so we preach and so you believed."[11] For Paul there really are no proofs for the resurrection claim aside from the active faith of communities, which are themselves the "body of Christ."

The appearance stories are not normally used in the tradition to prove that the resurrection is true. Rather, they are presented as a sign of commissioning to preach the gospel. This is true of Paul, as we shall see presently, but also of the gospels. In both Matthew and Luke, the climax of the appearance scene is the commissioning of the disciples to go out and preach, to continue the work of Jesus.[12] Even in John 20, where proof of the resurrection seems to be at issue, John shows his extreme discomfort with the idea of using the appearance tradition in this way with his final telling comment, placed on the lips of Jesus himself, "Have you believed because you have seen me? Blessed are those who have *not* seen and yet believe" (John 20:29).

If the appearance tradition is usually taken as a sign of commissioning to preach the gospel, then we can well understand why Paul, the fourth evangelist, and others would have been reluctant to base their faith in the resurrection on the appearance stories. The earliest simple resurrection formula does not presuppose the appearance tradition. Rather, it is quite the opposite: the appearance tradition, with its orientation to the commissioning of disciples to preach, presupposes the resurrection tradition. After all, before anyone could be commissioned to preach, there had to be a gospel to preach. What was that gospel? That Jesus, who was crucified, had been raised by God from the dead — or so we might roughly summarize Paul's version of it. Thus, if we look carefully at *how these traditions are actually used* in the early church, we find that conceptually (if not also chronologically) the simple, primitive resurrection tradition has priority over the appearance tradition. In this sense, it is very unlikely that the resurrection proclamation arose in response to stories of Jesus' appearance. What, then, was the basis for the early Christian claim that God raised Jesus from the dead?

The answer lies in the nature of the resurrection claim itself. In Jewish tradition the idea that God would raise someone from the dead arose when Jews faced the disturbing reality that just and righteous people are some-

---

11. Willi Marxsen, *The Resurrection of Jesus of Nazareth* (Philadelphia: Fortress Press, 1970), 108–9.

12. As noted in ibid., 83–84.

times killed at the hands of their foes. In Isaiah 24–27 the prophetic voice utters a protest against the demise of faithful Jews: all who have died for Yahweh's sake shall someday be restored. In Dan 12:1–3 the context is again martyrological. In texts associated more with early Judaism, such as 1 Enoch 22–27 (third century B.C.E.); 1 Enoch 92–105 (second century B.C.E.); Jubilees 23:11–31 (second century B.C.E.); 2 Maccabees 7 (late second century B.C.E.); 4 Maccabees 7:3; 9:22; 13:17 et al. (first century C.E.); Wisdom of Solomon 1–6 (first century B.C.E.–first century C.E.); 2 Baruch 49–51 (first century C.E.); 4 Ezra 7 (first century C.E.) — whether a strict concept of resurrection is embraced, or, as in some of the later of these texts, something like redemption of immortal souls is implied — in this great variety of expressions, the fundamental existential concern is always the same: what happens to just and righteous people done in by a world full of injustice?[13] The very idea of resurrection arose in spurts and starts as Israel found itself suffering under successive episodes of foreign domination, during which just and righteous people were killed unjustly. Whether one needed or believed in the idea at all might well depend on how one felt about those domineering guests. So it was that in the first century, groups like the Sadducees, who were closely aligned with Roman authority, had no use for the idea of resurrection. But Pharisees, who greatly resented Roman rule, did. The followers of Jesus certainly would have agreed with the Pharisees on at least this point.

So the *presupposition* for any claim about resurrection is not appearance stories, empty tombs, and the like. Resurrection, as vindication, presupposes only that a righteous person has been killed in faithfulness to a divine cause. In a dissident Jewish context, this is all you need. The followers of Jesus could have said "God raised Jesus from the dead" on the day he died, and probably did. The only necessary presupposition for such a statement is the conviction that, should Jesus be killed, God *would* raise him from the dead. This conviction is one which Jesus' followers would have had the minute they decided that he was right about God and began to participate in the imperial rule of God that he proclaimed. Resurrection is the vindication of a life lost to the forces of injustice in the world. To the extent that Jesus' followers embraced his life as God's own work, the resurrection proclamation would have arisen quite naturally as the appropriate Jewish response to his untimely death.

In the traditional Jewish liturgy, the second of the Eighteen Benedictions says, "Blessed are you, Yahweh, who makes the dead to live." This is not very

---

13. For this litany of texts and a helpful discussion see George Nickelsburg, "Resurrection," *Anchor Bible Dictionary* 5:685–87.

far from the simple early Christian formulation, "God, who raised Jesus from the dead." Paul, in fact, uses the second benediction itself in Rom 4:17.[14] Such parallels suggest a setting in the life of the early church for this early formula: worship. If this is so, then with some imagination it becomes very easy to reconstruct when, where, and why the followers of Jesus first came to say something like "God raised Jesus from the dead." Following Jesus' death, his followers would have continued their practice of gathering, probably around a meal-setting, to speak of what they had heard and experienced in the company of Jesus. In the context of this nascent Christian worship, prayers would have been uttered in the traditional Jewish way. Among them one certainly would have heard something like, "Blessed are you, Yahweh, who raised Jesus from the dead."[15] They would have said this because they believed that Jesus had died for a divine cause. Later, they might even have sung a hymn, whose middle verses went something like...

> And being found in human form,
>   he humbled himself
>   and became obedient until death, death by crucifixion.
> Therefore, God has highly exalted him,
>   and given him the name that is above every name...
>   ...Lord Jesus Christ...

In this familiar pre-Pauline hymn (Phil 2:6–11), even with its bold christological claims, empty tombs and appearances are nowhere in sight. Jesus goes directly from crucifixion to heavenly exaltation, and the only prerequisite for this claim is "obedience until death."[16]

The Jewish traditional context for the resurrection claim is underscored by the course this tradition subsequently took in earliest Christianity. As I have already indicated, it is seldom linked with the appearance tradition, as though this could effectively validate the resurrection proclamation. Instead, as it comes to Paul in the rather developed form of 1 Cor 15:3–4, it has already become an *exegetical* tradition. These things are true because they happened "according to the scriptures." As surprising as it may be to find

---

14. Hoffmann, "Auferstehung Jesu Christi," 486.

15. Jürgen Becker, "Das Gottesbild Jesu und die älteste Auslegung von Ostern," in Georg Strecker, ed., *Jesus Christus in Historie und Theologie,* (Festschrift Hans Conzelmann (Tübingen: Mohr [Siebeck] 1975), 120–21.

16. One caveat: The pre-Pauline traditions tell us that these claims about Jesus were made very early on. We should not, however, be led to think that they were universal in early Christianity. The earliest Christians might have found various ways of expressing their conviction that Jesus had been right about God. A nonliturgical expression of that conviction would be something like Q, where the sayings of Jesus were collected, presumably, for further propagation.

evidence of such exegetical activity so early in the Christian tradition, its influence over this tradition is undeniable. Its power can be seen more clearly
in the traditions that led to the development of the gospels. As we have seen
in the last chapter, when Christians first began to describe the events around
the end of Jesus' life, they created a passion narrative — perhaps the earliest attempt at narrative writing in Christian circles — thickly studded with
scriptural quotations and allusions. Their exegetical work was not without
precedent. The result of their labors follows closely the pattern of persecution and vindication of the suffering righteous one worked out in the Jewish
martyrological literature of the period, whose elements included conspiracy,
false accusations, trial, obedience, condemnation, and ultimately vindication
and exaltation.[17] As much as we might like to think of the resurrection of
Jesus as an utterly unique event, which separates Christians even from the
Jewish roots of our faith, this does not do justice to the origin of the resurrection proclamation itself. When this proclamation is examined carefully as
it appears in early Christian tradition, we can see that this most central claim
of Christian faith is a response to the life and death of Jesus that is quite
understandable within the culture of ancient Judaism.

This, of course, is not to say that Christian claims about the resurrection
of Jesus were not without innovation. Every ancient resurrection claim is distinctive in some respects. After all, one must not assume that these ancient
poetic expressions of hope had taken on the quality of dogma, such that every
detail must be drawn into consistency. One of the distinctive things about
Christian resurrection claims has to do with timing. In most Jewish scenarios of vindication, resurrection is spoken of as a future event involving all of
God's faithful ones at some climactic point of history. But many Christians
spoke of Jesus' resurrection as a past event, involving only him. For some
early Christians, like Paul, this could only mean that the end had come and
that Jesus was but the "first fruits" of many others who would also soon be
raised (1 Cor 15:20–28).[18] But even this idea cannot be said to be uniquely
Christian. In the broader Hellenistic world, it was a commonplace to speak
of great heroic individuals who had been taken up to dwell among the gods
as a reward for and the vindication of a life well lived.[19] This tradition, too,
would have been influential in the Hellenized Jewish environment of the first
century, and it no doubt influenced the formulation of early Christian claims

---

17. This is shown clearly by George Nickelsburg in "The Genre and Function of the Markan
Passion Narrative," *Harvard Theological Review* 73 (1980): 153–84.

18. This is also the origin of the mysterious story found in Matt 27:52–53.

19. Adela Yarbro Collins, *The Beginning of the Gospel: Probings of Mark in Context* (Minneapolis: Fortress Press, 1992), 138–43.

about Jesus. In any event, it is clear that resurrection has a significance all its own in the ancient world that can well account for its genesis among the early followers of Jesus. It is not dependent on the appearance tradition. That is a separate matter, to which we shall now turn.

Jesus Appeared...

The Appearance Tradition

It has already been noted in passing that this is a distinct tradition in itself, with its own formal features as well as a probable setting in the life of the early church. The fact that all the references we have to the appearance tradition are associated in some way with the commissioning of apostles to preach suggests the context of mission activity as its place of origin. This may indeed be all we need to account for the rise of this tradition: it arose as a purely formal way of acknowledging the appointment of such persons as are named in the tradition to preach.[20]

But the content of the tradition, in my view, does not lend itself to a purely form-critical explanation. Unlike the resurrection tradition, in which early Christians made claims about realities existing solely in the transcendent realm — God's activity in redeeming someone beyond the grave — the appearance tradition makes a hybrid claim: that God has revealed the risen Jesus (transcendent realities) to certain living persons (historical realities). Moreover, one such person is actually speaking in 1 Cor 15:8, and he claims actually to have experienced the risen Jesus (1 Cor 9:1). So this tradition poses for us another sort of question: did Paul (and others named in various appearance traditions/stories) in fact have experiences which they took to be appearances of the risen Jesus?

What Happened to Paul?

Paul refers three times in his letters to direct experiences he claims to have had of the risen Jesus: 1 Cor 9:1; 1 Cor 15:8; and Gal 1:15–16. The third cannot really be called an "appearance" claim as such. Here Paul says, rather

---

20. This is the view of Rudolf Pesch, "Zur Entstehung des Glaubens an die Auferstehung Jesu," *Theologische Quartalschrift* 153 (1973): 201–28, esp. 214–15. Pesch has since withdrawn this view in the revised version of this essay that appeared in Paul Hoffmann, ed., *Zur neutestamentlichen Überlieferung von der Auferstehung Jesu*, Wege der Forschung 522 (Darmstadt: Wissenschaftliche Buchgesellschaft, 1988), 243. Cf. also the view of Marxsen, *The Resurrection of Jesus of Nazareth*, 92.

mysteriously, that God had chosen to "reveal his son *in me*" (*en emoi*). In spite of the tradition of translating this text as though it involved an appearance (RSV: "he ... was pleased to reveal his Son *to* me"), I can find no compelling reason not to read it more literally: "he ... was pleased to reveal his son *in* me."[21] And isn't this the way Paul thinks of Christ's presence in the life of the believer — as somehow dwelling *in* him/her?[22] Whatever this "inner" experience was,[23] it was apparently a powerfully moving one for Paul, since he immediately dropped what he was doing and went off to Arabia (Gal 1:16b–17) to propagate a movement he had previously violently opposed (Gal 1:13). Paul understood this experience as a commissioning to preach (Gal 1:15–16a).

Paul refers to this experience again in 1 Cor 9:1, only now he explicitly says "have I not *seen* [*heoraka*] the Lord?" That this is indeed a reference to the same experience is shown sufficiently by the fact that Paul links it to his status as an apostle, that is, one commissioned to preach. It may be that here Paul adopts the Christian practice of referring to such revelatory experiences as "seeing" the Lord, even though when left to his own manner of description he might word it differently. In 1 Cor 15:8 he is also following an established early Christian tradition in lining up his experience with those of other persons mentioned in the confessional formulae of 15:5–7. As in these formulae, Paul says Christ "appeared" to him as he did to Peter, James, the Twelve, other apostles, and at least five hundred other people. So, based on Paul's own references to his experience, one might well conclude that initially Paul may not have understood his experience as an "appearance" of Jesus, but simply as a revelatory experience, albeit a powerful one.

The question is, do these texts refer to something that really happened to Paul, which he eventually took to be an appearance of the risen Jesus? I see no reason not to take Paul at his word on this. After all, one must account for Paul's dramatic turnaround on the question of the Jesus movement somehow. And such things do happen. The history of religions is full of dramatic religious experiences that result in an equally dramatic change of course in the lives of those who have them. And Paul seems to have been a person who sought out and was accustomed to having such experiences, if one may

---

21. So Marxsen, *The Resurrection of Jesus of Nazareth*, 101–2.

22. See esp. Romans 8; however, it is curious that Paul here does not seem to be able to settle on whether he is speaking of the Spirit of God (8:9a) or the Spirit of Christ (8:9b).

23. One should be careful to limit one's presuppositions about what *en* might mean here; we cannot project onto Paul a modern psychology. Lüdemann perhaps risks this in *The Resurrection of Jesus: History, Experience, Theology* (Minneapolis: Fortress Press, 1994), by appealing to depth psychology as an explanation for Paul's (and Peter's) experience, even though the candor with which he deals with the resurrection in this book is generally laudable.

rightly take Paul's cryptic words in 2 Cor 12:1–5 as a reference to his own practice of mysticism.[24] And by Paul's own account, it may have been as the result of such an experience that he initiated his second trip to Jerusalem (Gal 2:2). Of course, the historian can neither confirm nor deny Paul's *interpretation* of his experience — that it was indeed an appearance of Jesus. But it seems reasonable to think, given the evidence, that Paul did have a dramatic religious experience, and probably on more than one occasion.

But what was that experience like? Are there any clues in Paul's letters that might shed light on these mysterious allusions to revelatory experiences?

For starters, we need not go any further than 1 Corinthians 15 itself. Recall that the point of this chapter is not ultimately the resurrection of Jesus, but rather the general resurrection of all believers at some future time, an idea which some in Corinth have come to deny. The argument goes like this: You will no doubt agree that Jesus has been raised from the dead (vv. 1–11). If that is true, then you must also agree that there will be a general resurrection; to deny one is to deny the other (vv. 12–34). If there are doubts about the specific way in which one might imagine this future resurrection, I will attempt an explanation (vv. 35–57). It is this last section that is of chief interest. The specific question he wants to address is raised in v. 35: "How are the dead raised? With what kind of *body* do they come?" Paul proceeds to answer this question by way of analogy, using the parable of the sown seed (vv. 36–41). Just so, he says, "what is sown a physical body, is raised a spiritual body" (v. 44b). But how? Through the power of Christ, the second Adam, who himself "became a life-giving spirit" (v. 45b). Just as Jesus, the archetype, became a spirit (*pneuma*), so also shall believers become spirits (vv. 46–49). Leaving aside for now the history of religions question of how this all works in the mind of Paul, it is enough to notice how the argument works on paper: believers will become like Jesus in receiving a "spiritual body" (*soma pneumatikon*). To be raised from the dead is to receive such a body. This will be true of the believer just as it has been true of Jesus.

But what is Jesus' spiritual body like? In 2 Corinthians Paul may provide other hints at his experience. In 2 Corinthians 3 he speaks of the "glory" (*doxa*) of the spirit that surpasses even the glory that shone in Moses' face when he descended from Sinai (vv. 7–11). It is luminous, it shines. In 3:18 this "glory" becomes the "glory of the Lord," in which the believer shares as he/she is gradually transformed into his "likeness" (*eikon*). Indeed, in Phil 3:21 Paul says that Jesus will return to change the Christian's lowly body

---

24. It is generally agreed that Paul is speaking of himself and his own experience in this odd passage; for a discussion of the sparse details, see Victor Paul Furnish, *II Corinthians*, Anchor Bible 32A (New York: Doubleday, 1984), 542–45.

(*soma tapeinoseos*) into a "glory body" (*soma tes doxes*) like his. Paul thinks
of Jesus' body as a glorious, luminescent body. This general impression of
"luminosity" is reiterated in 2 Cor 4:6, where Paul probably alludes to the
"inner" experience he had near Damascus that sent him off to Arabia:

> For it is the God who said, "Let light shine out of darkness," who has
> shone in our hearts to give the light of the knowledge of the glory of
> God in the face of Christ.

This piecemeal case can only be suggestive. But it seems at least to point
to a historical kernel in the fictive descriptions of Paul's "Damascus road"
experience in Acts 9, 22, and 26: the religious experience that so transformed
him had the quality of luminosity (9:3; 22:6; 26:13). The history of religions
is full of this type of religious experience, from a variety of cultures and a
variety of periods, from Isaiah, to St. Teresa, to Sri Ramakrishna.[25] It is not
unreasonable or unlikely to think that Paul also had such an experience.

One last question: how did Paul know that it was Jesus who "was revealed
in him"? Even if we could assume that Paul's vision took some recognizable
human form, we must remember that Paul had never seen Jesus, and so could
not automatically recognize him as the content of his vision. So, how did
Paul come to identify the content and significance of his visionary experience
as Jesus?

On the one hand, we must say that Paul did not have this experience in a
vacuum. When Paul "saw Jesus" there were already persons who were claiming that God had raised Jesus from the dead. Paul knew of such people and
was in relationship with them (albeit a hostile relationship). This provided
the interpretive context within which Paul could have come to understand
his vision as an appearance of the risen Jesus. He *could have* so understood
his experience, and did . . . but it was not *necessary* that he understand it so.
Why did he not conclude that it had been Elisha who had been revealed in
him, or Enoch or Moses, or even God? Why Paul concluded that it was in
fact Jesus who had appeared to him is, and shall remain, a mystery shrouded
deep in the psyche and soul of Paul himself. Here we have reached the limits
of historical investigation. All we can say is that on that day, for whatever
reason, Paul came to the realization that Jesus had been right about God,
that God had shone through in his life and ministry, and that the continuing
work of his followers was indeed the work of God.[26] And so he changed his

---

25. The immediate context for Paul is Jewish apocalyptic, in which visions are common (Hoffmann, "Auferstehung Jesu Christi," 494–96). But the broader cross-cultural context of such
experiences should not be overlooked.

26. It is not necessary to appeal to deep psychological forces in Paul to account for this change

mind. Paul the opponent became Paul the apostle, commissioned by God to preach the good news of Jesus Christ.

What Happened to Peter and James?

In 1 Cor 15:5–7 several other people are mentioned as having also received resurrection appearances. Among them are Peter (Cephas) and James. So we might ask the question: did these people, like Paul, also have ecstatic religious experiences, which they took to be appearances of the risen Christ?

With Peter and James the case is not so clear as with Paul. First and foremost, we have no first-hand statements asserting that they indeed had such experiences. At best, 1 Cor 15:5–7 is third-hand information: having had such experiences, (1) Peter and James might have said something to others about them; (2) others then repeated their claims in the form of a confessional statement; finally (3) Paul repeats the confessional statement in 1 Corinthians 15. What is more, this information comes to us in confessional formulae, whose purpose it was to confirm the authority of certain persons to preach. Peter and James are both significant enough figures in the early church that, even if they had not been so commissioned, everyone would have assumed that they had been. Finally, the political function of such claims in setting up apostolic lines of authority cannot be overlooked.[27]

On the other hand, the 50s C.E. is a little early for apostolic authority to have exercised an overwhelming power in shaping the tradition. As for the third-hand nature of our text, Paul himself might be a mitigating factor in assessing its historical value. After all, Paul in fact knew both Peter and James, visited them in Jerusalem, and fought with them in Antioch (see Galatians 1–2). In their common discussion of what it means to have legitimacy as an apostle (Gal 2:1–10), is it not likely that the topic of appearances would have come up? Paul, in repeating the formulae in 1 Cor 15:5–7, may be repeating material whose content he has personally checked out in conversation with Peter and James.

---

of heart. We need not say, for example, that Paul was deeply troubled about his persecution of the church, or already a Christian at some deep psychological level (so Lüdemann, *Resurrection*, 81–84), even though this might turn out to be true if we were able to probe Paul's psyche. Holding the psychological approach in abeyance should not suggest, however, that Paul's experience, especially its interpretation, was not deeply affected by his own subjectivity. His experience could in no wise be considered an "objective" event.

27. See Elaine Pagels, *The Gnostic Gospels* (New York: Random House, 1981), 3–32. See also her study "Visions, Appearances, and Apostolic Authority: Gnostic and Orthodox Traditions," pp. 415–30 in B. Aland, ed., *Gnosis: Festschrift für Hans Jonas* (Göttingen: Vandenhoeck & Ruprecht, 1978).

In view of the possibilities, it is worth noticing that there is at least one appearance story that features Peter and James, along with a third figure, John. It is, of course, the Transfiguration of Jesus in Mark 9:2–13. It has long been suspected that this story was originally a postresurrection appearance narrative, now transformed into the "Transfiguration" and transposed back into the life of Jesus.[28] James M. Robinson has noted that, as with Paul's allusions to the luminosity of Jesus' resurrected body, this narrative, too, assumes that the appearance of the risen Jesus would have had a luminous quality: "his garments became glistening, intensely white" (9:3a).[29] I would not suggest that the Transfiguration represents anything more than a highly stylized presentation of the appearance of the risen Jesus to these three, rather like the highly stylized account Luke creates of Paul's experience near Damascus. It is not likely, for example, that three persons could simultaneously have had the same sort of inner religious experience that Paul had. If the Transfiguration is a transposed postresurrection appearance story, it is likely that three different stories have here been brought under a single umbrella, establishing the authority of these three apostolic figures simultaneously.[30] The separate traditions around Peter (Cephas) and James in 1 Cor 15:5, 7 would suggest that here we encounter these trajectories at a much earlier stage in their development, when they had not yet been lumped together.

But taking the Transfiguration as part of the appearance tradition suggests something else as well: that, somehow not included in the 1 Corinthians 15 formulae, there was another appearance tradition related to John. Did John also have an ecstatic religious experience, which he came to regard as an appearance of the risen Jesus? In this connection it is worth noting that when Paul made his second trip to Jerusalem, he met with three persons there said to be "pillars" (*styloi*): James, Cephas, and John — precisely those names that

---

28. The theory was first espoused by Julius Wellhausen in *Das Evagelium Marci* (Berlin: G. Reimer, 1909), 71. In the large body of literature amassed on the subject since then, Wellhausen's view has become the *communis opinio*. In spite of Robert Stein's worthwhile effort to examine this hypothesis critically ("Is the Transfiguration [Mark 9:2–8] a Misplaced Resurrection-Account?" *Journal of Biblical Literature* 95 [1976]: 79–96), it is still, rightly, the dominant view. Given the choice between Wellhausen's theory and seeing the Transfiguration as a *sui generis* story of Christ's glorification, the former has greater plausibility. Stein, in underlining the differences between the Transfiguration and other resurrection stories, either ignores the exegencies of transforming the story from a postresurrection appearance story into an episode in the life of Jesus (e.g., in the resurrection appearances Jesus comes to the disciples, but in the Transfiguration he is already with them) or simply misstates the case (e.g., the term "Rabbi" is not appropriate to a resurrection account [cf. John 20:16!]).

29. James M. Robinson, "Jesus from Easter to Valentinus (or to the Apostles' Creed)," *Journal of Biblical Literature* 101 (1982): 9.

30. *Pace* Bultmann (*Geschichte*, 279), who thinks that perhaps only Peter was originally involved.

appear in the Transfiguration story.[31] What made them "pillars"? What distinguished them from others in Jerusalem, who surely had also been in the company of Jesus? Is it possible that what made them "pillars" was the fact that they all had experiences of the risen Lord? The Transfiguration, as an appearance story, would then have developed as a highly stylized representation of those experiences, offered together as an etiology for their commonly held authority.

If the Transfiguration was originally an appearance story reflecting older traditions about luminous appearances of Jesus to Peter, James, and John, why was it not preserved as such? Why was this appearance story redesigned as the *sui generis* story we have come to know as the Transfiguration?

In a 1990 article published for the first time in his *Gesammelte Aufsätze*, Hans Dieter Betz provides part of the answer.[32] Betz argues that the appearance tradition, far from being an asset to the early church, would have been viewed by some as a liability. The problem with such stories is that for someone with a little education and social standing, they would have sounded vulgar. All of our gospel writers, who, after all, can read and write and thus, would have been among the educated elite, might have experienced them in this way. The word *pneuma*, which Paul uses to describe the risen Jesus, is the same word ancients use to refer to disembodied spirits who wander the earth. For someone like Mark, these mysterious stories of ghosts (*pneumata*) and luminous appearances would have sounded embarrassingly similar to the graveyard spook stories that were so popular in common folk religion of the period, and in fact formed the basis of the more practical forms of magic.[33] The problem this posed for early Christians is illustrated by a point in the debate Origen would later have with Celsus over the merits of Christianity. Betz points out that Celsus never doubted the Christian claim that Jesus had appeared to the followers of Jesus; he only disputed what this meant. Jesus was no savior, said Celsus, but a mere ghost (*pneuma* or *biothanos*) condemned to wander the earth like so many other common criminals, barred from salvation![34] That made Christians nothing but a pack of common magicians,

---

31. The names are the same, but are they the same people? The James in this trio is normally taken to be James, the brother of Jesus, since this is the James to whom Paul refers in Gal 1:19. In the Transfiguration it is presumably James the apostle, the son of Zebedee (Mark 1:19), who is mentioned. The name is the same, but the person is not. Or is he? Could it not be that Paul identifies the James of Gal 1:19 as "the brother of the Lord" to distinguish him from the better known "pillar," one of Jesus' original apostles, whom he mentions without predication in 2:9?

32. Hans Dieter Betz, "Zum Problem der Auferstehung Jesu im Lichte der griechischen magischen Papyri," pp. 230–61 in his *Hellenismus und Urchristentum: Gesammelte Aufsätze I* (Tübingen: Mohr [Siebeck], 1990).

33. Ibid., passim, esp. 239–48.

34. Ibid., 234–39, and esp. 247–48.

manipulating the powerful spirit of an executed man (the spirits of violently executed persons are particularly potent[35]) to accomplish their illicit ends.

But it was not just opponents of Christianity who would have seen the appearance stories in light of their folk-religious character. Paul himself may have seen them in this way. He cannot be separated from this general religious mentality, which would have simply been assumed by almost everyone. For Paul, Jesus' spirit is a powerful presence[36] But, as with most things he uses, Paul puts his own spin on this tradition. For example, in Romans 6 Paul describes how the believer, through the ritual of baptism, might have access to the power of Jesus' spirit. But he does not offer access to that power only for power's sake (the whole point of ancient magic); rather, in baptism one receives power "to walk in newness of life" (6:4b), freed from the power of sin and enabled "to live for God in Jesus Christ" (6:6–11).[37] Of course, not all of Paul's followers appreciated such nuances. In 1 Corinthians 15 part of the problem must surely be that Paul's opponents have appreciated Jesus' resurrection only for its spiritual power, and not for its future, eschatological implications. Disregarding Paul's idea of a future, eschatological consummation of the Empire of God in which everyone will be included, they use the power of Jesus' resurrection, through baptism, to rescue individuals who have died (15:29), leaving the rest to rot in the grave.

In the next generation, the heir to this esoteric, folk-religious aspect of earliest Christianity became Gnosticism as it developed in the second century and beyond. As James M. Robinson pointed out in his 1981 SBL presidential address, the Christian Gnostic literature of the second century is rich with luminous appearances of the risen Lord.[38] Nor is it lacking in magical spells, techniques for ascent to the heavens, and ecstatic religious experiences. We must recognize that in some sense these were the rightful heirs of Paul, a Paul not cleaned up at the hands of Luke. For many years Paul was a favorite of early Gnostic Christians, a preference that was not entirely misguided.[39]

Though it is not my intention here to enter into a complete treatment of the tendencies and purposes enveloped in the resurrection narratives in the individual gospels, we are at least in a position now to see why the gospel writers treat the issue of the resurrection and appearances of Jesus in the way

---

35. Ibid., 241–42.

36. See ibid., 254–58, for Pauline parallels to folk religion and magic.

37. Betz also sees Paul differentiating himself on the issue of baptism, but he locates the difference in Paul's emphasis on the futurity of resurrection over against the magician's access to immortality now (ibid., 258–59). This, of course, is also true.

38. See the examples collected by Robinson, "From Easter to Valentinus," 10–17.

39. For the use of Paul among Gnostic Christians see Elaine Pagels, *The Gnostic Paul* (Philadelphia: Fortress Press, 1975).

they do. For example, is it any wonder now that Mark[40] — any literary clever-
ness aside — preferred to end his story with an empty tomb rather than with
appearance stories of the sort that might have been typified by the Transfiguration.[41] The luminous appearance of Jesus in the Transfiguration could easily
have led to the assumption that Jesus was merely a ghost, that is, if Mark had
chosen to use this story as an appearance story rather than as the "Transfiguration." So Mark simply leaves the matter of Jesus' appearance after his death
as a question — or better, as a point of decision on the part of the believer —
rather than risk the misperception that Jesus was just a ghost. Whatever Jesus
becomes in the Transfiguration, he is no ghost.

When Matthew comes to add his own appearance stories to supplement
Mark's empty tomb, all that is left of the older tradition of presenting Jesus as
a luminous spirit is an angel descending from heaven with a "visage like light-
ning."[42] Jesus himself has a body — or at least feet so physical as to be grasped
(28:9). He is no longer just a spirit. In Luke, too, one may perhaps see the
vestiges of a "ghost story" in 24:36–7, where the sudden appearance of Jesus
startles and frightens the disciples, who think they see a ghost (*pneuma*).
From then on Luke seems even more adamant to demonstrate the unam-
biguous physicality of the resurrected Jesus. "Handle me and see; for a ghost
(*pneuma*) does not have flesh and bones like I do." This, of course, directly
contradicts Paul, who argues to his folk in Corinth that "flesh and blood
cannot inherit God's imperial rule" (1 Cor 15:50).[43]

Finally, among the myriad incongruities in John's appearance stories one
may still see the same tendencies at work. Even though Jesus is able to pass
through doors (now twice, 20:19 and 26), and Mary is instructed not to touch
him, since he has not yet ascended (20:17[!]), John manages to create a Jesus
so physical that he borders on the macabre. "Here, stick your hand in my
side," he instructs Thomas (20:27). John's Jesus is not a ghost, but a corpse!
In the end, John dismisses the entire tradition as second rate to begin with:

---

40. The following remarks on the gospels draw from Robinson, "From Easter to Valentinus,"
9–12, and Betz, "Zum Problem," 248–53.

41. In so doing Mark does not totally avoid the folk-religious tradition; see Betz ("Zum
Problem," 245–47) on the significance of tombs as places inhabited by dangerous spirits. It is
noteworthy that the earliest images of the empty tomb (ca. 400 C.E.) are apotropaic ampoules
(Betz, "Zum Problem," 246–47). In using the empty tomb motif, however, Mark also accesses
the Greco-Roman hero cult tradition, in which heroes are frequently translated out of the tomb
to heaven as an act of vindication for their virtuous deeds (see Yarbro Collins, *The Beginning of
the Gospel*, 138–43). In so doing Mark was moving back to the original thrust of the resurrection
claim, that God would vindicate Jesus because he had been right.

42. Robinson ("From Easter to Valentinus," 14) suggests that 28:2–3 is left over from that
earlier tradition.

43. So noted in ibid., 11.

"Have you believed because you have seen? Blessed are those rather who have not seen, and still believe" (20:29). One can sense John's frustration with a tradition that is so easily misconstrued and misused.

So 1 Cor 15:5, 7 may reflect the historical reality that Peter and James, like Paul, also had ecstatic religious experiences, which they took to be appearances of the risen Lord. The Transfiguration may represent a vestige of that tradition, together with the claim that John, too, had such an experience, a luminous kind of experience, like Paul's. This could account for the fact that these three were designated "pillars" in the Jerusalem church. The popular appeal of such stories, with their connection to folk religion and magic, probably contributed greatly to the spread of Christianity. That folk tradition no doubt informed how many early Christians understood the new religion and its rituals, such as baptism. But this understanding of the appearance tradition, which eventually came to play a significant role in Gnosticism, proved to be problematic for the church, or at least part of the church. The canonical gospel writers all follow suit in treating the "pillars" tradition as the Transfiguration and replacing any of the older, luminous-type appearance stories with very physical appearance stories calculated to prove Jesus was no mere ghost. These more "physical" stories should all be seen as late, and, at least in part, generated by these apologetic impulses.[44]

If Peter, James, and John had the same sort of luminous revelatory experiences that Paul had, we might also ask of them as we did of Paul: how is it that they came to regard these experiences as appearances of the risen Jesus? Here the answer is not nearly so difficult to grasp. All three of these pillars had known Jesus and had been in his company. Long before his death, they had committed themselves fully to Jesus' vision of the Empire of God. They believed in his cause as God's cause. It was people like these who would have been the first to say, "God raised Jesus from the dead." To say this was simply to say what they had already said with their very lives: that Jesus was right about God, his cause was just, his vision true. Just as they had given themselves over to this cause during Jesus' lifetime, so now they would give themselves over to the belief that God would not allow the cross to remain

---

44. It should be pointed out that in adding such stories to the end of their narratives of Jesus' life, the gospel writers were doing more than *counteracting* the appearance tradition. For example, as with the earlier appearance tradition, so also these older stories connect the appearance of Jesus with a commission to preach. In some ways they do this more effectively than the older appearance tradition could have. By placing these stories at the conclusion of an account of Jesus' life and ministry, they made clear what it was that the church wanted to continue, and what it was that they had originally proclaimed as vindicated by God. In the gospel tradition, there is less a chance that the resurrection itself could have been severed from this program and viewed as a source of power in its own right.

as the final word on Jesus' life. They would continue the ministry of Jesus, bolstered by his spirit, in the confidence that God had raised him from the dead. All of this could happen quite apart from any remarkable, ecstatic religious experiences to motivate them. But when such experiences did come, they knew exactly how to interpret them. Jesus had appeared to them.

What Happened to the Twelve?

1 Cor 15:5 asserts that Jesus appeared to Cephas, then to the Twelve. If one can say with some historical credibility that Peter, James, and Paul all had ecstatic religious experiences, which they took to be appearances of the risen Jesus, what about "the Twelve"? Did they also have such experiences and so are named here?

"The Twelve" as a designation cannot be taken literally here. After all, Peter was one of the Twelve, but is named separately. So at best the formula could mean that Jesus appeared to Peter and then to the *rest* of the Twelve. I will take this term then in the less literal sense of indicating that collective body of authority-bearing persons chosen by the early church to carry on the task of preaching.[45] Whether this group had its origins during Jesus' own lifetime is a question that may be left aside for now; it is enough to note that, whatever its origins, in the early church "the Twelve" became a body bearing ecclesial authority. Did members of this body have an experience like those of Peter, James, and Paul?

Before proceeding with those considerations that have led me to answer this question in the negative, I want at least to acknowledge that there may be some small evidence to indicate that they did have such an experience. The Transfiguration is not the only epiphany story that might have been folded back into the life of Jesus by Mark, or by some pre-Markan sculptor of the tradition. It has often been observed that the story of Jesus walking on the water in Mark 6:45–52 may also have originally been told as a postresurrection appearance story.[46]

Unlike in the later, physical-type appearance narratives we find appended at the end of Matthew, Luke, and John, here Jesus appears in a mysterious, ghost-like form reminiscent of the earlier Pauline tradition of appearances.

---

45. That they were preachers I derive from the appearance tradition itself: it is always taken as a commission to preach (Marxsen, *The Resurrection of Jesus of Nazareth,* 91).

46. For Bultmann's endorsement of this view see *Die Geschichte der synoptische Tradition, Erganzungsheft,* ed. Ph. Vielhauer and Gerd Theissen, 5th ed. (Göttingen: Vandenhoeck & Ruprecht, 1979), 81. For a recent argument of the case see John Dominic Crossan, *The Historical Jesus* (San Francisco: HarperCollins, 1991), 405.

This is a pretty good ghost story. It is late at night (v. 48b: the fourth watch); the wind is blowing. Suddenly, an eerie figure appears walking on the sea. The disciples think they are seeing a ghost (v. 49: *phantasma*), and they scream (*anekraxan*). Only then does Jesus reveal his true identity with the epiphanic self-identification, "It is I" (v. 50: *ego eimi*). As the story closes, the disciples are left shaking in their sandals (lit: "deranged" [*existanto*]). This is just the sort of spooky appearance story Betz imagines to have thrived among those earliest Christians drawn to magic and folk religion. It is little wonder that it did not survive as a postresurrection appearance story, but rather, like the Transfiguration, was remolded and used instead as an episode in the life of Jesus.

But as interesting as these possibilities are, I nonetheless do not accept this story as convincing enough evidence for an actual experience, which the Twelve might have taken to be an appearance of the risen Jesus. The expression "the Twelve" clearly designates an authority-bearing institution in the early church. What could it mean to say that "Jesus appeared to the Twelve"? It could not mean that, collectively, they had the same sort of subjective, religious experience that Paul had. Such experiences are common with individuals, but group visionary experiences are rare. And in any event the formula does not say that Jesus appeared to the Twelve *all at once* (cf. v. 6, which does assert this for the five hundred plus). So perhaps the formula means to say that that each person in "the Twelve" had such an experience, so that having a visionary experience would have been a prerequisite to membership in this elite group. But this is not the way Luke understands membership in this institution. In Acts 1, the vacancy left by Judas is filled by a process of nominations, followed by the casting of lots (Acts 1:15–26). We are left with the conclusion that, according to this formula, each person already in "the Twelve" had been singled out for such an experience. But if this were really so, why are these persons not named, like Peter and James? In this statement it is clearly the *institution* that is at issue; it is the institution that gains legitimation through the formula, not the individual members of it.

This case is not at all like that of Paul, who, with nothing to gain and everything to lose, had an experience that sent him off to Arabia and on to a life spent propagating a movement he had previously opposed. When he says that something happened to change his life, it is obvious that he means that quite literally. In the case of the Twelve, however, we have an authority-bearing body working within the church, a church which comes to recognize appearances of the risen Jesus as experiences that convey authority. So both the Twelve and the church have everything to gain by the assertion that the risen Lord had also appeared to the Twelve. Including the Twelve in the appearance formulae probably derives from a decision on the part of the early church to expand the sphere of authority that was originally confined to the "pillars" to include the Twelve as well.[47] It is not so likely that it derives from an actual experience of the risen Jesus.

What Happened to the Apostles?

All that has been said about the Twelve above could also be said about the claim in 1 Cor 15:7 that Jesus also appeared to "the apostles." As with the appearance to the Twelve, I am not convinced that this represents a literal claim to be understood analogously to claims about appearances to Peter, James, and Paul.

As a designation, "the apostles" is more open-ended and less precise than "the Twelve." It is not at all clear who would be included in this group. Mark combines both terms, creating "the twelve apostles" in 3:16. But this is a late development. For Paul, it seems, anyone sent out (*apostello*) to preach is an apostle (*apostolos*). These include, for example, Andronicus and Junia (Rom 16:7). Even later, Luke could call Barnabas an apostle (Acts 14:4, 14). Noticing these Greek and Latin names, and their sphere of activity, Fuller suggests that "James and the apostles" might well represent those designated to preach primarily to Gentiles, while "Peter and the Twelve" would represent the Jewish team.[48] In any event, it seems clear that we have in this expression a second authority-bearing designation from earliest Christianity.

Could each of the apostles, whoever they might have been, have had the same sort of experiences Peter, James, and Paul had, and likewise taken them to be appearances of the risen Jesus? It is possible, but not likely. If that had been the case, why does Paul not mention them here? As long as he is piling up evidence for the resurrection of Jesus, why does he not add appearances to Andronicus, Junia, and Barnabas to the stack? It can only be that he, like other early Christians, did not understand the term "apostles" in this creedal formula primarily in terms of the individuals it embraces, but as a collective body, an *institution* of the early church. Just as with the Twelve, we have here an authority-bearing body already working within the church, a church which came to recognize appearances of the risen Jesus as experiences that convey authority. The inclusion of "the apostles" in this formula no doubt derives from an ecclesial decision to expand the sphere of authority beyond

---

47. Cf. Marxsen, *The Resurrection of Jesus of Nazareth*, 93. What 1 Cor 15:5 accomplishes in creedal form, the story of Jesus Walking on the Water, as a resurrection narrative, accomplishes in narrative form (cf. Crossan's conclusions, *The Historical Jesus*, 405–6).

48. Fuller, *Formation*, 40–41.

James to include others who could be trusted with the task of preaching. In saying that Jesus also appeared to the apostles, the church merely asserted that this decision to expand authority was taken under the guidance of the spirit of Jesus.

And What about the More Than Five Hundred Others?

Sandwiched between the statements about Peter and the Twelve and James and the apostles is a third statement, odd for both its form and its content:

> Then he appeared to more than five hundred brothers at one time, most of whom are still alive, though some have died. (15:6)

Formally, v. 6a conforms to the rest of the formulae insofar as it, too, uses the passive construction *ophthe* ("he appeared") to refer to the appearance itself. But it is different in content: here Jesus is said to have appeared to a *group* of people ("at one time").[49] This means that it cannot refer to the same sort of experience taken by Paul to be an appearance of the risen Jesus. Groups — large groups(!) — do not have the same sort of subjective, religious experiences Paul had. If there is a historical experience that lies behind this assertion, it must necessarily have had the character of a collective ecstatic experience, such as glossolalia. Is this plausible?

We know that such things did in fact happen in the early church. Paul himself gives us direct evidence for this based on his own experience with the church in Corinth. Paul mentions speaking in tongues several times in his discussion of Corinthian worship practices (1 Cor 12–14, passim). In fact, the worship scene has become so wild there that Paul worries that, should outsiders wander into their gathering unwarned, they might think the whole lot of them mad (14:23)! We also know that Paul thought of such things as manifestations of the "Spirit": "there are various gifts, but the same Spirit" (1 Cor 12:4).[50] Paul could also speak of the Corinthians as manifesting the "body of Christ" while they were engaged in such activities (1 Cor 12:27). So it is not inconceivable that an early Christian group might have interpreted an ecstatic worship experience as an appearance of the risen Jesus, however loosely this might be understood.

---

49. Verse 6b is not part of the confessional formula, but is usually taken as a comment of Paul. We will return to it presently.

50. Paul here speaks of the "Holy Spirit" and the "Spirit of God" (12:3), as well as simply the "Spirit." Elsewhere he can speak of the "Spirit of Christ" (Rom 9:2) or the "Spirit of Christ Jesus" (Phil 1:19). Paul has obviously not yet reached any consistent theoretical understanding of a phenomenon that remains to him a very real experience.

Does such an experience lie behind 1 Cor 15:6a? I think that this is likely. Paul seems to know persons who actually experienced the thing that is referred to in this formula, or so one might conclude from v. 6b. There are still people around to tell of it, and he might have heard about these things first hand. And the tradition may elsewhere reflect this sort of event. Acts 2:1–13 could well be a *highly stylized* depiction of such an event, if not exactly the one Paul is talking about here. We might understand the Acts story analogously to the Transfiguration in relation to the experiences of Peter, James, and John, or Acts 9, 22, and 26 in relation to Paul's experience. In any event, we know that such things did happen. It is not unlikely that early Christians could also have come to interpret such ecstatic experiences as "appearances."

What Really Happened?

How did the resurrection tradition begin in early Christianity? What were its origins and what did it mean to those who cultivated and guarded it so closely? I have tried to show that the answer to this question lies not in the gospel stories about Jesus rising up out of the tomb as a flesh-and-bones, walking, talking corpse. Rather, we come closer to the truth when we look carefully at the much earlier tradition about Jesus' resurrection and appearances that Paul uses in 1 Cor 15:3–8. What we learn from these traditions is that the early Christian belief in the resurrection of Jesus began in a simple act of proclamation in the face of great odds, that God had raised Jesus from the dead. This earliest proclamation was not grounded in anything other than the conviction among the followers of Jesus that God *would* raise Jesus from the dead, because Jesus had been right about God and should not have been killed. This was a very Jewish thing to say; it connects Christian faith to Jewish reflection on resurrection in a martyrological context that extends back centuries. It was not necessary for Christians to have had experiences of the risen Jesus, or to have discovered an empty tomb, in order to say this. They could have said it, and would have, even if Jesus' body had been thrown into a pile of corpses and never seen again.[51] The origin of Christian claims about the resurrection of Jesus was the conviction among his followers that he had been right about God.

But the early church was not just stubborn about its convictions. It was also a religious movement alive with spiritual enthusiasm. Leaders such as

---

51. As Crossan suggests in *Jesus: A Revolutionary Biography* (San Francisco: HarperSanFrancisco, 1994), 126–27.

Paul, Cephas (Peter), James, and perhaps also John, were among those who had ecstatic revelatory experiences in the period of Christian origins. Because early Christians believed that God would and had raised Jesus from the dead, such experiences could be interpreted and understood as appearances of the risen Jesus. Since these experiences were also taken as signs that those who had received them had been commissioned to preach the good news, the church gradually came to attribute such experiences to groups, such as "the Twelve," or "the apostles," as a formal way of recognizing their authority to preach. Finally, there were manifestations of spiritual enthusiasm in early Christian worship. This, too, came to be understood as the presence of the living spirit of Jesus among those gathered at such events. That is where historical investigation has led us. It is all we can say historically.

But there are still many questions left unanswered, and for the believer, they may seem to be the most important questions: Did Paul really see Jesus? Did Jesus really appear to Peter? to James? to John? Was Jesus really present in the ecstasy of early Christian worship? Did God really raise Jesus from the dead? These, however, are not questions for the historian. They lie beyond the historian's ken. They are the most important questions for the believer, because one can answer them only out of one's faith, one's conviction about who God is. Did the resurrection really happen? Would God raise Jesus from the dead? Was Jesus right about God? These are all the *same* question, and they must all be answered in the *same* way: with a decision, a risk, to believe in the God of Jesus. History can be of no further help here.

The resurrection is an event that, for Christians, *in reality* did happen. But the reality in which one can speak of such things at all is *not historical reality*. Rather, it belongs to those realities we call the transcendent. The claim that God raised Jesus from the dead is not presented in the New Testament as a historical reality, but as a rupture in history. That is the point of the earthquakes and darkening skies, the general chaos and disordering that comes as part of the gospels' accounts of Jesus' death. Here the steady march of history is broken. The resurrection is presented as God's breaking into history in order to redeem a life prematurely ended by historical forces and, in so doing, to redeem history itself from its demonic rebellion against the God made known in that gracious, gentle life. History says that Jesus' life and work came to an end on Golgotha. Christian faith claims that it did not. Herein lies the decision of Christian faith. It is not a decision about miracles or demonstrations of power, about corpses or empty tombs. For the earliest Christians, this was a decision about Jesus. Was he right, or was he wrong? Would God redeem his life, or would his ghost be doomed to wander the earth like so many other crucified criminals? In the mind of an ancient peasant, both are equally possible.

For Christian faith to be *faith*, this decision, this risk to believe in Jesus, must be embraced without fear. It cannot be bolstered with appeals to certain remarkable historical events that would seem to prove the case. For to insist that the resurrection was a *historical* event is to succumb to the urge to flee from faith, to embrace as true only that which can be proven historically or scientifically. To say, "I believe, because history proves that God raised Jesus from the dead," is not faith. It is a refusal to have faith. It is unfaith.

To believe in the resurrection is to have faith that God would redeem the life and work of Jesus from the death sentence imposed on it by history. It is to have faith that Jesus' ministry was the work of God, that his words were the Word of God. History cannot prove that these things are true. One can only risk asserting that they are true, and listen and watch for this same God in one's own life. This is all that the earliest Christians had to go on. It is all we have too. They understood that the resurrection of Jesus is a *challenge* to believe that history is not all there is to human existence. They understood it as a *call* to have faith that we live in the presence of a God whose gracious, loving character shone forth in the life of Jesus of Nazareth. They understood it as an *invitation* to live life as a faithful, trusting response to that God, extending that experience of gracious love to others, just as God had extended it to them in the ministry of Jesus. This challenge, this call, this invitation are still ours today.

Resurrection is not about the resuscitation of a corpse, that one great miracle that proves we are right after all. It is about the resuscitation of hope in the face of cruel realities. There is so much in our world that points in the direction of despair: war, hunger, racism, human degradation and abuse, fallenness. History easily suggests that if there is a God, if there is a reality that runs through and beneath it all, this reality is surely not a benevolent God. Resurrection is about the resuscitation of hope against all odds that there is indeed a God, and that God loves us beyond all our furthest imaginings. This is the God Christians claim to have met in the life and preaching of Jesus of Nazareth. If one cannot summon the faith and hope to believe that there is such a God, an ancient claim about one more savior rising from the dead will not be able to convince one that there is such a God after all.

The assumption that it could is perhaps the greatest error of Christendom. It is often argued today by evangelical theologians that without the miracle of the resurrection, it would be impossible to account for the rise and spread of Christianity, or even its survival past Good Friday. But this is precisely what differentiates those first followers of Jesus from his latter-day worshipers: they really believed that Jesus was right. They were convinced by what he said, excited about what he did, and chose to give themselves over to this person whom they experienced as gospel, completely. And they did all of this *before* Jesus' death. That is why they proclaimed the resurrection in the first place. For the earliest Christians the resurrection depends on whether or not Jesus was right about God. Their first commitment was to Jesus, his message, his gospel. For latter-day Christians, that Jesus was right depends on whether the resurrection is a historical event. This shift is crucial, for it involves a shift in first commitments: from message to miracle, from gospel to power. John the evangelist, who, writing near the end of the first century, had inherited from the tradition a host of miracle stories and resurrection tales, understood the danger this shift posed to authentic Christian faith. And so, after dutifully including many of these stories, he refuses to allow them to stand as the source and starting point for Christian faith. To Thomas, who demands proof of the resurrection before he will believe, John's Jesus offers the final word: "Have you believed because you have seen me? Blessed are those who have not seen, and yet believe" (John 20:29).

Conclusion

Is It a Sin to Be Liberal?

Liberal Christianity is as unpopular today as it has ever been, because the dominant spirit of our time attempts to smother free religious thought. On the other hand, it is a timely cause — as timely as ever — because it is a necessity for the spiritual life of our age. Every deep piety is reflective; every really deep thought is reverent.

— ALBERT SCHWEITZER,
Pilgrimage to Humanity (1947)

Is it a Sin to Be Liberal?

I am a liberal Christian. I mean this in the simplest sense, not as an ideological claim or in any technical sense. I just mean that anyone who reads the preceding chapters will probably conclude that I am a liberal, not a conservative. I would like to think, in my own naiveté, that the critical study of history and tradition could raise one above these labels that identify the combatants in the so-called "culture wars" that have become of late a dominant force in shaping the public discussion of religion and values in North America. But this is unlikely. The critical study of history and tradition is itself a liberal enterprise. And since critical study is necessary to understanding the texts and traditions Christianity has bequeathed to us, texts and traditions that come from a time removed from us by two millennia, from a place half way around the globe, from a culture we in the West can scarcely understand even today, it appears that the liberal label is almost inevitable. Then so be it. I am a liberal Christian. So is it a sin to be liberal?

It often feels like it is, especially when liberals are in the company of conservative evangelicals or fundamentalists. And since evangelicals and fundamentalists now comprise a majority of Americans who profess any Christian faith, this feeling comes over us liberals a lot. As I speak in churches around the St. Louis area, it is a rare occasion when I do not encounter the righteous anger of at least one or two conservatives in the audience. The radical wisdom of Jesus, the parables — these areas do not normally draw much fire. But when it comes to those things touching on traditional church doctrine, especially the death and resurrection of Jesus, I can always count on vocal, sometimes furious, opposition.

On a recent Sunday morning, after I had finished speaking to a group of adults in a local mainline church about the resurrection, a well-dressed gentleman, clearly agitated and deeply troubled by my remarks, stood to address me. He demanded to know whether I believed in the resurrection. I took my usual tack, and replied with an unequivocal, "Well, yes and no. Yes, in the sense that I believe what the resurrection signifies: that Jesus was right about God. But no, in the sense that I do not believe that anything special happened to Jesus' corpse after his death." Unimpressed by my attempt at a thoughtful response, he interrupted my explanation and, with scarcely veiled anger quivering his voice, reasserted: "What I want to know is whether or not you are a Christian!" I replied, "Of course I am, or so I try to be!" "How can you possibly say that when you clearly do not believe in the resurrection?" he shouted as he stormed from the room.

An awkward moment.

Fundamentalists and conservative evangelicals have a way of forcing such awkward moments on liberals. The circumspection liberals exhibit when struggling with ultimate claims about matters of Truth, the hesitancy, the blush in the face of so many things to consider, often appears like wishy-washy backfill by comparison to the self-assured claims of fundamentalists on every subject from the virgin birth to the resurrection. The legacy of the fundamentalist strain in American religion has been to inculcate in all of us the idea that tenacious certitude is the chief ingredient in strong religious faith. Doubt is the enemy. Questioning is dangerous. Education is suspect. Even after several years of formal study and teaching within a religious tradition that welcomes critical thought, I still find myself feeling vaguely anxious and inadequate in such situations. The feeling is the same one I recall having when I was being scolded by my father. But my own father was a religious liberal! It is not his voice I hear inside my head in such moments. It is the voice of some indistinct Father, some great cultural Patriarch, whose all-seeing eyes watch over the traditions of our people, like Washington's portrait in my third-grade classroom. His face appears wise and kind to those who acquiesce to the assumptions of our cultural canons. But to those who strain and pull against his spiritual grip, the furrows in his brow deepen into a stern warning not to go too far. Such a raw display of anger always makes me wonder whether I have gone too far.

But then something else usually happens as well. As the crowd is breaking up one person and then another comes forward, usually quietly and a little unsure, and says something like, "I had no idea that there were people in the church who think like you do. Why haven't I ever heard this before? Do ministers know these things?" When I explain that none of what I have said is original, that many theologians think this way, and that many pastors think this way as well, their surprised expression turns to relief, or sometimes to anger. After years of quietly keeping to themselves about such things, these folk are always surprised to find that their own attempts to work out an understanding of Christian faith that makes sense to them may not be illegitimate or aberrant after all. They are relieved to know that there is a real place in the church for them. They are angered to learn that there always has been room for critical thought in the church, but that pastors and theologians have often been too timid in the face of conservative opposition to make that clear. When I think of the great decline in membership that my own denomination, like many others, has experienced over the past twenty-five years, I wonder how many people just wandered away because they had given up on finding a place for their views in the church and assumed that organized religion was simply not for them. Why remain committed to an institution that makes you feel like it is a sin to think?

That we have arrived at such a situation after two millennia of Christian history is a pity. For if it started, ultimately, with Jesus and his followers, Christianity did not begin with uncritical deference to authority. Jesus and his followers used the best of Jewish tradition to criticize many cherished assumptions in their world about God, about human community, about how life might be lived and experienced more deeply. Jesus was not an intellectual, but he did think deeply about these things and did not defer to the automatic answers supplied by his culture. It is not a sin to think, to doubt, to ask questions. On the contrary, this is where it all begins for Christians. Jesus' questions are the same questions we have today. Who is God? How might we live together more faithfully to God? What gives life its meaning? Jesus addressed himself to such questions as these, but his answers will not be translated easily into our own situation. This itself will require much thoughtful consideration. It is not a sin to think. It is a necessary part of Christian faith today.

What Did Jesus Think?

As Jesus thought about life's ultimate questions, what did he come to believe about God, about human community, about the things that give life real meaning?

...About God?

Jesus believed in a God who is present in human life, not a distant reality. This is what it means to speak of the Empire of God as already present, "within you." God is as close as the human heart. And yet, this kind of closeness suggests limits to the concept of God's involvement in human life. Jesus did not experience God as a power operating in the world apart from human agency. God did not throw up a pillar of fire for Jesus to follow into the wilderness. God did not stop the world for Jesus. And though Jesus may well have been a healer, a holy person who could do for people what a shaman can do, there were many things that Jesus could not do, pray to God as he might. There were people he could not heal. There was pain that he could not stop. And there were powers in the world that would eventually overwhelm him. God could not save him from his fate. To know God as part of human life is not to know a disembodied power intervening willy-nilly at the convenience of those who call out for help, however just, however pained or pathetic their cries might be. Too many innocents have suffered and died, like Jesus himself, to think that God's presence in human life takes the form of a power that can save us from the evils that one human being can inflict upon another. To know God's power in the way Jesus knew it, as an Empire "within you," is to know God as a reality running through all of life, a basic, fundamental reality. When one responds to this reality and makes it part of one's whole life, everything changes. Sometimes even the world changes. Human life works better. It means more. It becomes richer and rises above the pettiness of our contrived realities because it becomes part of something more basic, more real, more true.

This basic reality that Jesus experienced as God had the character of love. This word has become so washed out and sentimentalized in our time that it seems hopelessly naive and corny even to say this. But our cynicism about this old liberal notion only underscores how difficult it really is to believe. Did Jesus believe it? I think he really did. He boiled his own faith down to just two propositions: to love God and to love one's neighbor (Mark 12:29–31). The writer of Matthew would later add: the second is like unto the first (Matt 22:39). This is true. To love one's neighbor *is* to love God. For to love God is to love love itself. That is why Jesus embodied love in his own life in a more radical way than the simple love of neighbor might suggest. He loved prostitutes. He loved sinners, traitors, tax collectors. He treated the shamed with honor and declared the unclean clean. He loved the unlovable. He loved his enemies. To love God is to be devoted to a basic and fundamental reality that runs through all of life and creation. The character of that reality is love. This is the reality that can give life its richness and ultimate meaning. This is the reality that beckons us to live better than we live. This is the reality that exists as already present, an Empire "within you," that can be as powerful in the shaping of human life and relationships as we want it to be.

But to know God in this way is to admit of divine limitation. Love does have limits. It cannot force its own way. Love cannot be coerced. It can invite, croon, cajole, mourn, weep, and summon all the persuasive powers love can afford. But it cannot force. This lies beyond the character of love.

If one risks the belief that God's nature is love, then one must be willing to accept the limitations that come with this faith.

Jesus lived with limitations. Perhaps his whole life was a struggle with limitation. He was not a person of means. His place in his world was marginal. He lacked the one thing that could guarantee him a place in the ancient agrarian culture of imperial Rome: land. Whatever place his family may have had, now it had little, and Jesus had none. He was a wanderer, homeless, without family in a culture where power and possibility came from family. Yet, in spite of these limitations, Jesus still found within himself the power to love. He experienced that power as an ultimate power, one that came not from himself, but from God. And so he embraced that power, lived it, spoke of it, storied it into existence, and surrendered to it, finally accepting its limitations and succumbing to the powers of fear and hatred that crucified him. This is how, even in death, Jesus could become an experience of God to others.

... About Human Community?

Jesus believed that the experience of God he had could be translated into human relationships and forms of community. That is why he began to speak about a new Empire of God. To speak about a new Empire, a reign, is to speak about life in its greatest corporate aspect, life *together.* How did he imagine this?

Picture a table. It is large and lavished with foods of every sort and drink. Around it are gathered the children of God. They are not your peers. They are brought here by another invitation. Each has been drawn to the table by the inviting power of God's love. They have come as they are, some in rags, some in rich finery, some washed, some not, some are alone, some sit as families, some speak your language, most do not. There is a man you know, who has so utterly destroyed his life and that of those around him that he seems beyond redemption. He waits. There is a woman whose shoulders curl in the permanent shape of shame. Her back is bowed, but her head is held high. She sits at the head of the table. There is a young child, thin and drawn, with hollow cheeks but eager eyes. She has already begun to eat. A beggar slips into a chair, unsure of his place but willing to risk it. He tries to blend in. And so it goes around this infinite expanse of table, containing practical things: food, company, belonging, care, honor — the necessities of life. Here they are offered to each; all have access to what is needed. This is the communal form of love.

Jesus' vision for what human community might be like came from his experience of God. If God is that fundamental reality running through all of life and existence, and if the character of that fundamental reality is love, then the finest, most authentic form of human community must in some way embody love. Jesus told many stories, parables offering glimpses of what authentic human community might be: the Great Feast, the story of a table that is opened to all; the Workers in the Vineyard, a parable of worth and work, in which all receive at the end of the day enough pay to meet their need, no more, no less; the Samaritan, where one's enemy becomes salvation and unexpected care renders the old maps of who belongs where utterly ridiculous; the Prodigal, a tale of lost and found, in which a brother must choose love over honor or risk losing everything. How can we imagine human life and relationships lived out of the fundamental reality of love? Jesus tried out scenarios in his parables. As stories, they are experiences of love manifest in relationships, not templates for community formation. They are not a blueprint, but invite further imaginative work: how might love be embodied in all our relationships?

This imaginative challenge is with us now more than ever. How might we imagine life together in such a way that the poor are blessed, the hungry fed, the depressed filled with laughter, and the abused made safe? How might we imagine a world in which the anxieties of those who live teetering on the margins of life, never knowing whether food will come tomorrow, or clothing and shelter, might disappear in a sea of enough? Does this seem too hopelessly naive? Perhaps it is. But anyone who risks the claim that in Jesus we have come to know who God is ought at least to remember that Jesus did dream such utopian dreams. He did not spell out a complete social and political program. Perhaps his peasant imagination was not quite up to that; or perhaps he simply did not live long enough to think through all the implications of what he was doing. But he did envision human life together in terms that are vastly different from those which Christian culture has agreed to settle for. Hard work, thrift, a day's pay for a day's work, competition in the marketplace — these modern values, as admirable as they may be, were not the building blocks Jesus imagined as the foundation for human life together. Love, care, mutual nurture of one another, mercy, redemption of the lost — these were the values Jesus claimed as ultimate values. Human relationships, if they are to be fully authentic, fully grounded in what is real and true, must be grounded in these values.

...About Life?

These are the values that Jesus believed give meaning to individual lives as well. Human relationships that are grounded in love do not just happen.

Communities of care do not simply appear with the wave of a hand or the desire of a well-wisher. People must decide to act out of love as though it were the ultimate reality running through and beyond all things. To believe in God is to believe in such a reality. It is to believe that what one can feel and taste and count and measure, what one can possess and hold and manipulate, what one can see and hear, these things are not all there is to life and existence. To believe in God is to believe in a transcendent reality, something that lies in and yet beyond all things. It is in giving oneself over to this transcendent reality that life finds its ultimate meaning. This is what Jesus meant in counseling others to give up their lives in order to find real life. To see the transcendent in life means seeing through the concrete realities that suggest themselves as so utterly important and determinative for one's daily plan. What is most urgent is not always what is most important.

Jesus' life was a failure, at least when measured against any common standard of success. He had no home. He held no job. He had no family, and few friends. He died a criminal, his body hung out in shame for all to see, and to think, "Thank God I did not turn out like that." How is it that so many have come to worship a person whose life we would still most surely despise if it were not the life of our "savior"? Perhaps it is that we have imbued Jesus with such mythic power and cultic strength that his life can sink quietly into the background, a mere comma in the Apostles' Creed that jumps quickly from "born of the Virgin Mary" to "suffered under Pontius Pilate" without so much as a glance back at Jesus' sorry life. That this is at least part of the truth about us is indicated by the great shock and offense that historical Jesus research always produces among folk not used to thinking about Jesus as a real person. The historian's Jesus is an offense because Jesus was an offense. Part of the reason we can worship Jesus today as "Christ," "Savior," "Son of God" is that we have run from the historical Jesus and his challenge to see through the shallowness with which we normally conduct our lives.

But this is only part of the truth. For when we bother to read the gospels, that offensive life and challenging voice are still there, clearly audible among the enthusiastic confessional claims of his followers who had been moved by his life and his voice. And through history there have been remarkable souls who have heard this voice and experienced this life in such a way that moved them to their own radical demonstrations of what life might be like if it were lived in response to a God whose nature is love — St. Benedict, Francis of Assisi, Catherine of Siena, Menno Simons, Sojourner Truth, Dorothy Day, Martin Luther King, Jr. We are moved by such lives and drawn to them because in them there is hope. The hope they offer is that this is not as good as it gets. Life can be richer. Human existence can become more meaningful. There is a transcendent reality that can transform us if we will but let it. Jesus' life is one that draws to it a worshiping community because, even in its failure, it allows us to see through the pretense of meaning we erect around the great trophies to be won in a successful life. Jesus experienced intimately a transcendent quality to existence that was more real, more satisfying, more hopeful than what life — even a successful life — can offer. It is this transcendent quality that we call God. Its nature is love. This is what Jesus knew.

Appendix I

History, Method, and Theology

What do we mean when we use the term "history"? What sort of discipline is historical research, and is it still a viable discipline today? And how does the theologian make use of history in the discipline of theological reflection? Though these questions are of an abstract nature and thus take us too far afield of our main topic to be included in the text of the preceding chapters, they are nonetheless critical to the work I have presented, all the more so in light of the recent historical Jesus debate, which always seems to return to issues of method.

Appendix 1A: History

History as Objective Fact and Subjective Experience

I have used the term "history" throughout this book without much qualification, perhaps, at times, too loosely for those who pay close attention to matters of method. What do I mean by "history"? Usually, I have used "history" to refer quite simply to certain events which took place in the past, in our case, the remote past. This, of course, may seem at first to be a naive view. Hopefully it will not turn out to be. By using the term in this way I wish simply to assert that people did indeed say and do certain things in the past, and that these things do have real effects on the present, *our* present. And if this is true, it is legitimate for someone to have an interest in such things. An interest in the past is born legitimately of the desire to be fully aware of one's own present historical context.[1] This desire may, of course, be wholly self-serving and even perverse. One may engage in historical work to justify one's present, to deceive oneself and one's foes. This postmodern criticism of

---

1. Joyce Appleby, Lynn Hunt, and Margaret Jacob, *Telling the Truth about History* (New York: W. W. Norton, 1994), 271. I am indebted throughout to Appleby, Hunt, and Jacob for their perspective on history and historical research.

history and historians is not unjustified. But one's interest in the past need not be self-serving. Those who wish to assess *critically* their own place in the world of the present must also pay close attention to the past. For example, it is a fact that European Americans kidnapped Africans and brought them to North America to work as slaves. That bit of history has profound implications for how we regard matters of race in American culture today. To ignore this or to pretend that we all begin life with a clean slate unaffected by this history would be wrong, both factually and morally. History demands an act of remembering from its heirs.

History, in this sense, has an objective quality. That is, it is a fact that certain things did happen in the past while other things did not. In this objective quality is rooted a resistance to falsification, to which anyone interested in the past is obligated to yield. However, this objective quality to past events can be misleading. For it suggests that knowledge about the past can also be possessed of a certain objectivity. This is not true. It is not true because of the way in which the past is made available to us not as an object, but as the memory of a human subject.[2] We have access to history only through *historical experience*. This means that when we speak of history we are in practice dealing with the subjective human experiences of past events and the memories they evoke. History will never be available to us as an object, for events pass away even as they occur. All that remains is the memory of them, and their effect on human subjects. Thus, even though the historian must yield to the resistance against falsification that comes with the objective fact of an event, he or she cannot ultimately deal with history as an object, but as subjective human experience.

Finally, the historian, in trying to reconstruct actual past events by listening to the subjective human memories of them, does not do so from a distance, as though he or she were not also involved in those events. Insofar as the past is also resident, by way of its effects, in the historian's present, the historian must also deal with the fact that he or she also encounters past events as an experiencing subject. Indeed, it is usually the historian's personal interest in a past event that draws him or her to its investigation in the first place. This is certainly true of the present work: as a Christian I am deeply interested in Jesus and can encounter him as a figure from the past only as someone who is deeply involved in the continuing effects of his life and work in the present. This adds yet another layer of subjectivity to history as we

---

2. This is mitigated somewhat by physical evidence, e.g., the yield of archaeological investigation. But only somewhat. For archaeological remains must also be interpreted, usually through the corroborative use of literary evidence and much imagination.

can know it. The objective fact of a past event compels me to resist its falsification in my own interest, but it does not free me from the limitations
imposed by the fact that I cannot know it apart from my own experience as
a human subject.

The Discipline of Historical Research

All of this means that historical research does not present itself as a discipline analogous to the various disciplines of natural science. It is like science
in the sense that it aims to discover something factual. But unlike the natural
sciences, historical research has no here-and-now object, something that can
be handled, manipulated, scanned, or otherwise tested.[3] Its subject matter is
the very subjective recollection of passing human events. As in the natural
sciences, the historian must employ reasoned, inferential analysis to arrive at
a plausible construal of the past. His or her ideas about what was said or
done must be defensible relative to the evidence without special pleading.
But unlike the natural sciences, historical research cannot rely on certain
universals, such as Newton's gravitational laws, to help establish the facts of
the case. The historian is constantly involved in making reasoned judgments
about what happened, but there are no universal laws in the realm of human
behavior to help guide these judgments.[4] The historian must consider the evidence, but the construal of evidence into a plausible scenario always involves
making numerous subjective decisions about people and how they behave,
or even about a particular person, his or her personality, the sense one has
of him or her. So it is with historical Jesus research. It is not science. It is a
humanistic discipline involving one subject's experience (the historian) of another (Jesus) as mediated through other experiencing subjects (the followers
of Jesus, early believers, and others).

Yet many people who approach a work of history approach it with scientific expectations. They look for a clear starting point, for scientific controls,
for repeatable procedures that could guarantee the reliability of the results.
Historical research cannot provide such guarantees. Consider how a historian actually goes about his or her work. One gathers the evidence, all of
it, or as much of it as can be mustered. One tries to grasp the whole, to
see everything at once. One begins to weigh it, sort it, assign relative factual

---

3. This insight, and many others, is from R. G. Collingwood's classic study, The Idea of History (Oxford: Clarendon, 1946), 233. It is echoed by Appleby, Hunt, and Jacob, Telling the Truth,
252.

4. Collingwood, The Idea of History, 234; also Appleby, Hunt, and Jacob, Telling the Truth,
259.

value to each witness, to look for patterns, plausible relations, scenarios. In this process there is no automatic starting point, no control. The historian must first of all decide on what constitutes evidence for a certain past event, then on what bits of evidence are reliable. Finally, he or she must settle on the few things that appear to be crucial to understanding what happened. But why do *these* things appear to be crucial, while others do not? This depends entirely on the historian's ability to see significance in certain events and to make that significance apparent to others. History is a discipline, but a disciplined *art* that requires considerable ability to synthesize information. It is not simply a matter of recovering a thing, "history," that lies resident in certain authoritative texts, waiting to be discovered. "History" must always be reconstructed. The historical information provided by certain texts and the reliability of that information must always be tested and established.[5]

This is as true of the historian who works with biblical sources as it is of any secular historian. After all, even the biblical text itself must be critically reconstructed from various ancient manuscripts using methods that are no different from those of historical research in general. Each manuscript must be evaluated for its authenticity and value. The various readings of different manuscripts must be collated and compared and judged for their accuracy. Human judgments are used to establish, test, and confirm virtually every sentence of the New Testament. Apart from the subjective work of historical reconstruction we would have no Bible at all. Anyone who works in any way with the Bible cannot escape the subjective work of the historian. There can be no trade-off, for example, between biblical theology and historical Jesus theology, on the grounds that the latter is too subjective, while the former offers a clear objective starting point: the text. Such a view today would have to cope with the rather embarrassing presence of an apparatus at the base of each page of the Greek New Testament in which the reliability of each reading is weighed on a scale of "A" (certain) through "D" (uncertain). Is Jesus proclaimed as "the Son of God" in Mark 1:1? "C": "there is a considerable degree of doubt."[6] Scripture offers no easy escape from human subjectivity.

This view of history as more of an art than a science, as a subjective, humanistic discipline rather than an objective, scientific enterprise is not the view that grew up with the rise of modern historiography in the eighteenth and nineteenth centuries. Nor is it the view that persists even today in the popular imagination.

---

5. For a masterful description of the actual working process of the historian, see Collingwood, *Idea of History*, 234–45.

6. K. Aland et al., eds., *The Greek New Testament*, 3d ed. (New York: United Bible Societies, 1975), xiii (the quoted phrase), 118 (for the variants on Mark 1:1).

The Modern View of History and Its Demise

The popular view of history finds its origins in the intellectual revolution that began in the seventeenth century, known as the Enlightenment. This was the dawning period of modern science, with its stress on reason, method, and objectivity. The study of history began to flourish as a discipline during this period, as did many other intellectual pursuits, but it did so very much under the influence of the scientific paradigm. This wedding of history to science had a profound impact on how people would come to view historians, and even history itself. History came to be understood as a thing, an object waiting to be discovered, like other objects of scientific investigation. The historian came to be seen, like the scientist, as a kind of heroic figure, objective, neutral, a dispassionate observer of the truth. As in the natural sciences, historians, too, searched for the universal principles governing history. The more one could know about history, the more one could see of the progress of history, with its own laws of human development. With proper insight into these universal laws, one could see, as in the natural world, a kind of evolution of humankind as it passed, gradually maturing, through its various inevitable stages. Historians strove for the big picture, a kind of metahistorical narrative in which all events could somehow find their place and meaning.[7]

In the twentieth century, under the influence of philosophers and historians such as R. G. Collingwood, William Dilthey, Karl Popper, and, later, cultural historians such as Clifford Geertz, this view of history and historians has completely collapsed. In an "Epilegomenon" to his brilliant opus, *The Idea of History*, Collingwood showed how in the actual practice of historical research history turns out to be not at all like a science, in that it has no object properly speaking and that the historian cannot take even the first step without involving him- or herself in making subjective judgments about the sources, their reliability, and how to construe their information. The historian's chief faculty is not objectivity, he argued, but a certain a priori imagination.[8] Karl Popper demonstrated that any notions about the supposed progress of history could only amount to special pleading on the part of those who, having emerged victorious from the struggles of the past, chose to proclaim their triumph as the triumph of some greater good, even God. This, he argued, was nothing more than self-congratulatory idolatry.[9] And the idea of a historical metanarrative ran aground on the shoals of particularity, as

---

7. For an account of how history came to be wedded to science in the eighteenth and nineteenth centuries, see Appleby, Hunt, and Jacob, *Telling the Truth*, 52–90.

8. Collingwood, "The Historical Imagination," pp. 231–49 in *Idea of History*.

9. Karl Popper, *The Open Society and Its Enemies*, vol. 2: *The High Tide of Prophecy: Hegel Marx, and the Aftermath*, rev. ed. (Princeton: Princeton University Press, 1966), 259–80.

the later *Annales* school and the newer cultural historians underscored the
utterly complex and culturally specific way in which events unfold and gain
their significance.

The Postmodern Critique of History

For these early twentieth-century philosophers of history, seeing through the
pretense of "objectivity" in historical research to a more accurate description of the historian as an involved subject did not mean giving up on
history altogether. Historians like Collingwood simply called for a more realistic assessment of the limitations of historical research and the necessity of
public discourse and other checks on the work of individuals such as himself.
More recently, however, critics of history have not been so hopeful. Among
late twentieth-century intellectuals, especially the newest intellectual wave of
postmodernist thinkers, a thoroughgoing skepticism about history as a viable
discipline has taken hold. They have held history to its modernist roots and
its claims to objectivity and discredited it by showing how poorly it measured
up to its own standards of truth.

The roots of this less sanguine approach are to be found in the work of
the linguistic philosopher Ferdinand de Saussure, who raised the epistemological problem of the relationship between language and its supposed referent.
When pressed, we cannot show any real direct connection between words
and the things they portend to reference. "T-r-e-e" is not a tree. Building
on his work, cultural critics like Jacques Derrida and Michel Foucault argued
that the words of historians do not really present us with anything of the
past, but merely discourse about the past. At best, such historical discourse
is simply the motiveless play of words and phrases without any real referent
(Derrida). At worst, it is a smoke screen erected to mask the historian's stake
in the present, and ultimately the will to power, which lies at the root of any
claims to Truth (Foucault). It is not only religious conservatives who harbor
suspicions about the newest phase of historical Jesus research. The new intellectual left is also concerned with what it sees as yet another modernist
attempt to establish the Truth, which will, of course, inevitably correspond to
what the historian him- or herself is, or would like to be.

The Pragmatist Approach to History

So is history, having failed to live up to the modernist goal of seeking after
and attaining objective truth, no longer a viable discipline? It should be obvious by now that I am convinced that historical research can be pursued

meaningfully, though not, of course, with the modernist goal of establishing once and for all the real truth about what was said and done. The limitations of historical work are to be taken seriously. Still, I believe that it is possible, through disciplined historical work, to produce useful, if imperfect, knowledge. In this I find aid and comfort among the growing number of philosophers and cultural critics who are turning again to the turn-of-the-century American philosophical movement known as Pragmatism. Drawing on the work of Charles Peirce, William James, John Dewey, and others, these neo-Pragmatists are finding a way around the impasse created by the modernist demand for objectivity and the postmodernist resignation to radical relativism.[10]

The Pragmatists saw well that knowledge is contextual, that particularity, novelty, and contingency characterize the human condition far more than the modernist dream of the great metanarrative could account for. They saw that all knowledge is fallible and open to correction through further investigation and discussion. But they rejected the notion, accepted by modernists and postmodernists alike, that all meaningful knowledge must be rooted in secure, fixed, objective foundations in order to be valid. They argued, rather, for the intersubjective, communal, and social nature of some kinds of knowing. Peirce, for example, anticipated the postmodernist denial that language has a direct correspondence to that which it signifies. In his "Critical Review of Berkeley's Idealism," he argued that although one must distinguish between a thing and one's mental perception of it, this distinction does not thereby become an insurmountable barrier to knowing anything. Rather, whenever several minds are constrained by observation and critical thought to agree that something exists as such and has a certain character or quality, then one may posit this as true and useful knowledge, however provisional it may turn out to be.[11] For the Pragmatists, the distance between things and our subjective perception of them need not lead to epistemological skepticism. For we do not need to know something in itself in order to know something useful about it. To know something by its effects upon us is to know something pragmatic, and thus important.

History is an area of disciplined inquiry that can benefit most from this pragmatic way of thinking about knowledge. Historical events, after all, are

---

10. My attention was drawn to the Pragmatists and the latter-day neo-Pragmatists as a way around this impasse by Appleby, Hunt, and Jacob, *Telling the Truth*, esp. chapter 7: "Truth and Objectivity" (241–70) and chapter 8: "The Future of History" (271–309).

11. Charles S. Peirce, "Critical Review of Berkeley's Idealism," in Philip P. Wiener, ed., *Values in a Universe of Chance: Selected Writings of Charles S. Peirce* (Garden City, N.J.: Doubleday, 1958), 74–88.

known only through their effects. We could not ever know history as an object, a thing in itself. We must know historical events, if we can know them at all, subjectively, in their effects as we and others experience them. Indeed, should we try somehow to objectify history or its sources or to place ourselves in a place of objective neutrality vis-à-vis the past, it is not at all clear that the resulting knowledge would be superior to knowledge derived from procedures which would take more seriously the subjectivity of historical experience. To the contrary, it is the subjectivity of both the historian and the subject matter of history that makes possible useful knowledge of the past.

Let us consider, for example, the subjectivity of the historian relative to historical events. Without his or her own subjective interest in the subject matter there would be no historical investigation in the first place. Apart from certain persons' interest in Jesus, there would be no historical investigation of his life. Moreover, without the historian's effort to imagine a world two millennia and half a globe away, to listen to ancient words, and to use the imagination to connect words and events into meaningful scenarios, nothing could be learned of Jesus. Learning involves first and foremost an act of will: to listen, to think, to experience things outside oneself. Without this subjective interest, this willingness to be impacted by the past, to feel its effects, nothing could be learned at all.[12]

And what of the things that are the object of historical investigation? They are not really things, objects, at all, but also acting, willing subjects — or at least the lingering expression of such. The texts we use as sources cannot be treated as objects liable to our own manipulation. If we do so treat them, we risk distorting them. We must understand them for what they are, *someone's* expression, the result of someone *else's* will to create something. We may use them, but we may not twist them into something we wish they were, something we need for our own purposes. We would like, for example, to have objective historical reports of the person in whom we are most interested, Jesus. But the texts we have are not this. To treat them so is to do violence to those who created them. They are artifacts, the remains of the effect Jesus had on people in certain times and places. We can learn something useful from them only if we treat them realistically, without collapsing their interest into ours. As they give answer to their question — what does Jesus mean to us in our time? — we cannot assume that they are simultaneously answering our own question about the meaning or effect of Jesus in our own time. This question we must ask in conversation with the texts,

---

12. Popper, *The Open Society*, 302.

using historical criticism to separate their questions from ours and learning from them what we can within the limits posed by this different interest and agenda.

And finally, there is Jesus himself. Though the effects of his life and words have resulted in traditions and texts, these cannot lull the historian into the feeling that he too is an object thoroughly knowable in himself. Jesus is a subject to be encountered, like any other human subject, knowable only in his effects on ourselves and others. The knowledge we must settle for is only the sort of knowledge we can ever have with respect to another person. We can hear his words, observe his deeds, and attempt through our own imaginative effort to understand them within the context of his world. But this person, Jesus, encounters us in a limited way. We cannot penetrate beyond the words and deeds by which he manifests himself; our knowledge of him must rest in the effects his life produces on others.

The subjectivity of historical work poses limits on the historian. But in it lies the only real possibility for useful knowledge from the past. The idea that, since human events from the past have a certain objective quality about them, they could be treated as objects for investigation was itself a flawed idea. The objective fact of another's existence does not free one to treat him or her as an object. Another person must always be treated as an acting subject, with a will and a right to speak his or her own words. This is true of living persons, but also persons long dead, whose words and deeds live on in memory and the artifacts of history. The habit of treating the remnants of the past as objects has probably contributed more to the distortion of the past than to its fair representation, for it freed the historian from the necessity of allowing people of the past to speak and act for themselves. They became objects, susceptible to our manipulation. This is probably true of the Bible more than any other artifact of history. For we do not even think of it as belonging to any other voice than our own. It has become "our Book." But it is not our book in this sense. Its texts come from another time and place, from subjects with a mind and will of their own. We can learn from these ancient voices, but only if we open ourselves to their effects, settling for the kind of knowledge that can come from the interchange of two acting, willing subjects.

Checks on the Historian's Will

To be completely realistic about the problem of historical research, however, it must be admitted that a historian's encounter with his or her sources is not really like an encounter with another person. The will that produced these sources is now long dead, no longer able to assert itself, to counter the historian's queries with its own, to correct and redirect the conversation. The back and forth between the historian and his or her sources is a conversation that must occur within the imagination of the historian. This loads the weight of the conversation entirely into the subjectivity of the historian, and thus will inevitably distort it. This means that responsible historical research must be carried on in a way that minimizes this potential distortion and maximizes the resistance to falsification that comes with the objective fact of past events. But how is this to be done?

There are two checks on the historian's will that must be attended to constantly in any historical work. The first is the evidence itself. The evidence of the past can exercise a check on the whim of the historian, provided it is treated according to critical, agreed upon standards and rules.[13] Of course, evidence of the past never simply falls readily into place. The historian must constantly use his or her imagination to construe the evidence into a plausible scenario of the past. This was Collingwood's insight on the central role of imagination in the process of historical research. But he distinguished imagination from mere fancy. The imaginative work he recognized was the disciplined, reasoned, inferential analysis that yields to the evidence at every turn.[14] Without the historian's imagination, no history would be written. But without the disciplining of that imagination, no useful, realistic history would be written. It is a delicate balance.

So the second check on the subjective will of the historian is just as important as the first, viz., other historians. Just as one is constrained by the evidence, so also one is constrained by *communis opinio* about the evidence, how it might be treated responsibly, and what sort of interpretation it can reasonably bear. Not that a community of scholars cannot itself be misled about something, or fail *en masse* to see the truth of a certain matter. Indeed, most historical work, as with other humanistic disciplines, aims at constant innovation in an attempt to move the consensus to a new and more adequate position. What a community of peers can do is offer a check on the whim of the individual historian by requiring of him or her an adequate, public defense of any new proposal. This, of course, presumes that individuals in the guild of scholars do not hoard privileged information (as has sometimes been the case in biblical studies), and that peers can be honest with one another about biases and presuppositions (as has often not been the case). With cul-

---

13. Appleby, Hunt, and Jacob, *Telling the Truth*, 225; see also 259–60.
14. Collingwood, *Idea of History*, 240–42; cf. also Appleby, Hunt, and Jacob, *Telling the Truth*, 255 and 259–60.

tivation, however, collegial work and peer review can function as they should in the shaping of useful knowledge of the past.[15]

Principles of Historical Methodology

Given the nature of history and historical research as I have just described it, I would offer the following general principles as the basis for sound historical methodology:

1. One should always approach one's sources (especially written sources) as subjects, not objects liable to one's own manipulation. A text should not be regarded as anything other than the expression of another subject's will, with an agenda that may or may not be consistent with one's own.

2. One should embrace limitation. The historian is limited by the fleeting character of the past: one can never know events as they were, but only in their lingering effects. One can never know other persons as they are in themselves, but only in those things they say or do and their effects. One can never escape one's own perspective and the limitation that comes with one's own finite way of experiencing things. The historian must eschew any claims to objective, immutable truth, even while venturing to propose useful knowledge about something of the past.

3. One should raise to awareness one's own interest in the subject of one's inquiry and take account of its possible distorting effects.

4. One should work collegially in a group of peers who share access to information and can engage in open, free discussion.

5. One should treat one's sources professionally, embracing scholarly consensus whenever possible and avoiding idiosyncratic positions. Departures from the *communis opinio* should be defensible with reasoned, inferential arguments.

---

15. Appleby, Hunt, and Jacob, *Telling the Truth*, 194–97; also 261–62, 282–91. This point is central to their thesis. In making it they acknowledge their debt to the Pragmatist tradition (especially Peirce), and more recently to Helen Longino, *Science as Social Knowledge: Values and Objectivity in Scientific Inquiry* (Princeton: Princeton University Press, 1990).

Appendix 1B: Method

Every historian should have a method for doing his or her work that includes clarity about how one should regard the sources, how one intends to treat the sources in such a way that yields information, and how one goes about construing that information in a realistic and meaningful way.

Working Assumptions about the Sources

For the most part I have made use of common scholarly opinion about the sources and their treatment in the historical work presented here. I have, however, occasionally embraced minority opinions or my own innovations where necessitated by the evidence. Here are some of my basic assumptions about the sources.

Markan Priority. I assume that the consensus about the relative order and dependence of the three synoptic gospels is correct: that Mark wrote first, around the time of the destruction of the Jewish Temple (ca. 70 C.E.), and that Matthew and Luke made independent use of some form of Mark's work, and so wrote a generation or so later (ca. 80–100 C.E.).

The Sayings Source, Q. I also assume that Matthew and Luke had a second source, of which they also made use independently of one another, namely, the document referred to as Q. I am also convinced, along with a number of Q scholars, that Q passed through one or more editorial stages, and that John Kloppenborg's hypothesis of an earlier, more sapientially oriented version of Q, and a later, more apocalyptically oriented version, in which one finds most of the typically apocalyptic flavor of Q, is basically right.[16] Though his work has been met with some general skepticism about our ability to be so precise about the history of a document that must be reconstructed from fragments, his detailed arguments and analysis of the texts remain to my way of thinking the most convincing proposals. Since Q does not mention the disastrous event of the Temple's destruction, I assume that it had reached the basic form in which Matthew and Luke encountered it before the year 70 C.E. The general time frame of 50–60 C.E. is a reasonable rough estimate of the period in which this document arose.

Special Matthew and Special Luke. The material that is peculiar to Matthew or Luke, that is, derived neither from Mark nor from Q, should not be overlooked simply because it is not found in the earlier synoptic sources. Some of

---

16. John Kloppenborg, *The Formation of Q: Trajectories in Ancient Wisdom Collections;* Studies in Antiquity and Christianity (Philadelphia: Fortress Press, 1987).

this material, to be sure, is late and derives from the communities in which these gospels grew up. However, some of this material may be quite old, even extending back to Jesus himself. We know that the oral tradition of Jesus' sayings was carried on well into the second century, after the first gospels were written. The Matthean and Lukan Special Material no doubt contains some of this material. Through critical analysis this material can sometimes be identified.

The Gospel of Thomas. There is currently no universal consensus on the relationship of the Gospel of Thomas to the other gospels, Matthew, Mark, and Luke, with which it shares so much in common. My own position is laid out in my earlier book, *The Gospel of Thomas and Jesus.*[17] I refer the reader there for a defense of the position that the Gospel of Thomas represents a gospel tradition that is basically autonomous to the synoptic tradition. It is, however, a cumulative document, as any ancient sayings collection would be. There are earlier and later traditions incorporated into it, and some of these traditions might have been influenced by more popular and widespread traditions known today from the canonical gospels, or by the local lore of Syria and Egypt, where this gospel was used most extensively. But the beginnings of this tradition could have been as early as Q (so, before 70 c.e.), since like Q it does not dwell on the destruction of the Jewish Temple. In *The Gospel of Thomas and Jesus* I argued, however, that Thomas began to assume its current shape and character over an extended period of time roughly contemporaneous with the writing of the canonical gospels (70–100 c.e.).[18] Any more specificity than this would be speculative, and attempts to date it decisively earlier or later have usually involved special pleading of one sort or another.

The Gospel of John. Following the consensus that has existed among New Testament scholars now for most of this century, I have not relied much on the Gospel of John for information about the historical Jesus. Where John appears to offer independent confirmation of information we have in the synoptic tradition or in Thomas, I have noted this. But determining this is no easy matter. The precise relationship of John to the synoptics has never been settled. For the most part, I have assumed that the author of John did not make direct use of the synoptic gospels (whether he knew them or not), but drew rather from a number of other sources know to him. In the case of the Passion Narrative, I have assumed, again, John's independence of the synoptic tradition, but cannot rule out a common early source from which John, Mark, and the Gospel of Peter all draw. I agree generally with John Dominic

---

17. Stephen J. Patterson, *The Gospel of Thomas and Jesus* (Sonoma, Calif.: Polebridge, 1993).
18. Ibid., 113–18.

Crossan's hypothesis of an early "Cross Gospel."[19] Thus, one cannot in my view regard John, Mark, and Peter as independent multiple witnesses to the events of the trial and death of Jesus. There are also numerous places in John where later redaction (Bultmann's ecclesiastical redactor[20]) may have produced points of agreement between John and the synoptics, which also give the false impression of independent attestation. These, too, are to be disregarded in my view.

The Letters of Paul. Paul seldom comes into the discussion of the historical Jesus, and his appearance here is likewise rare, for the simple reason that he rarely speaks of Jesus in any historical sense. For the most part, the Jesus who is important to Paul is a cosmic figure of mythic proportions. His earthly life and words pale in significance before this new role he has assumed in Paul's theology. Still, Paul can be useful, and not just for the occasional word of Jesus he passes on. Paul's voice is the earliest we hear in the Christian scriptures. What he says about Christian faith, about its view of God and of God-centered community life, all has its roots in the early Jesus movement, and ultimately in Jesus himself. I am not convinced, as many others have been in the past, of a radical discontinuity between Paul and the early Jesus movement. This somewhat novel position I have defended elsewhere, and so will not enter an explanation here.[21] Suffice it to say that I am influenced in a very general way by Paul's point of view on certain issues, such as his critique of hierarchy, his disregard for ethnic purity, his recognition of women as church leaders, and his generally countercultural posture. I assume that such things are deeply rooted in the Jesus tradition and come in some way, however indirect or inferential, from Jesus himself.

Non-Christian Sources. I have on occasion made reference in this book to certain non-Christian sources that mention Jesus. There is, however, a tendency to look to such sources with unrealistic expectations of finding here a more extensive and neutral account of things. The problem is that these sources, such as Tacitus or Josephus, are neither extensive in their accounts nor neutral. In the case of Tacitus, his bias is anti-Christian (anti-superstition), as is quite evident from his disparaging remarks. In the case of Josephus, he himself probably did not feel strongly one way or the other about Christianity. But the Christian monks who preserved his works for pos-

---

19. John Dominic Crossan, *The Cross That Spoke: The Origins of the Passion Narrative* (San Francisco: Harper & Row, 1988).

20. Rudolf Bultmann, *The Gospel of John: A Commentary,* trans. G. R. Beasley-Murray (Philadelphia: Westminster, 1971), passim.

21. "Paul and the Jesus Tradition: It Is Time for Another Look," *Harvard Theological Review* 84 (1991): 23–41.

terity were very biased toward Christian doctrine, and took great liberty with the Josephan passages that concern Jesus. They are brief (as we would expect from the non-Christian Jew Josephus), but quite doctrinally correct from the Christian point of view (as we would not expect from him). In using these sources I have tried to take account of their biases, just as one would do with the Christian sources consulted.

A Method for Working with the Sources

In working with these sources, especially the early Christian gospels, there are three problems that must be overcome if they are to yield any useful information for the historian interested in Jesus. First, they are all late, written one, two, even three generations after the death of Jesus. Second, the materials they contain were passed along orally for many years without any apparent modern historical interest, but rather in the context of believing communities and with a view to nurturing the faith and fidelity of those communities. And third, the sources themselves were not written with any modern historical interest in mind, but, just as with the traditions they encompass, were created in the interest of promoting Christian faith. All of this is discussed at length in the introduction to this book. We need simply to repeat here that history cannot be read off from any of these sources without considerable critical thought and discipline. How can one make use of these early Christian texts in such a way to yield useful historical information about Jesus?

Identifying Things Jesus Likely Said

It is common in historical Jesus research to use certain criteria for identifying authentic sayings of Jesus from within the entire corpus of things attributed to him. I have also used certain criteria, none of them particularly original. But in making use of such criteria, I have found that there are really two different sorts of criteria, distinguishable by how they might legitimately be used. On the one hand, there is a set of criteria that one might use to eliminate certain sayings or versions of sayings from consideration as things Jesus might plausibly have said. These I will call *negative* criteria. On the other hand, there is a second set of criteria that one might use to build a case for including certain sayings in one's view of the historical Jesus. These I will call *positive* criteria. These two sets of criteria are distinct from one another and, in terms of their application, do not generally overlap. I will deal with each set in turn.[22]

---

22. These ideas about criteria I first discussed in "Fire and Dissension: Ipsissima Vox Jesu in Q 11:49, 51–52," *Forum* 5, no. 2 (1989): 130–34.

The Negative Criteria: I have used the following criteria to eliminate individual sayings, or sometimes certain versions of a saying, from consideration as something Jesus might have plausibly said. In general they are related to the problem of identifying the interests of early Christians in the cultivation of the Jesus tradition, in both written and oral forms. Where those interests are distinct from interests one might plausibly find in Jesus himself, they should be taken as evidence that this material, whatever its general worth might be, does not come from Jesus. There are three negative criteria:

1. *The Redaction-Critical Criterion.* This criterion reflects the fact that each gospel writer presents the Jesus tradition in a literary context, with its own narrative, theological, or ideological framework. *One should eliminate from consideration any material that derives clearly from the redactional activity of an evangelist.*

2. *The Kerygmatic Criterion.* This criterion assumes that the interests of early Christians found expression not just in the written stage of the Jesus tradition, but also in the tradition of early Christian preaching about Jesus (the *kerygma*, broadly defined). *One should eliminate from consideration any material that derives clearly from early Christian preaching about Jesus,* such as:

   (a) apologia related to the death of Jesus (such as predictions of his death or resurrection, the fixing of blame on certain Christian enemies, etc.);

   (b) apologia related to the rejection of early Christian claims about Jesus, especially by non-Christian Jews;

   (c) the supra-signification of historical events known to have happened after the death of Jesus (*vaticinia ex eventu*, such as the destruction of the Jewish Temple);

   (d) statements reflecting the mythological claims that early Christians made about Jesus (e.g., Jesus as a descending/ascending messenger from heaven, as the Son of Man figure adapted from Jewish apocalyptic lore, or as a *theos aner*, or "divine human," the spawn of a human mother and a divine father, etc.).

3. *The Social-Historical (Form-Critical) Criterion.* This criterion assumes that the interests of early Christians and their communities were not restricted to purely religious issues, but had certain social dimensions as well. In part, this criterion comes from the older form-critical school,

which postulated that oral tradition survives only when it has a certain function and usefulness in the community, and that by studying the forms in which various traditions were passed along, we can learn something of the communal context (*Sitz im Leben*) in which these traditions were used. Recognizing that community life played a significant role in shaping and generating the tradition, *one should eliminate from consideration material which reflects a* Sitz im Leben *in the early church, insofar as such settings can be seen as distinct from any social-historical context one might plausibly imagine for the life of Jesus himself.*

The Positive Criteria: These three negative criteria can be used to eliminate certain sayings, or particular versions thereof, from consideration as things Jesus might have plausibly said. But in the end, they do not leave us with a leftover pile of "authentic" Jesus material. There will be many sayings that cannot be isolated to the hand of a particular gospel writer, or clearly related to a particular mythic framework, or associated exclusively with some social-historical episode in the life of an early Christian community. Even so, we would still have no particular reason to attribute them to Jesus, other than the fact that some early Christians did so. But early Christians attributed so many things to Jesus that he in fact did not say, the mere fact of attribution is not by itself a reliable historical indicator. Thus, we need another set of criteria that can be used positively (though not negatively) to argue for the historicity of particular sayings of Jesus. There are five positive criteria I have used:

1. *The Criterion of Multiple, Early Attestation.* The problem of connecting a saying to Jesus is in part the problem of linking something that appears in a document of the 50s, 60s, or 70s C.E. with someone who died in the 30s. If a saying appears independently in two or more documents we can at least be sure that it was current in the generation antecedent to the earliest of those two documents. That is a start. It cannot thereby guarantee that Jesus said it, but locating a saying earlier and earlier in the Jesus tradition lessens the doubtfulness of its attribution to Jesus. Therefore, *one should give careful consideration to sayings attested independently in two or more early Christian documents.* Some caveats:

   (a) The determination of independence is based on the premise of the two-source hypothesis, the basic autonomy of John, Thomas, the material particular to Matthew and to Luke (Special Matthew and Special Luke), and Paul's letters. It is also the case that some early church Fathers also drew independently upon oral traditions known to them, although this only seldom comes into play.[23]

(b) When a saying is attested independently in two or more documents, the tools of form criticism and tradition history should be used to arrive at a plausible earliest version of the saying, knowing that this will be only an educated guess, and that in most cases the most we can hope for is to capture the gist of a saying, not its original formulation on the lips of Jesus himself.

2. *The Criterion of Distinctiveness.* As with all people, Jesus was a mixture of what was unique to him and what was common of people in his culture. It is my assumption that people notice and remember the things that are unique and unusual about a person much more precisely than they do the common things about them. The common things go unnoticed and assumed; they can be filled in later from a store of common cultural knowledge. But the unique and unusual things stand out, tagging a person in the memory of others. For this reason, *special attention should be given to sayings that appear to be unique to Jesus or unusual.* Some caveats:

(a) Notice that this is a positive criterion, not a negative one. That is, the fact that something is not unique is no grounds for assuming that Jesus did not say it. I am quite sure that he said many common things, echoing the wisdom of others when he agreed with them. I am not particularly interested in constructing a unique Jesus. Nor am I interested necessarily in elevating to prominence the unique things about him at the expense of those more common things he would have shared with his culture. Both are important for understanding Jesus.

(b) The unique or unusual sayings in the Jesus tradition should not be used exclusively over against the common things we find in the tradition. It is quite certain that Jesus said common things too. But the unique and unusual sayings can help us understand Jesus' peculiar understanding of the things common to his culture. Thus, while their function should not be to define Jesus

---

23. For the independence of gospel traditions in certain of the Apostolic Fathers, see Helmut Koester, *Synoptische Überlieferung bei den apostolischen Vätern*, Texte und Untersuchungen zur Geschichte der altchristlichen Literatur 65 (Berlin: Akademie-Verlag, 1957). More recently on the nuanced situation of the *Didache* see Clayton N. Jefford, *The Sayings of Jesus in the Teaching of the Twelve Apostles*, Supplements to Vigiliae Christianae 11 (Leiden: E. J. Brill, 1989).

in his entirety, the unique or unusual sayings in the tradition do have a certain heuristic value in understanding his "take" on things.

3. *The Criterion of Embarrassment.* There are many things in the Jesus tradition that turn out to be rather embarrassing for early Christians, and so are difficult to imagine as having been created by them and attributed to Jesus. Such things would include, for example, Jesus' attitude toward his family as expressed in Mark 3:19–21, 31–35, pars. Absent another explanation for the presence of these sorts of sayings in the tradition, attribution to Jesus becomes less doubtful. *Therefore, particular attention should be given to sayings which would have been an embarrassment to early Christians.*

4. *The Criterion of Memorability.* This criterion takes into account the fact that all of what we have from Jesus would have circulated for many years orally before (and after) it was included in an early Christian document. *That means special attention should be given to sayings, stories (or versions thereof) which appear to have certain memorable qualities:* they are brief, clever, structured in threes, use catch-phrases, etc. Simple forms are to be preferred over more complex, highly structured forms of a tradition, such as allegorical renderings or versions heavily cross-referenced to scripture.

5. *The Criterion of Coherence.* I assume that the effect Jesus had on people was in some measure due to the fact that he was lucid, consistent, and coherent in expressing his views. Therefore, *special attention should be given to any corpus of material from diverse sources and tradition-historical streams that coheres with respect to ethos, attitude, theology, or any other meaningful category.* Of course, coherence always is in the eye of the beholder. This criterion, more than any other, risks the danger of circularity in the historian's argument. For this reason, many have downplayed this criterion as less crucial to the historical method than others. But in fact it is the most important. This *is* the work of the historian: using a disciplined imagination to find coherence in a mass of disparate material. It goes right to the heart of historical methodology and defines the work of the historian as a humanistic discipline. So it is best, in my view, not to run from this criterion (or feign to do so), but rather to embrace it in the central role it plays in all historical work.

I wish to underscore that this scheme includes negative and positive criteria, each with a distinctive use. There are negative criteria to be used in eliminating material from consideration. These criteria cannot be used positively, only negatively. That is, if something does not clearly come from the hand of some early Christian author, is not particularly kerygmatic, and serves no distinct early Christian social function, we still do not have any positive argument for ascribing it to Jesus. Such material would not yet be eliminated from consideration, but neither would it yet be attributable to Jesus. To assume so would be to assume some basic historical intention on the part of the gospel authors that should be doubted only when the evidence warrants it. But this is not so. We cannot assume that the gospel authors had any such historical motives as they wrote. Therefore, in addition to these negative criteria, we need positive criteria that might indicate some historical content that could be used in reconstructing the preaching of Jesus.

On the other hand, the positive criteria I have proposed cannot be used negatively. That is, no single one of these criteria should be used as a sine qua non for historicity, but rather, as a positive indicator, which mitigates against the historical problems endemic to the sources. The absence of one of these criteria, let us say multiple attestation, need not be taken as a fatal flaw and used to eliminate something from consideration. Our picture of the tradition, and the capricious process of oral tradition, is just too limited to allow us to use these criteria in such an absolute way. The Gospel of Thomas reminds us of just how limited our view is: prior to its discovery in 1945, there was only a handful of multiply attested items in the tradition. Now, thanks to Thomas, there are dozens. Or let us take the criterion of uniqueness. We know that Jesus was not always unique in what he said, and we might even be interested in some of the common ground Jesus held with other sages of antiquity. Still, one must build an argument for thinking that something bears some historical content. These criteria can be used to build such a case. Naturally, the more of these criteria one can invoke, the stronger the case will be. For example, a cluster of unusual, but similar sayings attested multiply and in various forms will be very attractive for the historian. The socially radical sayings I have discussed in chapter 3 would be such a cluster. The convergence of these criteria is what we are after.

Finally, it must be said that none of these criteria enable one to establish exactly what Jesus said. There is little hope or possibility that we could ever do this. Nor will these criteria enable one to distinguish between words of Jesus and those of his closest early followers, who had not yet begun to think of him in highly mythological terms. We must be content with tools that do not allow such fine distinctions. But these tools are good enough, for they do allow one to get at the gist of what Jesus said, in general and on specific occasions. Jesus was a teacher, not an oracle. And it is my assumption that he was a good enough teacher to see to it that some of those who followed him understood what he was saying and could convey his ideas to others. This is what we are aiming at: some sense of the thoughts Jesus expressed about his world, the people and forces within it, and ultimately about God.

Identifying Things Jesus Likely Did

The conventional criteria I have enumerated above are quite useful so long as one is dealing with words — sayings of Jesus. But they are not so helpful when speaking about things Jesus is thought to have done. The problem is not so much with the negative criteria. As with the sayings of Jesus, one can generally see in the gospels where Jesus' activity is simply a cipher for the life situation of later Christian communities. For example, Jesus' constant debate with the Pharisees in the synoptic tradition is clearly reflective of the situation of Christian communities in the latter half of the first century, after the Pharisaic party had grown to prominence and become Christianity's chief rival for the traditions of Israel. It is difficult, on the other hand, to imagine groups of Pharisees following Jesus around rural Galilee, challenging him at every turn. Such things are easily eliminated from historical consideration.

The problem arises with summoning any positive criteria to recommend this or that "deed" as historical. There are, for example, very few multiply attested deeds in the Jesus tradition. One reason for this lies in the nature of our sources. The Gospel of Thomas, which provides so much multiple attestation in the sayings tradition, is of no help with the deeds, for it is a gospel consisting only of sayings. But there may be other reasons for this phenomenon that we do not yet understand. Already Kähler sensed that the sayings embedded in the narrative of the gospels have a greater claim to historicity than the narratives themselves, in which the author's creative expression has freer rein.[24] In any event, we know that Jesus did do certain things and that part of his renown was owing in part to the remarkable things he did. The question is, how can we identify these things?

I have treated this problem in chapter 2, and so can be relatively brief here. While it is difficult to identify any single thing in the gospels that Jesus actually did, it is also true that the gospel writers regularly depict Jesus as doing certain types of things — Funk calls them "typifications."[25] In a sense, some of the same principles are involved in their identification as with the

---

24. Martin Kähler, The So-Called Historical Jesus and the Historic, Biblical Christ, trans., ed., and introduced by Carl E. Braaten (Philadelphia: Fortress Press, 1964 [German original published in 1896]), 82. More recently see the comments of Robert W. Funk, "On Distinguishing Historical from Fictive Narrative," Forum 9, nos. 3–4 (1993): 188.

25. "On Distinguishing Historical from Fictive Narrative," 193–98.

sayings. For example, Jesus is depicted with great frequency as engaging in the activity of exorcism. The frequency with which one sees this, and the fact that one sees it across a range of sources, amounts to a kind of multiple attestation for this "type" of activity. The fact that this activity was illegal, and not necessarily viewed as legitimate in the broader culture, meets the criterion of "embarrassment." And the fact that it can be seen as consistent with other behaviors, such as keeping company with other ne'er-do-wells of his time, might be seen as meeting the criterion of coherence.

Still, the approximation of these criteria is only that, an approximation. The deeds do pose a challenge to the historian. For discourse about "what happened when" is generally regarded with more freedom by both speaker and hearer than is an important saying. This may be illustrated with the telling of a good joke. The teller generally has considerable freedom in setting up the punch line, but if the punch line itself is blown, the whole thing falls flat. Just so, in looking at stories about what Jesus did we are generally dealing with a genre of utterance that is relatively free in form. With the recounting of deeds, we are listening more to the creative memory of the early church. Thus, we must be content, even more so than with the sayings, with receiving only the gist of things, the "types" of things Jesus was remembered as habitually doing. But this is enough to serve a useful purpose. Jesus did memorable things; people would have remembered them enough to convey something of how Jesus comported himself in relation to others, and what sort of things he did that moved them. This is what we are after: what *sort* of things did Jesus do that moved people to respond to him in the way that they did?

Writing History

It is one thing to identify pertinent evidence for what someone was like, but quite another to write history about that person. What does this entail?

First, it bears repeating that the discipline of historical research is a humanistic discipline, an artful task involving creativity and imagination. This, of course, does not mean that the historian can write willy-nilly according to his or her fancy. It is simply to recognize that the evidence we have for past events and persons seldom presents itself in cogent form. This is notoriously true of the problem of the historical Jesus. The evidence we have for him as a historical figure is fragmentary: individual sayings, a few events from his life, a handful of anecdotes, and memories of the kind of things he was apt to do. For the utter skeptic, it ought to be stated that this is as much as we have for many figures of the past, but it is sufficient for saying something meaningful and useful about them. This is true of Jesus as well. But a collection of evidence does not present itself to us as a complete picture, which we might observe from an objective distance. The historian must take this material and shape it, construe it into a plausible human profile. This takes a disciplined historical imagination.

In doing this imaginative work, the historian interested in Jesus must try to take in and integrate three *sources of information*.

First, he or she must take in the content of a large body of *textual evidence* from early Christian (and a few non-Christian) sources. The criteria listed above impose a discipline on the historian in the selection of this evidence. But in the end, the body of textual evidence is still considerable.

Second, the historian must be able to see this textual evidence within the *cultural context* of the ancient agrarian culture in which Jesus lived and made his impact. This means knowing about the characteristics of ancient agrarian societies in general and about Jewish life under Roman occupation in the first century in particular. Given what we know about Jesus, where he lived, his social status, etc., the historian must be able to imagine how such a person would have experienced the world around him.[26]

Third, the historian must be able to grasp something of *the insight Jesus had* about life, the world, and God. This, of course, is the least tangible of these three sources, and it is derivative of the first two. But it is nonetheless important as a source of information about him. Jesus was a teacher, a visionary, a prophet. He is remembered because he had an impact on people. If one is to understand something about him — indeed the most important thing about him — one must develop a sense for the insights he communicated to people. This involves reflection on the part of the historian, and so brings into the equation the insight and imagination of the historian much more deeply than someone devoted to an objective historical ideal might be comfortable with. But without this very humanistic source of information, the most important thing about Jesus *from a historical point of view* would be left aside. After all, Jesus is remembered because he reflected deeply on life, the world, and God. Anyone who lacks this capacity or fails to use it in his or her historical work, will not easily understand Jesus in his significance as a historical figure.

The historian's task is to commit to writing a synthesis of these three sources of information. In this synthetic task, there is no clear, objective starting point. The historian must decide where to start based on his or her own

---

26. This second area generally combines two of Crossan's three levels of inquiry, the anthropological and the historical (*The Historical Jesus: The Life of a Mediterranean Jewish Peasant* [San Francisco: HarperSanFrancisco, 1991], xviii–xxix). I generally agree with Crossan's approach, but would wish to hold these two areas closely together, thus affording less use of cross-cultural modeling and holding to a more strictly synchronic approach.

sense of the whole. There are also no set rules for how disparate pieces of information are to be integrated. This takes the work of imagination, which must be defended in the end with reasoned, inferential arguments. But the imaginative process itself — the capacity of one human being to make sense of another, to connect words and deeds, to form opinions — this process is not well understood.[27] And yet it is central to the historian's work. How others judge his or her work will depend ultimately on how compelling the historian's sense of the whole is. It is thus perhaps worthy of note that compelling writers have an unfair advantage over poor ones in this arena. But this only underscores the necessity of pursuing one's work within a collegium of peers, who can use their own expertise and grasp of the evidentiary material to see through elegant prose to the real issue of how the evidence has been understood and interpreted.

Appendix 1C:
Can Christian Theology Be Historical?

Christian Faith as Incarnational

Christian faith is rooted in the life of a historical person, Jesus of Nazareth. Christian belief is, as Crossan has so simply and succinctly described: "(1) an act of faith (2) in the historical Jesus (3) as the manifestation of God."[28] For precision's sake I would reword this only slightly: Christian faith is trust in the God we have come to know in the life of Jesus of Nazareth. This rootage in the life of a real person, a figure of history, is the primary expression of the incarnational aspect of Christian faith. God is known in the midst of this human life. But it leads also to a secondary incarnational aspect that is, in my view, key to the meaningfulness of Christian faith for those who embrace it today. That Christianity is rooted in a human life means that it comes out of an experience of human existence, an experience of being human that has the potential to connect with our own sense of being human. To embrace incarnational faith is to embrace the notion that God comes to us in the midst of human existence. God is not distant, but as near as life itself.

The difficult thing about truly embracing this incarnational aspect of Christian faith is that our experience of life is very subjective. We do not

---

27. What Collingwood called the historian's use of a priori imagination (*Idea of History*, 240–42.

28. John Dominic Crossan, *Jesus: A Revolutionary Biography* (San Francisco: HarperSan-Francisco, 1994), 200.

experience other people as objects, knowable in themselves, in their essence. We can know them only experientially, as one subject interacting with another willing, thinking subject, whose depths of being can be known only in part. And any knowing of an other can come only through one's own imagination, as one uses this creative capacity to construct the person who is saying and doing certain observable things. This is true of living persons, but even more so of figures of the past: we can know them only by imaginatively construing what they say and do into a person. Jesus of Nazareth can be known to us only in this very subjective way. Historical research is not impossible, but to do it one must embrace the subjectivity of human existence and realize that this will always be part of any historical work. Can theology be grounded in such a subjective undertaking?

The Desire for an Objective Theological Point of Departure

For someone committed to the idea that religion is about discovering a certain objective Truth about life, the world, even God, the subjective work of the historian will seem like very shaky ground, not at all suitable for theological foundations. What is needed is a certain clear, objective starting point that does not depend on the will of the theologian in any way. For some, the Bible is just such a starting point. This is true, for example, of the biblical fundamentalist, for whom the first article of faith is the objective inerrancy of the biblical text. The foundation for this claim is posited as the divine inspiration of the text, understood as the plenary dictation of the text's words to an author who is simply a scribe. In this way the text, this object before us, is seen as divine; the divine is objectified.

This strategy of turning away from history toward the biblical text as an objective starting point is not limited, however, to Christian fundamentalism. The subjectivity and uncertainty of historical work was also Martin Kähler's basic objection to the "so-called historical Jesus" of nineteenth-century liberal theology. In turning to the "historic, biblical Christ," Kähler sought to avoid the sullying effect that any human construal of events might have on the figure of Christ and his work. With the work of the historian, Kähler argued,

> what is usually happening is that the image of Jesus is being refracted through the spirit of these gentlemen themselves. This makes considerably more difference here than in any other field. For here we are dealing with the source from which the outpouring of the purifying Spirit is to proceed now as it has in the past. How can the Spirit per-

form his purifying work if he is not permitted to reach our ears and hearts without obstruction?[29]

This preference for the pure text of the Bible over the subjective work of the historian would become dominant in the generations after Kähler, as biblical and kerygmatic theology emerged as the new dominant theological paradigms in the West, and historical Jesus research fell into disrepute and was relegated to a bygone age.

To his enduring credit, Kähler was able to see through the pretense of objectivity thrown up by modernist historians of the nineteenth century. His error was in clinging to the ideal of a clean point of departure and turning to the Bible, the object we have before us, as a way of avoiding the polluting effects of human subjectivity. But there can in reality be no easy escape from human subjectivity by turning to the Bible. The Bible is in fact not free from human "obstruction." We know too much now about the history of the biblical text — its authors and their circumstances, its modern reconstruction through textual criticism, the history of the canon, the production and publication of versions of the Bible and their various uses — we know too much ever to suppose that here is a book free from human influence. With such a complicated history open for all to see, plenary inspiration is now an absurdity. One could perhaps rescue this history by christening it with the guidance of the Holy Spirit, and so shore up the claim of divine origins. But mingling the work of people with the will of God with the level of confidence necessary to substantiate such a claim would itself constitute an act of idolatry.

Every search for an objective starting point for theology is in the end idolatrous. For it seeks to find God in an object, a thing we could control and manipulate to our own ends. For Christians, the deeply pious feelings we have about the Bible pose the greatest danger in this sense. The respect and deference we rightly feel for these ancient texts that document Jewish and Christian faith — these pious feelings we have for the Bible can easily be mistaken for faith itself. But when faith in God is exchanged for faith in the Bible, the nature of faith is altered dramatically and fatally. For in so doing we have exchanged a relationship of trust in a living God for a very different kind of relationship: the possession of a text. Of course, it is much easier to relate to our possessions, objects of our own manipulation and power, than it is to relate to another subject, a will and power operating apart from ourselves and beyond our control. This is why biblicism is so attractive, in all its forms. It reduces God to an object we can easily use: to comfort ourselves, to

---

29. Kähler, *The So-Called Historical Jesus*, 57.

ground our systems, to answer all our foes just as we would have God answer them. But this use of the Bible is idolatrous. The Bible is not God; God is not an object. God does not submit to our desires in this way.

Historical theology, if pursued as though it were a quest for such an objective starting point, would also be idolatrous, however critical its methods. When thought of in this way as an objective science, the quest for the historical Jesus draws us again, seductively, toward the comfortable prospect of knowing God as an object. But as we have seen, history as a discipline cannot claim any objective starting point. It involves a subject encountering the remains of other acting subjects. Jesus, insofar as we meet him through historical work, is not an object, an objective starting point, but a subject, whom we shall know and understand only in part, and only to the extent that we can be open to his ideas and view of the world, as expressed in his remembered words and deeds. The Christian claim that we have encountered God in the life of a real human being forces us to abandon any hope of knowing God in an objective way. Incarnational faith means accepting the limitations that come with human subjectivity, including our ability to know only in part, provisionally, and without any ultimate assurance. Faith in God known in this way will always retain the character of trust, not possession.

An Existential Christology

How, then, shall we speak of Jesus as divine revelation? If one takes seriously the epistemological problems posed by the element of subjectivity that comes with one's encounter with any human life, it becomes impossible to speak of Jesus as a manifestation of the divine in any essentialist terms. We cannot speak intelligibly about Jesus' inner nature, his ontic relationship to God, his essence, or true being. Such speculative discourse attempts to establish the objective reality of Jesus' divine nature, something that is utterly beyond our capacity to do. Nor is there much point to the attempt. If we could somehow know about Jesus' inner nature, this would not change the terms in which one encounters Jesus, and thus is affected by him. Our experience of Jesus would still be limited to the subjective experience of his words and deeds. Hypothetical knowledge about his inner nature would not supply this subjective experience with a kind of objective quality, so that now the theological significance of his words and deeds would become self-evident. In any event, the fact of the matter is that the theological significance of Jesus was not self-evident. Most people who encountered him in the villages and on the roads of ancient Galilee did not see it at all. To some he was a teacher, to others a fanatic, and to others still, he was a criminal agitator. Very few people experienced Jesus and concluded that in him they had encountered God. So how is it that some did find God in Jesus and others did not? How is it that some make this claim today, and others do not?

To answer this question we must first ask what it means to make this sort of claim. It is a *religious* claim, that is, a claim that presumes there is a meaning to human existence, and that this meaning derives from a transcendent reality. But how shall we name that reality, or more fundamentally, how shall we know it? It cannot be known as other things are known, concretely, objectively. This is what it means to speak of a *transcendent* reality. Yet we can recognize it in the experience of meaningfulness itself in the course of a human life. We can recognize in those experiences that give life a sense of meaning and purpose a certain transcendent value, which, when we embrace it and give ourselves over to it, serves to cast human life and existence in a larger, more deeply meaningful framework. Thus, religious discourse always revolves around such experiences, looking for persons or events in which transcendence can be recognized and symbolized. In the theistic religions, such as Christianity, this transcendent reality of which we have been speaking is understood as God. Thus it is that certain persons and events come to be seen as revelatory of who God is. It is not that they are divine in some objective, self-evident way. It is that someone experienced in them that ultimate value he or she could only name as God.[30]

Of course, not everyone comes to embrace the same ultimate value in human life, and so there are differences in how one symbolizes the divine. For example, one who comes to value power as that experience in which life finds its ultimate meaning will search for persons and experiences which symbolize this conviction. This is what Roman imperial religion was about. It proclaimed the emperor to be divine because in him was symbolized that which Rome had come to recognize as that ultimate value in which life and existence finds its meaning: power. Other faiths had other symbols, each depending on the ultimate value in which they claimed to find ultimate meaning.

Now we may return to the question of why certain people claimed to find God in Jesus, while others did not. This decision to have faith in Jesus is really a decision about ultimate value. People who claimed to find God in Jesus did so because they had experienced in him something which gave their lives meaning, ultimate meaning such that this something, this value, could only be named as God. In his words and deeds they experienced a transcendence

---

30. I am indebted to Schubert Ogden for this perspective, as articulated especially in *The Point of Christology* (San Francisco: Harper & Row, 1982). The most relevant discussion to the point at hand is in chapter 2: "The Question Christology Answers," pp. 20–40.

that created for them a larger framework within which to live life with depth and authenticity. This claim, while it takes the form of a single assertion, is really concerned with two questions which come together in the experience of transcendence. The first is the question of what is ultimately real and valuable in the universe, viz., God. And if it is this fundamental reality that gives all of life and existence their true meaning, then a second question is always posed simultaneously: What is it that gives my life meaning and authenticity when I give myself over to it? Phrased otherwise, the christological claim is a response to two questions, neither of which has anything to do with Jesus' inner nature: Who/What is God? and Who/what are we to become in giving ourselves over to God? For Christians, both of these questions were answered in their experience of Jesus' words and deeds.

This way of thinking about Christology might be called "existential," as distinct from the "essentialist" approach. By the latter I mean to designate that way of posing the christological question that concerns itself with Jesus' inner nature and how this "essence" might be understood as somehow divine. An existential Christology does not concern itself at all with Jesus' inner nature, but with the experience people had of Jesus that moved them to a new understanding of life and existence. It asserts that the grounding for any christological claim does not lie in any objective reality to which one might appeal for proof for one's claims. It lies, rather, in the subjective experience of being "moved" by what Jesus said and did, and the decision to give oneself over to that ultimate reality by which one was moved as the fundamental value that gives all of life and existence its true meaning. This was true of persons who encountered Jesus in Galilee, but it is also true of people who encounter his words and deeds today. Every christological claim is really a decision: to recognize God in the experience of encountering another human life, and to give oneself over to that God in freedom and trust.

Historical Theological Method

The nature of christological claims suggests a method for doing theological reflection on the basis of historical research. This is what I have attempted to do throughout this book. It involves two steps. First, one must establish as much as possible the significant historical experiences people had of Jesus. What did people remember him saying? What did they remember him doing that caused them to stop and reflect? Second, one must then examine these words and deeds of Jesus for their theological content. On occasion their theological content will be explicit, for example, when Jesus says something directly about God or God's Empire. In most instances, however, it will only be implicit. One must then ask: What value or character is resident in those things that Jesus does or says and what would it mean to construe them as divine qualities? This basic structure would hold true of any historically grounded theological reflection, for the transcendent dimension of human existence is seldom self-evident. It must always be asserted and claimed about those ordinary, yet extraordinary, occurrences that we experience as meaningful.

This, of course, takes imagination. But imagination is the central ingredient in any reflection on the meaning of things. We could see this already in the discussion of the historian's task above (Appendix 1A: History). It is only through the power of imagination that one can understand what another person means by what that person says and does. It is only through the imagination that one can assess the claim that is being made on one's own person by another's words and deeds. And it is only through the imagination that the claims of others upon oneself can be felt as the claim of God. It is in this sense that Howard Thurman called imagination the *angelos* of God.[31] Like the artist, who uses imagination "as he reproduces in varied forms that which he sees beyond the rim of fact that encircles him," the believer uses imagination to see and experience more than is purely self-evident, "beyond the rim of fact that encircles him." Thurman's application of the idea is primarily ethical. It is through the imagination that the believer is able to stand in the place of another, to know the other's needs, and to respond in the service of God: "The degree to which our imagination becomes the *angelos* of God, we ourselves may become *His instruments*."[32] But his theological method is essentially what I am advocating: if God is not present to us in a way that is purely self-evident, then imagination is the means by which we can know God.

This method is also found in the New Testament itself. It is, for example, evident in Paul, who can say in defense of his own, apparently insignificant, life,

> But we have this treasure in earthen vessels, to show that the transcendent power belongs to God and not to us. We are afflicted in every way, but not crushed; perplexed, but not driven to despair; persecuted, but not abandoned, struck down, but not destroyed; always carrying in the body the death of Jesus, so that the life of Jesus might be manifest in

---

31. Howard Thurman, *The Inward Journey* (New York: Harper & Brothers, 1961), 120–21; see also Howard Thurman, *The Growing Edge* (New York: Harper & Brothers, 1956), 25–28.
32. *The Inward Journey*, 121 (emphasis original).

our bodies. For while we live we are always being given up to death for Jesus' sake, so that the life of Jesus may be manifested in our mortal flesh. (2 Cor 4:7–11)

Paul knows that life is not what it seems. He posits a transcendent reality that manifests itself in his very life, if he can summon the will to believe it. And he sees the transcendent in others as well. Later in this same letter he will write, "We regard no one from a human point of view, even though we once knew Christ from a human point of view, we know him thus no longer. So if anyone is in Christ, there is a new creation: the old has passed away. Look! Everything is made new" (2 Cor 5:16–17).

It is also this theological method that lies behind the gospels, which present the story of Jesus in the form of an actual life, and yet filled with significance that some are able to grasp and others are not. Perhaps one of the best illustrations of it is to be found in Matthew's famous interpretation of the last judgment, wherein Jesus, the returning Son of Man, separates the nations as a shepherd separates the sheep from the goats, the sheep on the right and the goats on the left. Then he will say to those on the right,

> "Come, O blessed of my Father, inherit the kingdom prepared for you from the foundation of the world; for I was hungry and you gave me food, I was thirsty and you gave me drink, I was a stranger and you welcomed me, I was naked and you clothed me, I was sick and you visited me, I was in prison and you came to me." Then the righteous will answer him, "Lord, when did we see you hungry and feed you, or thirsty and give you drink? And when did we see you a stranger and welcome you, or naked and clothe you? And we did we see you sick or in prison and visit you?" And the King will answer them, "Truly I say to you, as you did it to one of the least of these, my brothers and sisters, you did it to me." (Matt 25:34b–40)

The writer of Matthew here brings the transcendent into the midst of life. The transcendent reality of God's judgment does not lie in the distant future, but always in the present. But it is hidden, not at all self-evident, as an event imagined literally in some distant future might lead one to believe. Judgment comes in the present decisions one makes to hear the claim of another on one's life as the claim of God.

This is the sort of venture the historical theologian must make. History does not come packed with self-evident meaning, just as life itself is without meaning, that is, until one ventures to impart some meaning to it. Even the words and deeds of Jesus himself do not necessarily mean anything in themselves. Their meaning must be ventured in the imagination, the *angelos* of God. Jesus' words become the Word of God to us, his deeds the movement of God among us, when we recognize in them that ultimate reality in which life and existence are grounded and find meaning in our own lives by giving ourselves over to that reality in freedom and trust.

Appendix II

Listing of Evidence

Below is a list of all the sayings, parables, and typifying stories and statements I have used in this book as evidence for my views on Jesus. A few words of introduction may forestall misunderstandings it might inspire. First, since it derives directly from the pages of this book, I cannot claim that it is an exhaustive list of everything I would include, given further reflection. Secondly, I regard most of the sayings and parables in this list as representing in some form an original saying of Jesus — most, but not all. Occasionally I included items which I do not regard as strictly historical, but which contain elements consistent with Jesus' ideas (that is, something like a "gray" vote from the Jesus Seminar). Such points are noted in the discussion, but not in the list itself. Finally, it should be noted that virtually all of the items in the list of Typifying Stories and Statements fall into this category. None of these (with the exception, perhaps, of the Temple Scene) can be shown to depict actual events in the life of Jesus. Taken together, however, they suggest what was typical of Jesus' behavior, and of how others regarded and remembered him. The idea of "typifications" in Jesus tradition is explained on pp. 57–58 and in Appendix IB, pp. 271–72.

A. Sayings

Tax Collectors and Prostitutes Enter the Empire
  Texts: Matt 21:31
  Discussion: pp. 52, 66

Nothing Can Defile
  Texts: • Mark 7:15 • Thom 14:5
  Discussion: pp. 71, 85, 100

Blessed Are the Clean of Heart
  Primary Texts: • Matt 5:8
  Discussion: p. 72

On Adultery
  Texts: • Mark 10:2–12 • Luke 16:18||Matt 5:31–32 [Q] • 1 Cor 7:10–11
  Discussion: p. 77

A Prophet without Honor
  Primary Texts: • Mark 6:4 • John 4:44 • Thom 31
  Discussion: pp. 79, 110

If You Know What You Are Doing
    Primary Texts: • Luke 6:5+ (D)
    Discussion: p. 102

The Prayer of Jesus
    Primary Texts: • Luke 11:2–4 || Matt 6:9–13 [Q]
    Discussion: pp. 103, 114

Bread Not a Stone
    Primary Texts: • Matt 7:9
    Discussion: p. 104

Give without Expecting Return
    Primary Texts: • Luke 6:30 || Matt 5:42 [Q] • Thom 95
    Discussion: p. 104

Renounce the World
    Primary Texts: • Thom 110
    Discussion: p. 104

On Cares
    Primary Texts: • Luke 12:22–31 || Matt 6:25–33 [Q] • Thom 36
    Discussion: pp. 105–6

Foxes Have Holes
    Primary Texts: • Luke 9:58 || Matt 8:20 [Q] • Thom 86
    Discussion: pp. 91, 106

Become Wanderers
    Primary Texts: • Thom 42
    Discussion: pp. 65, 106–7

Ask for Food, Offer Care
    Primary Texts: • Luke 10:4–9 || Matt 10:7–14 [Q] • Thom 14:4
    Discussion: pp. 107–8

Unless You Hate Family
    Primary Texts: • Luke 14:26 || Matt 10:37 [Q] • Thom 55, 101:1–2
    Discussion: pp. 110–11

My Real Family
    Primary Texts: • Mark 3:35 • Thom 99:2
    Discussion: pp. 111–12

Why Call Me Good?
    Primary Texts: • Mark 10:18
    Discussion: p. 114

Love God, Love Neighbor
    Primary Texts: • Mark 12:29–31
    Discussion: pp. 114–15

Love Your Enemies
    Primary Texts: • Luke 6:27, 35a || Matt 5:44 [Q]
    Discussion: p. 115

Turn the Other Cheek
    Primary Texts: • Luke 6:29 || Matt 5:39–41 [Q]
    Discussion: p. 115

No Stone Left
    Primary Texts: • Mark 13:2
    Discussion: pp. 193–94

This House Destroyed
    Primary Texts: • Mark 14:58 • John 2:19 • Thom 71
    Discussion: pp. 193–94

Not Peace, but a Sword
    Primary Texts: • Luke 12:51 ‖ Matt 10:34 [Q] • Thom 16
    Discussion: pp. 196–97

B. Parables

The Leaven
    Primary Texts: • Luke 13:20–21 ‖ Matt 13:33b [Q] • Thom 96:1
    Discussion: pp. 135–36

The Mustard
    Primary Texts: • Mark 4:31–32 • Luke 13:19 ‖ Matt 13:31b–32 [Q]
       • Thom 20:2
    Discussion: pp. 136–38

The Tenants
    Primary Texts: • Mark 12:1–11 • Thom 65
    Discussion: pp. 138–41

The Vinyard Workers
    Primary Texts: • Matt 15:1–15
    Discussion: pp. 142–45

The Great Feast
    Primary Texts: • Luke 14:16b–24 ‖ Matt 22:2–13 [Q] • Thom 64
    Discussion: pp. 48–49, 85–86, 145–48

The Samaritan
    Primary Texts: • Luke 10:30–35
    Discussion: pp. 148–52

The Prodigal and His Brother
    Primary Texts: • Luke 15:11–32
    Discussion: pp. 152–58

The Hidden Treasure
    Primary Texts: • Matt 13:44 • Thom 109
    Discussion: pp. 158–61

The Beautiful Pearl
    Primary Texts: • Matt 13:45–46 • Thom 76
    Discussion: pp. 159–61

The Great Fish
    Primary Texts: • Matt 13:47–50 • Thom 8
    Discussion: pp. 159–61

C: *Typifying Stories and Statements*

The Wealthy Young Man
    Primary Texts: • Mark 10:17–23
    Discussion: p. 65

Jesus the Carpenter
    Primary Texts: • Mark 6:3
    Discussion: p. 68

A Prostitute Comes to Dinner
    Primary Texts: • Luke 7:36–50
    Discussion: pp. 66–67, 71

Jesus Eats with a Leper
    Primary Texts: • Mark 14:3
    Discussion: p. 71

The Syro-Phoenecian Woman
    Primary Texts: • Mark 7:24–30
    Discussion: 71, 72, 77–78

Jesus Exorcizes an Unclean Spirit
    Primary Texts: • Mark 1:21–26
    Discussion: p. 72

Unclean Spirits Cry Out
    Primary Texts: • Mark 3:11
    Discussion: p. 72

Jesus Accused of Spirit Possession
    Primary Texts: • Mark 3:30
    Discussion: p. 72

Jesus Exorcizes Legion
    Primary Texts: • Mark 5:1–13
    Discussion: p. 72

Jesus Exorcizes a Deaf-Mute Spirit
    Primary Texts: • Mark 9:14–29
    Discussion: p. 72

Jesus Makes a Leper Clean
    Primary Texts: • Mark 1:40–42
    Discussion: pp. 72–73

A Woman Accused of Adultery
    Primary Texts: • [John 7:53b–8:11]
    Discussion: pp. 76–77

Bartimaeus Healed
    Primary Texts: • Mark 10:46–52
    Discussion: p. 77

Mary and Martha
    Primary Texts: • Luke 10:38–42
    Discussion: p. 77

Jesus Rejected in Nazareth
  Primary Texts: • Mark 6:2–4
  Discussion: pp. 78–80

Jesus Eats with Tax Collectors and Sinners
  Primary Texts: • Mark 2:14–17
  Discussion: pp. 81–82

Jesus a Glutton and a Drunkard
  Primary Texts: • Luke 7:31–34 || Matt 11:16–19 [Q]
  Discussion: pp. 81, 83–84

Plucking Grain on the Sabbath
  Primary Texts: • Mark 2:23–28
  Discussion: p. 84

The Anointing at Bethany
  Primary Texts: • Mark 14:3–9
  Discussion: p. 84

Jesus' Disciples Do Not Fast
  Primary Texts: • Mark 2:18–22
  Discussion: p. 84

Jesus Eats with Unclean Hands
  Primary Texts: • Mark 7:1–23
  Discussion: pp. 84, 85

Jesus Mocks the Pharisee's Table
  Primary Texts: • Luke 11:37–41
  Discussion: p. 85

Take the Lowest Place at Table
  Primary Texts: • Luke 14:7–11
  Discussion: p. 85

Invite the Beggars to Dinner
  Primary Texts: • Luke 14:12–14
  Discussion: p. 85

Jesus' Family Comes to Take Him Away
  Primary Texts: • Mark 3:21
  Discussion: p. 111

The Temple Scene
  Primary Texts: • Mark 11:15–17 • John 2:13–16
  Discussion: pp. 192–94, 208

Works Cited

Abrahams, I. *Studies in Pharisaism and the Gospels.* Library of Biblical Studies. New York: Ktav, 1967.

Aland, K., et al., eds. *The Greek New Testament.* 3d ed. New York: United Bible Societies, 1975.

Appleby, J., L. Hunt, and M. Jacob. *Telling the Truth about History.* New York: W. W. Norton, 1994.

Arnal, W. "The Rhetoric of Marginality: Apocalypticism, Gnosticism, and Sayings Gospels." *Harvard Theological Review* 88 (1995): 471–94.

Bainton, R. *Here I Stand: A Life of Martin Luther.* Nashville: Abingdon, 1950.

Barr, J. "Abba Isn't Daddy." *Journal of Theological Studies* n.s. 39 (1988): 28–47.

Barrett, C. K. *The New Testament Background.* Rev. ed. San Francisco: Harper & Row, 1987.

Baur, F. C. *Kritische Untersuchungen über die kanonischen Evangelien.* Tübingen: Osiander, 1847.

Becker, J. "Das Gottesbild Jesu und die älteste Auslegung von Ostern." Pp. 105–26, in Georg Strecker, ed. *Jesus Christus in Historie und Theologie.* Festchrift Hans Conzelmann. Tübingen: Mohr (Siebeck), 1975.

Belo, F. *A Materialist Reading of the Gospel of Mark.* Maryknoll, N.Y.: Orbis, 1981.

Betz, H. D. *Essays on the Sermon on the Mount.* Philadelphia: Fortress Press, 1985.

———. *The Sermon on the Mount.* Hermeneia. Minneapolis: Fortress Press, 1995.

———. "Zum Problem der Auferstehung Jesu im Lichte der griechischen magischen Papyri." Pp. 230–61 in idem. *Hellenismus und Urchristentum: Gesammelte Aufsätze I.* Tübingen: Mohr (Siebeck), 1990.

Bonhoeffer, D. *No Rusty Swords: Letters, Lectures and Notes, 1928–36.* Ed. Edwin H. Robertson. Trans. Edwin H. Robertson and John Bowden. New York: Harper & Row, 1965.

Borg, M. *Jesus, A New Vision: Spirit, Culture, and the Life of Discipleship.* San Francisco: Harper & Row, 1987.

———. *Jesus in Contemporary Scholarship.* Valley Forge, Pa.: Trinity Press International, 1994.

———. *Meeting Jesus Again for the First Time.* San Francisco: HarperSanFrancisco, 1994.

———. "A Temperate Case for a Non-Eschatological Jesus." *Forum* 2, no. 3 (1986): 81–102. Reprinted: Pp. 47–68 in M. Borg. *Jesus in Contemporary Scholarship.* Valley Forge, Pa.: Trinity Press International, 1994.

Bradley, K. R. *Slaves and Masters in the Roman Empire: A Study in Social Control.* New York: Oxford, 1987.

Bultmann, R. *Die Geschichte der synoptische Tradition, Erganzungsheft.* 5th ed. Ed. P. Vielhauer and G. Theissen. Göttingen: Vandenhoeck & Ruprecht, 1979.

———. *The Gospel of John: A Commentary.* Trans. G. R. Beasley-Murray. Philadelphia: Westminster, 1971.

———. *The History of the Synoptic Tradition.* Trans. John Marsh. New York: Harper & Row, 1963.

———. *Jesus and the Word*. Trans. Louise Pettibone Smith and Erminie Huntress Lantero. New York: Charles Scribner's Son's, 1934.

———. *New Testament and Mythology and Other Basic Writings*. Selected, edited and translated by Schubert M. Ogden. Philadelphia: Fortress Press, 1984.

———. *Theology of the New Testament*. 2 vols. New York: Scribner's, 1951.

Brown, R. *The Death of the Messiah*. New York: Doubleday, 1994.

Butts, J. R. "Probing the Polling: Jesus Seminar Results on the Kingdom Sayings." *Forum* 3, no. 1 (1987): 98–128.

Carlson, J., and R. Ludwig, eds. *Jesus and Faith: A Conversation on the Work of John Dominic Crossan*. Maryknoll, N.Y.: Orbis, 1994.

Carlston, C. *Parables of the Triple Tradition*. Philadelphia: Fortress Press, 1975.

———. "Reminiscence and Redaction in Luke 15:11–32." *Journal of Biblical Literature* 94 (1975): 368–90.

Cerfaux, L. "Les paraboles du royaume dans l'évangile de Thomas." *Muséon* 70 (1957): 307–27.

Childs, B. *Introduction to the Old Testament as Scripture*. Philadelphia: Fortress Press, 1979.

Collingwood, R. G. *The Idea of History*. Oxford: Clarendon, 1946.

Collins, J. J. *The Scepter and the Star: The Messiahs of the Dead Sea Scrolls and Other Ancient Literature*. New York: Doubleday, 1995.

Conzelmann, H. "Gegenwart und Zukunft in der synoptischen Tradition." *Zeitschrift für Theologie und Kirche* 54 (1957): esp. 227–96. ET: "Present and Future in the Synoptic Tradition." *Journal for Theology and the Church* 5 (1968): 26–44.

Corley, K. *Private Women, Public Meals: Social Conflict in the Synoptic Tradition*. Peabody, Mass.: Hendrickson, 1993.

Countryman, L. W. *Dirt, Greed, and Sex: Sexual Ethics in the New Testament and Their Implications for Today*. Philadelphia: Fortress Press, 1988.

Crossan, J. D. *Cliffs of Fall*. New York: Seabury Press, 1980.

———. *The Cross That Spoke: The Origins of the Passion Narrative*. San Francisco: Harper & Row, 1988.

———. *The Dark Interval: Towards a Theology of Story*. Sonoma, Calif.: Polebridge Press, 1988.

———. *Finding Is the First Act: Trove Folktales and Jesus' Treasure Parable*. Semeia Supplements. Philadelphia: Fortress; Missoula, Mont.: Scholars Press, 1979.

———. *In Fragments: The Aphorisms of Jesus*. San Francisco: Harper & Row, 1983.

———. *The Historical Jesus: The Life of a Mediterranean Jewish Peasant*. San Francisco: HarperCollins, 1991.

———. *In Parables: The Challenge of the Historical Jesus*. Sonoma, Calif.: Polebridge, 1992.

———. *Jesus: A Revolutionary Biography*. San Francisco: HarperSanFrancisco, 1994.

———. *Raid on the Articulate: Cosmic Eschatology in Jesus and Borges*. New York: Harper & Row, 1976.

———. "The Seed Parables of Jesus." *Journal of Biblical Literature* 92 (1973): 147–48.

———. *Who Killed Jesus?* San Francisco: HarperCollins, 1996.

———. "Why Christians Must Search for the Historical Jesus." *Bible Review* 12, no. 2 (April 1996): 34–38, 42–45.

Deissmann, A. *Light from the Ancient East*. Trans. Lionel R. M. Strachan from the 4th (1923) German ed. New York: George H. Doran, 1927.

Derrett, J. D. *Law in the New Testament*. London: Darton, Longman, & Todd, 1970.

———. "Workers in the Vineyard: A Parable of Jesus." *Journal of Jewish Studies* 25 (1974): 64–91.

Dibelius, M. *From Tradition to Gospel*. Trans. Bertram Woolf. New York: Charles Scribner's Sons, 1971.

Dodd, C. H. *The Parables of the Kingdom*. New York: Charles Scribner's Sons, 1961.

Douglas, M. *Purity and Danger: An Analysis of the Concepts of Pollution and Taboo*. London: Routledge & Kegan Paul, 1966.

Dudley, D. R. *A History of Cynicism from Diogenes to the 6th Century A.D.* London: Methuen, 1937.

Eco, U. *Semiotics and the Philosophy of Language*. Bloomington: Indiana University Press, 1984.

Elizondo, V. *Galilean Journey: The Mexican-American Promise*. Maryknoll, N.Y.: Orbis, 1983.

Fallon, F. T., and R. Cameron. "The Gospel of Thomas: A Forschungsbericht and Analysis." Pp. 4195–4251 in W. Maase and H. Temporini, eds., *Aufstieg und Niedergang der Römischen Welt* 2/25.6. Berlin/New York: de Gruyter, 1988.

Finley, M. *The Ancient Economy*. Berkeley: University of California Press, 1973.

Fredriksen, P. "What You See Is What You Get: Context and Content in Current Research on the Historical Jesus." *Theology Today* 52, no. 1 (April 1995): 75–97.

Frei, H. *The Eclipse of Biblical Narrative*. New Haven: Yale University Press, 1974.

Fuchs, E. *Studies in the Historical Jesus*. Naperville, Ill.: Allenson, 1964.

Fuller, R. *The Formation of the Resurrection Narratives*. Philadelphia: Fortress Press, 1971.

Funk, R. W. "The Good Samaritan as Metaphor." Pp. 74–81 in J. D. Crossan, ed. *Semeia 2: The Good Samaritan*. Missoula, Mont.: Scholars Press, 1974.

———. *Honest to Jesus: Jesus for a New Millennium*. San Francisco: HarperSanFrancisco, 1996.

———. "How Do You Read? (Luke 10:25–37)." *Interpretation* 18 (1964): 56–61.

———. *Language, Hermeneutic, and the Word of God: The Problem of Language in the New Testament and Contemporary Theology*. New York: Harper & Row, 1966.

———. *New Gospel Parallels*. 2 vols. Philadelphia: Fortress Press, 1985.

———. "On Distinguishing Historical from Fictive Narrative." *Forum* 9, nos. 3–4 (1993): 179–216.

———. *Parables and Presence*. Philadelphia: Fortress Press, 1982.

Funk, R. W., and R. Hoover. *The Five Gospels*. New York: Macmillan, 1993.

Funk, R. W., B. B. Scott, and J. R. Butts, eds. *The Parables of Jesus: Red Letter Edition*. Sonoma, Calif.: Polebridge, 1988.

Funk, R. W., and M. Smith, eds. *The Gospel of Mark: Red Letter Edition*. Sonoma, Calif.: Polebridge, 1991.

Furnish, V. P. *II Corinthians*. The Anchor Bible 32A. New York: Doubleday, 1984.

Gerrish, B. A. *The Old Protestantism and the New*. Chicago: University of Chicago Press, 1982.

Grey of Fallodon, Viscount. *Twenty-Five Years*. 2 vols. New York: Frederick A. Stokes Co., 1925.

Gryglewicz, F. "The Gospel of the Overworked Workers." *Catholic Biblical Quarterly* 19 (1957): 190–98.

Hadas, M. *Three Greek Romances*. Indianapolis: Bobbs-Merrill, 1964.

Harmon, A. M., trans. *Lucian* (8 vols.). Loeb Classical Library. Cambridge: Harvard University Press, 1979.

Harris, W. V. *Ancient Literacy*. Cambridge: Harvard University Press, 1989.

Hedrick, C. W. *Parables as Poetic Fictions: The Creative Voice of Jesus*. Peabody, Mass.: Hendrickson, 1994.

Hengel, M. *Crucifixion in the Ancient World and the Folly of the Message of the Cross.* Philadelphia: Fortress Press; London: SCM, 1977.

Héring, J. *The First Epistle of St. Paul to the Corinthians.* London: Epworth, 1962.

Herzog, W. *Parables as Subversive Speech: Jesus as Pedagogue of the Oppressed.* Louisville: Westminster/John Knox, 1994.

Hoffmann, P. "Auferstehung Jesu Christi: II/1. Neues Testament." *Theologische Real-enzyklopädie.* 1:478–513.

Holtzmann, H. J. *Die synoptischen Evangelien.* Leipzig: Wilhelm Engelmann, 1863.

Horsley, R. A. "The Death of Jesus." Pp. 395–422 in Bruce Chilton and Craig A. Evans, eds. *Studying the Historical Jesus: Evaluations of the State of Current Research.* Leiden, New York, London: Brill, 1994.

——. *Jesus and the Spiral of Violence.* San Francisco: Harper & Row, 1987.

——. "'Messianic' Figures and Movements in First-Century Palestine." Pp. 276–95 in James H. Charlesworth, ed. *The Messiah: Developments in Earliest Judaism and Christianity.* Minneapolis: Fortress Press, 1992.

Jacob, I. and W. "Flora." Vol. 2, 803–17 in D. N. Freedman, ed. *The Anchor Bible Dictionary.* New York: Doubleday, 1992.

Jacobson, A. *The First Gospel: An Introduction to Q.* Sonoma, Calif.: Polebridge, 1992.

Jefford, C. N. *The Sayings of Jesus in the Teaching of the Twelve Apostles.* Supplements to Vigiliae Christianae 11. Leiden: E. J. Brill, 1989.

Jeremias, J. *Jerusalem in the Time of Jesus.* Philadelphia: Fortress Press, 1969.

——. *New Testament Theology.* 2 vols. New York: Charles Scribner's Sons, 1971.

——. *The Parables of Jesus.* 2d Eng. ed. New York: Charles Scribner's Sons, 1972.

——. "Zum Gleichnis vom verlorenen Sohn." *Theologische Zeitschrift* 5 (1949): 228–31.

Johnson, L. T. *The Real Jesus: The Misguided Quest for the Historical Jesus and the Truth of the Traditional Gospels.* San Francisco: HarperSanFrancisco, 1996.

Jones, W. T. *A History of Western Philosophy.* 5 vols. 2d ed. revised. San Diego: Harcourt, Brace, Jovanovich, 1975.

de Jonge, M. "The Use of the Word 'Anointed' in the Time of Jesus." *Novum Testamentum* 8 (1966): 132–48.

Jülicher, A. *Die Gleichnisreden Jesu.* 2 vols. Tübingen: Mohr (Siebeck), 1910.

Kähler, M. *The So-Called Historical Jesus and the Historic, Biblical Christ.* Trans., ed., and introduced by Carl E. Braaten. Philadelphia: Fortress Press, 1964.

Käsemann, E. "The Beginnings of Christian Theology." *Journal for Theology and the Church* 6 (1969): 17–46.

——. "The Problem of the Historical Jesus." Pp. 15–47 in idem. *Essays on New Testament Themes.* Studies in Biblical Theology. Trans. W. J. Montague. Naperville, Ill.: Allenson; London: SCM, 1964.

Kee, H. C. "A Century of Quests for the Culturally Compatible Jesus." *Theology Today* 52, no. 1 (April 1995): 17–28.

Kennedy, A. "Leaven." Pp. 2752–54 in *Encyclopaedia Biblica.* London: Adam and Charles Black, 1902.

Kloppenborg, J. S. *The Formation of Q: Trajectories in Ancient Wisdom Collections.* Studies in Early Christianity. Philadelphia: Fortress Press, 1987.

Kloppenborg, J. S., M. W. Meyer, S. J. Patterson, and M. G. Steinhauser. *A Q–Thomas Reader.* Sonoma, Calif.: Polebridge, 1990.

Klosinski, L. *The Meals in Mark.* Ann Arbor, Mich.: University Microfilms International, 1988.

Koester, H. *Ancient Christian Gospels: Their History and Development.* Philadelphia: Trinity Press International; London: SCM, 1990.

———. "Jesus the Victim." *Journal of Biblical Literature* 111 (1992): 3–15.

———. *Synoptische Überlieferung bei den apostolischen Vätern.* Texte und Untersuchungen zur Geschichte der altchristlichen Literatur 65. Berlin: Akademie-Verlag, 1957.

Lake, K. *The Apostolic Fathers.* Loeb Classical Library. Cambridge: Harvard University Press, 1912.

Lenski, G. *Power and Privilege.* New York: McGraw-Hill, 1966.

Lévi-Strauss, C. *Structural Anthropology.* Garden City, N.Y.: Doubleday & Co., 1967.

Lewis, I. M. *Ecstatic Religion: An Anthropological Study of Spirit Possession and Shamanism.* Penguin Anthropology Library. Baltimore: Penguin Books, 1971.

Lietzmann, H. "Der Prozess Jesu." *Sitzungsberichte der Preussischen Akademie der Wissenschaften in Berlin* 14 (1931): 313–22.

Lindars, B. *New Testament Apologetic: The Doctrinal Significance of the Old Testament Quotations.* Philadelphia: Westminster, 1961.

Lindbeck, G. *The Nature of Doctrine.* Philadelphia: Westminster, 1984.

Longino, H. *Science as Social Knowledge: Values and Objectivity in Scientific Inquiry.* Princeton: Princeton University Press, 1990.

Lord, A. *The Singer of Tales.* Cambridge: Harvard University Press, 1960.

Lüdemann, G. *The Resurrection of Jesus: History, Experience, Theology.* Minneapolis: Fortress Press, 1994.

Lührmann, D. *Die Redaktion der Logienquelle.* Neukirchen-Vluyn: Neukirchener Verlag, 1969.

Mack, B. *A Myth of Innocence.* Philadelphia: Fortress Press, 1988.

Malina, B. *The New Testament World: Insights from Cultural Anthropology.* Louisville: John Knox Press, 1981.

Martyn, J. L. *History and Theology in the Fourth Gospel.* 2d ed., rev. Nashville: Abingdon, 1979.

Marxsen, W. "Jesus Has Many Names." Pp. 1–15 in idem. *Jesus and the Church: The Beginnings of Christianity.* Selected, translated, and introduced by Philip E. Devenish. Philadelphia: Trinity Press International, 1992.

———. *The Resurrection of Jesus of Nazareth.* Philadelphia: Fortress Press, 1970.

———. "When Did Christian Faith Begin?" Pp. 76–95 in idem. *Jesus and the Church.* Selected, translated, and introduced by Philip E. Devenish. Philadelphia: Trinity Press International, 1992.

Mattill, A. "Good Samaritan and the Purpose of Luke-Acts: Halévy Reconsidered." *Encounter* 33 (1972): 359–76.

Miller, R. J. "Battling over the Jesus Seminar: Why the Ugly Attacks?" *Bible Review* 13, no. 2 (April 1997): 18–22, 47.

———. "Historical Method and the Deeds of Jesus: The Test Case of the Temple Destruction." *Forum* 8, nos. 1–2 (1992): 5–30.

Murphy, F. J. *The Religious World of Jesus: An Introduction to Second Temple Judaism.* Nashville: Abingdon, 1991.

Neusner, J., W. S. Green, and E. Frerichs. *Judaisms and Their Messiahs at the Turn of the Christian Era.* Cambridge: Cambridge University Press, 1987.

Nickelsburg, G. W. E. "The Genre and Function of the Markan Passion Narrative." *Harvard Theological Review* 73 (1980): 153–84.

———. "Resurrection (Early Judaism and Christianity)." Vol. 5, pp. 684–91 in D. N. Freedman, ed. *The Anchor Bible Dictionary.* New York: Doubleday, 1992.

Niebuhr, R. *Interpretation of Christian Ethics.* New York: Harper & Brothers, 1935.

———. *The Irony of American History.* New York: Charles Scribner's Sons, 1952.

Oakman, D. *Jesus and the Economic Questions of His Day.* Studies in the Bible and Early Christianity 8. Lewiston, N.Y., and Queenston, Ont.: Edwin Mellen Press, 1986.

Ogden, S. *The Point of Christology.* San Francisco: Harper & Row, 1982.

Ong, W. *Orality and Literacy: The Technologizing of the Word.* New York: Methuen, 1982.

O'Niell, J. C. *Who Did Jesus Think He Was?* Leiden: E. J. Brill, 1995.

Orchard, B. B., and T. Longstaff, eds. *J. J. Griesbach: Synoptic and Critical Studies 1776–1976.* London: Cambridge University Press, 1979.

Osborne, D. "Women: Sinners and Prostitutes." Paper presented at the SBL Pacific Coast Region, Long Beach, Calif., April 1987.

Pagels, E. *The Gnostic Gospels.* New York: Random House, 1981.

———. *The Gnostic Paul.* Philadelphia: Fortress Press, 1975.

———. "Visions, Appearances, and Apostolic Authority: Gnostic and Orthodox Traditions." Pp. 415–30 in B. Aland, ed. *Gnosis: Festschrift für Hans Jonas.* Göttingen: Vandenhoeck & Ruprecht, 1978.

Patterson, S. J. "The End of Apocalypse: Rethinking the Eschatological Jesus." *Theology Today* 52, no. 1 (1995): 29–48.

———. "Fire and Dissension: Ipsissima Vox Jesu in Q 12:49, 51–53?" *Forum* 5, no. 2 (1989): 121–38.

———. *The Gospel of Thomas and Jesus.* Sonoma, Calif.: Polebridge, 1993.

———. "The Gospel of Thomas and the Synoptic Tradition: A Forschungsberichte and Critique." *Forum* 8, nos. 1–2 (1992): 45–97.

———. "Paul and the Jesus Tradition: It Is Time for Another Look." *Harvard Theological Review* 84 (1991): 23–41.

———. "Wisdom in Q and Thomas." Pp. 187–221 in L. G. Perdue, B. B. Scott, and W. J. Wiseman, eds. *In Search of Wisdom: Essays in Memory of John G. Gammie.* Louisville: Westminster/John Knox Press, 1993.

Patterson, S. J., J. D. Crossan, and M. Borg. *The Search for Jesus: Modern Scholarship Looks at the Gospels.* Ed. Hershel Shanks. Washington, D.C.: Biblical Archaeology Society, 1994.

Peirce, C. S. *Values in a Universe of Chance: Selected Writings of Charles S. Peirce.* Ed. Philip P. Wiener. Garden City, N.J.: Doubleday, 1958.

Perrin, N. *Rediscovering the Teaching of Jesus.* New York: Harper & Row; London: SCM, 1967.

Pesch, R. "Zur Entstehung des Glaubens an die Auferstehung Jesu." *Theologische Quartalschrift* 153 (1973): 201–28.

Pitt-Rivers, Julian. *The Fate of Shechem or the Politics of Sex: Essays in the Anthropology of the Mediterranean.* Cambridge: Cambridge University Press, 1977.

Popper, K. *The Open Society and Its Enemies.* Vol. 2: *The High Tide of Prophecy: Hegel Marx, and the Aftermath.* Rev. ed. Princeton: Princeton University Press, 1966.

Porton, G. "Diversity in Post-Biblical Judaism." Pp. 57–80 in Robert A. Kraft and George W. E. Nickelsburg, eds. *Early Judaism and Its Modern Interpreters.* Atlanta: Scholars Press, 1986.

Rauschenbusch, W. *Christianizing the Social Order.* New York: Macmillan, 1912.

Reimarus, H. S. *Fragments.* Trans. R. S. Fraser. Ed. C. H. Talbert. Philadelphia: Fortress Press, 1970.

Riley, G. J. "The Gospel of Thomas in Recent Scholarship." *Currents in Research: Biblical Studies* 2 (1994): 227–52.

Ritschl, A. *The Christian Doctrine of Justification and Reconciliation.* Trans. H. R. Mackintosh and A. B. Macauley. Edinburgh: T. & T. Clark, 1902.

Robinson, J. M. "The German Discussion of the Later Heidegger." Pp. 3–76 in idem and John B. Cobb, Jr., eds. *The Later Heidegger and Theology*. New Frontiers in Theology 1. New York: Harper & Row, 1963.

———. "Hermeneutic since Barth." Pp. 1–77 in idem and John B. Cobb, Jr., eds. *The New Hermeneutic*. New Frontiers in Theology II. New York: Harper & Row, 1964.

———. "Jesus from Easter to Valentinus (or to the Apostles' Creed)." *Journal of Biblical Literature* 101 (1982): 5–37.

———. *A New Quest of the Historical Jesus*. Studies in Biblical Theology. Naperville, Ill.: Allenson; London: SCM, 1959.

———, general editor. *The Nag Hammadi Library in English*. 3d rev. ed. San Francisco: HarperSanFrancisco, 1988.

Sanders, E. P. *The Historical Figure of Jesus*. Harmondsworth: Penguin, 1993.

———. *Jesus and Judaism*. Philadelphia: Fortress Press, 1985.

———. *The Tendencies of the Synoptic Tradition*. Society for New Testament Studies Monograph Series 9. Cambridge: Cambridge University Press, 1969.

Sanders, James. "Tradition and Redaction in Luke xv.11–32." *New Testament Studies* 15 (1969): 433–38.

Schaff, P., ed. *Nicene and Post-Nicene Fathers of the Christian Church*. Vol. 4: *St. Augustine: The Writings against the Manichaeans and the Donatists*. Edinburgh: T. & T. Clark; Grand Rapids: Eerdmans, 1988.

Schleiermacher, F. *Das Leben Jesu*. Ed. K. A. Rütenik. Berlin: Georg Reimer, 1864.

Schottroff, L. "Das Gelichnis vom verlorenen Sohn." *Zeitschrift für Theologie und Kirche* 68 (1971): 27–52.

Schottroff, L., and W. Stegemann. *Jesus and the Hope of the Poor*. Trans. Matthew J. O'Connell. Maryknoll, N.Y.: Orbis, 1986.

Schüssler Fiorenza, E. *In Memory of Her*. New York: Crossroad, 1988.

———. "Redemption as Liberation: Rev. 1:5–6 and 5:9–10." *Catholic Biblical Quarterly* 36 (1974): 220–32.

Schweizer, E. "Antwort an Joachim Jeremias, S. 228–231." *Theologische Zeitschrift* 5 (1949): 231–33.

———. "Zur Frage der Lukasquellen, Analyse von Luk 15, 11–32." *Theologische Zeitschrift* 4 (1948): 469–71.

Schweitzer, A. *The Quest of the Historical Jesus*. Trans. W. Montgomery. London: Adam and Charles Black, 1948.

Scott, B. B. *Hear, Then, the Parable: A Commentary on the Parables of Jesus*. Minneapolis: Fortress Press, 1989.

———. "The Prodigal Son: A Structuralist Interpretation." Vol. 2, 185–205 in *Society of Biblical Literature Seminar Papers (1975)*. Missoula, Mont.: Scholars Press, 1975.

Sellew, P. "The Gospel of Thomas: Prospects for Future Research." Pp. 327–46 in John D. Turner and Anne McGuire, eds. *The Nag Hammadi Library after Fifty Years: Proceedings of the 1995 Society of Biblical Literature Commemoration*. Nag Hammadi and Manichaean Studies 44. Leiden: Brill, 1997.

Shorto, R. *Gospel Truth: The New Image of Jesus Emerging from Science and History, and Why It Matters*. New York: Riverhead Books, 1997.

Smith, D. E., and H. E. Taussig. *Many Tables: The Eucharist in the New Testament and Liturgy Today*. Philadelphia: Trinity Press International; London: SCM, 1990.

Smith, M. "Palestinian Judaism in the First Century." Pp. 67–81 in Moshe Davis, ed. *Israel: Its Role in Civilization*. New York: Harper & Row, 1956.

Smith, W. C. *The Meaning and End of Religion*. New York: Harper & Row, 1978.

Stein, R. "Is the Transfiguration (Mark 9:2–8) a Misplaced Resurrection-Account?" *Journal of Biblical Literature* 95 (1976): 79–96.

Strauss, D. F. *The Christ of Faith and the Jesus of History: A Critique of Schleiermacher's "Life of Jesus."* Trans. and ed. Leander Keck. Philadelphia: Fortress Press, 1977.

———. *The Life of Jesus Critically Examined.* Trans. and ed. P. C. Hodgson. Philadelphia: Fortress Press, 1972.

Taylor, V. "The Order of Q." *Journal of Theological Studies,* n.s. 4 (1953): 27–31. Reprinted: pp. 90–94 in Taylor. *New Testament Essays.* Grand Rapids: Eerdmans, 1972.

———. "The Original Order of Q." Pp. 246–69 in A. J. B. Higgins, ed. *New Testament Essays: Studies in Honor of T. W. Manson.* Manchester: Manchester University Press, 1959. Reprinted: pp. 95–118 in Taylor. *New Testament Essays.* Grand Rapids: Eerdmans, 1972.

Theissen. G. "Jesus' Temple Prophecy: Prophecy in the Tension between Town and Country." Pp. 94–114 in idem. *Social Reality and the Early Christians: Theology, Ethics, and the World of the New Testament.* Trans. Margaret Kohl. Minneapolis: Fortress Press, 1992).

———. *Sociology of Palestinian Christianity.* Philadelphia: Fortress Press, 1978.

Throckmorton, B. H. *Gospel Parallels.* Nashville: Nelson, 1979.

Thurman, H. *The Inward Journey.* New York: Harper & Brothers, 1961.

———. *The Growing Edge.* New York: Harper & Brothers, 1956.

Tuckett, C. M., ed. *The Messianic Secret.* Issues in Religion and Theology 1. Philadelphia: Fortress; London: SCM, 1983.

———. *The Revival of the Griesbach Hypothesis.* Cambridge: Cambridge University Press, 1983.

Vielhauer, P. "Gottesreich und Menschensohn in der Verkündigung Jesu." Pp. 51–79 in W. Schneemelcher, ed. *Festschrift für Günther Dehn.* Neukirchen, Kreis Moers: Buchhandlung des Erziehungsvereins, 1957.

Weiss, J. *Jesus' Proclamation of the Kingdom of God.* Trans. Richard Hiers and David Holland. Philadelphia: Fortress Press, 1971.

Weisse, C. H. *Die evangelische Geschichte kritisch und philosophisch bearbeitet.* 2 vols. Leipzig: Breitkopf und Hartel, 1838.

Wellhausen, J. *Das Evagelium Marci.* Berlin: G. Reimer, 1909.

Wilckens, U. *Die Missionsreden der Apostlegeschichte.* Neukirchen: Neukirchener Verlag, 1960.

———. "Der Ursprung der Überlieferung der Erscheinungen des Auferstandenen." Pp. 56–95 in W. Joest and W. Pannenberg, eds. *Dogmen und Denkstructuren.* Festschrift E. Schlink. Göttingen: Vandenhoeck & Ruprecht, 1963.

Wilder, A. N. *The Language of the Gospel: Early Christian Rhetoric.* New York: Harper & Row, 1964. Reprint: *Early Christian Rhetoric: The Language of the Gospel.* Cambridge: Harvard University Press, 1971.

Williamson, C. M. *Has God Rejected His People? Anti-Judaism in the Christian Church.* Nashville: Abingdon, 1982.

Winter, P. *On the Trial of Jesus.* 2d ed., rev. and ed. T. A. Burkill and Geza Vermes. New York and Berlin: De Gruyter, 1974.

Witherington, B., III. "Buyer Beware!" *Bible Review* 13, no. 2 (April 1997): 23–26, 47.

Wrede, W. *The Messianic Secret.* Trans. J. C. G. Greig. London and Cambridge: James Clarke; Greenwood, S.C.: Attic Press, 1971.

Yarbro Collins, A. *Crisis and Catharsis: The Power of the Apocalypse.* Philadelphia: Fortress Press, 1984.

———. *Beginning of the Gospel: Probings of Mark in Context.* Minneapolis: Fortress Press, 1992.

Index of Scriptural References

297

JEWISH SCRIPTURES

Index of Authors

Abrahams, I., 151
Agee, J., 119
Aland, B., 227
Aland, K., 254
Appleby, J., 251, 253, 255, 257, 260, 261
Arnal, W., 140

Bahrdt, K. F., 31
Bainton, R., 29
Barr, J., 103
Barrett, C. K., 61, 62
Barth, Karl, 5, 37, 38, 43, 45, 53, 169, 174
Baur, F. C., 18
Becker, J., 221
Belo, F., 103
Betz, H. D., 105, 229–30, 231, 234
Bonhoeffer, D., 190–91
Borg, Marcus, 14, 45, 63, 73, 170, 199, 208
Braaten, C. E., 35, 36, 271
Bradley, K. R., 62
Brown, R., 200 169, 174, 199, 228, 233, 264
Bultmann, R., 5, 27, 28, 37, 38, 100, 101, 136, 137,
Burkill, T. A., 200
Butts, J. R., 44, 171

Cameron, R., 22
Carlson, J., 45
Carlston, C., 139, 153
Case, S. J., 168
Cerfaux, L., 158
Charlesworth, J. H., 196
Childs, B., 43
Chilton, B., 192

Cobb, J. B., 124
Collingwood, R. G., 253, 254, 255, 256, 260, 279
Collins, J. J., 196
Conzelmann, H., 174–75, 198–99
Corley, K., 66, 67, 84
Countryman, L. W., 69
Crossan, J. D., 6, 41, 45, 47, 48, 63, 64, 73, 83, 84, 86, 90, 97, 108, 128–29, 130, 132, 135, 139, 158, 160, 170, 174, 176–77, 182, 200, 205, 233, 235, 237, 264, 273, 274

Davis, M., 196
Deissmann, A., 182
de Jonge, M., 196
Derrett, J. D., 144, 150
Derrida, J., 256
de Saussure, F., 256
Devenish, P. E., 46, 56, 87
Dewey, J., 257
Dibelius, M., 136–37
Dillenberger, J., 124
Dilthey, W., 255
Dodd, C. H., 120, 121, 126, 127, 129, 135
Dostoevsky, F., 212
Douglas, M., 69, 70
Dudley, D. R., 61, 92

Ebeling, G., 124
Eco, U., 134
Elizondo, V., 210
Evans, C. A., 192

Fallon, F. T., 22
Farmer, W., 18
Finley, M., 62